THE RISE AND FALL OF
WORLD ORDERS

MANCHESTER
UNIVERSITY PRESS

The rise and fall of world orders

TORBJØRN L. KNUTSEN

MANCHESTER UNIVERSITY PRESS
Manchester and New York

distributed exclusively in the USA by St. Martin's Press

Copyright © Torbjørn L. Knutsen 1999

The right of Torbjørn L. Knutsen to be identified as the author of this work has
been asserted by him in accordance with the Copyright, Designs and Patent Act 1988

Published by Manchester University Press
Oxford Road, Manchester M13 9NR, UK
and Room 400, 175 Fifth Avenue, New York, NY 10010, USA
http://www.man.ac.uk/mup

Distributed exclusively in the USA by
St. Martin's Press, Inc., 175 Fifth Avenue, New York, NY 10010, USA

Distributed exclusively in Canada by
UBC Press, University of British Columbia, 6344 Memorial Road,
Vancouver, BC, Canada V6T 1Z2

British Library Cataloguing-in-Publication Data
A catalogue record for this book is available from the British Library

Library of Congress Cataloging-in-Publication Data applied for

ISBN 0 7190 4057 4   *hardback*
      0 7190 4058 2   *paperback*

First published 1999

05 04 03 02 01 00 99   10 9 8 7 6 5 4 3 2 1

Typeset in Sabon
by Carnegie Publishing, Lancaster
Printed in Great Britain by
Biddles Ltd, Guildford and King's Lynn

Contents

Part Two *Déjà vu*

List of figures, maps and tables

Acknowledgements

Some projects are like wisdom teeth: they are slow in coming, they are difficult to keep clean, they sit deep and are hard to extract. This book is one of those. Over a decade ago I wrote a Ph.D. thesis on great powers in the modern world-system the argument of which has haunted me ever since. It often intruded on other, more narrowly focused, projects; constructively informing them in some ways, but also side-tracking them in others. (In short, it has made a big nuisance of itself, and I hope it is not too naively Freudian to assume that the completion of this book will finally rid me of this incubus.)

During the course of this project I have accumulated large debts and small to several institutions and individuals. First of all to the Graduate School of International Studies at the University of Denver where it all began, to David Bayley and Peter van Ness. I also owe a great debt to the Fernand Braudel Center at Binghamton University, especially to Immanuel Wallerstein for his interest, his kind hospitality and his willingness to share his insights at a formative, early phase of this project. I am also indebted to the Center for International Studies at the University of Southern California which generously awarded me a postdoctoral stipend – notably to then CIR director Tom Biersteker. I am also happy to express my appreciation to friends and colleagues at George Mason University, in whose Department of Public and International Affairs I taught for a handful of years – especially to Louise White for her unfailing support. I am also grateful to the George Mason International Institute for research funding at a crucial stage. Finally, I owe many thanks to the university of Trondheim, notably to Dagfinn Slettan whose administration of a grant from the Norwegian Research Council allowed me to read up on theories of nationalism and identity formation.

The argument of this book came together during my brief tenure as a guest researcher at the Nobel Institute in Oslo. I am greatly indebted to Geir Lundestad, Odd Arne Westad, the Institute's staff and my fellow guest researchers – especially to Chen Jian and Immanuel Geiss – for providing a stimulating research environment which probed the fertile soils where history and social sciences overlap.

Bernt Hagtvet, Mark Katz, Jon Lauglo, Espen Moe, Jonathon Moses, Anita Schjølset and others have read parts of the manuscript and offered constructive criticism as the various probes and fragments finally came together into a book. Erik Noreen and Peter Wallensteen provided more help than they may realize for pushing me to publicly defend my final organizing claims before a friendly audience in Uppsala. Jennifer Bailey has not only commented on the manuscript in its various incarnations, she has also been tolerant of my flighty preoccupations with theory and history and my domestic delinquencies. Also, special thanks to an unnamed guard at the Oslo Central railway station who miraculously helped me retrieve my diskettes and laptop computer, and to Irene Caroline for being her effervescent self.

Torbjørn L. Knutsen
Las Palmas

To Sigvald and Irene
who never met

Introduction: the rise and fall of great powers

> When I come to study what has been, at different times and epochs
> of history among different peoples, the effective reason why ruling
> classes have been ruined, I note the various events and men and
> accidental and superficial causes, but believe me, the real cause, the
> effective one, that makes men lose power is that they have become
> unworthy to exercise it. (de Tocqueville 1970[1893])

In order to probe a topic as vast as the rise and fall of world orders it is
important to have clear and simple definitions of the key concepts used. Thus,
it is a problem that the term 'world order' is a notoriously slippery one. Most
discussions around world order refer to a stable pattern of relations among
sovereign states. These discussions have a problem. For states are groupings
of people, and people can be grouped in many ways. As investigations of
non-Western societies and of Western societies in the past suggest, most of
these groupings are not states at all. World order, then, conveys more than
stable patterns of state relations. What additional factors need to be considered
in discussing world orders? This is one of the key questions of this book.

If the key concept of world order is inadequately clarified at the beginning
of this journey, it is all the more important that other key concepts are all the
more precisely defined. The 'world' in this study is defined within narrow
temporal and spatial boundaries. First of all, the 'world' is limited in time to
the modern ages; it is understood as a sphere of social action which took shape
in the sixteenth century and which ended in the second decade of the twentieth.
The world is limited by the Italian wars (1494–1529) at one end and by World
Wars I and II (1914–18/1939–45) at the other. This world was marked by the
rise and expansion of the West. Through modern history, the world, under the
aegis of Western powers, became progressively unified and integrated. At the
same time, the world became increasingly unequal in terms of the distribution
of wealth and force.

'Order' exists when a relatively stable pattern of human relations characterizes the international scene. Such stability, it is claimed here, is upheld by

rules of international conduct. Since order is the outcome of rules, the nature and origins of these rules will be an important focus in the discussions which follow. Different authors have different views about these rules. However, they tend to agree on one thing: that the rules, whether they are formal or informal, are in the main defined by the most powerful actors in the system. This point harmonizes with the notion that wealth and force are unequally distributed among states – that some states are weak, while others are strong; some are small while others are great and powerful.

'Power', then, is a decisive background determinant of order and is here defined in the commonest of ways: as the ability to influence others. This ability is commonly identified as a composite of military force, economic wealth and command over public opinion.[1] 'Great' power is understood not in a Rankean[2] but in a Braudelian sense. For Braudel, the evolution of the modern world has been attended by a division of the world into three regions or zones: a Western core zone of powerful territorial states; a peripheral zone of weaker and poorer social formations; and an intermediate zone (Braudel 1984, pp. 39ff.). Great powers are, in this study, found only in the core zone of the modern world. And the great powers which are selected here are the leading core states of Braudel's modern world – Spain, the United Provinces, England and the United States.[3]

Two comments on power are in order before the run-through of key terms is complete. First, this simple definition of power as a composite of military, economic and normative capabilities helps shine some additional light on the concept of world order. At the very least, it allows world order to be probed in terms of the key resources that states draw on in their interaction and in the kind of interaction which actually take place among states. Thus, *military interaction* can be considered one aspect of world order – i.e. violent interaction in which states muster their punitive capabilities and project their military power in wars and skirmishes. Also, *economic interaction* can be considered an aspect of world order – initially this kind of interaction concerned barter and trade, but it rapidly became more complex as Western states developed money, banks and systems of exchange, credit, finance and insurance. Finally, *societal interaction* must be considered an aspect of world order – as a rudimentary society which cannot be reduced to military or economic inter-action, but which must be understood in terms of rules, norms and values (Bull 1977, pp. 13ff.). Every society possesses some kind of rules and norms which specify the rights and duties of its members. The most essential evidence for the existence of an international society is the formalization of norms and rules into a recognized body of international law. Although all states do not obey international law all the time, they obey it often enough for law to constitute an important formative fact in modern international relations. This point (that state behaviour is influenced by social realities other than military threats and economic promises) is extended by the claim that international actors are influenced not only by formal institutions (like law), but also by informal institutions (Kratochwil 1989; North 1990; Katzenstein 1996). Indeed, not only are states and state leaders conditioned by such social institutions, it is these which infuse material realities with purpose and direction. Rules, norms, values, obligations, decency, dreams and commonality of purpose provide meaningful ends in the light of which political leaders activate force and wealth. Such informal institutions provide political purpose towards which material resources are harnessed and applied (Finnemore 1996; Adler 1997).

Second, it is important to note that the Braudelian understanding of power harmonizes with the notion that capabilities like wealth and force are unequally distributed among states. This difference in capabilities is expressed in a hierarchical ordering of states. At the apex of the hierarchy are the most powerful states in the world – this amounts to very few, at the most a handful, of great powers. Below the great powers are the lesser states, ranked by capabilities and status. The most obvious difference between the great powers and the lesser states is their difference in resources and capabilities, and in their abilities to influence others. In addition there is a not-so-obvious difference between greater and smaller powers: namely, the various ways in which they benefit from the extant world order.

The final key terms of this study are 'rise' and 'fall' – these are among the looser historical terms, to say the least. Sometimes the terms are employed simply as synonyms for international change. But on other occasions they involve a cyclical vision of history. Here, the rise and fall of world orders denotes a cycle – a periodic repetition of macropolitical themes and constellations through time.

One of the most discussed patterns of periodicity identified in the international relations literature concerns the regular emergence of great wars. In contrast to the Middle Ages, when warfare was endemic in the West, the Modern Ages are marked by conspicuous recurrences of large-scale wars – by 'cycles of conflict' or 'waves of great wars'. This tendency for modern war to arise in great waves is noted by Robert Mowat, who explains that from the fifteenth century on

> social and political changes are discernible, which may be taken to begin modern history. In this modern period, from about 1491, warfare is far less common than in the Middle Ages. Nevertheless, war does arise, war on the grand scale, as it were in great waves, with long intervals of general or comparatively general peace between the waves. Each wave of great wars is

ended by diplomatic action, by a peace treaty or peace congress. Every such
war, as brought to an end by diplomacy, is followed by about thirty or forty
years of peace. (Mowat 1928, p. 1)

Boundaries of the world

Different studies of world orders entertain different notions of the world whose
order they venture to probe. Robert Keohane (1984) tends to focus on a
comparatively short time span – with tentative expeditions into the sixteenth
and seventeenth centuries, he largely covers the last two hundred years,
with industrial England and the United States as cases of hegemony. Peter
Taylor (1996) includes the United Provinces among the great powers, thus
extending the analysis back to the mid-1600s. Immanuel Wallerstein (1974)
begins his analysis with imperial Spain in the early 1500s. Fernand Braudel
(1977) dips into the Renaissance by including fourteenth-century Venice and
sixteenth-century Antwerp and Genoa as ordering powers. Modelski and
Thompson (1996) venture as far back as the turn of the millennium and show
how European Renaissance orders may have been affected by impulses from
Sung China.

   This study follows the example of Wallerstein and begins with the 'long
sixteenth century'. This choice coincides with Geoffrey Barraclough's selection
of the Italian wars as representing an important origin in Western politics.
Furthermore, it greatly simplifies the basic notion of the relevant 'world' as
framed by two great events. The first occurred around the Italian wars; the
second around World War I. The first great event marks the beginning of the
modern world; the second marks its end (Barraclough 1976).

Boundaries in time

The Renaissance, the Reformation and the Italian wars are signposts which
mark the entrance into the modern world.[4] Before the Italian wars, long-term,
large-scale economic and political dynamics were dominated by world empires.
Afterwards, economic and political dynamics involved territorial states and
capitalist interaction on a global scale.

   Together with the new imperialism, and the commercial revolution, World
War I marks the closure of the modern world.[5] The first warnings of this
closure emerged towards the close of the nineteenth century. It was then 'little
more than an intermittent stirring in the womb of the old world' (Barraclough
1974, p. 24). After 1918 changes rapidly accumulated to produce a new,
contemporary world which 'acquires a separate identity and an existence
of its own; it advances towards maturity with unexpected speed after 1945'
(Barraclough 1974, p. 24).

These two ruptures in the past – the Italian wars and World War I – constitute the temporal encasement of Part One of this study. Together, they frame the discussion of the hegemonies of the modern ages: the sixteenth-century Iberias, the seventeenth-century United Provinces, the eighteenth- and nineteenth-century Great Britain.

Boundaries in space

Between the Italian wars and World War I lies the chequered history of the modern world; the age of the great powers. It has been convincingly shown that world orders existed before the Italian wars – thus, Macedon, Rome and Han China can be said to enjoy all the hallmarks of world orders. However, the world orders which have existed since the Italian wars – i.e. the modern world orders – have been peculiar in that they have been global. Macedon, Rome and Han China were regional orders; they covered only parts of the globe. The Spanish, the Dutch and the British orders were all global in scope. Modern world orders are based on a global, oceanic system. Their global nature was ensured by the advent of new technologies which revolutionized the nature of sea power in the long sixteenth century and created global webs of transport and communication. This rise of sea power was ensured by the design of new types of ships and new methods of navigation that were made in the Mediterranean world.[6]

Second, this advent of sea power was the chief propellant of the rapid rise of Europe. The rise and expansion of the European world created a gap between the West and other regions in terms of economic wealth, military force and socio-economic modes of knowledge and thought. Simply put, the modern world was rapidly divided into three successive zones: the core zone, that is the region about the centre, which is marked by affluence and splendour. Next come the intermediate zones about this central pivot. And finally, there are the wide peripheral areas, which, in the division of labour characteristic of the increasingly interdependent modern world economy, are subordinates rather than participants (Braudel 1977, p. 82).[7]

Third, the history of modern world politics has largely been an account of the interactions of territorial states. The state has been the key institution through which Western societies have regulated their populations, their relations with each other and their interaction with non-European peoples. The territorial state – along with the will to make rapid technological and economic progress and the capacity to translate this progress into political power on a global scale – is a characteristic feature of the modern era. The institutions of the state and their unrivalled organisational efficiency have distinguished the Christian West from the rest of the world since about the long sixteenth century. Since then, these institutions have been partly imposed upon, and partly emulated by, the rest of the world.

Finally, the history of the modern world orders can be seen as 'the expansion of the international society of European states across the rest of the globe, and its transformation from a society fashioned in Europe and dominated by Europeans into the global international society of today' (Bull and Watson, 1984, p. 1). This expansion of European economic processes and political institutions has also meant the worldwide diffusion of European culture. Extra-European regions have become the recipients of Western norms and values (denoted by terms like rationality, individualism, equality and liberty) and by rules for social behaviour (as specified by European legal codes or, more subtly, by the Christian ethic).

This diffusion of Western values has increasingly come to define the notion of modernity. The epochal sense of the term 'modern' is associated with the nineteenth century. However, the threshold marking its beginning is often put around 1500. The modern age, then, can be seen as a long process. A variety of specifications exist as to its characteristic properties. Most of them involve the notion of a formalization of human rationality. It is generally agreed that 'modernity' is marked by an effort to demystify, secularize and subject natural forces to rational explanation and to human control – to develop 'objective science, universal morality and law' in the words of Habermas (1981, p. 9). Modernity began at the time of the Renaissance, the Italian wars and the Reformation; it evolved with great rapidity during the European Enlightenment of the eighteenth century; it reached its confident apogee on the eve of World War I.

The result of these developments was a unique international system, European in origin, composed of an interstate system (dominated by military interaction) and a world-economy (dominated by economic interaction) and informed by Christian, Western values. This modern system is the main focus of Part One of this study. Part Two discusses the advent of a contemporary or postmodern world order.

Cycles of world order

Mowat identifies four 'waves of great wars' in modern history – an observation which has been empirically substantiated and elaborated by several subsequent authors (Wright 1965; Toynbee 1954; Farrar 1977; Gilpin 1981; Modelski 1987; Goldstein 1988).[8] These are the Italian wars (1494–1529), the Thirty Years War (1618–48), the wars of Louis XIV (1672–1713) and the Napoleonic Wars (1791–1815). Contemporary history offers an additional fifth wave in the two World Wars of the twentieth century (1914–45).[9]

The beginning of each of these waves of great wars marks the destruction of a definite world order. The conclusion of each such wave marks the beginning of a new world order – an order which pertains to the wider world political system of which the states system is a part (Bull 1977, p. 21). A world order, then, is fixed in time by waves of great wars. And five distinct world orders can be identified during the course of modern history:

1 a sixteenth-century Iberian world order (an order dominated by the Iberian great powers) which existed between the Italian wars and the Thirty Years War;

2 a seventeenth-century Dutch world order which existed between the Thirty Years War and the wars of Louis XIV;

3 an eighteenth-century British world order which existed between the wars of Louis XIV and the Napoleonic Wars;

4 a nineteenth-century British world order which existed between the Napoleonic Wars and World War I;

5 a contemporary, American world order which emerged from World War II.

Each world order is here conceived of as a pattern of periodicity or a cycle, and seen in terms of the three simple phases of growth, stagnation and decline. This is not so different from propositions presented by several other authors – such as Wright (1965), Toynbee (1954), Gilpin (1981), Wallerstein (1984) and Modelski (1987) among others.[10] The first phase of a world order emerges after a wave of great wars. In this phase the distribution of power is such that interstate conflict does not readily trigger large and drawn-out wars. The world order is therefore relatively stable. It is important to note that this stability is not explained in balance-of-power terms. Rather than being the outcome of an even distribution of capabilities among the great powers, this postwar stability is the result of an uneven concentration of power. During this first phase, the world order is stable because the hierarchy of power is fairly obvious. The international system is dominated by a single great power. The members of the state system agree on who is pre-eminent among them; they understand that to challenge this pre-eminent great power to a contest of force would mean rapid defeat. Very simplified, one could say that during this first phase, the world order is 'managed' by a leading state or a hegemon. Thus, there is an intimate connection between the rise (and fall) of the world order and the rise (and fall) of 'systems-managing' great powers.

This first, relatively stable phase of the world order is called the phase of hegemony. The 'concert system' which emerged from the peace conference in Vienna in the wake of the Napoleonic Wars is often cited as an appropriate example of hegemony. It involved an international system grounded in principles which were espoused by a pre-eminent England, institutionalized in the political and economic practices of that power and subsequently emulated by others (Cox 1987, pp. 111, 129ff.). The constellations which followed the peace treaties of Utrecht (1713), Westphalia (1648) and, to a certain degree, Cambrai (1529), it is argued in this study, also approximated the hegemonic constellation.

In its second phase, the world order is marked by greater instability and an increase in interstate violence and war. This phase is called the phase of challenge because the pre-eminent core power is increasingly challenged – it is displaying slower rates of economic and military growth than some of the other great powers; it is criticized for its self-serving foreign policies. As a result its pre-eminence is flagging. The gap in wealth, force and authority which exists between it and other great powers is narrowing.

The third phase of the world order is marked by a more equal distribution of capabilities among the great powers. This is the phase of decline. It is so denoted because the pre-eminent state is declining relative to other powers. During this final phase, the interstate system is characterized by greater equality among core states. And as a consequence of greater equality comes greater uncertainty about the ranking order of the great powers. Since the rules of international behaviour are ultimately enforced by the great powers, it becomes increasingly unclear which of them it is that defines and enforces the rules of interstate behaviour. Thus, conflicts arise more frequently. These can no longer be solved by the pre-eminent state alone, they must be tackled through cooperation or balance of power – or not at all. War does not necessarily occur among the great powers with greater frequency in this phase, but diplomacy becomes more complex, more difficult, more intense and its stakes grow higher.

The thirty or forty years of peace which follow every wave of great wars correspond to a new world order's relatively peaceful, hegemonic phase. This phase is undermined by an increase in conflict and wars which mark the phase of challenge. This is, in turn, followed by a reduction of interstate violence as a balance-of-power principle establishes itself among the great powers. Finally, a new wave of great wars destroys the declining world order altogether.

Wars, great powers and hegemony

The sketch above provides a quick presentation of a few central definitions of the argument and a brief synopsis of the conceptual scheme which guides it. But some of its implications should already be evident: that the rise and fall of world orders is tightly related to waves of global warfare and to the rise and fall of great powers. That world orders may be described as a global process consisting of three successive phases – hegemony, challenge and decline. That these phases represent an evolution from a hegemonic constellation to a balance of power. That these phases describe an evolution from hierarchy to anarchy – or, perhaps, better: from relative order based on hierarchy in the initial phase of hegemony to relative anarchy based on greater equality of power in the concluding phase of decline.

The sketch also shows that waves of great wars are seen as having a formative impact on world order. On the one hand they destroy established world orders; on the other, they provide the conditions for new ones. The major reason is that all wars create coalitions. Great wars create great coalitions. Great wars force great powers to become military allies; they make independent and sovereign great powers into coalition partners. By virtue of long-lasting struggles against a common enemy, the great powers draw a distinction between 'us' and 'them'; the states assume a common identity as 'friends' against a mighty common 'foe'. Their understanding of world politics is shaped by this common experience.

From each winning coalition emerges a powerful, leading state. This state, as Mowat suggests, emerges pre-eminent and wields a particular influence on the final phases of the war and on the new world order which emerges in its wake. Spain emerged pre-eminent from the Italian wars; the United Provinces emerged pre-eminent from the Thirty Years War; England emerged pre-eminent both from the wars of Louis XIV and from the Napoleonic Wars. The pre-eminent state dominates international conduct in the wake of the wave of great wars. It becomes the leading power of a new postwar world order.

It is argued here, that these states – Spain, the United Provinces, England I and England II, respectively – were so pre-eminent in the aftermath of the great waves that they constituted hegemons. And that the immediate postwar period is best described as a hegemonic condition.

Hegemony means pre-eminence in power. However, before exploring the hegemonic condition further, it is important to recall that power is here defined in terms of three components: military force, economic wealth and command over public opinion. The debate about the rise and fall of great powers has tended to emphasize two of these: i.e., the military and the economic aspects of power. Paul Kennedy's famous book, *The Rise and Fall of the Great Powers*, for example, focuses entirely on the interaction of military force and economic wealth; it excludes the normative aspects of power altogether.[11] Kennedy discusses five hundred years of international relations without ever considering the importance of the normative aspect of power. In this neglect lies the main shortcoming of an otherwise outstanding analysis.

This shortcoming is most obvious in Kennedy's analysis of late cold war politics. He portrays the United States and the Soviet Union as two great powers. This portrayal is not untrue. But it is incomplete enough to be mis-leading – so misleading, in fact, that Kennedy forecast the demise of the United States at a time when it in fact was the Soviet Union which was on the cusp of collapse owing to deteriorating economic and political performance and the erosion of trust in civil society (Seligman 1992, pp. 170ff., 1997).

This point is so central to this study that it is worth elaborating upon – even at the peril of elaborating excessively on a point which will be introduced later in the story. Kennedy did not stress clearly enough that the two superpowers were, in fact, quite incompatible actors in important respects. He did not recognize sufficiently that the Soviet Union was the inferior actor in the cold war world order because he routinely excluded the normative aspects of power from his analysis. The USA was always strong in terms of normative power, whereas the USSR was weak.

At the risk of overstating the point, it can be claimed that this crucial difference between the two superpowers may be traced back to a difference in capital. The Soviet Union developed its physical and its human capital in impressive ways during the first half of the twentieth century – the development of machines, tools and other productive equipment was especially rapid during the early Stalinist era.[12] The United States, too, developed its physical and human capital by leaps and bounds during the first half of the twentieth century. However, the United States also developed its 'social capital'.

Both the USSR and the USA conspicuously developed their physical and human capital during the first half of the twentieth century – i.e., they made changes in resources and material so as to make tools that facilitate production, and they educated their workers in ways which gave them knowledge, skills and capabilities to act in new, more productive ways. But of the two powers, only the USA developed its social capital in ways which sustained a dynamic and trustworthy order. This difference in capital development shines some important light on the different fates of the two superpowers in the second half of the twentieth century. The long and the short of it is that American society has been marked by trust and orderly and continued socio-economic development, whereas Soviet society has not.

Throughout the cold war, the US made itself the confident, credible and trustworthy advocate of liberal, democratic values; and it enjoyed the support of its own citizens as well as that of US allies and trading partners. The Soviet Union advocated Marxist–Leninist doctrines and met with less enthusiasm. Under Stalin's dictatorship, Marxism–Leninism was sustained by fear-induced passivity. The Stalinist practice replaced consensus with force, dialogue with terror and trust with fear. The Soviet ideology grew rigid and formulaic; it lost active support both at home and among the USSR's primary allies and trading partners. The difference between the USA and the USSR in power over opinion was notably stark and consequential in the divided Europe of the cold war. For whereas liberal, democratic ideas were embraced and emulated by American allies in Western Europe, Marxist–Leninist ideas were resented by Soviet allies in Eastern Europe and had, on occasion, to be reinforced by troops and tanks. Most West Europeans saw the USA as a legitimate great power; most East Europeans saw the USSR as a conqueror and an oppressor. When the Soviet Union suffered economic decline in addition, it was thrown into a grave crisis and, finally, into a tailspin towards collapse.

There is an essential difference between great power based on force and great power rooted in consent. And only the latter qualifies as 'hegemony'. This recognition provides the key to the great power status of the United States in the twentieth century – and also to England in the nineteenth and eighteenth centuries, to the United Provinces in the seventeenth century and, to some degree, even to Spain during the sixteenth century.

One reason why these great powers could dominate, in turn, the world without triggering a balance-of-power reaction was that each case of dominance occurred in the aftermath of waves of great wars. The other great powers were exhausted by warfare, and the pre-eminent power was so superior as to be unbeatable. But another reason for this anomaly is that the dominant power temporarily possessed a substantial social capital and enjoyed a high degree of trust in international society. More concretely, the pre-eminent power expressed common values and norms developed among coalition partners during the wave of great wars. In this sense, the pre-eminent powers were 'hegemonic'. This second reason for postwar dominance is so compelling – and the importance of the consensual aspect of political power is so neglected in international relations analysis – that it deserves to be more closely explored.

Hegemony has been a much-used word in international relations analysis in recent years. However, many authors who apply it have overlooked the consensual connotation which informs the term. Hegemony has in much recent international relations scholarship too often been used as synonymous with great power. According to the ancient usage, however, hegemony means something more than greatness. And a hegemon is more than a great power. To be hegemonic means to possess the authority of command. It includes a notion of primacy based on a component of just and legitimate leadership. Pre-eminence in wealth and force is a necessary but not a sufficient precondition of hegemony. Hegemony involves pre-eminence which is sustained by a shared understanding among social actors of the values, norms rules and laws of political interaction; of the patterns of authority and the allocation of status and prestige, responsibilities and privileges.

In this conception of hegemony lies a key to the rise of world orders and to the unopposed pre-eminence of one distinct great power. This power is militarily strong – stronger than the others – materially wealthy, *and* it is normatively influential: it expresses a code of values, norms and rules for social conduct that other great powers embrace. Why does one power have such normative influence? Why does it set the tone for the political discourse of its age? Why does it articulate the political sentiment of the times? Partly because it is strong and wealthy. By being Number One. By being the best, the strongest, the wealthiest. It is seen by others as possessing a keen knowledge of the creation of wealth and power. Its military techniques, its economic processes, its political structures are emulated by others who see in its institutions a blueprint for the development of their own power and prestige. But also – and this is a simple answer which has been much neglected in recent debates – a power exerts a unique normative influence because it stresses the universal application of its values. It represents good values and norms – virtues like freedom, decency, honesty, equality. It articulates these values with great sincerity. And it grows more sincere the more it is admired, flattered and wooed by others.

In this conception of hegemony lies also a key to the demise of world orders and the decline of great powers. A pre-eminent power declines when its military strength and economic wealth become more equal to those of other core states. But its loss of authority and command of public opinion – at home and abroad – are also a decisively important component of decline. Hegemony, as defined above, has a moral component. A hegemon owes its commanding position to its effective articulation of globally relevant values, norms and rules of social interaction. If it loses this normative authority, it will also forfeit its commanding position.

Conclusion

The reason for probing past hegemons and for comparing past world orders is, of course, to obtain a greater perspective on and more knowledge about international politics in general. But the study is also guided by the hope that this probing of past orders will shed some light on the cold war and the recent transition to a post-cold war world. It agrees with John Gaddis's claim that

> if we are to grasp the nature of the post-World War II international system, then we will need an analytical framework capable of accounting for the rise and fall of great powers; but also one that incorporates variations in the nature of power and the influence it produces, as well as the limitations on power that permit peripheries to make a difference, even when things are being run from very powerful centres. (Gaddis, 1997, p. 27)

The four waves of great wars identified by Mowat – the Italian wars, the Thirty Years War, the wars of Louis XIV and the Napoleonic Wars – can easily be completed by the two World Wars of our own century (1914–18/1939–45). This fifth wave of great wars is not discussed in the first part of this study for reasons which are elaborated upon below: the decades which followed 1914 brought a transition from modern to contemporary history. They suggest a transition from an epoch marked by elitist control of power resources to an age marked by mass access to them – to an age of mass democracy in which political power was vastly disseminated into the hands of those who control air power, nuclear weapons, micro-electronics, cathode-ray-tube means of instant communications and global webs of finance and systems of information, intelligence and military command. Although the evolution of a *Pax Americana* after World War II displayed the central features of previous world orders, international relations are today so different from previous ages that it would be foolhardy to expect an exact repetition of great power dynamics. The American world order is included in this project; but it is discussed in Part Two as a case *sui generis*.

Nevertheless, the key to the rise of great powers – and to the establishment of world order – still lies in the moral influence which the pre-eminent state exerts on other great powers. The problems are (and here lies the key to decline) first, that the pre-eminent power must be second to none in wealth and in military force; and second that its moral authority must be beyond reproach. Once its military arsenal lags, and once its material wealth declines, it will also lose moral power. And if the pre-eminent power disintegrates at home, it will lose the domestic consensus which gives it authority and power over public opinion abroad. The disintegration of political consensus at home has always augured a reduction of moral authority abroad.

In 1989, on the heels of the collapse of Communism in Eastern Europe and the end of the cold war, an exuberant US President Bush announced the birth of a new world order. This was a premature and vastly misleading statement. Although the old world order was quickly fading, no new world order was then ready to be put in its place. Nearly a century ago Antonio Gramsci, seeking to understand the great changes that swept his world, sighed that he was living in an age where the old order was waning but the new was yet to be born. In 1989, Bush would have done better to paraphrase the old Italian Communist.

Notes

1 The classic discussion of this conception of power is still Russell (1938). A more detailed discussion is found in Chapter 3 of this present volume.

2 This study uses the same (limited) concept of great powers as Paul Kennedy (1987, p. xvi) – i.e. Western European states such as Spain, the Netherlands, France, Great Britain, Russia and, currently, the United States. This use of the term originates with Leopold von Ranke who, in his essay 'Die grossen Mächte', argued

that European states invented a novel, multi-polar international order and who sought to survey the fluctuations of this order. His purpose was to show the 'evolution of the modern ages' (Ranke 1872, p. 4), which he did by explaining why certain countries rose to a pre-eminence which they subsequently lost.

3 This narrow focus does not imply a total neglect of the other zones. First, because systematic relationships between the core and the peripheral zones constitute an important aspect of modern international interaction – a substantial part of the great powers' wealth was, for example, extracted from colonies in the periphery. Second, because the line which divides the haves from the have-nots is not fixed. Individual states may cross it, given time and appropriate circumstances. States move in and out of the world's zones – as when England moved into the core zone towards the end of the seventeenth century, and relegated Holland to semi-peripheral status; or when the United States evolved from being a peripheral colony in the eighteenth century to becoming the world core in the twentieth.

4 The Italian wars (1494–1529) mark a natural point of origin for the modern world-system. The wars marked a towering rupture with medieval political practices in several respects. They marked the first occasion on which gunpowder was used on a substantial scale. The use of artillery caused catastrophic losses for cavalry troops – and meant, in turn, that the old warrior aristocracy lost its leading role in warfare and its high position in civil society. Instead, kings and princes were encouraged to build their armies from the cheaper (and less powerful) infantrymen, whom they equipped with the new, deadly handguns.

This military revolution encouraged the growth of several new monarchies in Europe. It marked the advent of a plurality of independent territorial states and the rise of a European interstate system. It also marked the growth of more permanent military establishments and the strategic coordination of the three key components of the modern army (cavalry, infantry and artillery) financed by a central exchequer.

Such political-military changes were attended by economic transformations. As war grew in scale and cost, the monarchs of Europe needed more income. Taxes were the traditional source of royal income. But as the aristocracy declined in wealth and status, the kings were driven towards new, wealthy urban groups. In order to tax these groups more heavily, the monarch granted them more influence in domestic affairs. The monarch increasingly included them in deliberations over matters of national expenditure as advisers in royal councils, a function they assumed at the expense of the old aristocracy (Poggi 1978). Thus, changes in the fiscal apparatus of Europe's new monarchies encouraged the growth of new, semi-representative political institutions (Schumpeter 1976, p. 141).

Long-distance trade emerged as a second, new and promising source of royal income in the fifteenth and sixteenth centuries. The monarchs of Western Europe noticed soon enough that their fiscal income increased in proportion with mercantile profits. Thus, they found it in their interest to encourage trade and colonialism by royal privileges, subsidies and new commercial laws. The chief example of royal encouragement of private enterprise was the chartered company, a venture which forcefully encouraged Western exploration overseas and which greatly fuelled the Western surge of discoveries and colonialism.

On the basis of their new-found wealth, the monarchs of Europe began to rival the princes and emperors of other regions in splendour and power. By the early sixteenth century, Europe was as wealthy and as strong as the Turkish empire. The extent of European power stretched past the East African coast to the Indian Ocean and to South East Asia in the east and the Americas in the west. The modern weapons, wealth and culture of Western Europe were beginning to dominate the politics of the globe (Wolf 1982).

This domination was greatly enhanced by the spread of a new technology of interchangeable printing type in the second half of the fifteenth century. It revolutionized the storage and dissemination of thought and ideas, and played a central role in the diffusion of secular Renaissance values and in the making of the Reformation. Bibles were among the first books that obtained a vast dissemination by the new technology. This was not always a good thing: for as churchmen and kings in different regions of Europe found differences in each other's Bible translations and commentaries, they realized that there existed great disagreements about basic interpretations of doctrine. A German monk named Luther played a particularly important role in spreading this realization. He was courageous enough to argue in print against the pope. In the severe controversy which ensued, Luther first presented his arguments in Latin, but then took to German. His claims were immediately disseminated and had an entire continent in ferment.

All kinds of additional texts very soon rolled off the presses in the new print vernacular (Anderson 1983). Fables, romance novels, sundry handbooks, maps and navigation tables. And, last but not least: translations of Greek and Latin classics. All these texts were spread during the time of the Italian wars – indeed, since soldiers were hired from far away to participate in the fighting, books were among the valuable objects they brought with them as booty.

Although the Italian wars finally destroyed Renaissance Italy, they also helped disseminate its secular culture to the rest of Europe, thus helping to change the Continent and the world forever.

5   The second rupture of Western history began in the years that led up to World War I. The military, economic and intellectual upheavals which occurred in the later years of the nineteenth century ignited historical processes and cast up the social institutions of a new, contemporary international order. Improvements in economic and military capabilities gave rise to new modes of production and destruction. The rise of mass society integrated the populations of the world into new economic and political processes; new ideologies and normative codes disseminated by new means of communications and guided by new modes of political mobilization and mass control, provided the precondition for mass society – of liberal-pluralist types on the one hand, and of totalitarian varieties (Communism and Fascism) on the other.

Closely associated with these tendencies was an unprecedented expansion of international interaction. One of the characteristic features of contemporary world politics is that many of its most formative events had their origins far away from Europe; that the old, Continental cockpit of international relations was superseded by a wider world stage.

Two decisive chains of events foreshadowed the characteristic features of the new, contemporary world. The first was the rise of the East–West conflict. It began in the last years of the nineteenth century, when the United States expanded beyond its western borders and developed its own sphere of influence in South America and the Pacific; simultaneously, Russia expanded south-eastwards and created a vast empire which, at the turn of the century, infringed upon the ambitions of the Pacific powers. When Europe exhausted itself during the two World Wars of this century, America and Russia came to loom as newly arrived giants on either side of the Old World. After World War I, this development was reinforced by an ideological division between Wilsonian and Leninist visions of a new world order. After World War II, this ideological contest was accentuated and consolidated by an inflexible, world-scale military and economic rivalry.

The second decisive chain of events was the emergence of the north–south conflict. In the final years of the nineteenth century, European power in Asia and Africa stood at its zenith; but half a century, two world wars and a contested process of decolonization later, only the vestiges of European domination remained. Between 1945 and 1960, no less than forty countries with a population of eight million revolted against European colonialism and won independence. It was an unprecedented reversal in human history in both size and rapidity. This change in the position of the nations of Asia and Africa and their relations with Europe on the one hand and with the USA and the USSR on the other amounts to a decisive rupture in the history of the world (Barraclough 1974, pp. 153–99).

6 The most basic innovations occurred in Iberia – in Portugal and Spain – which is, in many ways, a gateway into the modern world. Fifteenth-century Spain is still medieval in many ways; the seventeenth century is modern. From the vantage point of the 1990s, the towering figure of Christopher Columbus shades almost all others from our view of this century. It is most fitting that it is an Italian who cuts such a dominant figure, since he thus can be made to represent the continuity with the dominant power of the Renaissance: Italian city-states. Furthermore, Columbus traversed the distance between the Old World and the New in more than one sense. Not only did he cross the Atlantic to discover an (for his contemporary Europeans) entirely new world; he also crossed the invisible line of demarcation between the Middle Ages and the modern ages. In this sense he was a traveller in time as well as in space.

7 An elaboration of this sketch is found in Braudel (1984, p. 3). A formal application is found in Wallerstein (1974, 1979, 1989). It should be noted already here, that whereas Braudel and Wallerstein focus on the dynamics of the world-economy, I also include an interstate system and an epistemological system – a 'system of knowledge and thought' (Foucault 1973). The long sixteenth century did not only see the advent of the capitalist world-economy, it also saw the evolution of the modern territorial states and their systematic interaction, and it witnessed the advent of a new, modern mentality.

8 This point is further discussed in Chapter 2 of the present volume. It could be argued that a study such as this ought to have included a presentation of the literature on war cycles. Such a presentation would cover much of the same ground as Goldstein (1988, pp. 99–123) and would be most unlikely to improve upon his excellent discussion.

9 It is argued below that just as the Italian wars can be 'taken to begin modern history' (Mowat 1928, p. 1), so World Wars I and II can be seen as its end. This argument is convincingly presented in Barraclough (1976). It will also be repeated in the second part of the study.

10 Wright (1965) argues that 'major wars' have occurred with great regularity throughout modern history, and been followed, first, by a period of general peace,

then by a cluster of 'minor wars' and, finally, by another period of peace. Toynbee (1954) claims that a phase of 'general war' is followed by a 'breathing space' which deteriorates into a conflictual era of 'supplementary wars' until a more lengthy 'general peace' is established. Gilpin (1981) maintains that great 'crises' have recurred with great regularity through modern international history and that each crisis is resolved through 'hegemonic war' which re-establishes an equilibrium in the international system – for a while. Wallerstein (1984) explains that 'world wars' have regularly broken out during the course of the modern world system, and that they have been followed by phases of 'hegemonic maturity', 'declining hegemony' and the ascent of rival hegemonies. Modelski (1987, 1989) claims that phases of 'global war' are regularly followed by phases of 'world power', 'global problems' and 'coalitioning' respectively. Different authors, then, present their arguments in widely different discourses. Wright and Toynbee may be said to represent a traditional realist paradigm, Gilpin a neo-realist approach and Wallerstein a 'revolutionist' world-systems approach (Knutsen 1997). Yet, these arguments by six influential authors show a remarkable similarity in content – as Table 1 below demonstrates.

Table 1   *Six authors' views of war periodicity*

Wright	*Toynbee*	*Gilpin*	*Wallerstein*	*Modelski*	*Knutsen (this study)*
major war	general war	resolution of systemic crisis	world war	global war (macrodecision)	wave of great wars
peace	breathing space	systems equilibrium	hegemonic maturity	world power (implementation)	phase of hegemony
minor war	supplementary wars	redistribution of power	declining hegemony	global problems (agenda setting)	phase of challenge
peace	general peace	systems disequilibrium	ascending hegemony	coalitioning (core alliance)	phase of competitive disruption

11 As the subtitle of Kennedy's book indicates: *Economic Change and Military Conflict from 1500 to 2000.*

12 Paul Kennedy is not alone in seeing the industrialization of the Soviet Union as 'something unprecedented in history'. For example, during the period covered by Stalin's two first five-year plans (1928 to 1937), the coal output of the USSR more than trebled (from 35.4 million to 128 million tons) and steel production more than quadrupled (from 4 million to 17.7 million tons). 'Electricity output rose sevenfold, machine-tool figures over twentyfold, and tractors nearly fortyfold. By the late 1930s, indeed, Russia's industrial output had not only soared well past that of France, Japan and Italy but had probably overtaken Britain's as well' (Kennedy 1987, p. 323 see also Kennedy's table 28, p. 299).

Part One
Patterns of the past

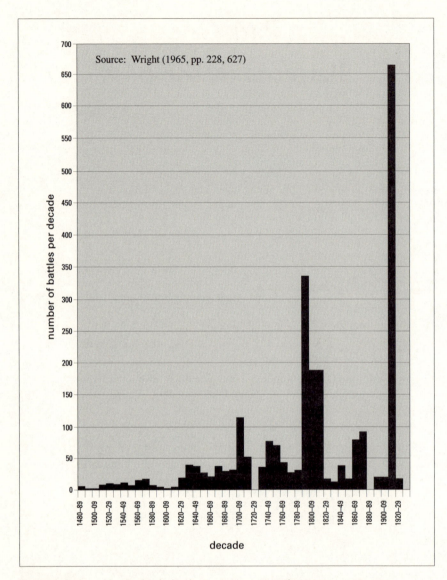

Figure 1 Number of battles fought by the great powers (Wright 1965, pp. 228, 627)

1

The wave of great wars

War, says Heraclitus, is the father of things. From the clash of
counterpitched forces in the moment of mortal danger ... arise new
and most consequential developments. (Ranke 1872[1833])

Great powers emerge from great wars. What kind of wars are great wars? And
how do they stimulate certain states' growth into greatness? The answer to
the first question is that great wars are 'hegemonic struggles' (Gilpin 1981,
pp. 186ff.). They are wars of a kind which has occurred with rough regularity
every hundred years throughout modern history. To these regular waves of great
wars belong: the Italian wars (1494–1529), the Thirty Years War (1618–48),
the wars of Louis XIV (1672–1713) and the Napoleonic Wars (1791–1815).

The second question requires a more complex response. It goes without
saying that great wars have great destructive effects on human lives and on
material wealth and that great wars deal devastating blows at extant world
orders. Thus, the Italian wars destroyed the city-state system of Renaissance
Italy; the Thirty Years War exhausted Spain and destroyed the sixteenth-
century world order; the wars of Louis XIV exhausted the United Provinces
and irrevocably disturbed the seventeenth-century world order; the Napoleonic
Wars exhausted France and brought about the demise of the *ancien régime*.

It is less immediately apparent that great wars also have constructive consequences. It was during the waves of great war that new world orders were
erected. During the Italian wars the semi-medieval Iberian powers rose to world
pre-eminence. During the Thirty Years War, the United Provinces emerged as
the dominant great power of the seventeenth-century world order. During the
wars of Louis XIV Great Britain rose to pre-eminence in the eighteenth-century
world order. The Napoleonic Wars nearly brought England to its knees; however, the country assumed the leadership of an anti-French alliance, defeated
France and re-emerged as the pre-eminent actor of a new, nineteenth-century
world order.

Why did these states emerge from the waves of great wars as pre-eminent
states? Several answers may be offered to this question. One answer is that the
wars stimulated processes of state- and nation-building. Another is that the

wars offered opportunities for far-flung expansion. Yet another is that war made it possible for new, proud, revolutionary regimes to project worldwide a moral message which would serve as an alternative to the corrupt ways of the old established states.

Wars and wealth

New, ascendant states profited from the great wars. Spain, the United Provinces and England (twice) benefited from the waves of great wars. Very briefly told: Spain was stimulated by the Italian wars to intensify its profitable ventures in the Americas. The United Provinces improved their agriculture and industries during the Thirty Years War and greatly expanded their foreign trade in both foodstuffs and manufactures. England profited from both the wars of Louis XIV and the Napoleonic Wars – the first stimulated shipping and agriculture, the second industrial growth.

An examination of the war conduct of the ascending states reveals some significant commonalities. First, the major battlefields were located at a safe distance from the ascendant states. This simple fact is decisively important, for it means that the new states' factors of production – land, labour and capital – were not destroyed by battle. It was the other, older, great states which saw their capital plant ruined, their land destroyed, their labour force killed, maimed or transformed into refugees. And as their opponents' factors of production were destroyed, their productivity reduced and their wealth diminished by war, the ascending states emerged relatively stronger by comparison.

Second, wars offer, among other things, opportunities. The ascending states were all sea powers that grabbed the opportunities which war handed to them. They kept their distance from the nearby, Continental battlefields and engaged instead in far-away conflicts while Continental powers had their main attention diverted elsewhere. Great wars, and the destructive effect they had for their Continental competitors, provided the ascending powers with opportunities for expansion. The hegemons have all been major colonial powers. They have been West European territorial states surrounded by a mantle of empire, the foundations of which can be traced to waves of wars which afforded the ascending states opportunities for expansion. War brought increases in trade, and the subsequent peace provided them with a vested interest in protecting the freedom of the seas upon which their commerce depended.

Third, during the great wars, the ascending states all fought in distant, overseas regions. Here, their armed forces vanquished all other actors. On the one hand, their navies proved superior against competing European powers, because these were distracted by great land wars on the Continent. On the other, their sailors and soldiers were superior to indigenous troops, because these had the disadvantage of less lethal technologies and less discipline. In short, the waves of great wars provided opportunities for colonial conquest. Spain, the United Provinces and England (twice) all increased their overseas possessions substantially during the course of the waves of great wars.

Fourth, most ascending states were slow to engage in Continental wars. True, Spain did not wait long before it intervened in Italy to contain the adventures of the French king Francis I. But the United Provinces engaged only intermittently in the Thirty Years War. And England initially kept out of the wars against Louis XIV and Napoleon.

Fifth, the ascending states not only joined the great wars late: once engaged in a grand European alliance, they tended to participate lightly in the military operations. With the significant exception of Spain, the ascending states emphasized not the military but the economic aspects of the war effort; they tended to see their role as that of a supplier of money and materiel to other states. This role greatly benefited their domestic economies, for instead of using their men as soldiers and sending them abroad into battle, the ascending states applied their citizens at home as workers.

Sixth, the ascending states were built around expansive urban centres, usually around a single big, productive, splendid, wealthy city – Seville, Amsterdam or London. Braudel noted how such urban centres provided a dynamic, wealth-creating and administrative core to the ascending state. Great cities are always wrought with contrasts. In the urban environment opulence and devastation exist side by side. Here, religious belief is sometimes intensified and organized into fanatical movements; yet, agnosticism is also a characteristically urban phenomenon. People who inhabit great cities must learn early on to deal with such contrasts. Every member of a great city must learn quickly how to deal with the myriads of total strangers with whom they constantly have to deal. City societies would soon unravel unless their great variations in fortunes, interests and opinions were contained by some moral code which militated against the meddling in the affairs of others. Cities could not exist without common norms and rules of social conduct. On one level, city dwellers may appear to be callous, self-centred individuals who do not look twice at an unknown person lying in the street. But on another, city dwellers display unique degrees of tolerance and trust when dealing with perfect strangers. Tocqueville observed this. He noted that in great American cities, social codes and modes of association became 'the mother of action, studied and applied by all' (quoted in Fukuyama 1995, p. vii). Urban life is wrought with economic, political and ideological tension; but it also contains subtle mechanisms which balance and contain the tensions – shared basic values, commonly shared norms, codes of routine behaviour and professional standards of conduct. Great cities are, on the whole, marked by tolerance, liberty and trust. 'City air liberates' is a slogan with roots back in the early Middle Ages.

Seventh, during waves of great wars, ascending states receive streams of refugees from the war-torn Continent. The atmosphere of tolerance and liberty of the ascending urban centres attracted members of minorities who were persecuted elsewhere. Thus, in the late fifteenth and early sixteenth centuries, workers and business professionals from Italy settled in the Iberias. During the seventeenth century, when the religious wars swept Europe, and Protestants and Jews suffered persecution on a predominantly Catholic Continent, refugees scrambled for entry into the more peaceful and tolerant Dutch society. During the eighteenth century many political radicals fled from absolutist Europe and settled in England; such migrations increased during the repressive reconstruction which followed the French Revolution. These migrants were, as a rule, young and endowed with intellectual and entrepreneurial skills. They added their energies to the political economy of the ascendant states. They contributed to the political and economic diversity of its cities and to the cultural vibrancy of their adopted nation. And one notable effect of this migration was that, as the new states emerged in the ascendant, the complexities and diversities of their core cities were complemented by religious and ethnic diversity.

Eighth, all great wars alter the political economies of their participants. The states' modes of production, procurement and distribution are restructured to meet the demands of war. Spain, the United Provinces and England (twice) were no exceptions. In all cases the great wars encouraged the government to intervene in the civil economy and regulate the infrastructures and the patterns of production. This intervention adapted the civil economy to the geostrategic purposes of war. And its effect was not only to strengthen military performance, but also to enhance economic performance. Such intervention regularly improved the country's performance in certain key industrial sectors, such as mining, metallurgy, shipbuilding and transport.

Ninth, by producing supplies for lease or sale, the ascending states increased both their wealth and their power. Habsburg Spain, the United Provinces and England enhanced their economic as well as their military capabilities during their respective waves of great wars. They emerged from these wars as great commercial powers; they commanded land forces of unrivalled efficiency, and were sea powers second to none.

Finally, wars create patriots. The successful struggle against a mighty common foe enhances the unity and cohesion of a state. All the ascending states discussed here experienced their societies becoming more tightly knit during the course of the respective wave of great wars. As the wars ended, the ascending societies were characterized by a high level of social solidarity undergirded by a common code of values, norms and rules of social conduct.

Wars, wealth and foundation myths

Wars create patriots. The protracted struggle of the new, ascending states against foreign enemies consolidated the nations' political mythology and accentuated the extant distinction between 'us' and 'them'. The waves of great wars thus helped consolidate the moral unity within states. Also, it instilled some measure of community in the interstate coalition of which these new states were members. The long-lasting struggles against a common enemy drew a sharp dividing line between 'us' and 'them' on an international scale.

A closer examination of the four waves of great wars in modern history indicates that the experience of a great war made a lasting impression on the statesmen, the politicians, the soldiers and often the common citizens who lived through it. The common experience of war informed the political understanding of an entire generation whose conception of a postwar world order was drawn largely from what they believed to have happened in the recent past (May 1976, pp. 18, 190). But such an examination also reveals another common factor: that ascending states which entered them had, prior to the war, been shaken by deep economic and political transformations. And the common experiences which resulted from these previous domestic upheavals were exacerbated by the participation in great foreign wars later.

Together, domestic upheavals and foreign wars consolidated a common political mythology which contributed greatly to the unity of the ascending powers. Spain, the United Provinces and England all went through a formative phase of domestic upheaval some decades before they emerged as great powers on the world scene. These domestic upheavals created a common mental outlook which unified the inhabitants of the new states socially and justified their political regimes. Furthermore, the new states had scarcely put their house in order before they were engaged in major *inter*national upheavals – in waves of great wars which further consolidated the new political regimes. The militant and anti-Islamic brand of Christianity expressed by sixteenth-century Spain informed the general outlook of the interstate relations of the century. The Dutch arguments for free international trade by states and (chartered) companies were echoed by most seventeenth-century powers. The English vision of a free (and, later, self-equilibrating) world economy was embraced by eighteenth- and nineteenth-century great powers. The peace conferences which formally ended each wave of great wars were important fora of influence. For by helping determine the conditions of peace, the ascendant powers could, in fact, help define the key rules of international interaction in the postwar system.[1]

The rise to international pre-eminence of Spain, the United Provinces, England I and England II were all preceded by domestic upheavals and by deep economic and political transformations. The advent of Spain was attended by strife which engulfed the Iberian peninsula in violence and disorder for centuries: the *reconquista*. The second half of the fifteenth century saw both the final phase of this struggle to expel the Moors from the Peninsula and the union between Castile and Aragon (1469). The sixteenth century witnessed a violent and protracted struggle in the Netherlands during which seven Dutch provinces signed a treaty of confederation in 1579. In the seventeenth century, the British Isles were shaken by violence and civil wars after which England emerged as a great unified monarchy. In the final decades of the eighteenth century another 'great transformation' (Polanyi 1957) of revolutionary proportions shook England and brought forth a new socio-political structure in the early 1800s.

These domestic upheavals constituted crucial state- and nation-building processes. Spain emerged from them as a monarchy supported by a confident landed aristocracy. The United Provinces emerged as a confederation of independent provinces dominated by a merchant oligarchy. England emerged as a constitutional monarchy supported by a nobility of socially active, noble landowners – an order which was later modified by parliamentary reforms around the time of the Industrial Revolution.

In addition, these upheavals were fecund mythogenic events. Each produced a distinct political mythology which helped unify a new, emerging society and justify and stabilize a new regime – which were additionally legitimized by rapid economic advances that attended their consolidation. Sorel (1959), an early explorer of political mythologies, notes how a unifying mythology is often forged on the anvil of violent struggle. Sahlins (1989, p. 271) agrees and explains that the identity of a modern nation, 'like ethnic or communal identity, is contingent and relational: it is defined by the social or territorial boundaries drawn to distinguish the collective self and its implicit negation, the other'. Colley (1992, p. 6) applies this argument to the formation of modern states, and writes that the members of a society decide who they are by reference to who they are not. 'Once confronted with an obviously alien "Them", an otherwise diverse community can become a reassuring or merely desperate "Us"'.[2] By selecting, isolating and emphasizing certain aspects of the life of another nation, and by making these aspects symbolize what they themselves are not, a people reinforces its identity. Such identity-building fabrications are easily affected during war, when emotions are strong, reason is weak, stakes are high and choices seem clear and simple.

Sorel adds another point: that the original struggle is commonly remembered and revered. Acts of remembrance are often standardized into ritualistic celebrations in which decisive political events are celebrated as birth pangs of nationhood and sovereignty and key participants – generals or delegates – are revered as heroes and founders. Such formal ceremonies of remembrance contribute importantly to a nation's self-definition. They keep a nation's political history alive. And they introduce new generations to the values, norms and rules which its political mythology articulates. All these are mechanisms of socialization and contribute to the maintenance of a nation's political consensus.

All great powers possess political mythologies.[3] These justify their regimes and consolidate a popular consensus. They sustain people's social identity and they inform their habits of mind and their patterns of political thought and action.

Christian Spain and the Muslim other

The origins of the political mythology of sixteenth-century Spain lie in the late medieval *reconquista* of Muslim territories. Egged on by the crusading sentiment of the age, the Christian kings of south-western Europe reconquered the Iberian peninsula during the twelfth century.

The foundation myth of Spain was the product of a climate of intense medieval Christianity and ruthless methods. It included accounts of the exploits of legendary heroes – like El Cid. The struggle was largely completed by the end of the thirteenth century, with only the small Muslim kingdom of Granada existing as a tributary to Castile until 1492. The long Christian crusade against Islam provided a formative, collective experience which fuelled the evolution of distinct social institutions and instilled a unique mentality among the settlers. The reconquest occurred in leaps and bounds. The size of the territories, and the difficulties inherent in cultivating the arid soil of the Iberian highlands, forced the conquering kings to hand over vast areas to the noblemen who had assisted them. This practice created a unique society of great *latifundios*. It yielded a feudal-like political economy controlled by aristocrats whose great powers were reinforced by strong military orders and by the Church.

Under the impact of the long struggle with its Islamic 'other', Iberian Catholicism developed a particularly intense and belligerent Christianity. It portrayed all human existence as participation in a great morality play produced by a divine master dramatist. Finished in idea before it was enacted in fact, this great drama evolved around an infinitely complex, cosmic plot authored by an omniscient God before the world began. It was completed down to the last syllable of recorded time. God had created the world and placed mankind in it; in God's appointed time, this world would come to an end – the earth would be swallowed up in flames and good and evil men would be separated: the former would be saved, the latter would suffer eternal damnation.

On this attitude rested the immense spiritual power of Spain's political mythology. For although the key assumption of the attitude was that good

men go to heaven and bad men go to hell, there was also the assumption of
original sin: that all men are born sinful. They are therefore always at risk lest
they are instructed by the Church. This attitude provides one of the keys to
sixteenth-century politics. The Church and State – both of which derived their
just powers from the will of God – were constituted among men to teach them
submission and proper behaviour and to repel the Muslim threat. The fear of
Islam was accentuated in the late 1400s by a wave of Ottoman expansion, and
was boosted in the early 1500s by Spain's encounters with the expansionist
policies of Sulaiman the Magnificent (1520–66).

The Dutch, the Spanish and the deep blue sea

While the Christian *hidalgos* were reconquering the Iberian peninsula from the
infidels, the inhabitants of the windswept North Sea lowlands of the great
European plain reclaimed new land from nature – from marshes, bogs and
river plains. This difference in socio-economic conditions was reflected in
different political mythologies. The people of the Netherlands were informed
by generations of hard work, pragmatic calculation and extensive cooperation.
By the fourteenth century, there existed a number of productive, political units
in the area – some of them below sea level. Their distinct, collective experience
contributed to a set of unique institutions. In several provinces, these institutions evolved around the functions of building and maintaining dikes, pumps
and canals.

This experience of a continuing struggle against the sea provided fecund
mythogenic conditions for the development of distinct outlooks, practices,
attitudes and habits of mind. The Dutch were quite conscious of their unique
predicament. They were intensely aware of their unique history – that they
had built dikes to trap the sea and windmills to remove it; that they had used
canals, dikes, polders and wind-driven pumps to push back the North Sea itself,
and recovered new soil which they slowly cleansed and converted to fertile
fields.

The Dutch had not one but two enemies: the struggle against the sea was
only one factor which contributed to their political mythology. The other factor
was the long bitter war against Spain. During the fifteenth century, the Netherlands had been an entrepreneurial and wealthy region in the Habsburg empire.
In the early sixteenth century both Charles V and Philip II taxed the Dutch
when they needed to raise funds for military expeditions. Increasingly, the
Dutch perceived Spain as an exploitative, threatening, alien other. First, they
protested at Spain's insensitive violations of their old economic and religious
liberties. Then they fought them. Finally, they pressed for independence. In the
1560s, a series of armed conflicts began – that the Dutch later called the Eighty
Years War, and that historians call the Revolt of the Netherlands. In 1579

several northern provinces formed 'a closer union' to coordinate the struggle for liberation.[4] In 1581, they rejected the authority of Catholic king Philip II and named the Calvinist William of Orange Stadtholder of their new republic. In the long anti-Spanish struggle which followed, the Dutch union was forged ever more tightly.

It can hardly be overemphasized that the period between 1575 and 1650, which was the most intense period of land reclamation, was also a period of war during which the Dutch won their independence from Spain. The struggle for territorial and for national reclamation were parallel processes; both informed the distinct Dutch mythology in decisive ways.[5] When the Dutch compared their simple Calvinist virtues with the opulent and luxurious habits of Spain's Catholic nobility, they saw themselves as ennobled by their industry and their simplicity. This notion was reinforced by symbol-laden tales from the New Testament which featured fishermen, shipbuilders and simple people of occupations with which the Dutch could easily identify. It was also reflected in the growing strength of the Calvinist movement and in their emphasis on homely Christian virtues of modesty, cleanliness, frugality and hard work.[6]

If the Iberian other was Islamic, the Dutch other was Catholic (the Dutch themselves were predominantly Protestant). Catholics were perceived by the Dutch as aristocratic, oppressive and corrupt (whereas the Dutch saw themselves as bourgeois, free and pure). Like other Christian citizens, the Dutch often portrayed their most popular leaders as guides of a chosen people; of a nation blessed and protected by God. However, their portrayal was influenced by a unique Dutch experience which cast the common biblical tales in a maritime light. The Dutch commonly compared their statesmen to Noah, Jonah or Moses. And these leaders would, in turn, portray their adherents as a tried and tested people, divinely blessed and predestined to inherit a land which was not merely reclaimed but redeemed – and in the process morally transformed.

By the seventeenth century, Dutch society was religious, urban, literate and wealthy. It was sustained by a tradition of cooperation and informed by a common code of social conduct which reflected the values and norms of the urban merchants, tradesmen and artisans. Two central features of this common code are suggested by the concepts of liberty and reason. The notion of 'liberty of conscience' was one of the central features of the Dutch code – the importance of which had been insistently stressed by Calvinist rebels during the long Dutch war of liberation from Spain, and which worked as a magnet on persecuted minorities during the religious wars and the Thirty Years War.

But not all Dutch were Calvinists, and not all Calvinists were virtuous. The Dutch owed their pre-eminence less to austerity than to hard work, and less to piety than to the rational calculations of their commercial and financial institutions – calculations of risk (which gave rise to insurance schemes) and profit (which produced joint-stock companies). And here lies a second striking feature of the Dutch code of social behaviour: its rational, legal and peaceful forms of commercial procedure. The Dutch may have been not only the first bourgeois society, but the first really *modern* one. According to Toulmin (1990), the responsibility for the characteristically 'modern' ways of thinking about nature and society must be attributed to the 'new philosophers' of the seventeenth century.[7] A significant number of them were Dutch thinkers of high quality; others were exiled intellectuals who lived and worked in the urban centres of the Netherlands – the most 'rational', 'individualist' and tolerant spot of the age. The faith in reason and individual liberty lay at the base of a unifying Dutch code of social behaviour.[8] One contemporary observer noted that:

> what made that contemptible spot of Ground so considerable among the principal powers of *Europe* has been their Political Wisdom in postponing everything to Merchandise and Navigation, the unlimited Liberty of Conscience that is enjoy'd among them, and the unwearied Application with which they have always made use of the most effectual means to encourage and increase Trade in general. (Mandeville 1989[1714], p. 202)

Britain, the Glorious Revolution and empires

The civil war which caused so much human misery in seventeenth-century England also provided one of the most fertile mythogenic conditions in the political history of the Western world. It may be argued that the first concept of a nation developed in England. 'Not only was there a common name and myth of ethnic descent, but also a variety of historical memories and traditions', explains Anthony Smith (1991, p. 56). 'There was also a growing sense of a common culture revealed in the English language'.

This concept of a national community matured during the Civil War and the Glorious Revolution. From those uncertain times emerged a unique mythology of a 'glorious revolution' – usually adorned by tales about Cromwell's military republic, the restoration of the Tudor monarchy, the flight of king James II and the arrival of William III. This rich national mythology derives much of its political appeal from the foundational idea of a rationally constructed social contract.

The primary author of this idea was Thomas Hobbes, a philosopher who was deeply marked by the chaos, fear and destruction of the age. During the English Civil Wars, Hobbes envisioned a ruleless and violent state of nature where the life of man was 'solitary, poore, nasty, brutish and short' (Hobbes 1951[1651], p. 186). The only way out of this intolerable condition, he argued, was to form a society (and a government) through a solemn compact between the ruled and their rulers that defined the rights and duties of each.

After the wars, John Locke (1960[1689]) gave Hobbes's bleak vision of a social contract a kinder, gentler interpretation. Also, he grafted on to it two new components. First, he criticized the old doctrine of absolutist rule. Second, he defended the idea of parliamentary democracy. By referring to accounts of old Saxon traditions and applying them to contemporaneous conditions, Locke gave the political mythology a foundation where no clear line existed between history and political speculation. In the process, he devised a labour theory of property – a brilliantly simple argument which justified the acquisition and accumulation of private possession.

Locke's contract philosophy was published in the immediate aftermath of the English Civil War. It harmonized beautifully with Dutch and English commercial interests who helped install the Dutch Prince William on the English throne (1688/89). His accession was then fashioned (partly by William himself and partly by subsequent Whig historians) into one of the most persistent political myths of Western politics (Israel 1993). The myth explains how King James II forfeited his right to the English throne and how Prince William of Orange was invited to assume the throne in his 'personal capacity' as the husband of its heir, Princess Mary. It thus justified a military operation which has all the hallmarks of a Dutch invasion and a *coup* (Israel 1993). Furthermore, it flattered the English by claiming that they were a chosen people, rescued in the nick of time from Catholicism by a prince who expressed the constitutional will of a Protestant God – fortuitous deliverance from Spanish armadas and gunpowder plots are often additionally invoked to consolidate this claim of divine protection. Finally, and most decisively, it sustained a practically workable solution to a long and bloody conflict between England's fiscal and governmental institutions. The Glorious Revolution limited the power of the Crown by forcing the new Dutch king to honour his commitments in domestic affairs. This produced a marked increased in the security of private rights, and greatly improved the general conditions for investments and trade (North and Weingast 1989).

The myth of the Glorious Revolution sanctioned the principles of constitutional monarchy and parliamentary rule. It also expressed the virtues which had so encouraged the Dutch economy: godliness, property, industry, thrift, patriotism, individual liberty and tea drinking. Locke demonstrated why and under which conditions government is useful and ought to be accepted by all reasonable citizens as a voluntary obligation. Such virtuous attitudes – which were also expressed by Milton, Cumberland and other writers – were disseminated throughout English society by an expansion of primary education. It struck deep roots in the rapidly growing middle classes.

At the threshold of the eighteenth century, the myth of the Glorious Revolution was reinforced by the great wars which England fought against Continental powers, particularly France. William of Orange had originally been driven to covet the English throne by his desire to contain Louis XIV. Once installed as king, he immediately harnessed the power of the island in his old effort to combat the expansionist ambitions of French absolutism. The efforts were crowned with great success. Not only did he organize a series of great alliances and conduct wars which eventually exhausted France, he also welded the war-ravaged inhabitants of the British Isles into a nation. The wars which followed the accession of William III (1689) unified England and Wales and Scotland (1707) and invested the key symbols of the new 'United Kingdom' with patriotism. It was in violent turn-of-the-century opposition to France that the British found their distinct identity as a nation. Later, as the Anglo-French rivalry spread to other corners of the world, the Britons also 'defined themselves in contrast to the colonial peoples they conquered, peoples who were manifestly alien in terms of culture, religion and colour' (Colley 1992, p. 5).

At the turn of the nineteenth century, France once again played the role of the primary alien other whose threatening nature helped consolidate the British consensus and legitimize the government and its policies. The wars against France also helped stimulate the Industrial Revolution and justify a political addition to the old free-market mythology: against the statism of Robespierre and the militarism of Napoleon, the British insisted that government ought to be as small as possible, and that its sole purpose should be to ensure civil law, social order and individual freedom. This would provide optimal conditions for a social division of labour which would, in turn, guarantee the efficient production of wealth and the just distribution of property. After the Napoleonic Wars, the British argued that liberal-democratic institutions maximized humankind's potential for developing and using its unique capacities. This involved a restoration of the basic claim of the Western humanist tradition, man was no longer seen only as a consumer of utilities but as a doer, a creator, an enjoyer of his human attributes (Macpherson 1973, pp. 8ff.; 1977, pp. 44ff.; Colley 1992, pp. 177ff.). It also implied a vision of man as a *homo faber* that informed economic theories of the nineteenth century – political economists from Smith and Ricardo through Marx to Mill all anchored their social theories in it.

Wars, values and global expansion

Spain, the United Provinces, England I and England II were shaken by great domestic upheavals (often reaching the proportions of civil wars). These upheavals nourished a proliferation of tales and myths which imposed meaningful interpretations on past events and expressed hopes and ambitions for the future. They were birth pangs of new states – with lean and effective regimes which rapidly expanded their domestic wealth and their foreign influence.

These states had scarcely consolidated their domestic institutions before they were embroiled in great international conflicts and wars. One effect of these wars was to consolidate the new societies even more firmly. Another was to increase their power – raise their output of wealth, stimulate their production of weapons and weapons systems, induce them to enhance their armed forces and project their new, efficient power on a global scale. A third effect was to pull the ascendant state into the vortex of international conflict, providing it with a unique opportunity to exercise a formative influence upon world affairs.

The ascendant state played a growing role in world affairs. It forged alliances and exercised increasing influence on its coalition partners during the struggle against a common mighty foe. Later, this influence would climax during the peace conferences which were organized by the winning coalition after the war. Through alliance management and peace diplomacy the ascendant power wielded political influence which stretched well beyond the war and far into the postwar period. In fact, wartime cooperation and peacetime diplomacy helped set the tone for the postwar relations. And peacetime diplomacy laid the groundwork for a new, postwar world order.

The religious universalism of Spain

These tendencies – the wartime alliance management, the peacetime diplomacy and the growth of a common outlook among states – are noticeable in the case of the Italian wars. When the French king Charles VIII invaded Italy in 1494, the Spanish monarchs were not the only ones who perceived a serious challenge. Other European kings, too, sensed the threat. King Ferdinand of Aragon soon managed to work these common sensations into an anti-French alliance. A Holy League between Spain, England, the German Empire and the Papacy emerged in 1495, designed to check the advance of Charles VIII. 'In building up this coalition, Ferdinand laid the foundations of a diplomatic system that was to maintain and extend Spanish power throughout the sixteenth century' (Elliott 1977, p. 130).

This said, it must be added that this tendency towards alliance management is weaker in the case of sixteenth-century Spain than in later cases. For although the Spanish monarchs – first Ferdinand and later Charles V – made the Pope a reluctant agent, negotiated alliances with England and chased the French troops from one north Italian state after another, the war produced no clear and lasting alliance. For when Charles V's imperial troops destroyed the better part of French chivalry at the battle of Pavia and captured the French king, he frightened Europe's other rulers and lost their support. Indeed, the monarchs of Europe protested at the tough demands which Charles V forced upon vanquished France in the Treaty of Madrid (1526).

At this precise moment, however, one decisive event suspended their defection: the armies of Ottoman sultan Sulaiman the Magnificent advanced from Belgrade, destroyed the Hungarian forces and moved towards Vienna. When King Francis I of France opened up negotiations with Sulaiman, the rulers of Europe recoiled; and when he initiated a degree of cooperation with the sultan that approached a formal alliance, all good Christian monarchs were scandalized. When Ottoman armies destroyed Hungarian forces on the plain of Mohacs (1526) and tore westwards towards the gates of Vienna, they again approached Charles V. At an opportune moment, Charles V proposed a reasonable settlement of the Habsburg–Valois struggle. This time the peace conditions were sanctioned by other rulers. The so-called 'Ladies' Peace' of Cambrai[9] was signed in 1529 and terminated a series of great battles over Italy and consolidated Spanish pre-eminence in Europe.

Sorel claims that at the core of every political mythology lies a distinctive notion of an important difference between 'us' and an alien 'other'. Few cases illustrate this notion better than sixteenth-century Spain. The idea of a Europe spiritually united in Christendom and politically unified by Spain was suggested to Charles V by his tutor Guillaume de Cièvres and, later, forcefully expressed by his brilliant counsellor Mercurio de Gattinara. 'God has set you on the path towards a world monarchy', Gattinara exclaimed when Charles became Holy Roman Emperor in 1519. The impending Muslim invasion represented a unique opportunity to fulfil this grand ambition: a common enemy in the face of which European unity would be the most logical response. Spanish lawyers developed a doctrine which held that relations between Christian rulers were different from those between non-Christian societies. Thus, the preamble of the Treaty of Cambrai refers to the Italian wars as a 'great error' which unnecessarily divided Christian kings. Then it notes that a new and dangerous situation has been created by 'the invasions made by the Turk, enemy of Christendom'. Furthermore, it explains that it is imperative for the rulers of Europe to 'remedy errors, wrongs and objections which resulted from the war'; it calls upon all nations to convert the common forces of all Christian kings, princes and potentates to repel the Turk and other infidel enemies out of Christian faith.

The bourgeois republic of the Dutch

The Dutch political mythology was deeply anchored in Christian values. But it also had a clear, selfconscious Protestant interpretation – which was much reinforced by recurrent threats from Spain and other Catholic powers. Furthermore, whereas the political mythology of Spain expressed the views and interests of a rural warrior aristocracy, that of the Netherlands reflected the values and norms of an urban oligarchy of merchants, tradesmen and artisans. The Dutch mythology emphasized liberty – especially liberty of conscience but also liberty of travel and trade which became famously expressed in the Dutch doctrine of the freedom of the seas. It stressed rational rules, negotiations and cooperation as a key to rational and orderly action.

Dutch attitudes are reflected in contemporary discourse on the norms and rules of international interaction. They are most apparent in Grotius's monumental work on international law – his *Law of War and Peace* (1625). Grotius rejects power politics as inimical to commercial interests; he emphasizes travel, trade, free access to the open seas and rational interaction among peoples.[10] He founds his argument on the claims that humankind is rational and 'naturally sociable'. From these axioms he develops his important concept of state 'sovereignty' and his elaborate defence of the idea of a legally anchored world order. Grotius insists that the territorial state is subject to no exterior controls and amenable to no considerations other than those of its own, rational self-interest. But he also demonstrates that on those terms, it is in the interest of each state to accept the rule of law – for if a state is to preserve its existence, there must exist a community or a society of states which obey common rules of international conduct. Thus, international law – 'that obligation which arises from mutual consent' (Grotius 1853, para. 16) – is for Grotius the only basis for a stable international order.

Grotius's writings on war and peace must be seen as a reaction to the chaos and savagery of the Thirty Years War. He noted that kings and generals were losing control of their armies and that the several constituent conflicts of the war deteriorated into orgies of violence 'of which even barbarous nations would have been ashamed' (Grotius 1853, para. 28). As the war progressed, Dutch arguments were accepted by many European monarchs.[11] And when diplomats from all over Europe met in 1648 to formally conclude the war, Dutch ideas affected their discussions. And when the peace Treaty of Westphalia was finally concluded, it gave concrete expression to the Grotian vision of a community of sovereign but cooperating states (Bull 1990, p. 75).

The market economy of the English

The English political mythology, like the Dutch, hinged on notions of anti-Catholicism, individualism and rational cooperation. But it added a clearer concept of social contract and an accompanying claim that the duty to obey government was conditional upon the government's ability to protect individuals and their property. The purpose of government, claimed the English, was to ensure individual freedom, civil law, social order and the sanctity of contracts. If a government fulfilled its purpose well, it would provide optimal conditions for a social division of labour which would, in turn, guarantee the efficient production of wealth, the just distribution of property and self-adjusting social equilibrium.

According to this logic, which was applied to national as well as international society, trade was at the bottom of wealth as well as power. 'To sum it up in a few words', wrote Daniel Defoe in 1728 'Trade is the Wealth of the World; Trade makes the Difference as to Rich and Poor, between one Nation and another' (cited in Plumb 1950, p. 21). Trade makes wealth; wealth can be translated into naval power; naval power could protect trade – which would engender more wealth which would strengthen naval power, and so on in a never-ending beneficial cycle (Heckscher 1931: 2, pp. 20ff.).

To encourage trade, and thereby enhance the nation's wealth and power, the government lowered taxes and removed tolls, both on the imports of raw materials and on the exports of English manufactures.[12] These were policies which reflected the interests of the rapidly growing commercial and manufacturing classes – which most readily embraced the values and norms of the Glorious Revolution. But the lower classes also embraced the British mythology. It was consolidated in the popular mind by the great wars which England fought against France. In the early 1700s, Magna Carta, Parliament and the Church of England became national symbols and contrasted with pride against the royal absolutism and Catholicism of the Continent. And beer and roast beef came to represent the freedom and prosperity of the English – and were contrasted to the wine and *ragoût* of the French.

The influence of the English mythology on the early eighteenth-century world is relatively easy to trace. For when the great powers of Europe were invited to the peace congress of Utrecht in January 1712, the wars of Louis XIV were already settled behind the scenes by England and France alone. The actual peace terms were largely the work of one man: British Secretary of State Henry St John – later Viscount Bolingbroke. His pre-eminence at the Utrecht conference (1713–15) is a key to the nature of the document it produced. By extension it is also a key to the nature of the world order it guaranteed: a balance-of-power system which allowed Britain to retreat from the quarrels on the Continent and devote itself to trade – the permanent preoccupation of the people and the constant concern of its government.

Through the eighteenth century, these attitudes were consolidated by great expansions in agriculture and manufacturing – they are well expressed in Adam Smith's famous *The Wealth of Nations* (1965[1776]), and attained their most extreme expression in Jeremy Bentham's vision of the self-equilibrating society. To the basic themes of liberty, property and rationality Bentham added the concepts of economic utility and natural harmony. If every man were free to maximize his own private pleasure and minimize pain, then 'the greatest happiness of the greatest number would result'.

The influence of these arguments on the early nineteenth-century world can be identified with ease. Foreign minister Viscount Castlereagh dominated the great peace conference in Vienna (1815) as Bolingbroke had dominated that of Utrecht a century before; and like Bolingbroke before him, Castlereagh worked to define rules of international conduct that agreed with Britain's commercial interests. The final treaty was largely Castlereagh's work – and was rather similar to the ideas of Utrecht. The settlement was built around the concept of a balance of power which allowed Britain to remain remote from the quarrels on the Continent while focusing its attention on the growing world market in manufactured goods. 'Continental states could not ignore Britain, but British statesmen could relegate continental issues to a subsidiary position: this was part of the explanation for Britain's greatness' (McKay 1983, p. 340).

Dawns of new world orders

Colinvaux (1983, p. 16) observes that the rise of a great civilization is always preceded by conflict and turbulence – 'by decades of strife at home, by signs of a turbulent expansionist society, by adventurous commerce'. This observation certainly holds true for the cases of pre-eminence discussed here.

When domestic turmoil was abating, the socio-economic energies they released were domesticated and channelled into economic and military purposes. In their moments of uncertainty, the emerging societies were regimented. Order was imposed on civil society by dictate and necessity. All available resources were mobilized in the interests of safety, efficiency and, ultimately, of victory and order.

These struggles were instilled in the Spanish, the Dutch and the English who were alike in their collective experiences of a formative sort. These events greatly informed the social practices which evolved. And in subsequent years, memories of them would remain inextricably associated with the characteristic social institutions of the nation. Individuals and events that attended these early upheavals would be included as lasting parts of the nation's foundational mythology.[13]

In the struggle against the Moors, Spain evolved a distinctly militant brand of Catholicism. The Dutch evolved, in their struggle against the Spanish, a political culture which emphasized freedoms of conscience and respect for secular law; England developed, through its struggles against absolutist kings, a distinct doctrine of constitutional monarchism tempered by respect for property and individual freedom. All these foundational mythologies were informed by Christian norms and values. But each was affected by the nature of the society in which it took root, and also by the nature of its enemies. Each would preserve the memory of the original struggle for 'freedom' and 'sovereignty' and cultivate that memory to justify its postwar order and its characteristic institutions. And through this cultivation, each political mythology preserved the image of old enemies and opponents. The new nations' cohesive pride had a flip side: a vision of a threatening other against whose evil nature one's own virtues could be ritually contrasted and celebrated. In the case of Spain the enemy was the Islamic culture of the Moor; for the Dutch, it was militant Catholicism; for the English it was autocratic rule – especially in its French, absolutist and Catholic form.

Significant elements of each of these political mythologies were diffused to other states during the endgame of each respective wave of great wars. The wars themselves provided a major belt of transmission. For great wars are not won so much by single states as by coalitions of states cooperating against a common foe. Furthermore, it is the winning coalitions that determine the settlement of great wars – who decide the conditions of armistice, preside over the peace conferences and who provide the premises to peace treaties.

The winning coalitions define the rules of the interstate conduct of postwar eras.[14] The coalition members have tended to be oceanic powers (whereas the losers have tended to be continental powers). They have been open seafaring societies whose expanding economies have relied heavily on shipping, commerce and colonialism. But their leaders not merely projected their nations' naval capabilities to distant corners of the globe; they also sought to subject the general traffic on the seas to a codex of rules or laws under which long-distance trade and commerce could be protected.

The existence of such a growing codex of international law suggests that a mutual understanding and a common political discourse evolved among the great powers. The terms of this discourse may have varied from one system to the next – thus the Treaty of Cambrai (1529) defined a European political system in religious terms, whereas the Treaty of Westphalia (1648) inscribed European politics in the secular terms of sovereign states. However, three things cannot be much in doubt. First, *that* such a common discourse existed. Second, that this discourse was routinely applied in a common 'public sphere' which was transnational in scope and sustained by the regular diplomatic interaction among great powers. And third, that after Westphalia, this discourse only applied to a particular type of social formation: namely, to well-functioning, modern territorial states. To qualify as such a state it was necessary to control a clearly demarcated territory and to possess a comparatively fair and efficient government which maintained order within the territory. Furthermore, it was necessary to demonstrate a certain degree of cultural and moral cohesion which could sustain reliable adherence to the government and its rules and laws.

All hegemons were cohesive, well-functioning states. The waves of great wars contributed greatly to their cohesion and the increase in their relative wealth and power. War would also contribute to their political consolidation – wars would fix their boundaries and make their governments appear efficient and heroic champions of order. Wars would also strengthen the moral consensus of the nation and the legitimacy of its government. Finally, the waves of great wars would help bring an ascending, well-functioning state to international pre-eminence among the great powers. By the end of their respective great wars, Spain, the United Provinces, England I and England II presided over the major military forces of the emerging international systems. Their superior position in their respective hierarchies of power guaranteed them pre-eminence in the interstate system and was reflected in their unsurpassed international prestige.

Notes

1 These two tendencies – the growth of a common outlook within the victorious alliance and the normative impact of the ascendant state on this common outlook – have been more apparent in the later than in the earlier cases of great wars: they were more pronounced in the Thirty Years War than in the Italian wars; they were even clearer in the wars of Louis XIV; and clearer still in the wars against Napoleon. The influence exerted by the British at the peace conferences at Utrecht (1713) and Vienna (1815) was greater and longer-lasting than that exercised by the Dutch at Westphalia (1648) and by the Spanish at Cambrai (1529).

2 The distinction between 'Us' and 'Them' can be observed in our earliest historical evidence – e.g. on ancient Sumerian and Accadian tablets – and has led some authors to claim that the practice of drawing this distinction is as old as humanity itself. This insight into the mythogenic potential of conflict and war was notably emphasized by German romantics like Herder and Fichte. Carl Schmitt added to this notion by invoking the concept of the 'Other'. Any state, argues Schmitt (1979, pp. 26ff.), defines itself through struggle by distinguishing sharply between friends and enemies, between *Freund* and *Feind* (between 'Friend' and 'Foe'), 'Self' and 'Other'. Schmitt's ambiguous political affinities in interwar Germany notwithstanding (Bendersky 1983), his argument has been embraced, in recent years, by poststructuralists.

3 Sorel warns against confusing mythological accounts of the past with historiography. Myths are not descriptions of events, he emphasizes, but tales endowed with symbolic significance. His important point is that a myth can never be rationally refuted. It exists in the collective imagination of a group. It is, in the final analysis, 'identical with the convictions of a group, being the expression of these convictions in the language of movement; and it is, in consequence, unanalysable into parts which could be placed on the plane of historical descriptions' (Sorel 1959, pp. 57f.).

4 This confederation was formalized by the Treaty of Utrecht (not to be confused with the treaty of the same name which formally ended the wars of Louis XIV in 1715).

5 The maritime and the anti-Catholic themes are masterfully entwined in Jost van Vondel's celebrated play *Het Paascha* (1612) which uses the exodus of the Jews from Egypt as an allegory of the liberation (and redemption) of the Netherlands.

6 All countries of sixteenth-century Europe had laws of capital punishment; but only in the Netherlands was this sentence executed by drowning. Also, all countries built correctional facilities to deal with swelling hordes of destitute migrants, beggars and petty criminals. However, only Holland introduced as odd a reformatory as the 'water house' – a small cell that the rising tide would fill with water in less than half an hour unless the unfortunate incarcerees bailed out and pumped for their lives. The water house, notes Schama (1987, pp. 15, 23), offered the inmates a simple choice between drowning or being Dutch!

7 These 'new philosophers', writes Toulmin (1990, p. 9f.):

> committed the modern world to thinking about nature in a new and 'scientific' way, and to use more 'rational' methods to deal with the problems of human life and society. Their work was therefore a turning point in European history, and deserves to be marked off as the true starting point of Modernity.

8 Max Weber (1930) argues that there was a strong and logical connection between the Calvinist ethos of the Dutch republic and its successful economic performance. First, Weber finds that the Calvinist ethic encompasses a utilitarian aspect: honesty is useful because a reputation for honesty enhances one's creditworthiness. Second, Weber finds in Calvinism an inward-looking frugality which encourages capital accumulation – an aversion to spending money on consumer goods, coupled with notions of duty and industry, must inevitably lead to savings and investment in the longer haul (Samuelsson 1957). Honesty, frugality, together with a goal-directed rationality constituted, in Weber's mind, the core of the bourgeois code.

9 So called because the Peace was negotiated by the mother of French king Francis I and by Margaret of Austria.

10 Grotius spells out these premises quite clearly at the beginning of his book. He explicitly refutes the old claims that man is an animal and that might makes right. 'Man is, to be sure, an animal, but an animal of a superior kind', he writes. But in contrast to other animals, he continues, man is endowed with reason, speech, 'a faculty of knowing and acting in accordance with general principles' and a natural 'sociableness' (Grotius 1853, para. 6).

11 Grotius's definition of sovereignty had great influence on the French court – cardinal Richelieu echoed Grotius when he claimed that French participation in the war was not only saving German liberties from Habsburg impositions, it was also rescuing the European state system. Also, Griotius was the favourite political theorist and jurist of Sweden's Gustavus Adolphus. These are important points, because the Thirty Years War concluded with the victory of France and Sweden over the Austrian Habsburgs; and it was France and Sweden that presided over the writing of the important Treaty of Westphalia.

12 These reforms ought not be confused with a policy of free trade; clearly, Walpole thought in mercantilistic terms and believed that English manufacturers should be protected – thus the Irish could not export their wool to anywhere but England and were forbidden to make their own cloth.

13 The concept of a political mythology is discussed in Chapter 2, note 7, and Chapter 4 of the present volume.

14 By the definition used by Susan Strange, winning coalitions who determine the rules of international interaction have 'structural power' (Strange 1988, pp. 24ff.).

2

The phase of hegemony

The strongest is never strong enough to maintain his mastery at all times unless he transforms his strength into right and obedience into duty ... Yielding to force is an act of necessity, not of will; at the very most, it is an act of prudence. (Rousseau 1971[1762])

Spain, the United Provinces and England (twice) experienced severe domestic turmoil before they emerged as pre-eminent great powers. During the course of this turmoil, they managed to convert the energies released by it into formative experiences in state- and nation-building. In a remarkably short period, these new states evolved socio-economic institutions of great efficiency and strength.

These new states had scarcely put their own house in order before they became embroiled in major international upheavals and wars. Participation in these wars served to reinforce their fast and furious ascendancy. As they were flung from social revolution at home into the vortex of great-power wars abroad, the energies which had been developed within civil society spilled over the nations' boundaries and affected interstate relations in decisive ways. Their economic wealth, their military strength and their moral decisiveness translated into steadfastness, efficiency and a determined foreign policy.

The rapid development of wealth, force and moral decisiveness attracted international attention. The paths of evolution of the ascending states became blueprints for progress which other states sought to recapture. Their social institutions became images of efficiency and success. Their economic and political theories became recipes for development and were studied by other peoples who sought to engineer comparable growths in wealth, might and prestige. In a word, Spain, the United Provinces, England I and England II emerged from the waves of their respective great wars as hegemonic actors in the postwar order.

On punitive pre-eminence

Waves of great wars are violent events which bring destruction and disease upon millions of individual inhabitants in the participating states. The states are regularly exhausted, often destroyed, during these wars. Sometimes, however, states evolve and prosper during war. This is commonly true of the leaders of winning coalitions. Some states in the past have emerged from the scene of violence, confusion, destruction and great human suffering empowered and enriched. Then they emerge as pre-eminent military powers in a postwar world order.

Spain, the United Provinces and England (twice) emerged from their respective waves of great wars with substantial land forces. These countries did not build up the biggest land forces of their time, as is indicated by Table 2.

Table 2 *Fluctuations in land power, 1475–1914 (number of soldiers of the great powers with figures of coalition leaders in italic)*

Year	Spain	United Provinces	England	France	Russia	Germany
1475	20,000	—	25,000	40,000	—	—
1555	*150,000*	—	20,000	50,000	—	—
1595	200,000	20,000	30,000	80,000	—	—
1635	300,000	*50,000*	—	150,000	—	—
1655	100,000	—	70,000	100,000	—	—
1690	—	70,000	70,000	400,000	170,000	—
1710	30,000	130,000	*75,000*	350,000	220,000	—
1756	—	40,000	*200,000*	330,000	330,000	—
1790	—	—	45,000	180,000	300,000	194,000
1813	—	—	*250,000*	600,000	500,000	270,000
1850	—	—	*417,000*	260,000	800,000	200,000
1880	—	—	320,000	503,000	770,000	420,000
1914	—	—	380,000	846,000	1,300,000	812,000

Source: Kennedy (1987, pp. 56, 99)

They *did*, however, organize the qualitatively best forces of the age. Spain developed the most efficient military force in Europe during the Italian wars: the *tercio* which, with its regimental organization, 'was the most successful form of permanent troops in the sixteenth century' (Corvisier 1979, p. 50). Its efficiency was further enhanced by the introduction of the mobile siege gun, capable of firing iron cannon balls (McNeill 1982, p. 89).

At the end of the sixteenth century the Dutch, confronted by invading Spanish armies, developed an unprecedentedly efficient military organization. By 1600, the United Provinces were launching successful offences against Spain and recapturing Zutphen, Deventer and Nijmegen. The Dutch battle formations finally proved their superiority at Nieuvepoort in 1600 (Feld 1975). When the

Dutch army recovered 'dozens of fortified towns from the Spaniards through sudden strikes and obdurate sieges, each conducted with a technical precision and dispatch never attained before' (McNeill 1982, p. 134), monarchs and generals came from all over Europe to study the principles and the technologies of the new Dutch model army (Zwitzer 1984). The superior weapons systems and military organization developed by the United Provinces, both on land and at sea, provided the military basis of Dutch hegemony after the Thirty Years War.

England introduced new weapons systems and battle tactics during the wars of Louis XIV and emerged, improbably, as the leading land power of Europe (Chandler 1971). England possessed sizeable armies, superior commanders and great efficiency of organization. In addition, the Royal Navy, whose weapons systems and battleship formations were also vastly improved during the wars of Louis XIV, guaranteed England's first-rate soldiers global mobility. This unique combination of efficient armies and a Royal Navy of global reach ensured the material preconditions for England's eighteenth-century hegemony (Lossky 1971, pp. 155ff; Morgenthau 1978, pp. 186, 203).

During the Napoleonic Wars England's military capabilities were again strengthened and improved. After 1815, weapons systems and war tactics were changed by inventions that came so rapidly that soldiers could hardly keep pace. The application of the steam engine to trains and ships, for example, implied a revolution in military transport and communication. The widespread adoption of percussion caps and long bullets increased the rate of fire, improved the aim and vastly enhanced the efficiency of infantry. The introduction of the revolver and the repeating carbine created a new role for the cavalry; the use of rifled and breech-loading fieldpieces caused a revolution in artillery tactics. Such improvements compounded English superiority in military organization.

These new weapons systems were not extensively tested in Europe before the 1850s. However, they were applied in more distant battlefields where they demonstrated stunning efficiency. With the aid of the Royal Navy, England could land troops, horses and equipment in virtually any region in a matter of a few weeks – even a few days in some fortuitous cases. And if British soldiers were effective on the battlefields of Europe, they were invincible on other continents. In Africa, America and Asia, 'ridiculously small European contingents regularly played decisive roles, less because of their weaponry than because of their dependable obedience on the battlefield and their manoeuvrability in the face of an enemy' (McNeill 1982, p. 151).

And here lies a key feature of the modern, hegemonic condition. Although pre-eminent powers emerge from the waves of great wars with large and effective military forces, it is not the quantitative size of their armies which guarantee their continued pre-eminence; rather it is the mobility and the high quality of the forces.

Their great mobility is guaranteed by a superior navy. Their high quality is guaranteed by a variety of factors. Among the most important of these are technological pre-eminence, appropriate organization and good leadership. During their years of hegemony, the Spanish, the Dutch and the English (twice) possessed both the best and the largest navies of their respective ages. This is apparent from Table 3.

Table 3 *Fluctuations in sea power, 1500–1900 (number of large warships of the great powers with figures of coalition leaders in italic)*

Year	Portugal	Spain	United Provinces	England	France	Russia	USA	Germany	Hegemon's proportion
1500	5	4	—	6	4	—	—	—	—
1525	66	21	—	14	5	—	—	—	0.2[a]
1550	40	18	—	25	7	—	—	—	0.2[a]
1575	37	18	—	28	3	—	—	—	0.2[b]
1600	—	51	38	34	—	—	—	—	—
1625	—	60	114	40	15	—	—	—	0.5
1650	—	30	70	80	35	—	—	—	0.3
1675	—	20	63	60	90	—	—	—	—
1700	—	26	86	115	118	—	—	—	—
1725	—	17	42	120	36	34	—	—	0.5
1750	—	38	33	116	53	23	—	—	0.4
1775	—	60	11	108	75	17	—	—	—
1800	—	—	15	132	61	58	—	—	0.4
1825	—	—	—	100	41	39	4	—	0.6
1850	—	—	—	70	26	43	6	—	0.5
1875	—	—	—	40	16	14	—	2	0.4
1900	—	—	—	22	9	6	8	5	—

Source: Modelski and Thompson (1988, pp. 62–84, 114–24)
Notes: a. Here Spain is claimed to be the pre-eminent state – a claim which e.g. Modelski and Thompson (1988, pp. 152ff.) contest.
   b. Whether Spain or Portugal was the pre-eminent Iberian state is to some degree a moot point – especially as Portugal in 1580 became a part of Spain (as the result of a personal union under Philip II) and the Spanish King came to command both fleets (Elliott 1977, p. 266; also, Modelski and Thompson 1988, p. 324).

The importance of sea power for the hegemonic condition lies in three functions which navies, and navies alone, can perform. The first, and most obvious, function pertains to the punitive aspect of power: only great navies could transport the hegemons' superior troops and equipment to foreign shores while defending the route. Only navies could project punitive power;

only superior navies could command and control the world oceans by neutralizing their opponents and by subjecting their home bases to direct bombardment.

The second function pertains to the remunerative aspect of power. Modern hegemons have been empires, their power sustained by trans-oceanic traffic of a wide and varied nature – from pillage to trade and exchange. Only large navies could complement and protect the vast merchant fleets and the global networks on which this lucrative trans-oceanic traffic depended.

The third function pertains to the normative aspect of power. Navies represent military might which protects the nerves of imperial government – strong navies guarantee the smooth running contact between decision-makers at home and administrators abroad (governors, lawyers and bureaucrats and so on). In addition, the oceans are the highways of the world and strong and busy navies guarantee the safe transport of civilian goods, capital and people (business people, authors, scientists, theologians, teachers, students and so on) whose interaction constitutes a less formal, but indispensable, human network of a greater imperial community; without the intelligence and informal communications of this community, neither empires nor world-systems could exist. By easing and protecting a wide range of communications, navies assist in an important integrating two-way traffic which imports goods and impressions from abroad on the one hand, and exports commodities, ideas, values and lifestyles on the other. As Modelski and Thompson (1988, p. 3) note: 'There can be no global system without global reach and implementation. Only those disposing of superior navies have, in the modern world, staked out a good claim to world leadership'.

Modern hegemons are strong sea powers. They preside over a worldwide web of political and commercial communications which give them an acute interest in international stability and in freedom of the seas. The argument has been phrased in different ways by different powers. The formulation has varied with place and age – thus the Iberian polyhistor Vitoria (1934a; 1934b) insisted on a God-given right to travel and trade; the Dutch lawyer Grotius (1853[1625]) added that free trade would create order in a world of sovereign states; British economists like Smith (1965[1776]; 1982[1759]) and Bentham (1843) claimed that freedom of the seas was a necessary precondition for a self-ordering world market. But in spite of such variations, the argument retains a constant core: that freedom of the seas guarantees a stable world order.

On remunerative pre-eminence

Malthus once noted that 'the power of population is indefinitely greater than the power in the earth to produce subsistence for man'(1982[1789], 91). For him, the greatest problem that faced the human species was that population growth would eventually outstrip the human resource base.

One feature shared by Spain, the United Provinces and England is that they all escaped the Malthusian trap. Technological innovations which improved agriculture and industry provided an escape hatch in all three cases. After the 1480s, Spain evolved agricultural and industrial techniques which triggered an economic boom. The United Provinces developed systems of crop rotation which gave higher agricultural yields than in any other European country at the time (Braudel 1981). In the early 1600s, the Dutch also became Europe's leading producers of textiles, ships and other industrial goods (Wallerstein 1980, p. 42; Wilson 1957, pp. 41ff.; Steensgaard 1970; Postma 1975; Williams 1984, pp. 40ff.). For England the wars of Louis XIV coincided with rapid economic development; this levelled off somewhat after 1710 before the evolution resumed at an even more rapid rate in the last half of the century. In the eighteenth century, English agriculture was marked by enclosures and by great increases in the yields of plants and livestock. Eighteenth-century industry was characterized by an evolution which eroded the country's old guild structures and foreshadowed a quantum leap in British industry and trade. Workers in certain industries began to be collected together into factories in order to produce things in larger quantities through a more systematic division of labour. This development was most conspicuous in the re-export trades which dealt in colonial products. The wars against the French revolutionary Republic and, soon after, against Napoleon coincided with economic growth which was both greater than and different from any economic boom that had preceded it.

Such technological advances, often stimulated by military needs (Nef 1963), helped the great Western powers escape the Malthusian dilemma. But they had another effect as well: they encouraged the great powers' economic expansion. Technological advances spurred the development of new, effective means of destruction. With these new means at their disposal, Western powers were equipped to conquer and coerce vast regions of the non-Western world. The Iberias are a dramatic case in point. Explorers from Portugal and Spain mounted field guns on their ships and blasted their way along the African and American coasts. In this way they opened new sea routes to Asia and the Americas, founded colonies and made the Iberian peninsula the major point of arrival for colonial goods.

Technological advance also spurred another, intimately related source of economic expansion: it stimulated the development of efficient new means of production. Around 1500, the Spanish kings encouraged the shipyards to construct new, large ships and established state-run foundries to produce high-quality cannon and other metal supplies. The intention was to strengthen Spain's military capabilities, but the initiatives did more than that: they also gave a great stimulus to the shipping and industry of the entire peninsula. They became elements of an unequalled industrial boom (Davies 1961, p. 68).

Expansion of exploration and of long-distance trade went hand in hand. In 1492 Columbus first sighted the New World. His discovery triggered fifteen years of coastal expeditions which established the existence of an enormous American landmass. Then the pattern of discovery changed: around 1508, Spain began to establish permanent bases on the Great Antilles. Ten years later, the *conquistadors* launched a full-scale invasion of the great American interior. Cortés vanquished the Aztec empire of Mexico in 1519; Pizarro destroyed the great Inca empire of the Andes in 1533. From the hearts of the two fallen empires, the Spanish fanned out over the vast South American territories and conquered them for the Spanish crown. By 1540, after no more than twenty-five years of 'exploration', the great age of the *conquista* was over.

It is noteworthy that Spain's economic expansion paralleled the Italian wars. It is also interesting that the rate of imperial expansion increased after the wars. During the 1530s, an annual average of 670,000 ducats' worth of gold and silver was shipped back to Spain; during the 1540s, the annual average doubled to 1.2 million ducats' worth; and during the 1550s, it doubled again to over 2 million ducats' worth.[1] During these years, the Iberian-dominated Atlantic markets eclipsed those of the Near East and the Mediterranean (Clough 1964, p. 464).

The connection between war and economic expansion is also apparent in the United Provinces during the religious wars of the early seventeenth century. The refurbishment of Dutch defences was accompanied by a veritable industrial revolution and by rapid growth in trade, construction and industrial activity (McNeill 1982, pp. 128ff.). The size of Dutch cities grew rapidly; even the size of the provinces expanded as new land was drained and reclaimed (Parker 1981, p. 249; Barbour 1950). The nucleus of Dutch trade was the Baltic entrepôt business in salt, herring, wine and cereals. It burgeoned around 1600. At this time, Dutch traders began to engage in longer-distance trade: to French and German ports, to the Mediterranean, to West Africa and Indonesia. Soon, the Dutch built trading posts and factories around the Indian Ocean, at the outlet of the Amazon, in Japan (1609). Then they founded colonies of their own – Amboina (1605), Ternate (1607), Guyana (1610), the Guinea Coast (1612), Batavia (1618), Manhattan (1624), Pernambuco (1630) and other places (Boxer 1973).

This expansion was stimulated by the evolution of cheap, efficient cargo ships (the *fluit*), by the establishment of a chamber of assurance (1598) which supervised the registration of policies and settled disputes about claims, and a new *bourse* (1608); it was also fuelled by the founding of new banks – an exchange bank was opened in 1609, and discount banks were opened up in

Amsterdam (1602), Middelburg (1616) and Delft (1621). This expansion is expressed in the founding of Dutch trading companies – like the Levant Company (1581), the East India Company (1602) and the West India Company (1621).[2] Thus, during the course of a few bellicose decades, the United Provinces were transformed from a stubborn opponent of Catholic Spain to the workshop of the Western world and a first-class naval power dominating the trade of the Far East and the Caribbean.

The connection between war and economic expansion is also apparent in the case of England. After the Civil Wars, England challenged the maritime pre-eminence of the United Provinces – by trying to beat the Dutch as well as to join them.[3] The pace of English agriculture and industry quickened during the wars of Louis XIV. Manufacturing expanded and pulled new areas into a growing division of labour (Landes 1969, p. 57). Roads were built, rivers were deepened and increasingly controlled by canals and sluices to enhance communications and production at home; financial institutions and joint-stock companies were expanded to stimulate ventures abroad. Trade mushroomed and became a national preoccupation in the early decades of the eighteenth century. The government fanned this development by protectionist policies – by removing restrictions on the export of goods manufactured in England, while levying tolls and taxes on selected foreign imports (Knorr 1968). This policy brought remarkable economic growth.[4] A decade after the Peace of Utrecht, a network of English business was expanding eastward to Muscovy, Persia and India, south to West Africa and west to the plantations of the Americas. And with its formidable military might, England soon managed to draw this network into a mercantilist seaborne empire (Bowle 1977).

Even more ostentatious expansion occurred during and after the Napoleonic Wars. England's great effort to contain the ambitions of France was attended by such a remarkable expansion of industry and trade that later historians have referred to it as 'the Industrial Revolution'. Britain's industrial production doubled between 1825 and 1850, and it doubled again before the end of the century (Hobsbawm 1978, p. 341). This development changed the British economy; it rapidly took it away from artisanal production of woollen cloth into the industrial production of cotton textiles; it ignited a worldwide industrial system which was centred on the British Isles but which drew its raw materials from and unloaded its products upon the world at large.[5]

Coal was the fuel of the Industrial Revolution. Coal smelted pig iron – the production of which quadrupled between 1790 and 1810 and increased thirtyfold during the nineteenth century. Iron revolutionized both tool-making and the weapons industries. It also inaugurated an entirely new phase in global communications, because the production of steam engines, rails and, later, great ships was based on iron. Between 1825 and 1838, five hundred miles of track were laid in England; by 1843, over two thousand miles of track were in actual use. Business professionals immediately found railways and steam-ships to be useful ways of extending their markets. First at home and then abroad: for the expanding British industries called for more raw materials and wider markets than the islands alone could provide (Knorr 1968).

By mid-century, England had spun a network of economic linkages around the globe that satisfied the needs of its domestic actors. But it also served the needs of actors elsewhere in Europe and of client élites on the periphery of the world system (Gallagher and Robinson 1953). By the 1870s, England controlled nearly one-third of the world's commerce. Commanding a far greater total of the capital available for loans and investment, London was the financial capital of the world (Barratt-Brown 1970, p. 93; Woodruff 1967, p. 150).

On normative pre-eminence

A great power is great by virtue of superior military force and economic wealth. A hegemon is a great power which exercises remarkable command over inter-national public opinion. There is more to political power than the ability to punish and reward. The power of a state is not reckoned by mere counting of heads. Command over public opinion is as essential for political purposes as command of force and control of riches.[6] The Sultan of Egypt or the Emperor of Rome 'might drive his harmless subjects, like brute beasts, against their sentiments and inclinations: but he must, at least, have led his *mamelukes* or *praetorian bands*, like men, by their opinions', wrote Hume (1985[1777], pp. 32f.). The art of persuasion has always been a necessary skill of political leaders. Rhetoric has a long and honoured record in the annals of state leader-ship – indeed, Aristotle included the study of rhetoric in the study of politics, as have countless generations of subsequent political philosophers.

A hegemonic world order exists when the major members of an international system agree on a code of norms, rules and laws which helps govern the behaviour of all. This agreement reflects the rhetorical skills of a particular great power. The code has evolved within a specific context. It has a concrete historical foundation as well as distinct political appeals. The hegemonic code is the product of peculiar national experiences and is attended by specific notions, tales and political fantasies. It originally acted to arouse the collective will of a victimized and dispersed people and helped unify and organize it into a cohesive and sovereign society. It imposes meaningful interpretations on events in the past and gives hopes and ambitions for the future. During the wave of great wars this code – and the values, norms and rules which inform it – are disseminated to other powers.[7]

Advent of Christian colonialism

The foundational aspects of the political mythology of sixteenth-century Spain reflected the experience of the late medieval *reconquista* of Muslim territories. The eschatological aspects of Spain's political mythology expressed a particularly intense and belligerent Christianity. Affected by the long struggle with Islam, it held that relations between Christian rulers were different from those between non-Christian societies. Muslim rulers were commonly portrayed as bearing the mark of the Antichrist, whose dreadful empire would precede the coming of the Kingdom of God (Bloch 1961: II, p. 84).

For the Spanish, life on earth was just a temporary probation: a means to a greater end. The individual had worth and value to the extent that he furthered God's great purpose, which was to save men's souls. Each individual person could do nothing to alter the thrust of God's great drama. It was unalterable as to either good or evil (Becker 1932, p. 7). Individuals could do little but accept the role which they were assigned. However, they could play their part well or could play it badly. In order to assist humankind to play the role well – i.e., according to the divine text – God had, in his infinite benevolence, provided his only son, Jesus Christ, as teacher and instructor. Christ had sacrificed himself on humankind's behalf. And although humankind was helpless in itself, it could through Christ's sacrifice, God's mercy and by humility and obedience to his will, obtain pardon for sin and error and save its soul from perdition. Good, penitent and faithful people would be gathered with God and dwell in perfection and felicity forever. The evil and recalcitrant, by contrast, were reserved a place of everlasting punishment.

One of the most meritorious kinds of behaviour, salvation-wise, was to save heathen souls for God. This understanding was reflected in the self-image and the behaviour of Spanish monarchs (Fernandez-Santamaria 1977, p. 168) who justified their struggle against all foreign enemies in universal terms like 'holy mission,' 'God's will' and 'natural law'. Thus, when Charles V weighed anchor at Barcelona to wrest Tunis from the Turks, he referred to himself as 'God's standard bearer'. Later, this religious discourse justified the ambition of Philip II to seize all Muslim lands on the Iberias, to expand into Muslim North Africa and finally to conquer the New World. Letters written by the *conquistadors* show that many of them took their missionary duties seriously. Cortés, for example, believed 'that God had arranged the discovery of Mexico in order that Queen Juana and Charles V should obtain special merit by the conversion of its pagan inhabitants' (Elliott 1989, p. 39).[8] With reference to Christ's command to go out and 'make disciples of all nations', sixteenth-century monarchs listed the spread of Christendom among the most important motives for their colonial exploits.

During the sixteenth century, Spain exerted a great influence on the rest of Europe, partly through its formulation of Christian values and partly through its example. Spain articulated – perhaps more insistently than any other early sixteenth-century state – the basic views and values of the age. The foreign policies of Charles V and Philip II expressed these views. Both monarchs justified their conquests in Africa and the Americas in terms of a peculiarly belligerent Christian eschatology. When Iberian naval expeditions began to reap increasing material returns, they inaugurated the 'Age of Discovery'. This 'age' began with colonial rivalry between Portugal and Spain, but as more monarchs emulated the Iberian ventures, there evolved a fever of competitive colonization. Soon, other Christian kings realized that wealth and power awaited them in overseas expansion – a discovery which marked the advent of a new epoch in world history (Wolf 1982).

This Iberian doctrine of Christian imperialism was formulated early by Charles V's brilliant and ambitious adviser, Mercuriano de Gattinara. It was later popularized by Ginés de Sepulveda and, in a milder version, by Vitoria. All of them insisted on the God-given, innate superiority of Christian soldiers. Vitoria expanded on this point, arguing that relations between two Christian societies are different from relations between one Christian and one heathen society – Christians do not make each other slaves, he argued, whereas Christian soldiers may enslave heathens who are captured in battle (Vitoria 1934b, p. lxv). Sepulveda went further, claiming that Spain had an obligation to conquer heathen territories in the name of a Christian world civilization and to demand the institution of wardship over heathen peoples. This world-vision informed the Spanish conquest of the Americas, and it justified the long-standing effort to contain and conquer the great common enemy: the Ottoman Muslims (Bull 1977, p. 29; Parkinson 1977, p. 22). The theological arguments expressed by Gattinara, Vitoria, Sepulveda and others soon informed the expansionist rhetoric of other European lawyers who justified the imperialist policies of their monarchs – not just for a few decades, but for centuries.

The rise of bourgeois expansionism

In the United Provinces, the combination of Calvinism, reason and liberty encouraged accumulative thrift, organizational entrepreneurship and acquisitive genius. It also produced an environment conducive to artistic and scientific exploration, and augured the advent of a rational, secular approach to society and politics. Although Dutch mythology was grafted on to a strong Christian trunk, it was eminently compatible with secular values.[9] It was compatible with Dutch ventures in trade and commerce, and stimulated the development of the United Provinces as the first 'trading state' (Rosecrance 1986, pp. 75ff.; Israel 1989). It was compatible with the Dutch quest for learning and education,

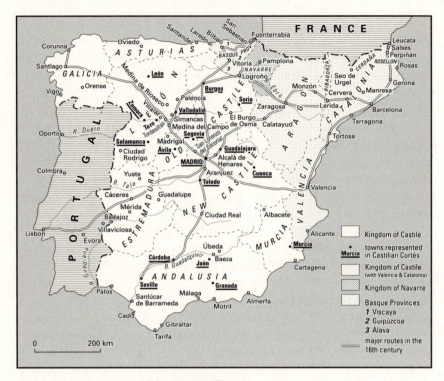

Map 1   Sixteenth-century Habsburg Spain (Elliott 1977, p. 16)

and helps explain why the United Provinces became the leading region in the intellectual life of seventeenth-century Europe. The United Provinces were the home of Huygens, Stevin, Lipperschey, Grotius and countless others. The intellectual vibrancy of the United Provinces was enhanced by its being a safe haven for scholars who fled religious persecution, oppression and war from all corners of Europe. Several French scholars settled in Holland in the early 1600s (like René Descartes, who arrived in 1618). Many traders migrated from Spain and the southern Dutch provinces which had remained loyal to Spain (like Baruch de Spinoza's father, Michael, who came to Amsterdam in the early 1600s). By the middle of the century, a great many of the powerful and influential Dutch were of southern origin (Schama 1987, pp 587ff.).

The Dutch were often ridiculed abroad. They were portrayed with scorn by labourers who saw the Dutch propensity for thrift as avarice, the acquisitive drive as rapacity and the entrepreneurship as exploitation.[10] Also, they were disdained by foreign nobles, who saw Holland as a chaotic society populated by an uppity, rebellious rabble.[11] However, in spite of this scorn, the practices of Dutch commerce, trade and manufacturing were emulated elsewhere. Dutch practices, norms and values spread and informed the urban middle class which emerged all over Western Europe and wedged itself between the old nobility and the working masses. The values and practices of the Dutch bourgeoisie emphasized travel, trade and free access to the open seas. They informed the views and actions of Dutch traders and artisans and found an unrivalled voice in the brilliant Dutch lawyer Huig de Groot – who became world famous in his own lifetime under his Latinized name, Hugo Grotius.

Few individual authors have articulated the Dutch political eschatology more consequentially than Grotius. And few individuals have done more to express a clear and convincing vision of modern international society. Grotius's monumental work on international law exerted a great influence on contemporary state leaders. Through Grotius, the Dutch political eschatology had a formative influence on the Treaty of Westphalia. The core idea of an international society was so clearly expressed in the Treaty of Westphalia that 'Grotius may be considered the intellectual father of this first general peace settlement of modern times' (Bull 1990, p. 75).

The Dutch contributed importantly to the vision of a new world order. Also, they greatly affected the formation of the modern world economy. They decisively formed modern institutions of credit, insurance, trade and manufacturing. Indeed, they assumed a leading role in a world economic process which began with medieval merchants, evolved through Renaissance banks and the Dutch international economy and ended with British industrialization (Barbour 1950; Wallerstein 1980; Braudel 1984). To this must be added a peculiar Dutch contribution to the socio-political ideals of the modern West: the bourgeois code of conduct. It became one of the distinctive Dutch contributions to seventeenth-century civilization (Wallerstein 1980, p. 65; Taylor 1996). In the long-term perspective, the Dutch war of liberation against Spain was the first modern reaction against old absolutism. Indeed, one of the much-neglected legacies of the Dutch is their example as a successful bourgeois alternative to dynastic absolutism ('tHart 1993). The Dutch mounted the first of the series of anti-absolutist revolutions which have broadened the definition of liberty throughout Western history.

It is worth noting that in the Dutch case (as in the Spanish) religion played an important socio-political role. The history of Dutch Bibles is worth closer scrutiny because it may well constitute a rich vein of social and political history. The first translations of the Bible into Dutch appeared at a remarkably early date – a printed vernacular version of the New Testament appeared as early as 1522 – suggesting the early existence of a living Dutch language. Also, Bibles were widely disseminated in Dutch society, suggesting high levels of general wealth and literacy. It is also worth recalling that the Dutch revolution had its direct origins in a religious revolt against Spain. The revolt quickly developed secular overtones – and the Dutch formulated, in subsequent years, a clear sense of political rights and duties. But the discourse in which these rights and duties were expressed had unmistakable biblical overtones. The distinctions between scripture, history and politics were effaced as Dutch demands for independence were fuelled by visions of a providential selection of a new people to be a light unto the nations of the world. From the 1580s onwards, the Dutch evolved a self-conscious, collective identity. They evolved a 'patriotic stead-fastness' and a 'community of the nation'. They developed 'a belief in themselves as a common tribe' which was based on a common religion, a common language and a common mobilization against Catholic Spain (Schama 1987, pp. 567f.). The Dutch also developed a common idea of nationhood – an idea greatly inspired by biblical descriptions of ancient peoples unified in faith and language and subsequently expressed in a rich vernacular literature.

The emergence of democratic imperialism

The English were among the first people to embrace Dutch bourgeois ideals. They proved nimble emulators of Dutch commercial, financial and fiscal prac-tices – as evinced by their early adoption of Dutch agricultural techniques and financial institutions and in the establishment (by a clever Dutch *coup*) of constitutional rule (1689).[12] However, rather than adopting Dutch ideas whole-sale, the English adapted them to their own particular circumstances.

In England, as in the United Provinces and Spain, the Bible played a signi-ficant role in the evolution of a distinct English nationhood. Henry VIII's Reformation – the breach with Rome and the establishment of an Anglican Church in 1534 – was an important contribution to the self-conscious, collective identity of the English. During the reign of Elizabeth I, printed vernacular Bible translations flooded the country; between 1570 and 1611 sixteen different editions were issued of the Bishop's Bible and seventy-five of the Geneva Bible. The Bible, together with the multitude of catechisms and the vernacular-based liturgy which all English people were legally bound to attend, instilled in all readers and listeners a common religious outlook, a common linguistic stand-ard and a common idea of nationhood.

These traits were strengthened by several wars against France. Thus, Eng-land emerged from the wars of Louis XIV as a confident and ingenious nation of great wealth and military pre-eminence. This was reflected in its independent diplomacy during the endgame of the war and in its influence on the peace Treaty of Utrecht. Economic arguments and political ideas spread from Britain during the wars of Louis XIV, and fanned across the Continent after Utrecht. The ideas which informed the values of England's rising middle classes in the late seventeenth century were readily embraced by the intellectual élites of

Map 2   Seventeenth-century United Provinces (Limm 1989), p. 2.

Europe in the early eighteenth. Discussions about English pre-eminence in wealth, power and civil liberties were stimulated by a considerable growth in European literacy, by an increasing demand for books, pamphlets, newspapers and magazines, and by greater ease of travel. French philosophers grew especially preoccupied with the political eschatology of England and the ideas which attended it. English ideals of individual liberty, the social contract, constitutional rule and parliamentary democracy were introduced into France in a fashionable package of anglophile sentiment which included a new style of fiction (the 'novel'), 'Gothick' horrors, picturesque ruins and *le jardin anglais* – in short, the whole apparatus of Continental pre-Romanticism was imported from England. By mid-century English social and political ideas fuelled their critique of France's absolutist monarchy.

The role of English ideas in this critique is most evident in the cases of Montesquieu and Voltaire, both of whom spent time in England. Crossing the Channel was for Voltaire a transition from 'a land of slavery, intolerance and darkness' into one of 'freedom, tolerance and enlightenment'. He remained the better part of three years in England. He developed a perfect command of the English language, and was constantly active in London's philosophical and literary circles. He was greatly impressed with what he saw, heard and read. In his *Lettres philosophiques* (1734) he introduced Bacon, Locke and Newton to the Continent in one of the most influential books of the century on social, economic and political thinking. The influence is also unmistakable in the case of Montesquieu. His *Spirit of the Laws* (1748) analysed English laws and governmental institutions and concluded that the unique stability and growth of English society were the result of a unique division of government into executive, legislative and judicial branches. Montesquieu warmly recommended every state to learn from this English system. Other French *philosophes*, too, embraced British ideals before they gradually evolved their own political ideas (Hampson 1968) – Rousseau, for example, greatly admired the political ideas of John Locke.

After the Peace of Utrecht, England became the master model of a modern, successful political system, more capable than any other state of harnessing the energies of its people at home and building up colonies overseas. The country was militarily strong, economically dynamic and normatively influential. In the final analysis, it was the English who sowed the seeds of the Enlightenment. But these seeds would soon take root in foreign soil, grow, adapt to local climates and would – through authors like Fergusson, Sidney and (later) Smith in Scotland, Mason, Jefferson and Madison in America, and Montesquieu, Voltaire and Rousseau in France – fuel political upheavals of historic proportions. Thus, England designed and cast the Enlightenment medal, the Americans embellished it, the French gilded it and wore it ostentatiously.

Political ideas cultivated by the British and Americans were adapted by French *philosophes* and helped bring French absolutism to its dramatic collapse at the end of the century. When revolution erupted in France in 1789, 'it would ensure in all its extreme insistence upon freshly discovered principles that France seized all England's clothes and surpassed England, at the public verbal level, a hundred times' (Hastings 1997, p. 97). After the French Revolutionary and Napoleonic Wars, Britain resumed its former leadership. It experienced rapid industrial development which strengthened the faith in a socio-economic system which was controlled, regulated and directed by markets alone. At the same time, Britons found their ambitions squeezed between the threats of revolution and reaction – by the threat of mass upheavals which demanded radical redistribution of domestic property, on the one hand, and by the re-establishment of an old order of feudal privilege and dynastic imperialism which was hostile to free trade and international competition, on the other.

To avoid revolution at home, Parliament passed a whole series of Reform Acts through the 1830s (Colley 1992, pp. 334ff.). To forestall frustration and conflict abroad, Britain withdrew from Continental associations. Even Britain's conservative Tory ministers soon found the illiberal policies of Continental monarchs and emperors repressive and reactionary. They saw no reason to cooperate with the Continental system. They broke with it – thereby hastening its collapse. Henceforth British foreign policy gravitated around two concerns: containing Russia in the Balkans and the Mediterranean and developing and defending colonial territories. A succession of foreign ministers – from Castlereagh and Canning to Palmerston and Disraeli – were consumed by these two basic concerns.

British merchants, manufacturers and politicians were informed by a mythology which praised the self-equilibrating properties of the free market. They insisted on a world order governed by 'fair competition' and 'free trade';[13] they perceived their ambitions to be hampered by the restrictions imposed during the wars upon the free and plentiful import of raw materials. They demanded the abolition of the Corn Laws and the Navigation Acts; they wanted free movement of money and goods, open access to foreign markets and to raw materials. These demands, which were set forth by British merchants, bankers and manufacturers, were backed by the general spirit of the country.

England was the world's greatest power – both in the world-economy and in the interstate system. But, it was not only gold, goods and weapons systems that made it a great power after Waterloo. The ideas it expressed and the ideals it represented were also important, for that 'made her a leader of world opinion' (Thomson 1978, p. 28). England was preoccupied with free trade, but not only for reasons of wealth; England was also the champion of higher principles like freedom and justice. People and politicians alike were consumed by the notion that the world was the oyster of the English in which they cultivated the pearls of free trade, free people and free institutions while 'striking Palmerstonian blows at protectionism, slavery and tyranny' (Halstead 1983, p. 24).

In the early decades of the nineteenth century the British were stirred by the values and norms of the Enlightenment. These values – of the natural right of all men to liberty, equality and the pursuit of happiness – were boosted into

Map 3   Eighteenth-century United Kingdom (Webb 1985, p. 6)

a tidal wave of democratic ideals by the American and French Revolutions, and they washed across Europe with great force during and after the Napoleonic Wars. England had few problems absorbing them into its political mythology and socio-economic institutions. The English adjusted to the democratic demands through a series of piecemeal reforms between 1828 and 1838, but they did not suffer any great upheavals.

England's parliamentary system was democratic in theory, flexible and responsive to popular demands in practice. Its parliamentary institutions were thus spared the great shocks that racked the monarchic regimes on the Continent in 1830 and 1848. Great Britain remained stable throughout these events, and emerged from them as the most ingeniously inventive nation in the nineteenth century in the art of politics. Also, by virtue of its political stability, its economic wealth and its liberal political rhetoric, it could present itself to the world as a paragon of progressive democracy. 'Other countries, envious of her success in combining democracy with stability, and self- government with responsibility, tried to imitate her parliamentary form of government just as they borrowed her industrial techniques and skills' (Thomson 1978, p. 29).

Hegemony

'Hegemony' is a concept which has long been a much-used term in the historical and social sciences, but which has been used in a variety of ways and often without any clear definition. The concept is invested with a plethora of meanings. One traditional usage, still applied with some frequency among historians, simply equates hegemony with 'dominance': the attempt by a territorial state to attain a dominant international position by the use of military might.[14]

Another usage infuses the term with economic rather than military overtones. According to this second usage – more common among social scientists than historians – 'hegemony' describes a 'preponderance of material resources'. 'Hegemonic states', writes Keohane (1984, p. 32) 'must have control of raw materials, control over sources of capital, control over markets, and competitive advantages in the production of highly valued goods'.[15] Wallerstein (1984, p. 38) pays attention to the normative aspects of power; he notes that hegemony is a situation 'in which the ongoing rivalry between the so-called "great powers" is so unbalanced that one power is truly *primus inter pares*; that is one power can largely impose its rules and its wishes (at the very least by effective veto power) in the economic, political, military, diplomatic, and even cultural arenas'. But even Wallerstein ultimately anchors hegemony in a country's economic basis. Hegemony ultimately 'lies in the ability of enterprises domiciled in that power to operate more efficiently in all three major economic arenas – agro-industrial production, commerce, and finance'.

In theory, the distinction between these conceptions of 'hegemony' is un-problematic. In practice, however, it is evident that a hegemonic condition can rest neither on a military nor on an economic base exclusively. 'Hegemony' also relies on a normative aspect of political power. A hegemonic condition is one in which a great power is tolerated as *primus inter pares* because it is perceived as legitimate. And it is so perceived because its primacy is sustained by a shared understanding about the values, norms, rules and laws of political interaction, about the patterns of authority and the allocation of status and prestige, responsibilities and privileges (Lundestad 1994, p. 385).

It is curious that those uses of 'hegemony' that stress the material dimensions of political power – the military and the economic – should have come to dominate contemporary debates in light of the fact that the concept is highly normative in its origins.[16] 'Hegemony' is rooted in the Greek word *hegeisthai*, meaning 'to lead'. To be 'hegemonic' means to possess the authority of command which ensures leadership – 'especially the leadership or predominant authority of one state of a confederacy or union over others ...'. The ancient use of the term conveys a primacy which is informed by a notion of just or legitimate leadership (Triepel 1938, pp. 4, 394ff.).[17]

The early English use of the term connoted a relationship of dominance, but not of a political kind. From 1656, there is a reference to 'the Supream or Hegemonick part of the Soul', meaning the master principle of the soul, or the predominant, spiritually guiding element of the individual. It was only in the nineteenth century that hegemony once again came to convey predominance of a political nature. By the early twentieth century, the term was largely purged of its ancient spiritual connotations. During the cold war, terms like 'hegemony' or 'hegemonic' were intermittently used in left-wing political discourse to de-scribe a policy of great powers that intended dominating other nation-states. Although these terms expressed an awareness of normative power, they were vulgarized by ritualistic use as an alternative to 'imperialism'.[18] All in all, the nineteenth- and twentieth-century usages have marked a steady vulgarization of the original concept.

The lessons of Chiron

In the 1920s, the Italian Marxist, Antonio Gramsci, reacted against this ma-terialist interpretation of the concept of hegemony, and sought to restore its original meaning. Gramsci used Machiavelli's discussions of the nature of political power as his vantage point.

In *The Prince*, Machiavelli recalls how Achilles was sent to Chiron, the centaur, to be taught the elementary principles of politics. Those instructed by a teacher who were half man and half beast soon learned 'how to act according to the nature of both', maintains Machiavelli (1961[1532], p. 99). His point is that no one can better appreciate the principles of political power than a creature who is half human and half bestial. For politics is half reason and half force, half consent and half coercion. In the exercise of political power there is always a mix of the two.

Coercion is associated with the material aspects – the punitive and the remunerative – of political power. First of all, the punitive aspect of power concerns a social actor's ability to punish (or to threaten to punish) another. It is the simplest aspect of power; and it is most commonly associated with the use of force. Punitive power represents coercion in its purest form: it denotes an actor's ability to destroy another's prized possessions. Second, the remunerative aspect of power concerns an actor's ability to reward (or to promise to reward) another – the ability to exchange a *quid* for a *quo*. It is associated with an actor's ability to create material wealth and with the economic functions of production and allocation. It is also associated with the denial of rewards, or the withholding of wealth and capital.

Consent is associated with a third, more intangible phenomenon: that is, the normative aspect of power. It concerns the power of symbols – words, images and signs – ideas and knowledge. It is vaguer than the punitive and the remunerative dimensions of power; it rests on more abstract and indeterminate concepts and it is the most complex and problematic of the three aspects of political power. Consent describes a particular state of a society's belief system. It can be defined as a shared understanding among the decision-making élite about the ordering rules of society.[19]

Hegemony and world politics

Of the two great eighteenth-century authors, the conservative Burke and the radical Rousseau, it is the latter who has most incisively affected the Western discussion of hegemonic power. For Rousseau informed the political thought of Marx and Engels, upon whom Gramsci drew for his epochal elaborations on the concept of hegemony.

Gramsci drew on both Marx and Machiavelli. He drew on Marx to define hegemony as a kind of collective political consciousness. And he relied on Machiavelli to claim that the hegemonic condition exists in so far as society is ordered by the consensual and not by the coercive element of power. Also, Gramsci was influenced by Sorel's discussion of political mythology. He saw both Marx and Machiavelli as first-rate myth-makers, defining political myth as a consensus-making vision – as a 'concrete fantasy which acts on a dispersed and shattered people to arouse and organize its collective will' (Gramsci 1971[1947], p. 126ff.).[20]

Gramsci identified three different types of 'collective will' and saw hegemony as one such type. The first type Gramsci referred to as corporate consciousness, and portrayed it as common interest among people who share a specific material interest.[21] He used this concept broadly, applying it to workers within a particular industry and to the burgers of the medieval towns of Italy. The second type he referred to as class consciousness. It represents a merging of the corporate consciousness of a series of groups sharing a common position in relation to a society's productive apparatus. Members of a corporate situation subordinate their particularistic corporate concerns to a broader consciousness of social class (1971[1947], pp. 258, 269).

'Hegemony' was for Gramsci the third and highest level of collective will. Hegemonic consciousness arises at a point where one leading class sees the desirability of creating a broader coalition with other classes. In so doing it consents to making some concessions or compromises which attract the support of these other classes. It is the nature of hegemony neither to endanger the dominant position of the pre-eminent class nor to put the other classes in a systematically disadvantaged position. Indeed, the other classes perceive that the compromise may turn out to their benefit. Thus, a measure of support is created for the coalition and the compromise on which it hinges.

Hegemony, then, does not express the interests of any particular class; rather, it articulates the general interests of all of society. The terms in which hegemony is expressed are universalistic in character; they claim to apply to the whole of society. 'Hegemony', writes Gramsci (1971[1947], p. 244) is vested in 'the entire complex of practical and theoretical activities with which the ruling class not only justifies and maintains its dominance, but manages to win the active consent of those over whom it rules'.

Hegemony is maintained to the extent that social consent takes precedence over coercion. Idealtypically, hegemony exists when social order is guaranteed by consent alone; when the key members of society employ the same political discourse; when they possess similar beliefs and regard these as natural and good; when they agree about the allocation of authority, status and privilege; when they entertain a notion of unity with each other and with society as a whole. More abstractly, hegemony can be defined as a temporal universalization in thought of a particular power structure conceived not as domination but as the necessary and natural order of things.

Gramsci applied the concept of hegemony to the international sphere only on a few hurried occasions (1971 [1947], p. 416f.); he restricted the concept to the analysis of domestic politics (1971[1947], p. 240). More recently, however, Gramsci's concept has been broadened and applied to international politics as well. Wallerstein (1980, p. 113), Cox (1982) and others have explored the notion of a 'hegemonic world order'. This exploration sees hegemony as a world order which is historically founded by an individual state that is militarily strong, economically wealthy and normatively dominant. It explains that hegemony cannot be built on force and affluence alone. 'To be hegemonic', writes Cox,

> a state would have to found and protect a world order that was universal in conception, i.e., not an order directly expressing the interests of one state but an order that most other states could find compatible with their interests given their different levels of power and lesser abilities to change that order. The less powerful states could live with the order even if they could not change it. (Cox 1982, p. 45)

'Hegemony' means something more than greatness. Pre-eminence in wealth and pre-eminence in force are necessary preconditions for hegemony, but they are not sufficient. A hegemonic condition involves pre-eminence which is sustained by a shared understanding among great powers about the values, norms, rules and laws of political interaction; about the patterns of authority and the allocation of status and prestige, responsibilities and privilege in international politics.

Hegemony and peace treaties

A state is hegemonic to the degree that it can found and maintain a world order which is universal in conception and which most other states find compatible with their aims and interests. The basic conception which other states accept and the values and norms which attend the hegemonic condition vary with time and space. They are products of the geographic region in which the hegemon is situated and of the historical experiences which have formed its outlook – thus the Spanish order reflected a militant interpretation of the Christian gospels; the Dutch order expressed an anti-Catholic insistence on liberty and civic rights; the British order articulated faith in the beneficial effect of free trade and of constitutional democracy.

At the peril of stretching this argument beyond endurance, its central point may be put succinctly: the norms and values which inform a hegemonic condition are a universalization in thought of the norms and values which have emerged from the political history of a pre-eminent great power. These basic norms and values express working arrangements which a ruling élite or class has obtained with other groups of society and which harmonize with its interests. And since the élite owes its dominant position to the exercise of power, it follows that its norms and ideas are in some degree tainted with power and with the socio-political values which legitimize and sustain it.

Hegemony is power which hinges on consensus of values, norms and rules of social conduct. The political mythologies of hegemons influence their respective world orders. Each hegemon in the past has exercised a formative impact as a result of its pre-eminence during the endgame of the wave of

great wars. Spain affected interstate relations during the Italian wars, the
United Provinces had some influence in the final stage of the Thirty Years
War, England exercised decisive influence as the leader of anti-French coali-
tions against Louis XIV and Napoleon.

This influence was especially great during the conferences which concluded
the peace. On peace conferences like Vienna (1815), Utrecht (1713), Westphalia
(1648) and, even, Cambrai (1529) the rules of interstate conduct were reformulated and the reformulation was generally accepted by the participant great
powers. By influencing peace conferences, the hegemons also had a lasting
influence on the international relations afterwards.

First, they exerted great influence by virtue of their pre-eminence in punitive
power. The ascendant powers were among the most efficient land powers of
their day. However, it was in sea power that the hegemons showed their
punitive pre-eminence. Estimates by Modelski and Thompson (1988) show
that at the peak of their pre-eminence, the hegemons possessed around half
of the total sea power available in the international system. This is evident
from Figure 2 below.

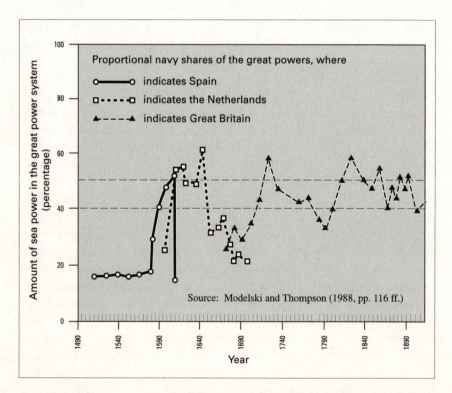

Figure 2 Sea power concentration through modern history (Modelski and Thompson 1988,
pp. 116ff.)

Second, the hegemons were the most efficient economies of the age. They harnessed the energies of their people at home and established economic institutions of unequalled productivity. Also, they channelled their national energies outward and built empires in far-flung corners of the world. All hegemons were empires. And they all exercised a great pull on other countries simply by virtue of their enormous preponderance of force and wealth. The hegemons had all enhanced their power capabilities during the great wars, whereas other great powers had emasculated themselves.

However – as has often been greatly underestimated in recent international relations scholarship – the hegemon also exerted great normative power in world affairs. In order to appreciate the origins and the nature of this power, it is helpful to discuss more closely the major peace treaties which mark the formal end of the preceding wave of great wars – and thus also mark the beginning of the phase of hegemony. Each major peace treaty – Vienna (1815), Utrecht (1713), Westphalia (1648) and, to some degree, Cambrai (1529) – was the outcome of a great multilateral conference the participants in which consciously sought to end a major period of war and establish a new, stable international order. They established the outcomes of the war – the losses and the gains. Also, they legitimized these outcomes (Randle 1973). But they also did more. By Holsti's (1991) account, the participants in such conferences

> were the ones who not only settled the terms of the preceding war, but who also tried to hammer out – never ignoring their own state's vital interests – some sort of system or set of procedures that would either prevent future armed conflict or that could help manage or limit it. (Holsti 1991, p. 22)

In a word, they established new world orders. The participants in these conferences established the norms regarding the use of international force, modes for ordering and governing the interaction of states, terms of settlement which precluded wars of revenge by the losers, ways of avoiding issues which might generate conflict in the future, procedures for resolving conflicts if they nevertheless should break out.

During the conference, the ascending hegemon exerted significant influence on the proceedings. Since its vital interests are preserved by the final treaty, the general agreement which is reflected in this document constitutes the basis of its hegemony.

After the conference, the hegemon articulates and exemplifies a code of social conduct which other powers seek to import and emulate. It expresses values, norms and rules which are emulated by other actors, partly because these appear better than their own and partly because other actors want to follow a fashion, to flatter and court the favour of the victorious and powerful.

Hegemony and Podsnappery

Norms and rules are always tainted by power. The ideas of what is just and fair are never remote from the basic interests of political actors. In the words of Lasswell (1936, pp. 30, 235): 'Any well-knit way of life moulds human behaviour into its own designs'. Any orderly society entertains a mute, organic consistency between values and interests. 'They do not foster ideas that are hostile to their fundamental working arrangements', writes Hofstadter (1948, p. viii).[22] Thus, a slave-owning society does not question the moral validity of slavery; a carnivorous society does not challenge the practice of raising cattle for slaughter; a private ownership society does not reject the sanctity of property; an affluent trading state does not question the doctrine of freedom of the seas. And in this observation lies a clue to one of the most elusive and misunderstood properties of the hegemonic condition, a feature which commonly attends pre-eminence and which is regularly confused with hypocrisy or conspiracy.

All states treat their own values as absolute standards. All hegemons treat their own values as standards laid down by nature itself. Since the Spanish, the Dutch and the English were all Christian powers, their norms and values were expressed in a Christian discourse. They all justified their rules and laws as divinely inspired. They all explained their pre-eminence in terms of God's protection. They all saw themselves as chosen by God to help Him fulfil His great plan and make all peoples His disciples.

The norms and values of these Western states have merged with a traditional Christian discourse and have, in turn, informed and justified their values and social rules. For example, there have been few varieties of the religious experience in which the Western emphasis on human individuality has assumed a more important role than in Christianity. Since the Reformation most notably, evangelical Christianity has emphasized self-scrutiny and reform through will. It has identified the moral power of the Christian message with the moral – some would say political – power of the messenger. To be 'changed', it was understood, was to be visibly so, and also to, in turn, effect changes in others. A doctrine so inspiring could not remain confined to the sphere of religious life.

Past discussions of colonial expansion may have exaggerated the nefarious ulterior motives of Western states as they imposed their Christian, mercantile and, after the 1700s, rational values on others and insisted on their own rights. Hegemons rarely insist on their national interests; rather they emphasize their global responsibilities.

Since hegemons treat their own values as a natural standard of divine inspiration, they are sceptical about rules, laws and values which deviate from their own quiet, unselfconscious mythologies and assumptions. They regard them as uneducated, primitive, quaint or unnatural. This may be perceived by outside observers as smugness, disdain or hypocrisy. That such smugness may constitute a blanketing, conceptual fog which obtrudes analysis by commination is suggested by Dickens (1985[1864–65], p. 179). In *Our Mutual Friend*, the following exchange occurs where Mr Podsnap explains, 'with a sense of meritorious proprietorship', to a foreign gentleman:

'We Englishmen are Very Proud of Our Constitution, Sir. It Was Bestowed Upon Us By Providence. No other Country is so favoured as This Country ...'

'And *other* countries', said the foreign gentleman. 'They do how?'

'They do, Sir', returned Mr Podsnap, gravely shaking his head; 'they do – I am sorry to be obliged to say – as they do!'

Mr Podsnap demonstrates the pitfalls of ignorance of other cultures. More to the point in this context, he suggests a fundamental blinkered satisfaction with the *status quo*. He certainly indicates a remarkable absence of domestic conflict of values. The nation's mythology is completely absorbed by its citizens; its distinct value system is entirely and unselfconsciously taken for granted; there exists an all-encompassing consensus as to the rules of the domestic game.

Mr Podsnap also suggests the conceptual fog which attends the smug self-satisfaction of hegemons. Other world actors, foreign gentlemen who stand outside of the hegemon and look in, have frequently noted the self-absorption and the arrogance which dominates its people. The sixteenth-century Spanish were half envied and half ridiculed by the French and the Dutch; the seventeenth-century Dutch were considered odd and stuffy by the English – although their wealth was generally envied and their economic efficiency emulated;[23] the eighteenth-century English were considered boisterous, insensitive and disorderly by Continental visitors.[24]

Because they confuse their own political mythology with the natural state of affairs, hegemons regularly express a remarkable inability to understand the seething mix of hatred, admiration and ridicule that they inspire abroad. They are not in the habit of examining closely their own myths, rules, laws and values. They simply take them for granted. Thus, *The Times* could naturally assume that England was the centre of the civilized world by informing its readers as a matter of course: 'Fog in Channel – Europe Isolated'.

Notes

1 This expansion is reflected in Table 4 below.

Table 4 *Imports of bullion to Spain by decade,*
1511–60 (in ducats)

Years	Value of bullion
1511–20	2,627,000
1521–30	1,407,000
1531–40	6,706,000
1541–50	12,555,000
1551–60	21,437,000

Source: Hamilton (1934, p. 34)

2 This expansion is also reflected in Dutch fiscal records. For example, from the 1580s, all ships had to pay 'convoy and licence money' to the Dutch republic. And although the receipts are incomplete (owing to evasion and smuggling), the records at Rotterdam and Amsterdam, reflected in Table 5 below, suggest an unmistakable growth in Dutch seaborne commerce during the religious wars in Europe.

Table 5 *Receipt of 'convoy and licence money' in some*
Dutch ports, 1580–1649 (in Dutch guilders)

Years	Receipts from		
	Rotterdam	Amsterdam	Other ports
1580–89	250,000	250,000	—
1590–99	400,000	300,000	—
1600–09	500,000	300,000	—
1610–19	550,000	375,000	—
1620–29	800,000	350,000	600,000
1630–39	1,050,000	450,000	500,000
1640–49	1,200,000	675,000	850,000

Source: Oldewelt (1953)

3 On the one hand, the Commonwealth and the Protectorate sought to disrupt the Dutch trade system, e.g. by severing the links which the Dutch had established with settlers in English colonies. On the other hand, the British sought to emulate Dutch techniques – by emulating the fourfold rotation of crops, by copying the *Verlagssystem* (Kriedte 1983, pp. 36, 95f.), by building their own institutions of trade, credit and finance – of notable importance were the passing of the Navigation Acts in 1650 and 1651 and the creation in 1694 of the Bank of England (Kennedy 1987, pp. 80), by establishing a British system of entrepôts and a set of specialized trading companies.

4 This expansion is apparent in Table 6 below.

Table 6   *British shipping involvement in overseas trade, 1686–1773*
(in thousands of tons by region)

Region	1686	1771–73	Change (as percentage)
Northern Europe	28	74	+164
East India	12	29	+142
Northern Europe and the British Isles	41	92	+124
America and the West Indies	70	153	+118
Southern Europe and the Mediterranean	39	27	−31
Total	190	375	+97

Source: Davis (1962, p. 17)

5 This expansion is reflected in the development of British foreign investment which is summarized in Table 7 below.

Table 7   *British foreign investment by region 1830–70 in £ millions*
(and as percentage)

Region	1830		1854		1870	
	£	%	£	%	£	%
Europe	73	(66)	143	(55)	193	(25)
USA	10	(9)	65	(25)	207	(27)
Latin America	25	(23)	39	(15)	85	(11)
British Empire	2	(2)	13	(5)	262	(34)
Other regions	—	—	—	—	23	(3)
Total	110	(100)	260	(100)	770	(100)

Source: Kenwood and Lougheed (1971, p. 43)

6 Classical discussions are found in Russell (1938), Carr (1964), Morgenthau (1975) and many others.

7 These notions will be discussed in greater detail later in this chapter (pp. 59ff.) and in Chapters 4 (pp. 128ff.), 7 (pp. 193ff.), and 10 (pp. 287ff.). Suffice it to say here that the notion of a hegemonic code may be clarified by Sorel's concept of 'political mythology', and the notion that such a code imposes meaningful interpretations on the past and arouses hopes and ambitions for the future may be clarified by Sorel's (1959[1908]) distinction between the foundational and the eschatological aspects of a political mythology. The *foundational* aspects of a political mythology address the past. They provide an account of how a particular political order was founded. They contain educational tales about the character and behaviour of national heroes – about the exploits of El Cid, Maarten Tromp, the Duke of Marlborough and Horatio Nelson. These heroes are revered by members of society. This reverence is often expressed in re-enactments or ritual celebrations of their exploits, the primary effect of which is to socialize new

members into the common values, norms and rules and generally lend legitimacy to the extant order. Every people has its national myths. All great powers possess foundational mythologies which inform and sustain their identities, their habits of mind and their patterns of political thought and action. These are part and parcel of the history of any country; they are usually too specific to be exported abroad to take root in outside communities. Thus, it is not the concrete, historically anchored, foundational aspects of a political mythology which are diffused through the international society, but rather the vaguer, *eschatological* aspects. These eschatological aspects of mythology focus on contemporary events or on the future. They envision the establishment of a new order, but are often vague on details – usually they simply depict the future order as an expansion of the old to new territories. Yet, eschatological mythologies may embody a clear set of norms and values. And they often prescribe a distinct set of rules for human action which, if followed, promise to yield a just and good society. On the one hand, such eschatologies are regularly used by great powers to justify expansionist policies. On the other, they may serve to strengthen the resolve of outside peoples who see themselves as victimized and coerced by them.

8 In his letters to Charles V, Hernan Cortés emphasized the importance of informing the Pope about the American discoveries, so that measures could be taken for the conversion of the natives. But soon pleas for the conversion of the natives were darkened by the ease with which ecclesiastical dignitaries allowed themselves to be corrupted by the opulence and the power they enjoyed in the New World. His hope remained, however, that there would arise in Mexico a 'new church, where God will be served and honoured more than in any region of the earth' (Elliott 1989, pp. 38f.).

9 For example, whereas Iberian theologians held that God's glory was best served by religious contemplation, Dutch thinkers maintained that the divine glorification should be performed by all human faculties in honour of God's works. No less an authority than Calvin encouraged scientific research as penetrating deeper into the wonders of nature than mere contemplation. The Calvinists 'were enthusiastic supporters of science and learning. Reformed theology not only tolerated scientific research ... but even demanded it' (Hooykaas 1963, pp. 262f.). This is certainly confirmed by the remarkable developments affected by seventeenth-century scientists like Huygens, Lipperschey and others.

10 A derisive portrait along these lines is drawn in Molière's comedy, *Le Bourgeois Gentilhomme*.

11 G. W. Leibniz maintained that Holland had taken in the world's outcasts. He explained in his *Consilium Aegyptiacum* [1671] how the Portuguese Jews fled from Spain, the Socinians fled from Poland and the opponents of Charles II fled from England ... and settled in Holland. Leibniz explained that this influx might, in fact, have been to Holland's advantage. For each refugee, argued Leibniz, 'brought with him his knowledge: the arts, the commerce, the manufacturing industry of his country – all those things which necessity and hunger, that mistress of the arts, that excitress of the mind, obliged them to concentrate on one single point'. By their effort Dutch power 'weak at the beginning' finally acquired 'the stability which we admire and which it would be difficult to overturn today' (quoted in Riley 1996, p. 248).

12 The parallels between the Dutch war of independence and the American Revol-

ution have been largely overlooked, as have the example of the commercial Dutch republic for the theory and practice of American politics – as even a cursory browsing of the *Federalist Papers* suggests.

13 As List (1927) was among the first to note, free trade is always in the interest of those who are strong enough never to fear competition.

14 Thus, Napoleon's attempts to dominate the Continent are sometimes presented as an effort to establish a universal republic under the guidance and hegemony of France.

15 This is the view of the theory of 'hegemonic stability'. It is also the view of many Marxists who claim that after World War II 'the United States attained a position similar to that held in the nineteenth century by Great Britain, which, because of its dominant role in the world economy, could exercise worldwide influence to its own advantage for almost a century' (Senghaas 1985, p. 303). But see also the discussion in Lebow and Strauss (1991).

16 In the 1970s and 1980s, the recognition that wealth and force alone cannot erect and sustain political order led to the development of several new ideas and approaches in the field of international relations and political economy. Among these were the so-called 'regime theories' which assert that, in everyday interaction, international order is maintained by basic 'principles, norms, rules and decision-making procedures around which actor expectations converge in a given issue area' (Krasner 1982, p. 185). These basic rules prescribe legitimate and proscribe illegitimate behaviour in order to limit conflict and, ensure equity or facilitate agreement (Keohane 1982; Nau 1990).

17 This discussion relies on *The Compact Oxford English Dictionary* (1992, p. 753) – from which the quote is taken – and on Triepel's (1938) teutonically thorough exposition.

18 During the 1970s this third usage was in vogue among left-wing (often Maoist) critics of the Soviet Union who needed a special term to distinguish the (aggressive) expansion of the Soviet Union from the (friendly) expansionism of non-Soviet socialist powers.

19 The appreciation of the consensual aspects of power is already present in the political philosophy of the ancient Greeks. Order and social stability do not lie in the use of force, argues Plato (1987, pp. 74ff.), but in citizens' realization that the laws of society are good, just and necessary. Aristotle reiterates this point in his *Politica*. And in *Rhetorica* he puts it into a larger context, explaining that political science is founded on rhetoric – which 'is a combination of the science of logic and the ethical branch of politics'. Rhetoric, explains Aristotle, is the art of public deliberation and persuasion. And 'the main matters on which all men deliberate and on which political speakers make speeches are some five in number: ways and means, war and peace, national defence, imports and exports, and legislation' (Aristotle 1941 [*c*. 300 BC], p. 1337).

Political deliberations presuppose a social context. They require a political society (a *polis*, in Aristotle's words) in which there is both a common language and a set of shared understandings that permits certain words and arguments to persuade an audience to judge or act in a particular way. For Aristotle, a society marked by consensus about political values and norms is the necessary pre-condition for rhetoric – i.e. for the logical, ethical and peaceful political discourse.

Several reiterations of this view are expressed in modern political thought.

Montesquieu (1990[1748]), for example, argues that, for a polity to be stable, its citizens must agree that its state is legitimate and its laws are just. Burke (1988) claimed that any stable social order hinges on a consensus about the traditional political values, norms and rules. This consensus is greater than the mere sum of a society's constituent individuals, he claimed; it involves a network of social visions and obligations, historically formed by generations of social interaction.

Burke's (1988[1790], pp. 194f.) idea that society is a 'spiritual community' founded on partnership and sanctioned by history has become a key axiom in the conservative tradition of political thought. Rousseau – whom Burke considered a 'deranged eccentric' and an 'insane Socrates' – contributed importantly to the radical tradition of political thought by a similar argument. 'The strongest is never strong enough to be always master, unless he transforms strength into right and obedience into duty', claims Rousseau. Then he pinpoints a key notion in the concept of hegemony: 'Yielding to force is an act of necessity, not of will; at the very most it is an act of prudence ... Let us agree, then, that might does not make right, and that we are obliged to obey only legitimate powers' (Rousseau 1971[1762], 2:519f.)

20 Gramsci was also influenced by Hegel's notion of an epochal 'spirit' and by Croce's idea of the 'ethico-political'. In order to view Gramsci in his proper historical context, it is important to recognize that he was part of the debate which attended the crisis of Marxism around 1900 (Laclau and Mouffe 1985). Among the participants who harboured similar notions were Kautsky, Plekhanov, Luxembourg and Bernstein; however, the independent Marxist Georges Sorel (1959) deserves a special mention in this context, for Gramsci found much value in Sorel's discussion of the collective consciousness of mass movements – notably in Sorel's concept of political 'myth' (Gramsci 1971[1947], pp. 126ff.). Also, avowed anti-Marxists participated in this debate about the importance of normative, cultural and collective aspects of power. Max Weber (1930), for example, wrote his anti-Marxist treatise on the legitimizing impact of norms on social behaviour, *The Protestant Ethic*, under the impact of this debate.

21 The individuals given to economic-corporate concerns concentrate on their own collective interests, obstructing the evolution of higher regional, national or class consciousness, Gramsci claimed (1971[1947], pp. 53, 173).

22 A relevant discussion is presented by Schumpeter (1954, pp. 33ff.) who imaginatively compares the Marxian concept of 'ideology' to the Freudian notion of 'rationalization'.

23 An ambivalence which is well represented e.g. by Leibniz, who at one moment complains about 'this mercantile spirit which the Dutch push to the point of the most sordid avarice' and at the next praises them for 'the sobriety which characterizes them' ... (Leibniz's discussion is found in *Consilium Aegyptiacum*, pp. 356ff and discussed in Riley 1996, pp. 246ff.).

24 In 1727, a Swiss traveller typically wrote home:

> I do not think there is a people more prejudiced in its own favour than the British people, and they allow this to appear in their talk and manners. They look on foreigners in general with contempt, and think nothing is as well done elsewhere as in their own country. (Plumb 1950, p. 33)

3

The phase of challenge

As soon as we have to recognize that someone possesses virtues which entitle him to be put on a pedestal ... then at last we say: 'Right, set him up!' But even while we're putting him there, and while he himself thinks we are enchanted by his eminence, we are knotting the noose in the *lasso* which is to drag him down at the first favourable opportunity. The quicker the turnover among proprietors of pedestals, the more chance there is for everybody to have his little hour up on one in due course. (Multatuli 1987[1860])

The phase of challenge and prestige, the second phase of a world order, begins with a challenge to the hegemon. Imperial Spain, for example, was challenged to war by both Muslim and Protestant powers during the 1560s. Similarly, the United Provinces were challenged, primarily by England in the 1650s and 1660s. The First British Empire was provoked by Spain and France in the 1750s; the Second British Empire was challenged by both France and Russia from the 1850s.

These challenges erupted as military conflicts which took the hegemons by surprise. However, the hegemons quickly regained their resolve. They faced the challenge head on, redoubled their military efforts, and regained their preeminence. But in spite of their eventual success, the hegemons' role in world affairs was forever changed by the wars. The hegemons re-emerged from the conflict apparently as powerful as ever. But the challenge had shaken their prestige, and their dominance rested on more uncertain bases. The continued maintenance of global pre-eminence carried a higher price tag. Regardless of how well the hegemons recovered from the challenge, their resurgence never truly recaptured the golden age of hegemony. Rather, the hegemons enjoyed an Indian summer: a spectacular (but temporary) afterglow of former hegemonic splendour.

Challenge, response and Indian summers

In spite of ample warnings, international challenges caught the Spanish, the Dutch and the English (twice) by surprise. Indeed, the challenges were in all cases so unexpected and the hegemons so unprepared that they suffered defeat in the initial battles once war broke out. This added a sting of embarrassment to the confusion of surprise and struck severe blows at the hegemons' self-confidence and prestige.

Spain was badly shaken in 1559 when the Turks attacked the Spanish fleet, sank twenty-eight galleys and forced ten thousand troops to surrender. The following year, a Tripolitanian corsair ambushed and destroyed seven more Spanish galleys. In 1562 a Spanish squadron was surprised by a freak October gale off Malaga that crashed twenty-five galleys to pieces and cost about four thousand sailors their lives. In three years, the thin peel of Spain's naval defences was stripped and the fragility of Spanish sea power in the Mediterranean cruelly exposed (Thompson 1976, p. 13). These losses hurt the prestige of Philip II. Several foreign diplomats noted that the new Spanish king was challenged by an enemy he could not contain. And Habsburg prestige was wearing thinner by the month as reports reached the crowned heads of Europe about whole strips of Spanish coastline being deserted as populations fled inland from foreign raiders.

The United Provinces met with a similar fate some nine decades later. When the prestigious Dutch fleet first exchanged gunfire with the English navy in May 1652, the diplomatic world marvelled at the display of Dutch inefficiency, and Dutch naval prestige plummeted (Geyl 1964, p. 30).

England was shaken by a comparable set of events in 1739. Spanish ships attacked English vessels and provoked the so-called War of Jenkins' Ear. Subsequent skirmishes revealed astonishing inefficiencies in command structures and battle plans, and disclosed that England had too few ships to meet the demands of a large-scale naval conflict. As the Anglo-Spanish war drifted on incompetently (Plumb 1950, p. 72) at great cost to Britain's naval reputation, the situation was exacerbated when British land forces unexpectedly suffered defeats at the hands of the French (Kennedy 1987, p. 98).

England was visited by similar surprises during the Crimean War (1854–56). Its army showed evidence of an over-all incompetence that contrasted strongly with the achievements of earlier years (Mosse 1974, p. 130). The Royal Navy put on an unexpectedly poor display (McNeill 1982, p. 225). The embarrassment was compounded by events in China (1856–57) and India (1857–58). 'The impact of the [Indian Sepoy] Mutiny on Victorian England, then at the height of its confidence and prosperity, was sensational' (Bowle 1977, p. 267).

In all four cases, then, the hegemon was oddly unprepared for adversity. When war came, their initial response was embarrassingly inept. Poor performance triggered domestic debates about the purpose and the cost of foreign policy. And disclosures of foreign-policy blunders acted as a solvent on the government's authority at home and on the country's prestige abroad.

Challenge and response

The reasons for the hegemons' sub-standard performance in war lay partly in that they were caught off-guard and partly in that they had long neglected to keep their military forces in proper repair. The hegemons' initial responses to war were marked by confusion. However, once collected, they responded with resolve and force. They quickly rectified their poor initial showing, and prevented further blows to their battered prestige.

Spain is a clear example of a surprised hegemon whose prestige was greatly undermined by initial bewilderment. But Spain is also a good instance of how initial setbacks were followed by a policy of decisive rearmament, resolute resistance and ultimate victory. As soon as Philip II received news that the Turk had sunk twenty-eight of his galleys (1559), he ordered new ships to be built. Through the 1560s, Spanish dockyards were hard at work on new warships for the king. By 1570, Philip II supported well over 100 galleys – nearly three times the number of a dozen years before. In October 1571, Habsburg forces dealt Ottoman navy a decisive defeat off Lepanto in Greece. The Turks withdrew. The Spanish victory signified the end of a long contest which had locked the Spanish and Ottoman empires in combat in the Mediterranean for decades. It also marked the transition from the European empire of Charles V to the Atlantic empire of Philip II.

The Dutch repeated this basic pattern of events. The First Anglo-Dutch War (1652–54) opened with serious losses for the Dutch fleet. But efficient men immediately sprang into action, coordinating the work of the admiralty and various administrative commissions to equip new fleets for sea. After 1653, the year of national crisis, the Dutch navy grew steadily stronger. With passionate determination the Grand Pensionary set himself to improving the fleet, and after some initial disappointments he succeeded in making it so strong as to re-establish naval supremacy (Kossman 1961; Modelski and Thompson 1988). In 1667, the Dutch had their Lepanto: in a spectacular manoeuvre they sailed up the Thames and destroyed the English fleet in the Medway. 'The impression made by that successful attack was enormous. The prestige of the States' regime rose immeasurably' (Geyl 1964, p. 95).

Eighteenth-century England, too, conforms to the basic pattern. When the country suffered naval defeats in the opening battles of the War of Jenkins' Ear (1739), the Admiralty was jarred into action. The government consciously began to rely on control of the seas as its main punitive tool in international politics. King and Parliament increased England's military inventory and formed new alliances in order to manipulate the Continental balance of power. In 1756, just as the nation seemed to face imminent defeat on the Continent, new men-of-war were ready to replace the hastily converted old merchant vessels. England's fortunes of war changed dramatically. In India, Britain won a great victory over French forces in 1757; this was followed by further triumphs at Wandiwash and Bengal. In Canada, English forces defeated the French army and obtained control over Quebec. The French navy was defeated off Lagos and at Quiberon Bay. In the wake of such victories, England's international prestige was gaining a new zenith, reviving Elizabethan and Jacobean ambitions of far-flung exploration (Bowle 1977, pp. 135f., 151, 219f.).

A comparable pattern of events occurred in the Second British Empire. The initial blunders of the Crimean War (1854–56) convinced the government that it was necessary to modernize the fleet. They felt forced to seek new defences against the new, powerful Russian guns and the new exploding shells; they armoured their warships and introduced steam engines in naval vessels on a large scale. Great Britain ended up with the largest naval fleet of the age.

Indian summers

The phase of challenge opens with jarring battlefield defeats, and it closes with 'Indian summers' – i.e. with a resurgence of greatness and expansion, and by a resurrection of national glory, pride and confidence. In the case of Spain, this resurgence, initiated by the victory of Lepanto, marked the end of a contest which had long locked the Christian and the Muslim worlds in mortal combat. In the aftermath of Lepanto, Philip II proudly portrayed himself as the victor over the infidel Turk and the protector of Christendom.[1] During the 1570s, pride, ease and confidence again characterized Iberian life. The long years of ordeal seemed to be over at last.

Spain is a good example of a resurgent hegemon – the victory of Lepanto rekindled the crusading spirit of an earlier generation and triggered a new, ambitious and expansionist foreign policy (Elliott 1977, p. 239). Also, Spain is a good example of the costs which are regularly associated with such resurgence. The victory at Lepanto was the end result of long and costly naval preparations. Philip II's policy of decisive rearmament trebled Spain's defence expenditures in a single decade – from less than 2 million ducats annually in the years before 1556 to 4.5 million in the 1560s, to 8 million in the 1570s (McNeill 1982, p. 110).

During the 1660s, the United Provinces experienced a similar boost in spirit and splendour. The victory in the Medway (1667) enabled the Dutch to command the peace negotiations of Breda (1667) and produce a treaty which was quite advantageous to the Netherlands. It boosted Dutch self-confidence, inaugurated the most brilliant period of the republic (Blok 1907, 4: p. 339) and added stories and heroes to the nation's political mythology (Schama 1987). But the resurgence was purchased at a steep increase in military expenditure. In 1665–67 alone, the Dutch built over sixty warships. The defence budget of the Estates General, which had lain around a stable average of about 7 million guilders between 1650 and 1665, soared to 12 million between 1666 and 1671 (ten Raa and de Bas 1908–18).

In the late 1750s, the First British Empire experienced an Indian summer that was no less spectacular. The Royal Navy scored several prestigious victories on the subcontinent and in North America. The persons associated with these victories – Clive, Coote, Boscawen, Hawke and others – were immediately incorporated into the patriotic mythology of the nation. By 1760, French rule in India and in Canada was at an end. Not since the battle of Blenheim had England been so overwhelmingly victorious. However, the cost of victory was reflected in substantial increases in England's military budgets. Naval expenditure (which had amounted to an annual average of £1 million during Walpole's tenure) trebled between 1755 and 1765 (Mitchell 1962, pp. 389ff.) as England adopted a policy of naval superiority. King and Parliament increased England's military inventory and involved the country in warfare all over the world – alliance followed alliance with bewildering speed, and English money poured into the pockets of German princes with troops to hire.

In the 1860s, the Second British Empire overcame the interstate challenges mustered by Russia (in the Crimea) and France (in the colonies). These challenges were followed by a long and prestigious Indian summer. In the 1870s and 1880s, Great Britain appeared as the strongest and wealthiest actor in the world. It dominated the interstate balance of power. And whereas Continental states were embroiled in frequent wars during the last decades of the nineteenth century, the British Isles miraculously escaped these engagements. Also, Britain dominated the international division of labour. From the early 1870s, it had consolidated a far-flung empire which was the envy of other states. But this consolidation was attended by a substantial increase in military budgets. Whereas British defence expenditures had lain between £10 million and £15 million during the 1830s and 1840s, they jumped to £27.7 million in 1855 and remained at this higher level for the next quarter of a century (Mitchell 1962, pp. 396ff.).[2]

The cost of pre-eminence I: the home front

The hegemons met the challenge which was thrown at them. Suddenly recognizing the poor state of their armed forces, they launched ambitious projects of modernization and rearmament – initiatives which were often accompanied by thorough reviews of extant strategies and tactics and by reforms of traditional command structures. As a result, the hegemons' fortunes changed. And although they lost their first battles, they ultimately won the wars.

However, victory was purchased at a high price. The hegemons' decisive response to challenge and war imposed heavy financial burdens on the state. It demonstrated that political pre-eminence carries a high economic cost. It forced politicians to discuss how the costs could best be met, and also raised the question of the proper relationship between the states' foreign-policy commitments and their economic capabilities (Kennedy 1987).

Raising funds through loans and taxes

All hegemons considered two revenue-raising options: taxation and borrowing. The options carried very different implications. Taxation would raise state revenues and improve the country's ability to carry larger, military commitments. But it would alienate the general public. Spanish, Dutch and English rulers alike noted immediately that few issues concern private citizens more than their tax rates. Fearing that the tax option might trigger a political backlash, they all saw borrowing as their most attractive option. Besides, loans would make the needed funds more immediately available than taxes would.[3]

Philip II was the only ruler who sought to cover his increased costs with taxation. The reason is simple: he had no choice. International financiers considered Philip II a high-risk customer in the 1560s and were reluctant to do business with him.[4] He was therefore forced to rely heavily on taxes and tolls to cover his naval costs, which increased threefold during the 1560s. He levied new taxes and export duties; he increased the *encabezamiento* – a sales tax which had traditionally accounted for the major share of the Crown's revenue; he received the Pope's permission to collect a religious tax, the *cruzada*, and a 'subsidy' of 420,000 ducats a year for ten years. In addition, he imposed duties on the export of wool, salt and playing cards. In 1565, customs, taxes and subsidies amounted to nearly 2 million ducats a year (Braudel 1973, p. 1009).

Dutch and English leaders had the luxury of choosing among several alternatives. They were in a position to combine financial methods more freely. The Dutch Estates General covered the increased defence costs partly by short-term loans and partly by tax hikes (Parker 1974, p. 579).[5] And in the 1760s, the English met their increases in military expenditure[6] partly by foreign loans, and partly by increases in land tax, beer tax and various customs (Watson 1960, p. 72f.). Similarly, in the 1850s, they turned to a combination of loans and taxes to finance the mounting costs of new weapons systems (Thomson 1978, p. 126).[7]

Whether a hegemon relied on taxes or loans, its financial policy hinged on the assumption that the increase in defence expenditure was only a temporary phenomenon. They all expected that when the challenge was fended off and the world returned to normal, the military costs would decline to previous levels. Then new taxes would pay off the state loans over a reasonable period of time. However, this assumption was never met. Neither Spanish, Dutch nor English defence budgets declined to the manageable levels of the immediate pre-war period.

Different states relied on taxes and loans to different degrees to make budgetary ends meet. All of them increased taxes. Also, during their respective Indian summers, they enhanced their state revenues through colonial expansion. Their spectacular turns of military fortune fuelled a revival of domestic hyperbole which echoed the patriotic Podsnappery of the first phase of the world order. The recovered prestige was attended by a spiritual renaissance, reminiscent of the golden age of hegemonic consolidation, and infused the new colonial ventures with a vigorous optimism. However, the renaissance would soon prove shallow. The new-found brilliance would prove a nervous splendour. The budgetary statistics of the Indian summers strongly suggest that the energetic expansion of the period was ultimately propelled by a double need: to earn enough profits to ease the financial pressures on the state, but also to quench an emerging dissatisfaction with fiscal affairs which threatened to erode the popular support of the government.

Few political debates are as tightly packed with public emotion as those which involve fiscal issues. Fiscal debates concern the disposable income of citizens and strike at the very basis of every family's standard of life. But they also concern the most basic and burning of political principles: they raise the issue of social justice. Fiscal grievances may be directly sparked by egotistical concerns for one's wallet; but to be made politically respectable, they must be reformulated in general principles which touch citizens' hearts. People may protest and revolt because they are economically cramped; 'but to the world – and, save for a very few hypocrites, also for themselves – they must appear *wronged*' (Brinton 1964, p. 34). If 'cramp' undergoes such a moral transfiguration, then a government may have a revolt on its hands.

Few political issues lend themselves more easily to demagogic appeals to the ideals of equity and fairness than fiscal reforms. Philip II faced a dilemma which he shared with subsequent Dutch and English rulers: although a people may take great pride in their nation's international pre-eminence, they are often reluctant to contribute the money necessary to maintain it. Spanish, Dutch and English rulers all discovered that tax hikes could cover the states' foreign-policy commitments only at the risk of domestic unrest.

Trade and colonization

In addition to taxes and loans, the hegemons faced an obvious third method which could help them cover the climb in public spending: economic development. They could increase state revenues by stimulating foreign trade, business

and production. In the age of Philip II this option assumed the form of intensified colonialism. Thus his military build-ups of the 1560s were followed by
intensified extraction of wealth from the Spanish Americas – the influx of
American treasure had hovered around an average annual royal revenue
of about 650,000 ducats during the 1550s and 1560s; during the 1570s it rose
to an annual average of some 1.2 million. The Dutch naval build-ups of the
1650s were also followed by an expansion of foreign ventures (Stoye 1980,
p. 145).[8] Likewise, the English build-ups of the 1740s and the 1850s and 1860s
were followed by conspicuous expansions of trade and colonialism.[9]

The Indian summers, which followed the hegemons' military resurgence and
splendid naval victories, were attended by a neo-colonial thrust. At the time,
this expansion was celebrated as the beginning of a new golden age and a
rejuvenation of the hegemon's spiritual life. In hindsight this sudden outward
expansion is better interpreted as a nervous quest for funds to ease a mounting
burden of national defence costs which put a great strain on national finances
– and domestic order.

The cost of pre-eminence II: the world arena

After a generation of undoubted pre-eminence, Spain, the United Provinces
and England (twice) were suddenly challenged by violence and war. The
challenge dealt a catastrophic blow to the hegemon's international prestige;
the hegemon's losses in the war's initial battle demonstrated to the world that
it was neither omnipotent nor invulnerable.

Also, the challenge significantly eroded the hegemon's international legitimacy. By fighting wars for purposes of national defence, the hegemon
prominently displayed its own national interests and advertised its own
geostrategic goals. It broke out of the international community of common
interest and aroused the scepticism of other great actors. This erosion was
compounded by the hegemon's new colonial policy, which was no longer
sustained by innocent altruism, but was cast more in sordid terms of profit
and gain. As a result, the world's pre-eminent actor increasingly supported its
international position not on hegemony and consensus but on power and
prestige.

On the falling prestige of hegemons

'Power' and 'prestige' are related terms – both are political tools of dominance;
both are used by states to ensure the obedience of other states. The terms are
similar, but not synonymous. Power is a function of activating punitive, renum-
erative and normative resources to make an actor do what he would not
otherwise have done. Prestige does not involve the immediate activation of

material and spiritual capabilities; it is simply the 'probability that a command with a specific content will be obeyed by a given group or persons' (Dahrendorf 1959, p. 166).

An actor's power depends upon force, wealth and normative standards; it is an immediate function of resources and capabilities. An actor's prestige, by contrast, depends on a general recognition on the part of other actors that he possesses the ability to muster adequate force or wealth if the occasion should demand it; it is a function of other actors' perceptions. Prestige, then, is not power; it is the reputation for power.

It is prestige rather than power which is the everyday currency of international politics. Prestige is enormously important, because if an actor's strength is recognized, the actor can generally achieve its aims without having to use it (Carr 1964, p. 236). Consequently, when bargaining among national leaders is determined by the relative prestige of the parties, interstate conflict may be resolved without resorting to overt force or even to threats of force. The prestige of a dominant actor plays an important, ordering role in a hegemonic order.

Prestige hinges on the successful use of power – and especially upon victory in war. The prestige of Spain, for example, was primarily built on the country's victories in the Italian wars, on the military efficiency of its soldiers and sailors and on its role as the primary colonizer of the non-European world. Similarly, the prestige of the United Provinces and that of England were functions of the fact that they emerged from waves of great wars as the primary organizers of victorious alliances, and from the general perception that they were the strongest and wealthiest countries of their times.

When an actor of high prestige unexpectedly loses a battle, the event shakes the international order at its very foundations. Such a loss surprises other world actors and causes them to reconsider their perception of the dominant actor's power capabilities. Indeed, if the dominant actor makes an unexpectedly poor showing in warfare, that immediately lowers its prestige. This, in turn, invites the other actors to re-examine the traditional pecking order of international politics.

Not only were Spain, the United Provinces and England (twice) shocked by their initially poor response to the armed challenge, but other actors were also surprised. Their perceptions of the dominant actors were revised to include weaknesses and vulnerability revealed by these unexpected turns of events. The dominant actors' capabilities were re-examined. Their positions in relation to the other great powers in the systems were reconsidered. And as other states adjusted their perceptions of the hegemon, the entire international hierarchy of power – in which the hegemon had traditionally provided the standards of assessment and comparison – became more fluid and uncertain.

On the rising capabilities of others

Different countries display different paces of economic and military growth, and they accumulate political resources at different rates. If such different rates of growth and accumulation persist over time, they will erode the old international hierarchy of power. This tendency towards unequal development of states became increasingly apparent as the hegemons sought to deal with their sudden, initial challenge.

The tendency was not always immediately apparent. It was often soothed by the expansion, the opulence and the contentment of the hegemons' Indian summers. Nevertheless, the unequal development of states introduced limits to the hegemons' foreign policy, and emerged with increasing visibility during the phase of challenge. The hegemons emerged victorious from their initial interstate challenges; however, the ways in which they handled the challenges revealed weaknesses – chinks in the armour, which subsequent challengers would seek to exploit later on. As the hegemons displayed uncertainties and vulnerabilities, their prestige eroded. And since the hegemons were the pre-eminent actors of their age and sought to maintain the extant institutions of international conduct, this erosion of their prestige affected the nature of the world order. International politics was rendered more multifaceted and unstable as a result.

In the late sixteenth century, Spain was spurred by the spectacular success of Lepanto to contain the Protestant powers in the North Atlantic. The Spanish took on England, whose rulers were developing international ambitions which Philip II wished to contain – for example, Queen Elizabeth I (1558–1603) backed the United Provinces during the 1580s and encouraged Dutch efforts to sever the links with Spain and create a sovereign republic. However, Philip II appeared oblivious to the fact that these new English ambitions were sustained by a rapid development of England's economic and military capabilities. During the late 1580s, the competition intensified and escalated into a battle for the Atlantic between Catholic Spain on the one side and the Protestant powers of the North Atlantic (the Dutch provinces and England) on the other. Spanish offensives also drove France and England closer together, burying temporarily the long-standing differences which Spain had always encouraged. During Spain's Indian summer, then, the world order was changing from a unipolar constellation to a bipolar balance-of-power system.

Comparable realignments attended the Dutch Indian summer during the third quarter of the seventeenth century. This time France was the ascending state, whose rapidly evolving capabilities challenged the extant hierarchy of prestige. When the French king Louis XIV assumed full power (1661), France entered the interstate system in a new and forceful mode. The new French monarch was determined to seize some of the wealth of the Spanish

Netherlands. His lawyers were working overtly on a theory of devolution which would enable him to present a legal claim on the Provinces. His generals were covertly preparing a military conquest, for the king knew that he ultimately had to defend the seizure by means of force. He prepared for the onslaught by rearming France. He also prepared by enhancing the animosity between the Dutch and the English and by weakening the Dutch. Finally, he sought to gain the confidence of England's king (Charles II) and he adopted British-type laws of navigation against Dutch shipping. During the Dutch Indian summer, the seventeenth-century world order changed from a unipolar condition of Dutch hegemony to a configuration where two larger (England and France) and two smaller (Spain and Sweden) monarchies were vying with one weakened confederate republic for primacy in a rough balance-of-power condition.[10]

The Indian summer of the First British Empire coincided with comparable interstate realignments. These were, once again, paralleled by the development of French capabilities – or better: by the final recovery of France after the disastrous wars of Louis XIV. A conflict between England and Spain had erupted in the War of Jenkins' Ear already in 1739. This war widened rapidly, and soon France joined Spain. During the third quarter of the century, France evolved as the most uncompromising of England's enemies. And by the 1770s, the old world order was clearly eroded by the global rivalry between England and France – as was particularly apparent in the Anglo-French wars in the American and Asian colonies. England's position was complicated by a proliferation of international actors. In the heart of Europe, Frederick the Great made Prussia[11] a great power in European politics. Further east, Russia emerged as a major actor.[12] In the Americas, the North American colonists were about to form their own sovereign republic. In sum, England's preeminence was replaced by a new constellation, by a 'new and somewhat perverted balance of power' (Ogg 1981, 143; Schroeder 1996, pp. 5ff.). By 1760, the English hegemony was on the wane owing to its declining prestige on the one hand and to the rise of new actors on the other. The world order was becoming a constellation of five major state with competing interests. 'The rise of Prussia and the re-entry of Russia as a major protagonist forced state leaders to consider central and east European issues far more, and much of the diplomatic initiative after 1748 was taken by Austria and Russia' (McKay and Scott 1983, p. 29).

In the nineteenth century, the Indian summer of the Second British Empire was also accompanied by a realignment in international affairs. The Second English hegemony was anchored in an industrial and commercial base which the Continental actors could not surpass. However, the 1850s saw the rapid spread of industrialization to other parts of the world and the emergence of other industrial and commercial states. These were years of a temporary French resurgence and of a brief Russian bid for international power (Best 1982, p. 223). England during the 1820s had already torn itself loose from the Russian-led movement of Continental reconstruction. France followed a generation later. The triangular constellation of England, France and Russia (with England as the pre-eminent actor) dominated the world order for the first half of the nineteenth century. By mid-century, France, gathering strength under a new Napoleon, in an unlikely alliance with England, took on Russia, the stronghold of European reaction, in the Crimean War (1852–54).

The Crimean War broke up this constellation. No one was impressed with either the English or the Russian performance. The French, however, proved unexpectedly efficient and professional in their conduct. Consequently, by the end of the 1850s:

> French military prestige in Europe stood high. While French armies had acquitted themselves with credit ... neither the British nor the Russian military reputation had recovered from the Crimean *débâcle*. That of the Austrian armies, notwithstanding their defensive gallantry, had been somewhat tarnished at Magenta and Solferino. As for Prussia, her disorderly mobilization in 1859 merely confirmed the low esteem in which her armed forces were generally held. (Mosse 1974, pp. 134f.)

A cluster of additional conflicts erupted in the wake of the Crimean War and consolidated this impression. Of these, five wars which broke out in Europe between 1854 and 1870, France, Prussia, and Austria were each engaged in three, Piedmont in two (Thomson 1974, p. 238). One result of these wars was to diminish the prestige of Russia and France and to increase that of Prussia and Piedmont. In a word, the wars flattened the international hierarchy of prestige. The bipolar constellation from the eighteenth century re-emerged: Great Britain *v*. France.

The new, uncertain correlation of forces presented new strategic possibilities for minor actors in the international system. Piedmont, for example, found it expedient to ally itself with France to further its ambition and extend the sway of the house of Savoy from the Alps to the Adriatic. The Magyar nationalities saw an opportunity to take a long-awaited revenge against Russia so they allied themselves with Prussia. But the master manipulator of the interstate system was Prussia's creative Chancellor, Otto von Bismarck. He had decided to make Prussia the equal of Austria within the German confederation. From an early moment on, he realized that this could be achieved only through a policy of 'blood and iron', by a carefully equilibrated series of small, opportunistic wars – none of which would be large enough to distract England's monumental fixation on France as the major challenge to English dominance (Kissinger

1968). Bismarck knew, just as Frederick the Great had known, 'how to exploit the system's slackness and instability to the advantage of his lean but sinewy state. In fact, Bismarck followed Frederick's line of approach. Both men were products of a trough between two waves of movement toward hegemony' (Dehio 1963, p. 217).

By the 1860s, the two principles which had provided order to the Continent – English prestige on the one hand and the consensus concerning monarchic restoration on the other – had been removed. Two forces of change were introduced into the interstate system after the Crimean War: the imperial *grand dessein* of Napoleon III and, consciously hiding behind the French bravado, the pan-Germanic designs of Bismarck.

> Gone forever was the era of an ideological solidarity that could peacefully override the selfish interest of individual states. Its place was taken by increasing division and extreme instability. Now, as in a similar state of flux which had overtaken the system of states in the middle of the previous century, the richest prizes would again fall to those who were swift-footed and bold in exploiting kaleidoscopic changes ... From then on, the chess board of Europe was filled, square by square, with strong pieces, without adequate room for manoeuvre, confronting one another in uncanny immo-bility. No common ideological firmament spanned their conflicting interests, as it had in the tranquil days of the Restoration. (Dehio 1963, pp. 201–2)

Challenge

The second phase of an international order was introduced by an eruption of violence and war. The hegemons were forced to intervene to defend their geopolitical interests against the incursions of a challenger. After an extended period of relative peace, the hegemons were in no position to wage a large war against territorial states with weapons systems comparable to their own. Their military forces had lain fallow for a long time, whereas the forces of others had evolved and were often consciously groomed. When the hegemons engaged in battle, the initial result was an unexpected defeat which seriously damaged their prestige.

To compensate for their losses in prestige and re-establish their capabilities, the hegemons launched crash armament programmes. They succeeded in hand-ling the challenge at hand, and ultimately emerged victorious from the war. But they achieved this at a high cost. The rearmament programmes which brought the victories had to be paid for by taxes and loans. Spanish, Dutch and English rulers all discovered that if they relied too heavily on taxes to cover their foreign-policy commitments, they ran the risk of alienating parts of their populations. Their common experience conforms to the old verity, that a ruler's quickest road to unpopularity goes through excessive taxation. For, as Machiavelli (1961[1532], p. 92) observed, 'this will start to make his subjects hate him, and, since he will have impoverished himself, he will be generally despised'.

The hegemons covered their government costs by loans to the extent they could (which was minimal in the case of Spain). They did this by assuming that the defence expenditure they sought to cover was a temporary phenomenon. They reasoned that when the challenge had been fended off and the world returned to normal, military costs would fall to previous levels. And when this happened, taxes would pay off the state loans over a reasonable period of time. In all cases the appealing logic of this simple theory stumbled over an unfortunate fact which is presented in the next chapter: the defence budgets of the Spanish, the Dutch and the English would never again settle at the old, manageable levels of the days of hegemony. Fiscal difficulties had become a permanent, indeed a mounting, condition.

After the adjusting wars, all hegemons experienced a resurgence of expansionism and self-confidence. But in no case was this superiority as secure or as lasting as during the original phase of hegemony. The postwar era was in all cases a pleasant, relatively tranquil and flourishing period. But it occurred on the eve of larger challenges which were still to come. Its resurgence was not a new spring but an Indian summer. It signalled demise.

One of the reasons why this postwar climate presented new challenges for the hegemons lay in the development of the interstate system. The wars which the hegemons had just won had stimulated the rapid growth of other states. Some of these were new actors whose inclusion in the international system made interstate politics more complex than before and more difficult to manage. This development can be explained by the so-called thesis of unequal development. As Paul Kennedy[13] explains:

> The relative strengths of the leading nations in world affairs never remain constant, principally because of the uneven rate of growth among different societies and of the technological and organizational breakthroughs which bring a greater advantage to one society than to another. (Kennedy 1987, p. xv)

This thesis of unequal development is, in essence, a theory of uneven technological evolution. It does not alone explain the interstate dynamics which propel the world order out of the phase of challenge and into the phase of competitive disruption. The unequal development thesis must be complemented by an auxiliary claim: as the more rapidly growing countries become conscious of their higher rates of growth, they expect their increased capabilities to be recognized by others. The most rapidly developing states expect, in a word, that their international prestige will increase at a rate which reflects their increase in capabilities.[14]

Notes

1 That Philip's half-brother commanded the Christian forces added to the political mythology of the Habsburg empire – a mythology which was captured on gigantic canvases where the glorious victory was celebrated by some of most famous artists of the age: Titian, Tintoretto, Veronese and others.

2 It is quite unclear whether these substantial expenditures were in any way offset by colonial profits (Robinson and Gallagher 1983).

3 In theory, the choice was between taxation and borrowing. In practice, no hegemon saw the financial problems in terms of a sharp choice of either taxes *or* loans. They all realized that loans only represented a temporary solution; that the moneys borrowed would have to be paid back somehow with the nation's own assets. In practice, they relied on combinations of taxes *and* loans. They borrowed some, thus softening the impact of the steep increase in armament costs; and they raised taxes somewhat, believing that as soon as the armed forces were built up, the threat would be contained.

4 It must be recalled that Spain had defaulted on its financial obligations in 1557, and that this had rocked some of Europe's greatest banking houses. In the 1560s, Spain was largely considered insolvent. Since Philip II consequently had great difficulties obtaining new loans, he was forced to cover his mounting naval expenditures by taxes at home and by pillage abroad.

5 This combination of loans and taxes did not mean that the fiscal burden in the Netherlands was easy; indeed, during the second half of the seventeenth century, the Dutch became the most taxed people in Europe (Boxer 1973, pp. 71f.).

6 Great Britain's military successes in Asia and the Americas in the late 1750s were purchased at a steep price. In the dark year of 1754, £4 million sterling was spent on military supplies; by 1759, the expense had multiplied to over £12 million. In 1760 and 1761 the amount had increased to nearly £16 million and £20 million respectively.

7 The new weapons systems involved the introduction into the Royal Navy of new armour and machines. The costs of these measures were vastly exacerbated by Britain's compulsion to keep up with France. The French navy introduced a series of technical innovations in the two decades which followed the Crimean War; and when France launched an immense frigate, *La Gloire*, in 1859, England responded by laying down the *Warrior*. Public support for the build-up together with England's 'superior industrial capacity made it relatively easy for the Royal Navy to catch up technically and surpass the French numerically each time the French changed the basis of competition' (McNeill 1982, p. 227).

8 These Dutch ventures suffered greatly during the Second Anglo-Dutch War (1665–67), so that the Dutch commercial expansion appeared uneven and choppy (Israel 1989, pp. 213ff.).

9 In the 1760s, William Pitt, first Earl of Chatham, captured the most lucrative branches of French trade in North America, the West Indies, Africa and in India. He applied the resultant profits towards subsidizing his costly foreign policies and

consolidated the First British Empire into the bargain (Bowle 1977, p. 112). In the 1870s, Prime Minister Disraeli consolidated the Second British Empire – in 1872, on the tail of costly naval build-ups, Disraeli denounced Britain's anti-colonial stance and announced his conversion to an active policy of expansionist imperialism.

10   This realignment becomes more evident if one considers the key international developments after 1670. These can be briefly expressed in two great movements. First, the Anglo-French invasion of the Spanish Netherlands, which eased the traditional animosity between Spain and the United Provinces to such a degree that these two old arch-enemies began to cooperate in defence of common national security concerns. Second, after the Anglo-French invasion, the United Provinces did not succeed – in spite of great rearmament efforts – in re-establishing the favourable *status quo ante*. In the wars against England, 'in which her trade was broken, Holland found her master. She bowed to the Navigation Act and fell back into second place as a naval power' (Dehio 1963, p. 71).

11   In the first years of the eighteenth century, the new kingdom of Prussia rivalled only Savoy in Continental insignificance. Weak and small, Prussia had a disproportionately large army with a vigorous life of its own. It was an important vehicle for providing consensus to Prussia's heterogeneous society but it was reluctant to be involved in war. Under Frederick William I (1713–40) Prussia developed a civil service noticeable for its honesty and efficacy. The monarch sponsored a prosperous new middle class which deferred to the nobility, served the state and stood in awe of the army. With the nation's efficient army and its new found prosperity, Frederick II (1740–86), later called the Great, struck swiftly to the south-east, seized Silesia (1740) and thus unexpectedly doubled Prussia's population and added valuable industries. With one bold stroke he secured Prussia a strong bargaining position in Central Europe that allowed him to pursue his ambitions through intrigue, threats and balance-of-power politics. After the invasion of Silesia, Frederick provided a catalyst which fused together a number of conflicts into a set of simultaneous wars that launched new actors on to the world scene.

12   Russia and Prussia underwent similar reforms in the 1760s and 1770s. The top-heavy Russian structures were set in motion by Peter the Great (1689–1725). After his death, this momentum petered out during the confused regime of the three women who succeeded him. But in the last half of the eighteenth century the nation made powerful strides under the control of a fourth woman, Catherine II (1762–96). She turned the attention away from Central Europe and concentrated on expanding the Russian Empire at the expense of Poland and Turkey (Young 1965). Britain rejoiced because this manoeuver kept France occupied. Soon, however, Catherine would pose a major threat to Britain as well. She extended Russia's power to the Black Sea, giving her empire a second window on the world while threatening Constantinople from the sea: a large Russian fleet sailed all the way around Europe and destroyed the Turkish fleet in the Aegean (1770). The question was raised in London whether a Russian victory in a war with Turkey would benefit or damage British interests. Until then, British state leaders, who subscribed consistently to balance-of-power analyses, had viewed any Russian victory over the Ottomans as a blow to the French. But Russian penetration of the Mediterranean was quite another kettle of fish! London, accordingly, engineered diversions on the Continent. It allied itself with both Turkey and Prussia and encouraged Sweden to go to war against Russia.

13 This is an ancient argument in political theory. The first discussion of it is found
    as far back as Thucydides. A most influential discussion of this observation is
    found in Friedrich Engels's *Anti-During*. The most popular rendition is, made by
    Lenin (1939[1917], p. 119), who elevated the observation to a socio-economic law:
    the so-called 'law of uneven development'. As Gilpin (1981, p. 78) notes, it is not
    at all necessary to be a Marxist to accept the heuristic value in Engels's and Lenin's
    discussions – he sees Lenin's claim 'as a special case of the more general law of
    diminishing returns'. Kennedy appears to follow Gilpin's interpretation.

14 This concept of 'recognition' can easily be connected with Spinoza's notion of
    conatus (Knutsen 1997, p. 97) or Nietszche's discussion of *Thymos* (Fukuyama
    1992, pp. 181ff.), and thus find a theoretical anchor in classical theory. This
    concept can also be easily connected with Organski's 'power-transition theory'
    which has received empirical support (Organski and Kugler 1980).

4

The phase of
disruptive competition

'My other piece of advice, Copperfield', said Mr. Micawber, 'you know. Annual income twenty pounds, annual expenditure nineteen nineteen and six, result happiness. Annual income twenty pounds, annual expenditure twenty pounds ought and six, result misery. The blossom is blighted, the leaf is withered, the god of day goes down upon the dreary scene, and – and in short you are forever floored!' (Dickens 1986[1849–50])

It is often argued that great powers decline because they overextend themselves – because they stretch their foreign commitments further than their domestic economies can cover. Does the overstretch hypothesis help explain the demise of the Spanish, the Dutch and the (two) British world orders?

In order to answer the question, it is necessary to appreciate two things more fully. The first is the overstretch hypothesis itself; it is necessary to clarify the conditions under which great powers increase their commitments. The second is the international changes which took place during the third phase of world order. Each of the orders provided the socio-historical context for each of the hegemonic powers discussed here. And as each world order changed, new impulses drove the powers to stretch their foreign commitments – and in some cases to overstretch themselves. What impulses were these?

The overstretch hypothesis identifies two such impulses. The first is the principle of unequal development. It holds that different states evolve in different ways and at different paces, and that this affects the international hierarchy of power. Simply put, if one state (or alliance of states) increases its capabilities significantly, then it improves its position relative to that of other states and thus challenges the old international ranking order. International competition becomes more intense and increases the burden of pre-eminent powers. For 'rival powers are now economically expanding at a faster rate, and wish in their turn to extend their influence abroad' (Kennedy 1987, p. xxiii).

The second impulse is the postulate of zero-sum relations between wealth and force. It means that as states grow richer they also grow stronger; and as they grow stronger they acquire new commitments beyond their own borders. In order to meet its commitments, the state has to undertake larger and more costly protective efforts. At first, these commitments are relatively easy to sustain. But later they become burdensome. In order to meet its commitments, the old great power undertakes larger and more costly defensive efforts. But, ironically, these exertions do not make the leading power more secure; they actually render it more vulnerable. For as more is spent on defence, resources are channelled away from productive activities.[1] As a result, the economic growth of the once pre-eminent power slows down. This erodes the economic basis of its military capabilities. And as the power feels increasingly drained and vulnerable, the process of relative decline accelerates.

Do these two general principles help illuminate the decline of Spain, the United Provinces, England I and England II? The first section of this chapter suggest that they do. But it also suggests that a more concrete, comparative application of these two impulses can tease out common features which characterize the phase of disruptive competition – features which promise to add to our understanding of the decline and fall of great powers.

The changing international order

First, and most importantly, old pre-eminent great powers increase their international commitments during the third phase of world order. As a result, the powers demonstrably increase their military expenditures during this third phase. The simplest explanation for this is that their leaders perceive how the old order is challenged – that some states develop at a high rate, improve their position relative to those of other (often more established) states, demand greater recognition and thereby alter the old international ranking order. In a word, changes in the hierarchy of power trigger demands for changes in the hierarchy of prestige. These alterations render the international order unclear and make international competition more pronounced. These dynamics affect the old hegemons in particular, because it was they who shaped the system in the first place. When the system in challenged, the old hegemons strive to stop (or reverse) its erosion. Efforts to increase their power and prestige drive up their defence costs.

Three key dynamics are common to all four world orders. These are characteristic features which pertain to the level of the international system and which stimulate the pre-eminent powers in such a way that their leaders invest more resources in military might. These characteristics are: the introduction of new states to the interstate system, the instability of old enemies and the reintroduction of balance-of-power politics. These three systems dynamics are

simultaneous and intertwined. They reinforce each other. And they contribute
to increasing international unrest and cause a mounting sense of urgency among
the leaders of the pre-eminent powers.

The fall of old enemies – and the rise of new

During the course of the third phase of world order, the old hegemonic great
power is increasingly challenged. The hegemonic power is the primary representative of the old world order – it has significantly informed the values and
norms of the order, it has helped formulate its rules of conduct, and it has
benefited significantly from it. As the old order is challenged, the old hegemon
is at the focus of the challenge. However, since it is the order itself which is
challenged, the old hegemon is not the only great power which is under
pressure. The hegemon's primary allies sense the challenge as well. And so
does the hegemon's old primary foe.

The hegemon's foe is in a curiously difficult position. For as the old foe
evolved into the main and most conspicuous challenger of the hegemonic order
during the second phase of world order, the threats which it posed were met
and parried by the hegemon. During this rivalry, the two powers grew increasingly engaged in a duel-like, ritualistic rivalry which became a recognizable
part of the world order in its second and third phases. Thus, the long Turko-
Spanish rivalry was a conspicuous feature of the sixteenth-century world order.
The mutual animosity between Spain and the United Provinces was a comparable phenomenon in the seventeenth-century order. The worldwide rivalries
of England and France existed as a constant sideshow to the international order
of both the eighteenth and the nineteenth centuries.

The long and the short of it is that as the old world order is challenged the
old hegemon's traditional foe is put in a paradoxical predicament. Its challenges
cause the hegemon to react; these action–reaction dynamics affect the workings
of interstate relations, and the challenger is recognized as a great power in the
process. This gives it an odd stake in the very system that it challenges.
Furthermore, the hegemon's rival is, in fact, the first major actor to suffer the
effects of overstretch. One of the curious commonalities of the third phase of
world order, then, is not the demise of the hegemon, but the prostration of
the hegemon's rival. The clearest case in point is the way in which hegemonic
Spain witnessed the withdrawal of the Ottoman Empire from Mediterranean
affairs after Lepanto (1571). Also, about a century later, the hegemonic Dutch
Provinces observed how Spain entered into an irreversible decline in the aftermath of the Thirty Years War and abandoned its long struggle to vanquish
Dutch maritime and commercial power. Similarly, the First British Empire
witnessed the decline of its old Continental enemy, France – a decline which
ended in the French Revolution of 1789 (and the establishment of a new and

fortified French nation during the course of the 1790s). Finally, the Second British Empire saw the decline of both its old rivals during the third phase of its respective world order: first, France lost the brief Franco-Prussian War (1871) and had its ambitious regime replaced by a corrupt and indecisive Third Republic; then Russia suffered an unexpected defeat in the Russo-Japanese War (1904–05) and was subsequently shaken by revolution (1905 and 1917).

In all cases, the hegemons' primary challengers were themselves challenged during the third phase of world order. Their stature declined and the interstate system was affected as a consequence. The changes occasioned the remaining great powers to reassess and readapt to the changing situation. These reassessments were made all the more necessary by a progressive fragmentation of the interstate system – a process which was often attended by the rise of new states which struggled to find their place in a rapidly changing world. In the case of the sixteenth-century Spanish world order, new states emerged in the wake of the Counter-Reformation and the religious wars which followed. The reformed faith stimulated state- and nation-building in Scandinavia, the Baltic, the British Isles and Russia. From the Iberian point of view, the most significant new sixteenth-century actor was the consolidation of seven Dutch republics into the United Provinces.

The late seventeenth century saw the formation of several great powers. In Sweden the Wasa kings created from a rustic, backward society a standing army of such strength and efficiency that it emerged during the Thirty Years War as one of the strongest in Europe and vitally affected the Continental balance of forces. Later, Austria emerged as a great power during its wars against the Ottoman Turks. Further north-east, Russia was centralized and consolidated under the Romanov tsars. But from the Dutch vantage point, the most consequential of the new states were France and England. When the French king Louis XIV finally broke the aristocratic revolts which had long created disarray in his kingdom, he centralized the state around his own person in a unique brand of royal absolutism. When Oliver Cromwell emerged victorious from the English Civil War as Lord Protector of a dynamic republic, he ignited a socio-economic expansionism which threatened Dutch interests – an expansionism which was later continued by the restored Stuart kings. The relatively small Dutch republic could not maintain for long the balance among these new and expanding states.

The late eighteenth century was an age of exceptional turbulence. It saw both the development of the great democratic ideals in the middle of the century and their eruption in revolutions towards the end. The first of these revolutions erupted outside Europe: first in a war of secession in England's American colonies, and then in a wave of upheavals which swept through South America. In 1789 revolution erupted in France, where it irreversibly destroyed the institutions of Louis XIV's absolutism and produced a new French state. Prussia was another new state which emerged as a great power in this period.

The late nineteenth century witnessed the continued evolution of Prussia through a series of mid-century wars. Prussia's victory in 1871 concluded the unification of Germany. On the Continent, Germany's victory led to the prostration of France, as well as the unification of Italy. Outside Europe, the United States emerged, through a vicious civil war, as a great industrial power and a competitor to England in the markets of the world. Japan emerged as one of Asia's great industrializing powers whose political ambitions had great impact on European relationships (Kennedy 1987, p. 252) and world order.

Revival of balance-of-power politics

World orders are challenged when a state (or an alliance) rapidly expands its wealth and power and upsets the traditional balance of forces. The sixteenth-century world order was, for example, presented with a challenge when Philip II in the late 1560s began to escalate Spain's military presence in the Netherlands. This initiative internationalized both the Dutch struggle for independence and the French civil war and it fomented the religious rivalries in Europe.

Similarly, the seventeenth-century world order was challenged when, in 1670, England's king Charles II signed a secret anti-Dutch treaty with France's Louis XIV and gave France the occasion to abandon the old alliance system constructed by Richelieu and Mazarin. The eighteenth-century order was undermined by England's overwhelming victories over France in the Seven Years War (1756–63). The nineteenth-century world order was irreversibly altered in the 1860s and 1870s by the rapid development of Piedmont–Savoy and Prussia into the new territorial states of Italy and Germany – unifications which occurred about the same time in about the same place and formed, from a macro-historical perspective, one great event which reshaped Europe and altered England's role in it. They greatly affected the balance of forces among the major actors in the interstate system.

These instances of rapid expansion upset the hierarchy which marked the old world order. As one state significantly increased its capabilities, it improved its position relative to that of other states; it challenged the traditional hierarchy of order and rendered established powers insecure. Interstate relations increasingly came to operate on the principles of *Realpolitik* – on the maxim that government and state policies are matters divorced from moral considerations, to be dictated only by the necessities of power and judged only by success. Competing powers increasingly tested each others' wills and capabilities through diplomatic manoeuvre, shifting alliances and open challenges and conflicts. This was apparent in the 1560s, when Spain's intrusion into north-western Europe produced an English policy of counterpoise through which

Elizabeth intervened to maintain the military balance on the Continent. And when France, in the 1670s, abandoned Richelieu's and Mazarin's old alliance structures, it caused other European states to unify in a series of anti-French alliances. England's victories in the Seven Years War (1756–63), similarly, caused other states to cooperate against a militarily powerful actor.

The nineteenth century offers the most-quoted example of this kind of change. The key event was the Franco-Prussian War (1870–71). Briefly told, the German victory at Sedan concluded the unification of Germany (as the French defeat consolidated that of Italy). In effect, the German victory blew the old world order to pieces, and allowed another to develop into a new pattern governed by new dynamics. According to the old understanding of the early nineteenth-century European concert, no territorial acquisition was made without a general agreement among the great European powers; war was an evil to be avoided and diplomacy was a tool for keeping the peace and maintaining the public laws of Europe. When this common understanding collapsed, countries acquired new territory if they thought they could get away with it; war became another instrument of national policy and diplomacy was governed by a balance-of-power calculus. In Metternichean theory, the balance of power was a rational political mechanism trusted to maintain peace. But in Bismarckian practice, such peace was maintained only by all parties' constant readiness to go to war. The great powers were more willing to fight each other (Kennedy 1987, pp. 182, 196). War became, under the influence of ambitious state leaders like Bismarck and Cavour, an effective instrument of national policy. In a word, balance-of-power principles were reintroduced into Continental politics.

Challenges without and within

During the third phase of world order, the old hegemons faced increasing opposition from other powers. This opposition regularly spilled over into the hegemon's internal affairs. Spain, the United Provinces and the (two) English cases were all empires, and they all faced opposition from within as well as from without.

On the one hand, opposition came from within the empire itself – often from the empire's periphery; just as Spain was opposed in Italy and the Netherlands, so too the United Provinces were opposed in Brazil, Africa and the East Indies and the First British Empire faced opposition from North America and India. On the other hand, the empire was challenged from without. Partly, these challenges came from other great powers – which often sought to exploit the hegemon's colonial turmoil by supporting local rebels (as is notably evident in French aid to Indian and American rebels in the 1770s). Partly the challenges came from *new* great powers. Just as a rapidly developing England opposed

sixteenth-century Spain, so too Sweden, France and England opposed the
seventeenth-century United Provinces.

The most severe initial opposition to the Dutch was mounted by England
and was expressed in the great Anglo-Dutch rivalry which erupted in wars
during the 1650s and 1660s. By 1670 the Dutch perceived the English threat
to be greater than ever. The main reason was that England's newly restored
King Charles II (1660–85) initiated an unprecedented *rapprochement* with
Louis XIV of France.[2] The prospect of an Anglo-French alliance unnerved the
Dutch. It boosted their foreign-policy activities and made them invest unprecedented sums in army and naval defences. The Grand Pensionary, Johan
de Witt, was keenly aware of the changes which such an alliance would effect:
it would destroy the power constellation on which the entire seventeenth-
century world order depended. De Witt noted that the new English policy
greatly exacerbated the French threat: the interstate balance was already tilting
towards France, and King Louis XIV was eager to exploit his military advantage. Louis XIV considered Charles II's *rapprochement* a piece of good
diplomatic luck and cultivated the new Anglo-French 'understanding' with the
purpose of destroying the supremacy of the Dutch in the world economy
(McKay and Scott 1983, p. 25; Geyl 1964, p. 102). In June 1670, he obtained
Charles II's signature on the top-secret Treaty of Dover. Charles II agreed to
attack the United Provinces from the sea while Louis XIV launched an assault
over land.

These threats to sixteenth-century Spain and the seventeenth-century United
Provinces were paralleled by the difficulties faced by the First British Empire.
During the Indian summer of the 1750s and 1760s, England brought total
defeat upon France – its traditional enemy. Chatham waged the Seven Years
War (1756–63) towards a clear victory; he resurrected England's international
prestige, but purchased triumph at a high political cost. By vanquishing France
so thoroughly, he produced a revanchist drive among the French and ignited
fear of English predominance among the other powers of Europe. The major
effect of Chatham's victory, then, was to drive other states together into a
hostile coalition and leave England without allies on the Continent. Also, it
confirmed France's determination to seek revenge for the loss of French
colonial possessions in North America and India (Goodwin 1965, p. 5). The
rising opposition in North America and India to English colonial policies
represented a most welcome tool for the French. France had rebuilt its military
strength when British colonies were shaken by unrest. It seized the moment
and began to support the rebels in America and Asia. Thus, Britain was forced
to defend its possessions at opposite ends of the world. In the effort, Britain
dispersed its sea power beyond endurance. With its forces so thinly spread,
the Royal Navy was unable to regain its old competitive grasp on maritime

strategy. The principles which were so successfully employed in the Seven Years War were almost totally lacking (Lloyd 1965).

The Second British Empire was shaken in comparable ways. During the nineteenth century, England had seen itself as a power broker or 'balancer' of the Continent. It had managed to preserve the Continental order without dominating Europe militarily. This feat depended on widespread agreement about the rules of the European game – a phenomenon which was, in turn, predicated upon European countries remaining of roughly equal strength and upon England's ability to maintain its reputation of preponderance. Both of these conditions were undermined by the rapid socio-economic changes which swept Europe in the 1870s. The rapid spread of industrialism hastened the processes of production, communication, wealth and investment in Europe. But the effects of growing wealth and the mobilization of people all over Europe were different in different countries. Some new countries (like Germany) expanded at a rapid clip, whereas others (among them England) grew at a more modest pace. In the nineteenth century, industrialism exacerbated the uneven growth rates among states. It added fluidity to the already unstable Continental hierarchy of power. It made it impossible for England to manage the shifting European relations of power unaided (Webb 1985, p. 438).

In sum, the pre-eminent Spanish, Dutch and English states faced mounting opposition from other actors during the third phase of world order. By itself this is a prosaic observation. It assumes greater significance, however, when considered in a greater context. It is noteworthy that the old hegemon's traditional rival is not among the most conspicuous challengers in this third phase. It is also noteworthy that the old hegemon and the old hegemon's traditional rival decline together, and that the hegemon encounters its most ferocious opponents among the most recent arrivals in the great power system.

Summary

How does the international system change during the third phase? Several features of change leap to the eye. As some states expand their wealth and power more rapidly than others, the distribution of relative capabilities in the system changes. As states become more equal, the state system loses much of the steep, hierarchical structure which characterized the old world order. As the system structure becomes 'flatter', the international system changes from a predominantly hierarchical constellation (which characterized the hegemonic situation) towards a more anarchical situation (which characterizes the third phase of world order). This development is accentuated by the creation of new states (and the transformation of some old ones). As the number of states increases, the system allows more permutations and alliance possibilities, and international politics is rendered more complex. This growing complexity accentuates the anarchical situation (Waltz 1979, pp. 134ff.; Gilpin 1981, pp. 87ff.).

The old hierarchical system structure is replaced by a new, more anarchic structure in which order is increasingly maintained through balance-of-power dynamics. It is this anarchical situation which provides the context within which great powers overstretch themselves.

Increasing defence costs

According to the overstretch hypothesis, great powers decline because they overextend themselves – they stretch their foreign commitments further than their domestic economy can cover. This is explained in light of two principles: the principle of unequal development and the principle of a zero-sum relation between wealth and force.

The Iberian case substantiates the overstretch hypothesis nicely. The Spanish economy was burdened by a rapid escalation of military expenditure. As Table 8 shows, the military budget of Castile rose from about 2 million ducats annually in the 1570s to well over 7 million in the 1590s. During the final quarter of the sixteenth century, military expenditure consumed a steadily expanding share of the Castilian state budget. Table 8 illustrates the overstretch

Table 8   *Castilian military expenditure, 1559–94 (in millions of ducats)*

Year	A The defence of Castile	B The war in Flanders	C Military budget (A + B)	D Total state budget	E 'Military burden' (C as % of D)
1559	0.7	—	0.74	2.93	25.3
1566	1.1	0.48	1.58	4.58	34.5
1577	1.2	0.90	2.10	5.86	35.2
1588	3.4	2.73	6.13	10.49	58.4
1594	3.5	4.10	7.60	12.32	61.7

Source: Thompson (1976, p. 288)

claim: that the Habsburgs 'simply had too much to do, too many enemies to fight, too many fronts to defend' (Kennedy 1987, p. 48). This explanation is informed by the assumption that a zero-sum relationship exists between wealth and force (i.e., whenever vast sums are applied to military affairs, they are no longer available for productive investment).

Although the zero-sum principle sounds intuitively reasonable, it does present a problem: it cannot be true as a general principle. For example, some seventy or eighty years before, Spain was deeply involved in another set of hugely expensive wars – the Italian wars (1494–1529) – during which Spain's economy was *not* exhausted. Quite the contrary, the Italian wars coincided with an Iberian wave of innovative agriculture, expanding manufactures and an imperialist drive which yielded enormous profits. This is an unlikely occurrence if the zero-sum relationship between wealth and force is universally true. Also, it raises an awkward question: if Spain could bear hugely expensive wars during the opening decades of the sixteenth century, why could it not do so during the closing years?

The answer to this question does not lie in Spain alone. It lies in the international system. A full answer requires a detailed discussion of Castilian economics and of the sixteenth-century world economy of which Castile was a part. What is important here is to note the two general points which such a detailed discussion would cover. The first point is that the overstretch hypothesis is essentially a systems-level argument. Around 1500, Spain was among the most productive and entrepreneurial states of the international system; eighty years later it was not. Spain was still productive; but other countries were more productive. Thus, the overstretch argument involves a systems-level logic, in light of which wealth and force are relative concepts.

The second point is that sixteenth-century Spain represented a noteworthy variation of the overstretch theme. This is gleaned, for example, from the writings of Martìn Gonzàlez de Cellorigo. He contributed to the debate about the decline of Spain with a treatise entitled *Memoria de la Política Necesaria y Util Restauración a la República de España* (A Treatise on Necessary and Useful Policies for the Restoration of Spain (1600)). Here, he adumbrated the overstretch hypothesis. He asked whether the decline of Spain was caused by the heavy expenditures of the Crown, and answered that the problem did not lie with the expenditures of the Crown alone. Gonzàlez concluded with a more general proposition: that is, that the basic problem of the nation lay in the disproportion between expenditure and investment. Spain was replete with money but was not for that reason a wealthy nation, Gonzàlez argued. And the reason was that the nation's money was squandered on unproductive activities – pointless military ventures being one of them. The money could instead have been 'expended on things that yield profits and attract riches from outside to augment the riches within', concluded Gonzàlez.

In Gonzàlez's mind, it was a mistake to believe that Spain's wealth was reflected in its stock of precious metals – 'there is no money, gold or silver in Spain because there is so much, and it is not rich, because of all its riches', he wrote (Elliott 1977, p. 313). Instead, he considered wealth a function of the nation's productive capacity. In order to stop Spain's economic decline, he therefore thought it necessary to invest more money in projects which would enhance the productivity of the country's agriculture and its manufactures (*arbitrios*). Gonzàlez belonged to a school whose members called for projects designed to stimulate economic recovery. Because of these calls for *arbitrios*, they were called *arbitristas*. Their basic argument was not that different from the overstretch argument that e.g. Lippmann (1944) or Kennedy (1987, pp. 45–55) proposed nearly four hundred years later.

Variations on the overstretch theme

The overstretch hypothesis seems to illuminate well the Spanish case of decline. Does it also help explain the Dutch and British cases to a similarly satisfactory degree? On the face of it, it does. The Dutch and the (two) British cases are similar to the Spanish in one important aspect: when their defence efforts increased, owing to a rise in international conflict and uncertainties, their economies lost much of their competitive edge.

In the Dutch case, the United Provinces maintained a relatively stable defence budget through the 1650s, averaging 6 million to 7 million guilders per year; but during the 1660s arms expenditures increased steeply to an annual five-year average of around 18 million guilders for 1665–70. And while Dutch defence expenditures increased, the relative productivity of the Dutch decreased.

In the first British case, England had stable defence expenditures during the 1750s and 1760s of between £3 million and £6 million per year; but during the 1770s the expenditures skyrocketed and reached £15 million in 1785. At this precise moment, Britain also entered an era of economic turbulence so severe that British exports 'actually declined throughout the 1770s' (Kennedy 1987, p. 116). The Second British Empire had a moderate defence budget of between £25 million and £30 million during the 1870s and 1880s; this increased to £35 million in 1895; £66 million in 1905; and to £77 million by the outbreak of World War I. During these precise years, Britain was also losing its primacy in the world economy.

These two factors – increased military expenditures and relative economic decline – are the two basic indicators of overstretch. The logic of the overstretch hypothesis is that as a nation's moneys are unproductively spent for military purposes instead of being ploughed into productive investments, its economy will be starved of new capital and its efficiency and productivity will erode. This argument can easily be supported by historical statistics. Can it also be supported by historical case studies?

The Dutch variation

The overstretch hypothesis seems to suit the Dutch case. Like Spain, the United Provinces increased their navy significantly during the third phase of their world order. The Dutch navy counted seventy-eight global warships in 1660; this had increased to ninety-six ships in 1670 (Modelski and Thompson 1988,

p. 67). This increase in naval power cost a fortune and is indicated by the estimates in Table 9.

Table 9 *Dutch military expenditure, 1656–75 (estimates of five-year averages in millions of guilders)*

Period	A No. of global-power warships	B Army budget	C Requests for defending the Province of Holland	D Estimated expenses for entire Republic
1656–60	79	—	3.7	6.2
1661–65	88	—	3.5	5.8
1666–70	95	—	6.6	11.1
1671–75	77	—	10.8	18.0

Source: Modelski and Thompson (1988, pp. 65ff.); *Staat van oorlog* (various years); ten Raa and de Bas (1921)

The increasing military budget of the United Provinces was accompanied by noticeable hikes in taxes and tolls (Engels 1862, pp. 71, 120ff.; Geyl 1964, p. 269) and by a decrease in the relative productivity of the Dutch economy. By 1670, Dutch farmers were being overtaken by techniques pioneered in England and France. Industries and crafts in which Dutch entrepreneurs had once enjoyed a virtual monopoly were emulated and improved in other nations. Dutch fisheries and long-distance trade faced increasing competition from other great powers. These activities were also shaken by international conflicts and war.

Pieter de la Court noted this simultaneity between the rise in weapons expenditure and the decline in competitiveness. In terms reminiscent of the overstretch hypothesis, he warned against the militarization of Dutch politics. He explained in his *Interest of Holland* (1702[1662]) that the affluence of the Dutch nation was produced by trade, not war, and that the continued increase in military expenditures would spell insolvency for the republic. He adumbrated an argument which was formulated more succinctly some 330 years later: the United Provinces could not in the long run afford to divert 'vast amounts of money into military expenditure, producing the upward spiral in war debts, interest repayments, increased excise duties, and high wages that undercut the nation's competitiveness in the long term' (Kennedy 1987, p. 87).

Does the Dutch case substantiate the overstretch theory? Yes, it apparently does. It confirms the now familiar correlation between wealth and force. The Dutch, like the Spanish, experienced both rising military expenditures and falling economic productivity during the third phase of their respective world order. In the immediate aftermath of the Thirty Years War (1618–48), the United Provinces were among the most productive and entrepreneurial states of seventeenth-century Europe; towards the end of the century they were not. By 1670, the Dutch were still productive, but other nations were more productive – most particularly the English.

The first British variation

Does the overstretch hypothesis illuminate the first British case as well as it does those of the Spanish and Dutch? Like Spain and Holland during the third phase of their respective world orders, the English suffered from increasing competition abroad and economic uncertainties at home. Like Spain and Holland, England expanded its navy greatly. The Royal Navy counted 95 global-power warships in 1757, 118 in 1767 and 132 in 1787 (Modelski and Thompson 1988, pp. 69f.). That such an expansion was costly is reflected in England's naval budgets. They expanded from nearly £2 million in 1755 to around £3 million in 1765 and skyrocketed to £12 million in 1785 (Mitchell 1962, pp. 389ff.). This is illustrated in Table 10 below.

Table 10   *English military expenditure, 1755–95 (in £millions)*

	A	B	C	D	E
					'Military
		Army and	Military budget	Total state	burden' (C
Year	Navy	ordnance	(A+B)	budget	as % of D)
1755	1.814	1.576	3.390	7.119	47.6
1765	3.154	2.984	6.138	12.017	51.1
1775	1.765	2.114	3.879	10.017	37.4
1785	11.851	2.941	14.792	25.832	57.3
1795	9.626	16.647	26.273	38.996	67.4

Source: Mitchell (1962, pp. 389ff.)

The increase in Britain's military budgets was attended by severe economic turbulence. 'Exports, which had stagnated following the boom period of the Seven Years War, actually declined throughout the 1770s' (Kennedy 1987, p. 116). Contemporary observers noted the same thing, and a number of them noted with great unease the connection between increases in military expenditure and decreases in economic fortunes. In his book *American Independence, the Interest and Glory of Britain* (1774) John Cartwright expresses the fear that the military build-up would stifle Britain's economy. Adam Smith repeated this argument in his *Wealth of Nations* (1965[1776]). In rich and advanced countries, where 'soldiers are maintained altogether by the labour of those who are not soldiers, the number of the former can never exceed what the latter can maintain', Smith (1965[1776], p. 657) wrote. Both Cartwright and Smith presented arguments which harmonize well with the overstretch hypothesis. Smith even probed its explanatory principle in some detail. He claimed that investments in trade and industry are productive, whereas military expenditure is not. To his mind, economic investment and military spending compete for the nation's same scarce resources, and where one gets more the other must get less. This core notion was further elaborated by Jeremy Bentham. The wealth and well-being of a nation are built on production and trade; military expenditure robs the civilian economy of its investment funds, argued Bentham in his *Principles of International Law* (1843[1790s]).

Does the British case substantiate the overstretch hypothesis? It does on the face of it. The case confirms the correlation between wealth and force. However, a closer examination of the late eighteenth-century economy reveals a picture which is more complicated than Cartwright, Smith and Bentham assumed. It reveals that whereas some sectors of the English economy were in the throes of contraction, others were quite obviously expanding. Traditional forms of agriculture and manufacturing were in decline during the final quarter of the eighteenth century. However, new forms of agriculture based on the systematic use of newly enclosed land were increasing both in quality and yield; also, new industries based on the systematic use of engines and on new principles of labour organization displayed unprecedented productivity – first in the production of cloth and then in other goods. Indeed, it is quite apparent that the overriding trend of the age was expansion: that England was experiencing an increase in economic productivity of unprecedented proportions as the old tenant farmers were replaced by a new, more productive yeomanry and the old manufactories were replaced by the new, vastly more productive machinofactories.

Clearly, the first British case does not confirm the overstretch hypothesis. By the 1790s, when a political revolution was cleaning the old feudal structures of power out of France and changing the balance of forces on the Continent, a veritable Industrial Revolution was sweeping across the British Isles. This development was simultaneous with a rapid increase in England's defence costs. It began during the American and the Indian rebellions and gathered speed during the French Revolution and the Napoleonic Wars. Clearly, England's increasing defence costs did not stultify the rapid development of industrialism.[3] It is tempting to ask, with John Nef (1963), whether they instead stimulated it. Did state-funded projects, designed to enhance the defence preparedness and the military force of the nation, have a tonic effect on emerging industrial sectors in the civilian economy?

The second British variation
Does the overstretch hypothesis illuminate the second English case better than

it illuminates the first? No, not really. The nineteenth-century English case heaps more doubt upon the entire overstretch hypothesis.

Compared with the other great powers on the Continent, Britain was among Europe's greatest military spenders during the final quarter of the nineteenth century. The increase in its military expenditures was staggering. Britain's military budget tripled from £24.5 million in 1875 to £77.1 million by the outbreak of World War I. These years saw a rapid rearmament of its naval power. They also witnessed how England was increasingly challenged by the rapid spread of industrialization and rising productivity to other great powers. The British economy suffered a conspicuous decline when compared with the United States and Germany (Kennedy 1987, p. 231).

Table 11   *English military expenditure, 1875–1914 (in £ millions)*

Year	A Navy	B Army and ordnance	C Military budget (A+B)	D Total state budget	E 'Military burden' (C as % of D)
1875	10.5	14.0	24.5	73.0	33.6
1885	11.4	18.6	30.0	88.5	33.9
1895	17.5	17.9	35.4	100.9	35.1
1905	36.8	29.2	66.0	149.5	44.1
1914	48.8	28.3	77.1	192.0	40.1

Source: Mitchell (1962, pp. 396ff.)

Many late nineteenth-century observers criticized both the 'new imperialism', the 'new militarism' and the conspicuous naval build-up. Liberals like Lord Morley, Campbell-Bannermann and David Lloyd George opposed the Boer War because of the exorbitant costs it entailed. They feared that colonial wars and naval build-ups together would impose crippling burdens on Britain's declining economy. Others, still influenced by the free-trade theories of Bentham, Cobden and Bright, held that a peaceful policy based on the doctrines of free trade would not only relax international tensions, but would also bring greater profits to all countries that did likewise.

When calculated in absolute values, England's arms expenditure was staggering during the final quarter of the nineteenth century. However, England was also the world's leading industrial power. Its industrial productivity was so much greater than that of other European powers that it did not find such military expenditure a crippling burden to bear.[4] In fact, of all the states in Europe, 'Great Britain found it easiest to be a great power' (Taylor 1971, p. xxix). This claim is substantiated by Table 12, which shows that Britain's military expenditure consumed only 3.4 per cent of the national income at the outbreak of World War I. That this amounts to a surprisingly light military burden is confirmed by O'Brian (1988, p. 188 n99), who notes that Britain's military expenditure amounted to between 3.5 per cent and 4 per cent of its GNP towards the end of the nineteenth century – with a sudden rise to 6 per cent during the Boer War.

Table 12   *Great powers' relative share of world manufacturing output 1880–1913 and percentage of national income devoted to armaments, 1914*

	Great powers' relative shares of world manufacturing output (%)			Changes (%)	Percentage of national income devoted to armaments
Power	1880	1900	1913	1880–1913	1914
Russia	7.6	8.8	0.2	+8	6.3
Austria-Hungary	4.4	0.7	4.4	0	6.1
France	7.8	6.8	6.1	−22	4.8
Germany	8.5	13.2	14.8	+75	4.6
Italy	2.5	2.5	2.5	0	3.5
Great Britain	22.9	18.5	13.6	−40	3.4

Sources: Kennedy (1987, p. 202) and Taylor (1971, p. xxix)

Surely, if there were any merit to the overstretch hypothesis, the countries which bore the heaviest military burdens also ought to show the clearest lags in economic performance. However, this is not borne out in the economic statistics. Table 12 suggests that there is no correlation between military burden and economic performance. The British, who carried the easiest military burden (when calculated as a share of GNP), experienced the steepest decline in their relative share of world manufacturing output before the turn of the century (a decline from 22.9 per cent of total global output in 1880 to 13.6 per cent in 1913 represents a change of 40 per cent in Britain's disfavour – an average annual change of 1.25 per cent). Germany, on the other hand, whose economy bore a heavier military burden, went through a period of great expansion (and increased its relative share of world manufacturing output by 75 per cent in thirty-three years – from 8.5 per cent in 1880 to 14.8 per cent in 1913). Russia, which bore the heaviest military burden of all great powers, experienced a modest expansion in its relative share of world manufacturing output during the thirty-three years which preceded World War I – in spite of its defeat in the Russo-Japanese War and the paralysis wrought by the 1905 revolution.

Summary

The overstretch hypothesis throws clear light on the decline of Spain. Here a heavy military burden was attended by a decline in economic productivity. It also applies to the Dutch case. Here, too, an increasing military burden correlates with an economy suffering relative decline.

However, the overstretch hypothesis does not illuminate the British cases very well. In neither the first nor the second British case is it possible to demonstrate convincingly any correlation between a rising military burden and a falling rate of relative productivity. In the first British case, an increasing military burden coincided with an unprecedented *in*crease in productivity. And in the second British case, where the military burden was surprisingly light, the British economy suffered a sharp relative decline anyway. The only trustworthy inference that can be drawn about defence costs and the decline of great powers, then, is fairly vague and pedestrian: old, pre-eminent powers spend more on defence during the third phase of their respective world order.

Defence expenditures may still be a pertinent indicator – although the discussion has left some unclarity as to what it is indicative of. Clearly, defence burden alone is an insufficient indicator of decline – especially since there are instances in which rising defence expenditures have been attended not by a declining economy but by an expanding one.

Old hegemons' defence expenditures increase during the third phase of world order. The overstretch hypothesis suggests that the reason for this is that the old hegemons observe how the old world order is eroding, and that their national leaders are prepared to use military means to stop (or reverse) the decline. This explanation indicates two things which are worthy of further exploration: first, that the increased defence expenditures are investments in a greater cause – that is, the perceived necessity of shoring up the eroding world order. Second, it suggests that the mounting defence expenditures of the third phase can be portrayed as an effect of decline just as reasonably as a cause.

Domestic unrest

In order to clarify the relationship between cause and effect in the overstretch argument, it will be helpful to discuss more closely the factor(s) which push up a great power's defence expenditures. The first British case may throw a particularly interesting light on the issue, for it is the only instance in which a steep rise in defence expenditure does *not* end in decline – in spite of the fact that in the 1770s British foreign policies bore all the hallmarks of the overstretch syndrome. Most prominent among these was an increase in defence costs combined with economic uncertainties (Kennedy 1987, pp. 116ff.). This section begins with a brief discussion of the overstretch hypothesis, followed by a more in-depth investigation of changes, wars and budgets in the first British case.

Changes, wars and the (Dis)United Kingdom

One of the criticisms that can be levied against the overstretch hypothesis is that as a systems-level argument it cannot reliably probe the domestic mechanisms that push up military costs. In effect, the overstretch hypothesis simply invokes the old realist assumption that all states seek to either increase or conserve their power, and adds that this is a very costly habit. Apart from the axiom that defence expenditures represents unproductive investment, the overstretch hypothesis cannot really account for why a sustained increase in defence expenditures must invariably be followed by economic exhaustion. It simply assumes that whenever vast sums are applied to military affairs, then they are no longer available for productive investment. This seems like a reasonable assumption on the face of it. It is certainly a common axiom among liberal political economists. But is it true?

Around 1770, England was involved in big wars which threatened to stretch the country's economy beyond management and endurance. Big wars were not unprecedented for England. The country had been involved in hugely expensive wars eighty years previously; yet, on that occasion, its economy had *not* suffered – quite the contrary, England's wars against Louis XIV (1672–1713) coincided with an economically expansive age. It was precisely during these wars that England rose to economic pre-eminence.

Also, England would be engaged in massive wars soon after 1770. During the course of the 1770s and 1780s, England became involved in hugely expensive wars with France in America, India and the Continent. After 1790, England sought to contain, first, the generals of the French Revolution and, then, Napoleon Bonaparte. Why did these large-scale wars against Louis XIV and Napoleon not exhaust England? Why did England emerge from them as a victorious and pre-eminent power?

Chapters 1 and 2 propose an answer: a robust social consensus anchored in a distinct and relevant political mythology was forged on the anvil of large-scale war, and this consensus rendered England self-confident, productive and strong. Thus, the rise of pre-eminent power follows the rise of a strong state.

This answer, which addresses the rise of strong states and strong powers, may in turn pose new questions which address their decline. If the establishment of a cohesive society and strong state is attended by the ascendancy of hegemony, is hegemonic demise then accompanied by their dissolution? Is the erosion of social consensus and trust a common factor which accompanies all cases of hegemonic decline? And, finally, does the (re-)establishment of a robust consensus distinguish the first British case (which ended in the re-establishment of hegemony), setting it apart from the Spanish and the Dutch cases (which ended in decline)?

Domestic changes

During the final quarter of the eighteenth century, English society was marked by a dramatic increase in conflict and contention – clear signs of the weakening of the common norms and rules which sustain social consensus. This increase in civil unrest is plainly visible from a perusal of papers and periodicals, which brought regular reports on the increase in number and in violence of brawls and rebellions. Tilly (1995) observes that there was a marked increase in 'contentious gatherings' in England during the 1770s, and connects this with the growth of a war-making, increasingly interventionist state and of an industrializing, capitalizing, proletarianizing economy.

The one major force which lies behind this increase in conflict and strife, scholars agree, is the Industrial Revolution. The foreshadowing of this 'revolution' can be observed as early as in the 1740s. New techniques of seed drilling, crop rotation and animal breeding boosted agricultural productivity. The process of enclosure gathered speed and undermined age-old modes of small-scale cultivation. This produced a more efficient system of larger-scale agrobusiness. But it also created a growing class of poor, landless wage labourers. Stimulated by improved communications, the markets expanded for the most efficient producers.

What the enclosures did for the countryside, steam engines did for the cities. By the 1760s, economic and political innovations were beginning to alter English society. In the 1770s, industrial progress inaugurated a wholly new era based on machinofacture and wage labour at home. The Industrial Revolution altered England's socio-economic structure. On the one hand it made industrialists and bankers wealthy. On the other, it occasioned the collapse of old manufactures and filled the ranks of the paupers with bankrupt craftsmen. Landless labourers, squatters, colliers and cottagers littered the old countryside; propertyless proletarians huddled in the new industrial centres. Enclosures and machinofactures ushered in an Industrial Revolution which transformed English society in its most basic socio-economic structures. This occurred just as England was embroiled in costly foreign wars.

These socio-economic changes which marked the final quarter of the eighteenth century greatly enriched many entrepreneurs. But they also brought desperate misery upon untold millions of new paupers. The changes exacerbated old conflicts. They also added new tensions to a bewildered nation. They eroded social cohesion and laid bare a complex and turbulent society which was vertically divided between town and countryside and horizontally split between a variety of social strata. *The London Chronicle, The Gentleman's Magazine, The Annual Register* brought regular reports of brawls, rebellions and contentious gatherings in which people were wounded, killed and arrested.

Conflict and contention

Observers and politicians sought to identify the causes of this development. Several of them associated it with the rapid disappearance of decency and a common code of conduct. Two of the most famous observers were elected Members of Parliament in 1774 – representatives from Liskeard and Bristol, respectively. Both of them had first-hand experience of the characters, views and passions of the first statesmen of the age. Both participated in the ongoing parliamentary discussions of the mounting number of domestic and foreign misfortunes. The representative from Liskeard, a small borough in Devon, discussed issues concerning the very existence of the British Empire during the day – and he supported 'with many a sincere and silent vote, the rights, though not, perhaps, the interest of the mother country' (Gibbon 1994[1814], p. 184f.). During the night, he worked furiously on the first volume of his *Decline and Fall of the Roman Empire*, where some sense of the darkening world stage comes through in his narrative. This observer was Edward Gibbon. He read the history of Rome in terms of dark themes like immorality, licentiousness, political quarrels and the multiplication of religious feuds.

A similar analysis of the dangers of moral decadence was formulated by the representative from Bristol – whose politics Gibbon approved (Gibbon 1994[1814], p. 214). He saw society as greater than the simple sum of its individuals. He viewed a nation as an imagined corporation produced by common values and shared historical experience; as a spiritual community seasoned by history. This observer was Edmund Burke. In his *Reflections on the Revolution in France* (1988[1790]), he portrayed society as a 'partnership' – 'a partnership not only between those who are living, but between those who are living, those who are dead and those who are to be born' (Burke 1988[1790], pp. 194f.). He observed that the old, moral community was rapidly disappearing in Britain, and feared its dissolution.

Gibbon and Burke argued that there is always a dangerous contradiction between economic progress and social order. And their insight was substantiated by English events. For those inhabiting the summit of the social pyramid, the late eighteenth century was a golden age of growing wealth, power and privilege. But for those on the lower rungs of the social ladder, conditions worsened. Tenant farmers, smallholders and peasants were squeezed off their land by the enclosure movement and included in the mushrooming faceless, landless masses of labourers. Growing social inequality and increasing notions of social injustice and unfairness eroded the legitimacy of the myth of an original compact.

Veritable revolutions in social thought exacerbated this inflammable social condition. The expansion of primary education greatly enhanced English literacy rates and stimulated economic productivity as well as political participation. But it also had destabilizing effects: the spread of literacy gave more people access to radical pamphlets. The business of journals and newspapers expanded briskly in wake of increasing literacy. *The Times* and the *Morning Post* sharpened the political criticism of the well-to-do; *The Political Register* expressed the attitudes of the less affluent. *The North Briton* was an organ for the radical intelligentsia whose members sided with the impoverished urban masses.

The growth of the printed media, which had contributed greatly to forming a unified, imagined community at the beginning of the century, contributed to social fragmentation towards its end. While farmers, engineers, entrepreneurs and officers altered the material structures of English society, philosophers, dissenters and journalists were chipping away at the traditional system of thought. In an age marked by the American and French revolutions, thinkers, preachers and writers were finding new and urgent causes to fight for. Drawing upon the fresh, republican ideas of America and France, they were finding new and radically different ways of looking at society and the world. And they were communicating their discoveries, in print, throughout society. As Burke noted with trepidation, there was no end to the commentators and analysts who addressed the violent problems of the age.[5]

Early industrialism created a proletariat. But diversity of jobs and conditions of employment prevented the formation of a working class (Thompson 1978). Instead, the new urban centres produced another phenomenon which is too often confused with it: the city mob. Rife with poverty, disorder, blood sports and vice, the city mob constituted a tinder of disaffection waiting for a spark. Towards the turn of the century, city mobs often took the law into their own hands. Theatres, brothels and bars were regularly rifled by disgruntled punters. Crowds, often led by women, would break in and stop the sale of cereal above fixed prices. Bread and food riots grew endemic. Turnpike gates were repeatedly rooted up as another protest over another concealed tax. Machine-breaking to halt the installation of new technology was commonplace, as were strikes for higher wages. In the final quarter of the century, England was pockmarked with unprecedented disorder; 'foreigners were astonished at the licence permitted to the common people' (Porter 1982, p. 118). 'Each year brought fresh disaster and increased the national debt. From the early sixties there had been a steadily mounting volume of criticism of every aspect of English life' (Plumb 1950, p. 133).

New consensus

The tide turned during the 1780s. The reduction of domestic conflict after 1789 coincides with the French Revolution and the revolutionary wars.[6] This conforms to the old claim that extreme distress may unite a nation – in this case it also seems to have restored a certain level of domestic cohesion. Of course, distress alone does not convince citizens to put aside their grievances rationally and unite behind a common cause in light of which all will be better off. Distress alone does not end social conflict. Yet, it is tempting to propose that in this English case, distress combined with external threat contributed to restore internal cohesion and trust. This restoration was hardly the outcome of a simple, rational compact. It seems to have represented a larger coordination of extant conflicts, to have channelled them, focused them and projected them on to an old, common, external enemy – a militaristic, republican 'other' – and in the process enhanced the sense of common identity.[7]

This new sense of common identity was accompanied by increases in economic productivity, in political power and in moral resolve. An erosion of consensus accompanied the decline of England as a great power in the 1770s; the re-establishment of consensus attended England's re-ascent to great power status after 1789. The Industrial Revolution was an important force behind this development. First, it was the major force behind the destruction of England's old socio-economic institutions and the instigator of the turbulence and dissent of the 1770s and 1780s. But later it became a key force in the construction of new institutions. Clearly, the Industrial Revolution brought desperate misery upon English society – it converted millions of ordinary people into paupers and flooded the cities with poor, landless wage labourers; indeed, by the end of the century, pauperism mushroomed to become the biggest labour problem in village and city alike. But at the same time, the rise of a new industrializing, capitalizing, proletarianizing economy also created new fortunes among industrialists, bankers and entrepreneurs. And in doing so, it enhanced the productivity of England to such a degree that the country could sustain the massive military expenditures brought upon it by international conflicts and war.

The overstretch hypothesis suggests that the mounting defence expenditures of the 1770s hampered England's economy. In one sense this is true; in another sense it is incorrect. From one perspective, the English economy entered a period of decline in the 1770s; however, from another point of view, England entered a period of unprecedented expansion. On the one hand was the stagnating sector of manufactories – the 'sunset sectors' of the unravelling world order. On the other were the expanding sector of machinofactories – the 'sunrise sectors' and the harbingers of a post-Napoleonic order in which England would emerge into its second term as a pre-eminent great power and the hegemon of new world order based on new institutions of industrial superiority and worldwide trade. The inescapable conclusion is that, during the final quarter of the eighteenth century, England was falling and rising at the same time.

Relevance for great-power politics

This brief sketch of the policies and complex social conditions of late eighteenth-century England can be connected with the greater issue of the fate of great powers. Throughout the modern ages, a variety of scholars have observed that rising defence expenditures are present whenever great powers decline; and they have regularly supposed that the first is causally connected with the second. However, as the familiar story is told here, two additional factors are relevant to the performance of great powers: the rate of industrial development and the level of social consensus.

The rate of industrial development is causally connected with the power and prestige of great powers. And if a low rate of development and expansion is present in the Spanish, Dutch and second British cases (which all ended in decline), then one would expect a high rate to mark the first British case (which ended in the re-establishment of hegemony). By the same token, if the re-establishment of a high level of consensus is present in the case which ended in re-ascent, then one would expect it to be absent in the cases which ended in decline. The question then is: are these expectations borne out by empirical observation? And to answer the question properly, it is necessary to compare the three declining cases in some detail. It is natural to begin such a discussion with that case which appears to conform most closely to the overstretch hypothesis (and which presumably provides the greatest contrast to the first British case): namely, the Iberian empire.

Iberian decline

Gonzàlez, de la Court, Smith, Cobden, Kennedy and several other observers of decline have noted that the fall of great powers is invariably attended by rising defence expenditures. However, as the first British case shows, increasing defence expenditure does not always accompany great-power decline. In late eighteenth-century England, the Industrial Revolution stimulated the country's productivity to such a degree that it managed to cover its steadily growing defence costs. This development was attended by the (re-)establishment of social consensus. If the two developments are causally connected with England's ability to re-establish its hegemony, then one would expect both to be absent in the Iberian case, which experienced a sustained decline.

The expectation of economic stagnation is supported by historical evidence. In the early decades of the sixteenth century, Spanish industry was stimulated by the influx of treasure from the Americas and by the rising demand among the colonists for manufactured goods from Europe. During the 1560s and 1570s, the influx of American treasure allowed Philip II to wage the wars which ultimately contained the Ottoman challenge. However, this great flow of wealth from the Americas could not prevent the Spanish decline of the 1580s and 1590s. The rapidly increasing volume of American treasure was accompanied by an equally rapid increase in commodity costs. Prices in Spain had already begun to rise in the 1520s and they continued to rise until they had increased fivefold by the end of the century (Hamilton 1934). Other countries, too, experienced inflation as bullion from the Americas reached them through various channels of commerce. But Spain received the bullion direct and suffered the highest rate of inflation. This created a widening price gap between Spain and the rest of Europe. In the longer run it made Spanish commodities more expensive and more difficult to sell on the expanding world market.[8]

As Spanish commodities were priced out of the European market, the Spaniards themselves increasingly procured goods and services from abroad. As a result, vast fortunes leaked out of the country. Much Spanish wealth was used to pay foreign mercenaries (Italian, German and Dutch) or to pay Spanish soldiers who fought wars (and used their pay) abroad. Some wealth was used for display by the court and the ruling élite and this involved the purchase of foreign consumer goods – indeed, even if such commodities were bought in Spain they were often manufactured abroad. Seville merchants increasingly became retailers of foreign manufactures.

The long and the short of it is that a remarkably small share of the immense American treasure which reached Spain was invested in productive activities at home. As quickly as it came, the treasure left Spain via foreign purveyors of goods and services who, in turn, converted its value into productive capital elsewhere. It was primarily the north-western regions of Europe – particularly the 'fog belt' around the English Channel – which produced goods for Iberian consumers. And it was precisely in these northern regions that most of the important industrial innovations of the sixteenth century originated. Spanish manufactures fell behind those of the entrepreneurial states of north-western Europe. And while the northern nations went through waves of technological innovation, Spain did not.

There are clear signs that the economic stagnation which befell sixteenth-century Spain was attended by the steady unravelling of the empire's social consensus. This was first evident in Spain's provinces in Italy and the Netherlands. Rebellions in these overseas provinces were soon followed by strife and unrest closer to home. By 1580, rebellion had spread to Aragon, Catalonia, Valencia and Portugal. Martìn Gonzàlez de Cellorigo commented on this increase in conflict and strife in his *Memoria* (1600). He adumbrated the overstretch argument by connecting economic stagnation with the excessive expenditures of the Spanish Crown; but he also included other considerations. For example, he noted a tendency for Iberian entrepreneurs to retire early – to cash in their business earnings and buy land in order to emulate the more prestigious life of the *hidalgo*. This tendency weakened the Spanish economy, Gonzàlez reasoned. The country lost its entrepreneurs while they still had productive promise, and it lost productive capital as their accumulated wealth was retired from productive investment and locked into land.

As the old faith in progress and in easy profits was replaced by more defensive business attitudes, the Iberian economy stagnated. The *arbitristas* argued that in order to remedy the country's economic decline, it was necessary to invest more capital in the development of agriculture and manufacturing – a proposal which harmonizes nicely with the zero-sum logic of de la Court, Smith, Bentham, Cobden and Kennedy. But Gonzàlez did more. He also maintained that even if the King of Spain transferred his stocks of bullion from military purposes to investments in productive capital, it would not save the country. The rot went deeper still, he argued. The American treasure which had widened the gap between the rich and the poor of the nation had also cultivated among the rich an unfortunate attitude of mind that made them despise productive work. Ultimately, then, Gonzàles argued that the Spanish problem was rooted in mental or moral shortcomings.

The (Dis)United Provinces

Was there an industrial revolution in the United Provinces during the third phase of the Dutch world order? There was economic and technical development. However, comparable development occurred in other countries. And in some of these it had a quicker pace. Industries and crafts in which Dutch entrepreneurs had once enjoyed a virtual monopoly (textile finishing, paper-making, sugar-refining, glass-blowing, and so on) were emulated and improved upon by other nations – often under Dutch tuition (Williams 1984, p. 71). The English Navigation Act (1651) and the First Anglo-Dutch War (1652–54) severely depressed Dutch fisheries and shipping. The decisive 'mother trade' – the Dutch bulk commerce on the Baltic – was disrupted by the Swedish–Polish War (1655–60). After these wars, Baltic trade never recovered to previous levels. The volume of Dutch commerce fell, and the Dutch dominance over Baltic carrying slowly diminished. By 1670, Dutch farmers were being overtaken by techniques pioneered in England and France.

The symptoms of economic decline coincided with a steady increase in conflict and strife at home. The old notion of a common national interest was replaced by the new idea of individual self-interest. Within the Dutch republic, several provinces clamoured for increasing sovereignty. Within each province, many individual ventures demanded greater mercantile liberty. In 1651, the merchant oligarchs won an important political victory. In a palace *coup*, they managed to suspend the principal executive officer of the United Provinces, the Stadtholder – formally an elected officer of individual provinces, but in practice the quasi-monarchical head of the Dutch republic and the captain general as well as the admiral general of the union. Since the Stadtholder was always a member of the House of Orange, the suspension of 1651 removed the House of Orange from active politics. During the years which followed – the 'first Stadtholderless period' in Dutch politics – the merchant oligarchy dismantled several institutions of state and government functions. This was done in the name of individual freedom and greater economic efficiency, and it was associated with two social trends. First, after 1651 there was a tendency for the rich to get richer and the gap between the rich and the poor to widen. Second, there was an increase in contention and conflict between various social groups – as was noted e.g. by the historian Lieuwe van Aitzema, who connected this increase directly to the suspension of the stadtholderate: disputes which were earlier settled by the Stadtholder were now left unresolved, he argued.

The merchant oligarchs begged to differ. Their attitudes were famously expressed in Pieter de la Court's book *The Interest of Holland* (1702[1662]).[9] The book was a Panglossian treatise. It was devoted to the condemnation of the old form of government, and to the construction of a make-believe faith in individual and regional freedom. The causes of Dutch affluence lie in the unique liberties which the republic affords its citizens, de la Court explained. These liberties were usurped by the excessive government of the Stadtholder but regained when the stadtholderate was abolished, he continued. Consequently, it would be in the interest of all Dutch citizens to guard and maintain their newly regained freedom – notably the freedom to trade, he continued (Barker 1906, p. 303). Such sentiments were also apparent in publications such as the *Courante uyt Italien Duytsland &C* and *Nieuwe Tijdingen*. These *corantos* were essentially commercial newsletters. They were issued regularly and brought information on the availability and prices of various goods and services. But they also included political news relevant to economic transactions (and were, in fact, pioneers of the modern international newspaper). The *corantos* were written by and for the business community and their commentaries were biased by the self-serving profit motive of the merchant élite. However, the United Provinces had a comparatively high literacy rate, and the *corantos* circulated widely. They indubitably affected public opinion. Texts such as these not only contradicted the old political mythology of Dutch society, they also assisted in replacing it with the new free-trade philosophy of the merchant élite.

After 1651, the leaders of the republic turned Dutch politics on to a course dominated by narrow goals of liberty and economic gain. Domestic politics were dominated by efforts to dismantle state institutions which hampered business interests. Foreign policy sought to maximize mercantile expansionism – a policy which quickly fuelled jealousies abroad, especially in France and England. In the 1660s it became fashionable to maintain, with de la Court, that 'in all societies or assemblies of Men, Self is always preferred; so all Sovereigns or Supreme powers will in the first place seek their own Advantage in all things' (quoted in Rowen 1972, pp. 201f.).

At this time, domestic debates were accentuated by foreign challenges. Old political cleavages re-emerged – most significantly the old conflict between merchants and Orangeists. Unruly masses demanded that the stadtholderate should be re-established. The Prince of Orange was once again placed at the head of the Provinces' military forces. The historian van Aitzema complained in 1660 that vital functions of central government 'have now fallen into the hands of a few who are not qualified to perform them, or do not have authorization to do so, and hence are not responsible for their conduct of them' (quoted in Rowen 1972, pp. 197ff.). These were fighting words, and it grew increasingly dangerous to utter them in public. In 1666 an Orangeist plot was discovered in Holland and brutally put down. In 1672 the Orangeists got their revenge when Grand Pensionary Johan de Witt and his brother, Cornelius, were hacked to death by an angry mob.[10]

The Dutch case, then, shows a declining power which is marked by increasing defence costs, a stagnating economy and a notable increase in disputes and disturbances. The decline of common concerns and the rise of private interests is well illustrated by the Dutch and the English preparations before the Second Anglo-Dutch War. Both countries rearmed and restocked their armed forces by purchasing naval supplies in the Netherlands. The English bought Dutch on the logic that by buying as many war supplies as possible in the United Provinces they would turn the Dutch merchants' obsession with individual profit into a solvent of collective Dutch interest. As a result of this shrewd policy, English magazines were full when the war broke out in 1665, whereas those of the Dutch were scantily stocked. And this was not the end of it: for in 1670, when the French planned an attack on Holland, they emulated England's strategy. The French, too, purchased war materials in the United Provinces. And once more the Dutch penchant for short-term profit enabled their enemies to succeed (Barker 1906, p. 377). Nowhere is the Dutch loss of concern for the public interest more tragically displayed than in the fact that Dutch merchants were thus *twice* successfully recruited to act as the unwitting agents of enemy interests.

Decline of the Second British Empire

If the second British case is observed in isolation, it appears that something akin to an 'industrial revolution' swept across the British Isles during the final quarter of the nineteenth century. However, it had a very different content from that which began in the late 1700s. The late 1880s saw an evolution that was driven by systematic scientific research, by the development of new means of mass production and of new products destined for mass consumption. Yet, this 'Second Industrial Revolution' had many of the same social effects as the first. Like the first Industrial Revolution of 1775–1825, this second revolution of 1875–1900 spurred socio-economic uncertainties which, in turn, fed political upheavals and rebellions.

By the logic of the overstretch hypothesis, it is necessary to observe England in a larger, systems-wide context. And from this perspective, it becomes apparent that similar industrial revolutions occurred in other countries as well – most significantly in the USA and Germany, where the rate of economic growth was more pervasive than in England. In this larger, systems-wide perspective Britain can be seen as retreating from the forefront of economic development. In view of the superior rates of growth in the USA and Germany, Great Britain experienced a relative economic decline during the final years of the nineteenth century. This decline is indicated in Table 13 below.

Table 13   *Relative shares of global manufacturing output, 1880–1928 (in percentages)*

Country	1880	1900	1913	1928
Britain	22.9	18.5	13.6	9.9
USA	14.7	23.6	32.0	39.3
Germany	8.5	13.2	14.8	11.6
France	7.8	6.8	6.1	6.0
Russia	7.6	8.8	8.2	5.3
Austria-Hungary	4.4	4.7	4.4	—
Italy	2.5	2.5	2.4	2.7

Source: Bairoch (1982; cited in Kennedy (1987, p. 202))

This economic tendency was expressed in the public sentiment of the age. Competition with foreign rivals sparked a national debate about England's place in the world. After the economic recession of the 1880s came the psychological depression of the 1890s. The myth of England's economic supremacy was exploded. A new sentiment of self-doubt was reflected in books like A. Williamson's *British Industries and Foreign Competition* (1894), E. E. Williams's *Made in Germany* (1896) and F. A. Mackenzie's *American Invaders* (1902). Such books argued that English industry was not as technologically advanced as Germany's and America's; that the scale of English production was too small; that the workers had become lazy – they were eager to consume, but reluctant to work and resistant to innovation. Explanations for the growing British failure to match foreign competition included arguments which blamed foreigners for unfair practices – such as subsidies which German and American governments awarded to their own producers in order to lower the cost of their products. But they also included scathing reviews of England's own shortcomings. 'At the risk of being thought unpatriotic', the *Daily Mail* 'called attention to the numberless blows administered to our commercial supremacy, chiefly by reason of the superior education methods and the strenuous life of the American and the German' (5 May 1901).

It is significant that this debate was expressed in books and newspapers. For a notable improvement in education and literacy stimulated the advent of printed media. Written texts were an integral part of social communication in the mass society which emerged in England in the late Victorian age. Public opinion became an increasingly important element in national politics.[11] However, the public could be unpredictable. Social movements and political organizations had been introduced on to the English scene more rapidly than existing political institutions could absorb them. The old political framework, which had been made by and for an élite section of English society only, was suddenly torn asunder by the demands put upon it by a politically activated population.

Towards the end of the century, the skills of organization and oratory of Gladstone and Disraeli focused the public gaze on the processes of parliamentary politics. The two were great political opponents. But together they contributed to bridge the gap between the old élitist ruling apparatus and a new, more democratic system. Disraeli, during his one great ministry (1874–80), wooed the newly enfranchised middle and labouring classes and broadened his parliamentary base. He consolidated the support of the lower classes by pushing for social reforms concerning public health, factory regulation, trade unions, housing and education. However, his great reform programmes were constantly interrupted by foreign and imperial troubles. Unrest broke out in the Balkans; Russian intrigues in Afghanistan led to British intervention, war and to a revival of Palmerstonian fears of Russian expansionism. The economic recession of the late 1870s created an agricultural slump at home and revived the old policy of protectionism within the ranks of the Conservative Party. It created political instability abroad, and occasioned active British interference to support bankrupt regimes along the eastern Mediterranean such as Turkey and Egypt. It was accompanied by a sudden conversion, in 1872, from a staunch anti-colonial policy to a new, aggressive imperialism – and to several sub-sequent small wars against other colonial powers in Africa and Asia. But it was the troubles in closer provinces which dominated the parliamentary scene. After 1875, the fate of the Liberal Party hinged on Ireland.

The new turbulence in English society was reflected in the demise of the England's Liberal Party and the rise of the Labour Party. Time ran out on the liberals and their once dominant ideology. At the turn of the century, the old liberal ideology began to sag under the burden of social reality. It began, in the words of George Dangerfield, 'to give out a dismal, rattling sound; it was just as if some unfortunate miracle had been performed upon its contents, turning them into nothing more than bits of old iron, fragments of intimate crockery, and other relics of the domestic past' (1961, p. 8). The late 1880s and 1890s were not an age of liberal deliberations; it was an age of mass action – of great strikes in industry, including both the famous London dock strike (1889) and the Engineers' strike (1897).

As the Liberal Party declined, the Labour Party was ushered on to the parliamentary scene on a growing wave of various political organizations – among which the trade union movement was the most consequential. The entry of new, large layers of the population into a new consumer market of views and values was visible outside the established political institutions. One of these was the feminist movement, the internal division of which illustrates the larger trend towards the rapid proliferation of political ideas and causes. When feminists like Christabel Pankhurst resorted to extreme measures of protest – which included false fire alarms, cutting telephone wires, slashing pictures in public galleries, arson and throwing bombs – this, too, was a sign of the times.

Just as in the cases of Spain and the United Provinces, the last phase of the second British order saw a traditional socio-economic consensus being replaced by new material and spiritual institutions. But unlike the erosion of the first British order, the erosion of the second did not produce an equally cohesive and dynamic replacement. The process involved a phase of painful unrest, both at home and abroad, and political unpredictability – during which even the venerable Conservative Party supported mutiny in the army, and even the traditionally passive Edwardian women found themselves fighting police and burning houses.

Summary

During the third phase of world order, old hegemons desperately try to contain the unravelling of the old order. The international arena in which they act is marked by a more competitive international environment and by the return to balance-of-power politics. In this international environment, ageing hegemons fight rearguard struggles which invariably push up their defence budgets.

When this is said, two things must be added. First, that not all cases of increasing defence budgets end in decline. For example, although the first British case experienced rapidly increasing defence costs, it nevertheless bucked the declining trend. The primary reason for this was the Industrial Revolution. New technologies and new modes of organization enabled late eighteenth-century England to cover the rising defence costs. Innovation, in a word, ensured a mounting rate of productivity which enabled England to keep abreast of its rising defence expenditures. Thus, it was the hegemons in which increasing defence costs were *not* offset by economic innovation that suffered overstretch during the third phase of world order.

Second, all hegemons were empires, and in the third phase of world order the old sense of imperial unity was replaced by sedition and strife. Edward Gibbon noted this change of sentiment during his years as an MP. And it is hardly a coincidence that when he wrote his magisterial analysis of the decline and fall of Rome, he singled out domestic quarrels as a main cause of imperial decline and connected it with rebellion in distant provinces. In Gibbon's eyes – as in the eyes of many of his parliamentary colleagues – the threat of disorder and decline was all about them. They saw no clear distinction between domestic unrest and foreign conflicts. The MPs in London debated and decided on current affairs issues on a day-to-day basis, and they drew no clear distinction between domestic strife, imperial challenges and international conflict. From their point of view, riots at home were fed by colonial rebellions which were fanned by interstate rivals, the containment of which demanded immediate attention and substantial resources. The various political arenas intersected and interacted. The spheres of domestic politics and world affairs were in practice indistinct.

During the 1760s, rebels in India protested at the fiscal pressures of England's colonial administration. The situation worsened in the 1770s when native rulers increasingly opposed the ruthless operations of English trade monopolies. It grew precarious in the 1780s when major Indian actors (Haidar Ali Khan, the Nizam of Hyderabad and the Marathas confederacy most notably) entered into an anti-British coalition, defeated British troops and tore through the Carnatic. At the same time, but on the opposite side of the globe, American rebels defended their independence with military means. The English soon realized that naval pre-eminence alone could not defeat the rebel armies. To reconquer and hold the colonies, England had to rely on large-scale armies. But since it could not count on raising soldiers and supplies in the rebellious colonies, men and munitions had to be organized in Europe and transported across three thousand miles of ocean. This venture was economically expensive and strategically cumbersome. Especially since the rebels received French backing.

France, England's primary geopolitical rival, saw these troubles in India and America as opportunities to take revenge for its defeat in the Seven Years War. French politicians resolved to back anti-English rebels on opposite sides of the globe and to effectuate their revenge *only* overseas. The French strengthened their navy so as to engage England at sea and prevent English shipments of supplies and reinforcements from reaching their colonial destinations. And in this way France inflicted immense costs on England in terms of men, money and prestige. England eventually restored the *status quo ante* in India. In North America it suffered a humiliating defeat. However, although England lost the Americas, France did not win. The Anglo-French rivalry locked the two great powers into a global rivalry which carried momentous costs for both. These costs, which nearly broke the English, did, in fact, break the French. By 1782 French finances were creaking under the burden of the vast naval rivalry. In 1783, the costs of war 'interacted with the growing political discontents, economic distress, and social malaise to discredit the *ancien régime*' (Kennedy 1987, p. 121).

During the 1780s, French politicians became increasingly constrained as the nation grew preoccupied with domestic strife. At the end of the decade, revolution broke out in Paris. In London, the politicians at Westminster were reminded of the volatility of their own domestic situation: they were ragged, their windows smashed and their carriages pelted and rocked. And during the 1790s, when the ruling classes of England witnessed the mounting reign of violence and terror in Paris, they were gripped by the icy fear that the French Revolution would soon spread to England.

Rebellions in America and India intensified conflict and strife among and within the great powers. Ministers lost authority and control both in Paris and in London. Governments staggered on, riddled by financial problems posed by vast empires that had to be garrisoned and maintained. Leading politicians were portrayed as oppressors and crooks. In France, this deterioration ended in a full-fledged social revolution in 1789. In England, it nearly did so. The Gordon Riots – sparked by fear of Catholics and foreigners and brilliantly described by Dickens after the event in *Barnaby Rudge* (1973[1840–41]) – were as near revolution as England would ever come. Newgate gaol, the Fleet Prison, Clerkenwell House of Detention, King's Bench and Borough Clink were all burnt down in early June 1780 and the inmates set free. The targets of the mob rapidly broadened to include the Irish, the rich, Lord Mansfield, the Bank of England, Catholics, breweries and distilleries – the final destination of many thirsty rebels who died there from alcohol poisoning. For several weeks, mobs took over London and did ten times more damage to the English capital in eight days than the French Revolution did to Paris in eight years.

The final quarter of the eighteenth century, in which England experienced challenges on the international scene, trouble in distant colonies, rapidly rising military expenditures and economic uncertainties, was also an age of unparalleled social unrest at home. England, wrote Horace Walpole in 1773, was 'a gaming, robbing, wrangling, railing nation without principles, genius, character, or allies; the overgrown shadow of what it was' (quoted in Plumb 1950, p. 133). The intersection between colonial conflict and domestic corruption is nowhere more clearly reflected than in the fate of the mighty East India Company. The struggle for power and profit had undermined the company. In the 1770s, complete bankruptcy was added to the moral scandals. Parliament passed several India Acts which, in effect, transferred control from the company to the government. Subsequent investigations revealed malpractice and cruelties on such a scale that it made India, together with the American secession, the leading subject of political controversy for twenty years.

Unravelling of old orders

International dynamics change during the third phase of world order. The old hierarchy of power erodes, the international system becomes more anarchic in nature and increasingly marked by balance-of-power politics among the great powers. These international dynamics find parallels in the domestic life of the old hegemon. The hegemons experience a notable increase in defence expenditures. Their domestic affairs are marked by economic stagnation and increasing civil strife. Traditional cleavages – many of which were repressed and half forgotten when society was wealthy, the state strong and the nation self-confident – resurface. Revived antagonisms blend in with new conflicts and add to the internal strife of the declining nation. The old political mythology, upon which the legitimacy of its traditional institutions hinge, is challenged. Old values, norms and rules are scrutinized, criticized and questioned.

A satisfactory account of this complex process would require a deep discussion of each case followed by a systematic comparison between all of them. Space will not allow such an extensive examination here. In place of an exhaustive demonstration of each of the four cases, the argument can be indicated by a hurried sketch of the Iberian case.

The Iberian example of great-power decline

In the final quarter of the sixteenth century, Spain found itself with 'too much to do, too many enemies to fight, too many fronts to defend' (Kennedy 1987, p. 48). International competition intensified. King Philip II faced a rapid rise in defence expenditures – a steady increase from about 1.5 million ducats in the mid-1560s to well over 7.6 million in the 1590s outstripped even the fabulous import of American bullion. Philip II found it necessary to increase taxes substantially in order to cover the mounting costs.[12] Still, he was constantly short of funds. So he borrowed vast sums and thus loaded a rapidly rising national debt on to the weakening economy. It could not last.

The problems which plagued Philip II were more than a simple case of overstretch; Philip II could hardly have reversed the Iberian decline by simply reducing his military expenditures and making his books balance. It would not be enough to simply withdraw from foreign engagements and dismantle far-away fronts. The king's difficulties were more complex than that. They also involved popular unrest, stagnating competitiveness and a loss of moral fibre. When Martin Gonzàlez de Cellorigo explored the difficulties which confronted Philip II during the last years of the monarch's life, he noted the connection between the Crown's expenditures and economic stagnation; but he also observed that Iberian entrepreneurs adopted more defensive business attitudes than before. Gonzàlez recommended that in order to stop Spain's economic decline, it would be necessary to invest in more offensive projects which would enhance the development of agriculture and manufactures; but he also claimed that the Spanish problem was ultimately rooted in mental or moral deficiencies: he noted that former entrepreneurs cashed in the fortunes they had made in better times and adopted the ideals and airs of the aristocracy – which included the scorn of trade and manual labour.

Gonzàlez's argument was built on the notion that the worth of a society was determined by the 'constant and harmonious' proportion between the different classes of its citizens. By this criterion, Spain had reached its apex in the late fifteenth century. During the sixteenth century, Gonzàlez claimed, the proportions steadily worsened until, by his own age:

> our republic has come to be an extreme contrast of rich and poor, and there is no means of adjusting them one to another. Our condition is one in which we have rich who loll at ease, or poor who beg, and we lack people of the middling sort, whom neither wealth nor poverty prevents from pursuing the rightful kind of business enjoined by natural law. (Cited in Elliott 1977, p. 306)

In the absence of 'people of the middling sort' – of solid, respectable, hard-working men of business – to bridge the gulf between the rich and the poor, Iberian society polarized. The economy stagnated.

Ultimately, Gonzàlez blamed the influx of American bullion. The massive influx of easy money encouraged the vain emulation of luxury rather than merit. It led too many men to invest too much capital in landed property and government annuities (censos) and to live as rentiers. Gonzàlez argued that the massive reception of American wealth had encouraged too many able-bodied men to live the unproductive (but, according to traditional mythology, both attractive and honourable) life of the hidalgo – a point which was also made (with great comic/tragic flair) in Cervantes's *Don Quixote* (1605). Gonzàlez maintained that passive reception of American wealth enhanced the decadence of the nation, the spread of hypocrisy and immorality. The decline of Spain could not be stopped, he concluded, without a moral regeneration of Iberian society.

Such a regeneration was unlikely as long as the American treasure created greater inequalities, social injustices and blatant hypocrisies in the nation. American bullion had created a society marked by a juxtaposition of lavish luxuries and cruel poverty, a fervent profession of faith and an exceptional laxity of manners. The wealth from America did not trickle down; it did not spread throughout society. Spanish cities displayed spectacular splendours; but their ostentatious wealth existed side by side with gruelling poverty. As times grew tougher, deepening inequalities fuelled rumblings of dissatisfaction. When Philip II increased the fiscal pressures towards the end of the century, poverty and destitution fuelled banditry and rebellions against the ruling Castilian élite. The authorities responded with repressive measures which greatly exacerbated the situation. The unrest threatened to tear Spain apart, along old lines of cleavage which resurfaced towards the end of the century.

One of these was an old territorial cleavage which set Castile apart from the rest of Spanish society. Philip II presided over an empire built around a monarchic, Castilian core.[13] The tendency for offices of government to be bestowed on Castilians was paralleled by a rising feeling among other inhabitants of the empire that they were no longer fairly represented at court. The first to feel neglected were the peripheries of the empire – notably the overseas provinces in Italy and the Netherlands.

Another line of cleavage was religion. During the days of hegemony, this line was covered up by a common Catholic zeal directed against the Ottoman Empire. Strong anti-Islamic sentiment undergirded a common religious outlook and served as a constant reminder that Islam represented the hostile 'other', confirming the monarchs' claim that Spain's historic mission was to contain the infidel barbarians. This policy of Christian containment was expensive. But it represented a manageable burden which imperial Spain could carry as long as it nourished the political mythology which legitimized the institutions of the state. When the Spanish vanquished the Turks at Lepanto (1571), they were jubilant. However, their celebrations were short-lived. For with the Ottoman threat removed, Philip II no longer faced a clear and obvious rival. Motivated by resolutions from the Council of Trent to contain the Reformation, the king began to engage with new rivals. But these new enemies were other European states and did not easily fit the image of the fearful, mythological 'other'. The new foes were not different enough to be credible. The French, the English and the Dutch were fellow Christians. Furthermore, they were trading partners. Religious appeal did not rally the Spanish as effectively against known Christian states as it once had done against Muslim rivals. Also, Europe's other powers possessed weapons systems which compared favourably with those of Spain, and they applied these in light of similar principles of operation and on the basis of comparable national interests.

Foreign wars, then, no longer conformed to old mythological precepts and they no longer served the cause of domestic cohesion well. Factions emerged in Spanish politics. Internal rivalries marred Spain's old unity of political purpose. Resultless foreign wars, rising defence expenditures and debates about falling trade and increasing taxes fuelled domestic dissent. War no longer unified the empire; it exacerbated its internal conflicts.

The troubles first manifested themselves in the overseas peripheries of the empire. The ingredients of international competition, rising expenditures, stagnating productivity and moral dissolution are all visible in Philip II's policy towards his overseas provinces in Italy and the Netherlands. Both Charles V and Philip II had treated Italy as a rampart against the Ottoman Empire. But after the Turkish defeat at Lepanto, this geostrategic consideration faded. Italian provinces were neglected. Economic recession followed and brought ruin to many Italian fortunes. This sad evolution was attended by civic strife, political debate and a new religious orthodoxy. The tribunals of the Inquisition stifled the intellectual freedoms of the city-states – as evinced by the famous trials of Giordano Bruno and Galileo's conflict with the authorities of the Church – and depleted the last creative energies of the Renaissance.

Charles V and Philip II had in the past drawn on the wealthy Netherlands for supplies to help finance wars against the infidel Turks. After Lepanto, as Philip II drew on the Dutch to finance his new wars in the Atlantic, Dutch noblemen objected. These noblemen were not landed aristocrats of the Spanish type; their properties were not created through war and conquest, but through trade and finance. They were alienated by the way Philip II put their fortunes at risk by waging wars against some of their most important trading partners. They were offended by his efforts to outlaw Protestantism in the Dutch Provinces. They were angry that they had to pay increased taxes to finance the king's follies.

Because the Dutch rebellion included Protestant, even Calvinist, arguments, it represented a serious threat to the Iberian empire.[14] Also, the Dutch entertained clear political notions about the sovereignty of their provinces – as evinced in remonstrances written e.g. by Vrank and Althusius. By their visions of independence and freedom of religion and trade, the Dutch represented a serious moral challenge to Castile's Catholic mythology. On the king's treatment of the Dutch rebels depended much more than the fate of the Netherlands alone. If the Dutch problem could be solved in such a way as to keep the Netherlands a contented member of the Spanish monarchy, solutions might be found for the other peripheral provinces as well. If, on the other hand, the Dutch claims triumphed, that might stimulate rebels in Naples, Aragon, Catalonia and Portugal and cause the entire Spanish empire to unravel.

It was a distinct danger that the Dutch rebellion might spread to Aragon. The Aragonese noted in 1580 that whereas Charles V had held *Cortes* for the Crown of Aragon every five years, Philip II had held only one (in 1563). They interpreted this abandonment as part of a Castilian plot to deprive them of their monarch and their liberties. When Philip II held a second *Cortes* in 1585, it was too late. By then, the kingdom of Aragon had become one of the most ungovernable of Philip II's possessions. The king hesitated about invading. For not only was Aragon seething with rebellion, the spirit of sedition was also rising in Catalonia, Valencia and Portugal. But in 1591 the king finally dispatched twelve thousand men to crush a revolt led by the aristocrats of the city of Zaragoza. The operation was a military success. But it was a political disaster. It fed the animosity between a Castilianized absentee monarch and subjects who insisted on keeping their traditional liberties. Conflict, rebellion and war spread across the Iberian peninsula. The unifying religious discourse of Spain's old political mythology lost both relevance and potency and Philip II lost some of his former decisiveness.

A series of foreign-policy defeats delivered additional blows to the staggering empire. During the 1580s and 1590s, Philip II equipped a series of fleets to conquer England. But all of them met defeat. This did much more than weaken Spain's prestige abroad; it occasioned spiritual vexation at home. The Iberian monarchy had tied its legitimacy, if not its entire *raison d'être*, to an empathetic, Christian God. Shaken by a string of naval losses, the kings' advisers raised questions like: Why were the divinely protected Armadas repeatedly repelled by foul weather? Why did God allow this unnecessary loss of Christian soldiers? Was it possible that the Almighty did not favour the enterprise of invading England? Why, in that case, did the venture displease Him so much that He repeatedly smote the effort with destructive gales?

Spanish theologians who went about their business with honest devotion had been an asset to Iberian expansionism in the heady age of spiritual certainty. Now, in an age of uncertainty, they constituted a liability: they contributed to a paralysing religious introspection which imploded with full force during the 1590s.

Competition, unrest and moral dissolution

The decline of Habsburg Spain can be seen from many angles. It can be seen as an outcome of costly external conflicts and imperial overstretch. It can be seen as a function of internal conflicts between different orientations towards government.[15] Or it can be seen as a combination of external and internal factors. Neither view would be complete, however, without a discussion of the spiritual crisis which descended upon the Iberias during the final quarter of the sixteenth century. The old imperial consensus was challenged by doubt and strife from within and by alternative systems of political thought from without. Internal unrest, external conflict and moral dissolution interacted to hasten the decline of the Habsburg empire.

Spain is not unique in this respect. The same combination of factors also appear in the Dutch and the (two) English cases. On the one hand, there was the internal unrest. This marred the regular workings of society, reactivated old lines of conflict and introduced new social tensions. The new tensions were usually connected with the unequal growth of groups within the nation and a widening gap between the rich and the poor. On the other hand, there were the international factors. Most conspicuous among them was the replacement of the old world order with a more anarchic situation. This was accompanied by greater international competition which, in turn, drove up the defence burden of all great powers – that of the old hegemon as well as that of the hegemon's traditional rival. In the four cases discussed here, the hegemon's rival was the first to fold under the burden of increased competition. This prostration of the old foe had important consequences for the foreign policy of the old hegemon. With the demise of the old, obvious, opposing 'other' went a weakening of the hegemon's sense of political 'self'. Also, the demise of a distinctive great power from the system created a sudden need among the remaining powers to reassess and readapt to a new international constellation of forces.

International change and the decline of the hegemon's rival rendered the hegemon's international situation more uncertain. However, in no case did the hegemon immediately realize how profoundly the situation had changed. Indeed, when its citizens first became aware of the troubles of their traditional foe, they cheered and greeted it as a blessing – as when Spain extravagantly celebrated Lepanto as a historic victory which would deliver the nation from all future uncertainties. However, no hegemon quite understood the degree to which its traditional rival had helped undergird its domestic consensus and legitimize its political doctrines. In the longer-term perspective, the retreat of the old rival was a fatal blow to its hegemonic pre-eminence.

When the Turk withdrew from the western Mediterranean in the wake of Lepanto, Spanish statesmen found themselves without a threatening 'other' to legitimate their policies. In much the same way, the weakening of Habsburg Spain by the Thirty Years War was followed by the eruption of dissent in the United Provinces; after the decline of their traditional foe, Dutch politicians no longer seemed to agree either on the nation's doctrines of security or on

the role of the (largely military) office of the Stadtholder. Also, when the French
armies lay prostrate after their losses in the Seven Years War, quarrels erupted
among the Anglo-Americans about the size and the function of England's
armed presence in the Americas.

This chapter began with a critique of the traditional overstretch argument:
a comparative discussion of four cases of decline concluded that the overstretch
hypothesis was an unsatisfactory theory – it was noted e.g. that the second
British case was notably at odds with its explanatory principle. The chapter
continued with a more in-depth discussion of the Spanish case – i.e., with that
case which could be most satisfactorily explained by the overstretch hypothesis.
This case discussion then brought into focus social mechanisms which explained
the rise and fall of hegemonic great powers in more complete and satisfactory ways. Two of these mechanisms may prove particularly important: the
mechanisms of collective identity and those of a strong modern well-functioning
state.

On consensus and collective identity

As to the first mechanism, it should be recalled that in Chapter 1 collective
identities were seen as contingent and relational. The common claim that the
identity of a community is shaped through the interaction with others, lies at
the core of Sorel's (1959) notion of a unifying political mythology. This is an
old claim – its core point was expressed by Sulla, who wondered (in 84 BC
after Rome had defeated the armies of Mithridates) what would be the fate of
the republic 'now that the universe offers us no more enemies'. The point has
since been made by students in a wide variety of fields – in anthropology
(Redfield 1953; Barth 1969), theology (Smith 1985; Green 1985; Pagels 1995),
social psychology, politics (Todorov 1989; Campbell 1992; Colley 1992;
Jeppeson et al. 1996; Huntington 1997a) and others. It is commonly agreed
that some distinction between 'us' and 'them' is accentuated during conflict.
It is a common claim in social-science literature that wars create cohesion and
consensus of a common identity both within and among the member states of
a wartime coalition which emerges victorious. It is also claimed that members
of victorious states do not merely discover 'others', but that they fabricate
them. This fabrication is one of the core processes of foreign politics. It involves
selecting, isolating and emphasizing certain aspects of another community's
life, and making these aspects symbolize the difference between 'us' and 'them'
(Neumann 1996).

Such political fabrications thrive on tension and conflict. In the case of great
powers, processes of identity formation are greatly enhanced by the presence
of a threatening rival. For, as is claimed, e.g., in the distinctiveness theory in
social psychology, people define themselves by what makes them different from

others in a particular context. People define themselves by what they are not. In all cases of hegemony, the presence of a rival delivered contrasting grist to the hegemon's political mill. The construction of a common identity in Habsburg Spain must be understood by reference to a Turkish threat; similarly, the Dutch identity must be appreciated in contrast to a Spanish foe; the construction of an English identity must be considered in relation to Continental (primarily French) rivalries.

Also, all cases of hegemonic decline have been accompanied by the decline of a long-standing rival which has been construed as the hegemon's primary 'other'. One clear instance here is the case of Spain which was attended by the prostration of its long-standing Turkish enemy. However, the mechanism can be observed in all cases of hegemony. For as the threat of the primary foe dwindles – as the rival loses its central position in the mythological universe of the hegemon – the old notion of the 'other' is diluted, the idea of a collective 'self' is diffused and the basic consensus of society is weakened.

On modern, well-functioning states

As to the second mechanism, all instances of hegemony evolved around strong, well-functioning, modern states. Such states share four characteristic properties: a demarcated territory, a comparatively fair and efficient government which maintains order within the territory, a certain degree of cultural and moral cohesion which can sustain an adherence to the government and its rules and laws, and a high degree of integration between government and domestic society.

It was noted in Chapter 1 that while waves of great wars impoverished most states, they enhanced the cohesion, efficiency and wealth of the ascending hegemons. During the first phase of world order, external conflict strengthened the ascending hegemon's internal cohesion. But during the third phase, external conflict had other consequences. Rather than strengthening the collective identity of the nation, conflict fragmented it. Rather than enhancing the cohesion of society, it reduced it. Rather than consolidating the legitimacy of the government, it undermined it. Several solvents are involved in this weakening of national cohesion. Some of them may be identified by two fairly common concepts: the concept of the 'public sphere' and that of the modern 'market'.

In a well-functioning, modern state, political institutions are embedded in society through a 'public sphere'. This sphere is a modern phenomenon. As Poggi (1978, pp. 77ff.) explains, the growth of the public sphere involved a development away from a situation in which the validity of the law hinged upon divine authority alone, on the will of the prince or on consanguinity. In the public sphere, the law is derived 'not at all from force, only to a small extent from habit and custom, really from insight and argument' (Hegel 1952[1821], p. 294). A 'public sphere' is a realm of social life in which a public opinion can be formed and expressed as judgements, opinions and recommendations on affairs of state (Hegel 1952[1821], p. 204).

Kant, Hegel, Weber and Schmitt associate the 'public sphere of civil society' with the rise of the modern state – with the growth of modern capitalist markets and with rational state bureaucracies. At the core of their discussion lies the notion of the rise of the modern bourgeoisie – a distinct stratum of literate and knowledgeable citizens who constitute a *publicum* through their informed discussion of social and economic issues. When informed citizens confer in an unrestricted fashion – that is, with the guarantee of freedom of assembly and association and the liberty to express and publish their opinions – about matters of general interest, they prepare the basis of the public sphere. By Schmitt's account this sphere is public in a double sense. It includes an autonomous body of people who are free to deliberate without any external compulsion imposed upon them. Also, it is an open sphere. A few basic ground rules may apply – such as 'shared convictions as premises, the willingness to be persuaded, independence of party ties, freedom from selfish interests' (Schmitt 1985[1923], p. 5) – but deliberation in the public sphere is in principle genuinely open to all.

By this definition, public spheres existed in some measure in urban centres of sixteenth-century Iberia. This was a golden age of Spanish literature. Major Iberian cities (especially in Andalusia and Catalonia) were inhabited by urban educated élites who freely conversed about matters of general interest. True, sixteenth-century Iberian citizens could hardly be called a 'bourgeoisie', and their urban interactions would scarcely sustain a large and lasting public sphere in the modern sense of the term. Yet the foreshadowings are undeniable. Spain was a relatively recent social formation, and some of the regions reconquered from the Moors lacked the medieval systems of guilds and burgers which marked the more traditional feudal areas north of the Pyrenees. Contemporary observations clearly testify to the existence of a class of 'people of the middling sort' (to quote Gonzàlez's famous term) whose open discussions and interactions affected the economic, political and cultural life of Iberian society.

However, the Iberias did not give rise to the distinctly modern bourgeoisie. The growth of a proper bourgeoisie is associated with the growth of Dutch trade. Amsterdam, more than any other commercial city of its age, sustained the rise of the first modern bourgeoisie. Within the dynamic civil society of the long sixteenth century, the Low Countries evolved commercialized segments which were distinguished by a high degree of economic integration and a strong sense of patriotism. In the United Provinces 'a political élite, the "regents" of about 2,000 persons at the head of a larger oligarchy of perhaps 10,000 economic and political leaders' evolved (Taylor 1996, p. 49). A comparable development occurred a little later among the commercial classes of south-eastern England. In certain segments of London society these also evolved the unmistakable characteristics of a modern bourgeoisie. During the seventeenth century this development would be noticeable in other countries, too (Koselleck 1988; Habermas 1989).

In sum, each hegemon represented the most advanced society of its day. In the eighteenth century, few nationalities enjoyed greater liberties than the English; in the seventeenth, few people enjoyed higher levels of wealth and comfort than the Dutch. In the sixteenth, few societies possessed a more developed public sphere than the Iberias. Each instance of hegemony was grafted on to a pre-eminent sea power whose society was heavily commercialized and which grew to become the most free and dynamic society of the age. Each had a strong, well-functioning state and a productive economy at its core.

Decline and fall of great powers

In his great study of the fall of Rome, Edward Gibbon (1994: III, pp. 1062ff.) identified four principal causes of the ruin of the Roman Empire: hostile attacks, injuries of time and nature, abuse of materials and domestic quarrels. The first of these has been a perennial favourite among students of great powers. Academic discussions of decline have routinely been intertwined with interstate rivalries and fear of invasion. Practical discussions have had the same emphasis; state leaders who have sought to protect their nation have regularly had the military strength and dispositions of their enemies foremost in focus – in the cases discussed here, rivalries and fear of invasion have intertwined in the minds of great-power politicians during the third phase of world order. The two factors were nourished by a changing balance of forces among the great powers and a continued erosion of the international consensus about the values, norms and rules of interstate conduct. The world order came to operate on the principles of *Realpolitik*.

For Gibbon, however, the most formidable cause of imperial destruction was not hostile attacks but domestic quarrels. The cases of hegemony discussed here support his conclusion. All cases indicate that one of the most important conditions for the growth of wealth and power is a high degree of social consensus. A tight consensus appears to be one of the factors which attend the ascendance of all the hegemons discussed here. Furthermore, the dissolution of consensus appears to be the *only* factor which is regularly associated with hegemonic decline. Social consensus has waned when hegemony has declined (as is evinced in the cases of Spain, the United Provinces and nineteenth-century England). Also, a high degree of social consensus has been present whenever decline is absent (or reversed, as in the first British case).

On consensus, trust and liberty

Gibbon saw that consensus and cohesion gave unity, order and safety to an imperial society; that a common set of values, norms and rules for social behaviour was a necessary precondition for decisive foreign policies. More recent scholars have elaborated these notions. Fukuyama (1995, p. 26), for example, argues that consensus and cohesion involve common expectations among the members of a community of regular, honest and cooperative behaviour, based on shared social norms. In a word, consensus involves social 'trust'. The notion was commonly a useful complement to the concept of a 'social contract' in early modern political theory (Maitland 1911) – for example, in the case of John Locke (Gough 1973; Dunn 1985), who maintained that 'trust . . . is the bond of society' (Locke 1990[1667], p. 247). In this context, 'trust' is not seen as the outcome of considered reflection or evaluation. 'Trusting' is not a function of rational deliberation of options. Rather, 'trusting' is a habitual practice in modern societies.[16] It occurs without a second thought. It is taken for granted.

In high-trust communities, citizens can be allowed broad individual liberties. The reason is very simple: the underlying shared norms will ensure that although all individuals are nominally free to act as they will, each individual will nevertheless tend to behave like everybody else. The high level of consensus about a shared set of norms ensures that each transacting individual expects his interlocutors to fulfil his agreed-upon part of the bargain – i.e. it sustains a high degree of trust in society. Misztal (1996, p. 18) defines trust as 'the willingness of other agents to fulfil their contractual obligation that is crucial for cooperation'. This definition makes it clear that trust is a decisive precondition for efficient cooperation and economic growth. Consensus, trust and liberty work together to create a social environment in which rational individuals may cooperate to form (and spontaneously reform) contracts, associations and partnerships.

Without consensus and trust, spontaneous individual behaviour by itself will not occasion the lasting institutions which make up a predictable (and efficient) social division of labour. If a society lacks a basic moral frame that encases elementary transaction rules and upholds a common trust among society's transacting parties, then individual citizens will have to associate under a system of formal rules and specific regulations. Here, each transaction will have to be formally negotiated, explicitly agreed to and ceaselessly monitored. Such a contract society is more costly to operate. It has, according to Coase, Williamson, North and other economists, high 'transaction costs'.

In a high-trust, solidaric society, individuals communicate and cooperate within a common frame of moral reference, where interaction is based on a common set of shared social values – rather than on formal contract (Durkheim 1933, pp. 181f.). Here, cooperation is efficient in the sense that it entails low transaction costs. In a low-trust society, by contrast, where individuals communicate within a complex bureaucratic/legal apparatus which is based on formal contract and constructed to substitute for a common code of moral values, cooperation has high transaction costs. For, in the absence of trust, each individual transaction will have to be monitored, violators will have to be litigated against and punishment must be meted out and enforced.

In sum, a smoothly operating society does not work by itself. Its operation is smooth to the degree that its members obey common rules. If civil life is to be marked by order and predictability, and the economy is to be marked by efficiency and productivity, people must obey common conventions and social norms and rules. The third phase of world order is marked by the erosion of such norms and rules, and by an increase in unrest, strife and conflict – among states and well as within the old great powers. From the point of the view of the old hegemon, domestic affairs and international events intertwine. State leaders in an age of decline do not seem to distinguish sharply between 'inside' and 'outside' events; they note that the old order is unravelling on all fronts and levels.

Findings

This chapter began with the claim that the overstretch hypothesis hinges on two important assumptions: that is, the 'unequal growth' principle and the 'zero sum' principle. The first holds that different countries develop at different paces, and that the engine of growth which once benefited one state will soon benefit another state more. The second means that wealth and force evolve hand in hand; that those states which enjoy the fastest economic growth also tend, over time, to be militarily the most powerful.

The discussion revealed that the overstretch hypothesis in essence is a systems-level argument. As such it addresses the general dynamics among states, and it cannot be relied upon to uncover the dynamics within specific countries. Later, the discussion exposed two additional assumptions which inform the overstretch hypothesis. First, the hypothesis cannot be confidently applied to all kinds of international systems; it primarily applies to anarchical systems and does not necessarily address hierarchical systems – i.e., it does not apply to conditions of hegemony or 'concert'. The overstretch hypothesis applies to anarchical interstate constellations that are marked by competition and flux, and where order is maintained by balance-of-power dynamics. It is within such anarchical contexts that the fortunes of great powers most clearly wax and wane. At one moment a state is the unrivalled ruler of the world; the next it is besieged by setbacks and misfortunes.

Second, the discussion disclosed that overstretch cannot simply be prevented by intra-nation adjustments. This claim can be backed up on methodological grounds: it is an error of inference to claim that a great power can avoid the pitfalls of overstretch by reducing its military expenditures, for the overstretch hypothesis is essentially a systems-level theory and as such it cannot strictly apply to intra-nation dynamics. The claim can also be substantiated by empirical evidence. Consider the following question: could the United Provinces have halted their decline by reducing their military expenditures in the 1660s? Adherents of the overstretch hypothesis might be led to think that they could, for a reduction in defence costs would have brought the state's annual expenditures into balance with its annual income. However, this argument is devoid of systemic context. The fact is that, in the 1660s, the United Provinces were trapped in an international system which was characterized by increasing state competition. And if the Dutch had reduced their military budget in such a competitive situation, there would have been no incentive for the French and the English to follow their example. The Dutch would, in effect, have conducted a policy of unilateral disarmament.[17]

Is there nothing, then, that the government of a declining great power can do to avoid the painful symptoms of overstretch? The English experience suggests that there is one action which may remedy an overstretch scenario: if the situation cannot be put right simply by lowering military budgets, then it can be remedied by increasing the relative productivity of the nation. This, at least, is a lesson suggested by the first British case, where the mounting military expenditures of the 1770s and 1780s were financed by innovations brought forth by the Industrial Revolution.

When this is said, it should be added that it is not an easy remedy to activate. First, because industrial revolutions cannot be created simply by political command. Second, because such revolutions imply major socio-economic changes which, in turn, are fraught with dangers of destabilizing the established order. The English experience indicates that increases in productivity are associated with technological and organizational innovations which act as solvents on the existing order and the rules and laws which sustain it. Thus, the remedy which may cure a severe condition of overstretch may have serious side effects in the form of upheavals and conflicts which regularly attend the decline of great powers.

Assessment of the overstretch hypothesis

Do the findings of this chapter confirm or reject the overstretch argument? On the one hand, it is apparent that hegemons which decline, suffer from economic overstretch – Habsburg Spain is a classic case in point. On the other, it is also evident that overstretched economies do not always decline – as is suggested by the first British case. In the final account, it is hard to either confirm or reject the overstretch hypothesis. It is not a hypothesis in the positivist sense of the term. It is too general a formulation to be decisively tested.

It must be added that the discussion so far has drawn firmer verdicts as to the two constitutive assumptions upon which the overstretch hypothesis hinges. The first assumption – the so-called 'principle of unequal development' has proved to be a very useful and applicable principle. It has for example been a great help in accounting for the changes from a hierarchic towards an anarchic interstate structure during the course of the world order cycle. The second assumption, on the other hand – the so-called 'principle of zero-sum relations between wealth and force' – has turned out to be of lesser value. It is untenable as a general proposition. It stumbles on an ecological fallacy as it unconsciously draws inferences about domestic politics from an essentially systems-level model.

In addition, the discussion has identified important limitations to the overstretch hypothesis. The hypothesis leaves out the important precepts of public spheres and historical processes. First, public spheres matter in international politics as they do in national affairs. Civic cultures, and the values, norms and rules that they embody, represent international institutions that structure the behaviour of states and state leaders. International political outcomes are not simply reducible to mechanic models of billiard-ball interaction. International institutions influence international outcomes because they shape actors' powers, strategies, identities and goals.

Second, history shapes public spheres. The values, norms and rules which structure the behaviour of state leaders are products of historical developments. What comes first (even if it is in some sense 'accidental') conditions what comes later. This is not an original insight. It is taken for granted by revolutionists as well as liberals. Radicals constantly refer to Marx's famous formulation in the *Eighteenth Brumaire of Louis Bonaparte*: 'Men make their own history, but they do not make it just as they please; they do not make it under circumstances chosen by themselves, but under circumstances directly found, given and transmitted from the past' (in Tucker 1978, p. 595). Liberals often package the same basic idea into the concept of 'path-dependence': thus North (1990, pp. 98f.; Jervis 1997, pp. 155–61) claims that state leaders inhabit an existing institutional matrix, and that the decisions they make are informed by the knowledge and skills that this matrix makes available to them. Marx and North agree on the larger point: that social actors – state leaders, economists and citizens alike – make policy choices under circumstances that are not of their making, and that their choices in turn affect the circumstances under which their successors must make *their* choices.

Neither of these two observations is of earth-shattering originality. However,

their commonsensical nature alone is no guarantee that students of international politics accept them. Indeed, neither public norms nor history are much
considered in the neo-realist applications which dominated the scholarly study
of international relations during the final two decades of the twentieth century
(Knutsen 1997, pp. 269ff.).

Notes

1 This part of Kennedy's argument is formulated with greater formality and in
   greater depth by Gilpin (1981).
2 Charles II's primary aim was to enhance royal power at home. He was convinced
   that a successful liaison with France would help reduce his dependence on Parliament and assist in the implementation of absolutist policies at home.
3 Indeed, the rate of Britain's economic growth was higher than that of any other
   country – as is suggested by Table 14 below:

Table 14   *Relative share in world manufacturing output, 1750 and 1800
(in % of estimated total)*

State	1750	1800	Increase (%)
Great Britain	1.9	4.3	126
German states	2.9	3.5	20
Russia	5.0	5.6	12
Habsburg empire	2.9	3.2	10
France	4.0	4.2	5
Italian states	2.4	2.5	4
Other European states	2.1	4.8	128
Europe as a whole	21.2	28.1	32

Source: Kennedy (1987, p. 149)

4 Britain's defence expenditure is compared with that of the other great powers in
   Table 15 below:

Table 15   *Defence expenditure of the great powers, 1870–1914
(in £millions)*

Power	1870	1880	1890	1900	1910	1914
Great Britain	23.4	25.2	31.4	116.0	68.0	76.8
Germany	10.8	20.4	28.8	41.0	64.0	110.8
Russia	22.0	29.6	29.0	40.8	63.4	88.2
France	22.0	31.4	37.4	42.2	52.4	57.4
Austria-Hungary	8.2	13.2	12.8	13.6	17.4	36.4
Italy	7.8	10.0	14.8	14.6	24.4	28.2

Source: Taylor (1971, p. xxviii)

5 The dark mood of the age is still noticeable in the best-selling novels of the age: in the gloomy Gothic tales of Walpole, Beckford, Radcliffe and Chatterton.

6 Table 16 below indicates this increase in conflict and contention through the late 1700s. A climax of violence was reached in 1780 (with the Gordon Riots). Then the tide turned. Table 16 is a crude indicator of social conflict and unrest. The crudeness notwithstanding, it suggests how the rate of social unrest first increased steeply and then abated at a time when war broke out with the arch-rival France – first against republican revolution and then Napoleon.

Table 16   *Arrests and casualties in contentious gatherings in England,*
1758–1820 (selected years)

Year	A Number arrested	B Number wounded	C Number killed	Number of casualties (B+C)
1758	3	1	2	3
1759	24	4	1	5
1768	92	147	75	222
1769	45	19	9	28
1780	174	20	109	129
1781	10	25	11	36
1789	10	10	—	10
1795	33	6	2	8
1801	8	8	2	10
1807	9	32	32	64
1811	29	9	5	14
1819	156	12	5	17
1820	53	25	1	26

Source: Tilly (1995, p. 92)

7 This interpretation is supported by the fact that many British subjects, when they appeared to share distinctive features with this alien enemy, fell victims to the projection. It should be recalled that, although the Gordon Riots (1780) began as a protest against the policies of Parliament, they quickly broadened to include regular witch-hunts for everything which smacked of Catholicism and republicanism.

8 This argument about the increasing cost of commodities also applies to the cost of labour. As inflation included the most common consumer goods, it soon spread to include wage levels. Wages in Spain grew more rapidly than in any other European country and contributed to the country's inability to compete in the world economy. 'Wages in Spain lagged only slightly behind the soaring prices, while wages in the rest of Europe were kept far down. This also penalized Spanish industry, making its products too expensive to compete in the international market' (Stavrianos 1966, p. 111).

9 The book was written by la Court (but issued anonymously) at the instigation of the primary spokesman of the republic's mercantile interests, the mighty Grand Pensionary of Holland, Johan de Witt – who apparently contributed two chapters.

The text reflected the effort of Dutch politicians to define alternatives to the Stadtholder's traditional policies of *raison d'état* (Schama 1987, p. 254).

10 This was a grisly event whose dastardly details would later provide Alexandre Dumas with an enticing opening to his novel *The Black Tulip* (1850).

11 The Reform Bill of 1867 marks an important stage on the road to this new mass society, for it gave the first real impetus to creating a national system of free and compulsory education; another step was the Education Act of 1870, which set up locally elected school boards which could compel attendance up to the age of thirteen. Another decisively important step was the Secrecy of the Ballot Act (1872), for it struck a devastating blow at the old system of political clientelism and enabled newly enfranchised workers to vote freely without fear of reprisals from employer or landlord. The development was also stimulated by two Gladstonian reform Bills (1884 and 1885) which extended the suffrage to new, numerous layers of the lower classes and redistributed the seats in Parliament in favour of larger towns.

12 The rapid increase in taxation is shown in Table 17 below:

Table 17   *The rising burden of taxation in Habsburg Spain,*
1500–1600 (rounded index numbers; 1500 = 100)

Year	Price level	Tax level
1500	100	100
1520	115	105
1540	145	115
1560	220	140
1580	250	360
1594	305	530

Source: Vicens Vives (1971, p. 58)

13 Charles V had governed the Habsburg Empire by royal action based on conciliar advice gathered during unceasing travels all across his imperial territories. His son, Philip II, ended this ambulatory rule, and made the central Castilian city of Madrid the country's permanent capital (1561). Experts, advisers, courtiers, adventurers and sycophants were immediately drawn to the new capital, which rapidly expanded in members. The royal court expanded immensely and encapsulated the conscientious king in a pressure cooker of intrigues. Increasingly isolated in the castle of Escorial, Philip II grew distant from Madrid. And Madrid, in turn, grew distant from the rest of the Iberian peninsula. The establishment of the Spanish capital in Castile gave Philip's government a Castilian complexion which was increasingly resented in other regions.

14 It is worth noting that the Dutch noblemen were not at first Protestants. However, as Philip II was resolved to rule both property and faith from Madrid, Dutch demands for freedom of conscience were added to a rapidly growing list of grievances. This heightened the stakes of the conflict. For the Iberian empire was informed by a pervasive political mythology whose glue was militant Catholicism. The Catholic religion was a driving force in Spanish foreign policies. And as Dutch demands assumed Protestant overtones they grew increasingly repugnant to Philip II. So when the king sent the ruthless Count Alva to suppress the Dutch rebellion,

he discovered, to his dismay, that the Spanish hand of iron produced a soul of steel in the body that it gripped. By 1570, the Netherlands were in open revolt against the Catholic absolutism of Spain. The Dutch resented Spanish taxation, despised Spanish arrogance and feared the methods of the Inquisition. The resentments fuelled Dutch concerns about their traditional rights, their liberties and the religious toleration upon which their free trade, their booming industries and their growing wealth ultimately relied.

15 The political conflicts in late sixteenth-century Spain can be seen as a contest between a centralizing orientation represented primarily by the nobility of Castile and a decentralizing reaction represented by Catalonia and other 'peripheries' of the empire (Elliott 1977, pp. 245ff.).

16 This claim, that 'trusting' is a habitual practice in *modern* societies, is intended as a criticism of authors who treat 'trust' as a function of rational choice of sovereign actors. In this chapter 'trust' is not an outcome of universal reason and individual calculation; rather, it is an outcome of particular historical and social processes which emerge from habit and are secured by myth. The present study views 'trust' as a modern, Western phenomenon; it sees the growing significance of 'trust' as intimately related to the rise of individualism. In Western societies, sustained by a liberal mythology, where the ideal of personal freedom releases individuals from the constraints of ascriptive roles, trust becomes an important social phenomenon. Since all the cases discussed here are modern, I have seen no need to burden the text with an extensive discussion of the social-historical preconditions for the phenomenon of trust. However, such a discussion may be found e.g. in Seligman (1997).

17 A policy which England followed in the 1920s and 1930s and which, at the eve of World War II, earned the sobriquet 'appeasement'.

5

The rise and fall of
world orders

[Thomas Buddenbrook] was still a rich man, and none of the losses
he had suffered ... had seriously undermined the existence of the
firm. But the notion that his luck and his consequence had fled,
based though it was more upon inward feelings than upon outward
facts, brought him to a state of lowness and suspicion. He entertained, of course, as before, and set before his guests the normal
and expected number of courses. But, as never before, he began to
cling to money and, in his private life, to save in small and petty
ways. (Mann 1984[1901])

One of the most discussed patterns of periodicity in international relations
literature concerns the regular occurrence of great wars. Robert Mowat (1928,
p. 1) observed that four 'waves of great wars' have occurred in modern history.
This observation has since been empirically substantiated by several other
authors – some of whom have elaborated on Mowat's basic claim and developed macro-historical models which cast the history of the modern world
in great cycles of recurring world orders. They see each wave of great wars as
indicating the fall of one world order, but also as heralding the emergence of
another. Waves of great wars, then, can be seen as separating one world order
from another.

Four complete world orders may be distinguished in modern history – a
sixteenth-century Iberian order (which existed between the Italian wars and
the Thirty Years War); a seventeenth-century Dutch order (which lasted from
the Thirty Years War to the wars of Louis XIV); an eighteenth-century British
order (which existed between the wars of Louis XIV and the Napoleonic Wars)
and a nineteenth-century British world order (which lasted from the Napoleonic Wars to World War I). This chapter will draw on earlier discussions of
these four complete orders to outline a simple, four-phase model of the world
order cycle.

Cyclical patterns of modern world orders

Each world order was initially dominated by a single, powerful, leading state. It was a state which had profited from the wave of great wars and which, when the wars ended, emerged pre-eminent in the postwar world. This state was the hegemon. It was strong and wealthy – obviously, without such strength and wealth a single state could hardly have helped guide the world from a chaotic state of war towards a new postwar order. Yet, although military might and economic wealth made each hegemon extraordinarily influential in the aftermath of war, material power alone did not make it hegemonic. Wealth and might provided important preconditions for pre-eminence; but the key to hegemonic status lay in an additional factor: it rested in the social cohesion of its civil society. This cohesion was anchored in a reservoir of common values and norms which informed its public sphere. It undergirded the high degree of social solidarity and the common political mythology which sustained the key social institutions of the hegemon.

All the great powers discussed here grew towards pre-eminence during great wars. By the time the wars were concluded, each state had become a strong, rich and powerful international actor. Why? Why did Spain, the United Provinces and England ascend towards pre-eminence during a wave of great wars? Why did they emerge so strong and wealthy as to be hegemonic by the time peace was concluded? Liberal economic theories may suggest that the reason lay in resources which all four countries possessed – resources which are commonly portrayed as *sine qua non* conditions of economic growth. Modernization theories will emphasize the presence of relevant factors of production (often by stressing the traditional triad of land, labour and capital). These theories will often attach great importance to high rates of productivity in agriculture, of a certain economy of scale, of highly educated and skilled workers and of sophisticated capital (e.g. in the form of technology which guarantees relative efficiency throughout the production process). Spain, the Netherlands and England all possessed such factors. They possessed efficient economies which could sustain a strong political/military establishment.

The problem with this kind of argument is that none of these conditioning factors enters the economic world one by one and full-grown as from the brow of Zeus. All of them can be seen as the end result of a process of development. Each and every one of them can be seen as the outcome of a process which, in turn, requires some preconditioning factors of its own. Economic history, like all history, is a seamless web. Every strand of it is interwoven with other strands in a complex array of regress. The so-called 'relevant factors of production' do not always leap to the eye. They have to be selected by a discriminating economist. The criteria for such selection may always be questioned. And one way of questioning them is to point out that the items which liberal economists often list as preconditioning factors of growth – innovation, economies of scale, education, capital accumulation, etc. – are not really causes of growth; they are indications of growth. They *are* growth (North and Thomas 1973, p. 2).

Radical theories are, when push comes to shove, not so different from the liberal ones. When radicals discuss the causes of a state's wealth and power, they tend to present the factors of production according to some variation of the old Marxist appeal to the means of production and the skills and organization of labour. In addition they tend to add a dependence argument. They argue, as an echo of Anathole France's claim, that behind every major fortune lies a major crime. They submit that wealthy states have got their gains by exploiting those who are weaker and poorer than themselves.

The focus of this study is on hegemony – on an orderly international constellation justified by a generally accepted, universal conception of world order. Such a condition is not easily captured in purely material terms. As proposed in Chapter 1, a peculiar non-material factor is present in all cases of hegemony: viz., a high degree of social cohesion sustained by consensus as to the values, norms and rules of social behaviour – within the pre-eminent state as well as among the members of a hegemonic coalition. Chapter 4 concluded that this consensus is eroding as the relative power of pre-eminent great powers declines. The presence or absence of consensus thus appears to play an important role in the rise and fall of great powers. And the fortunes of great powers will, in turn, affect the nature of world orders.

On upheavals, identity, cohesion, trust and great wars

The formative forces behind a hegemon's social cohesion are found among the upheavals and reforms which have occurred in its political history. They are especially found in the age of turbulence, upheavals and reforms which shook them a generation or so before the waves of great wars which catapulted them into international pre-eminence. The Spanish *reconquista*, the Dutch War of Independence, the English revolution and the 'Industrial Revolution' are instances of such ages of upheaval for the Spanish, the Dutch, the first and second English hegemonies, respectively. During these ages of upheaval, societies were (re)defined, collective identities were consolidated and state interests defined. In each of the four cases, this was an intense period when new social institutions were forged and expressed in new cultural codes – in dress, songs, *fêtes*, emblems, flags, etc. This phase of turbulence was a formative moment in the development of the state.

These new institutions, and the symbolic expressions which accompanied them, were forged on the anvil of political (often bitter and violent) struggle.

When its history was subsequently recounted, it was told by the victorious party. And the victor's version tended to describe the struggle, portray the various participants, define their aims in a light which justified the outcome. This description was a mythogenic act, and the victor's version paved the ground for a distinct political mythology – an ethno-social discourse which preserved the symbols and the cultural memory of the struggle and which legitimized the causes it served. The myth expressed a formative collective experience. It helped consolidate a distinct collective identity which (in all the cases studied here) was subsequently reinforced by public acts of reverence. The political mythology encased the memories of struggle in a discursive shrine, and reinforced them in common, standardized, ritualistic celebrations in which decisive political events were collectively re-enacted in the public sphere as birthpangs of independence and statehood.

This formation of collective identity and statehood has been regularly accompanied by rapid economic growth and by developing notions of state interest. What fuelled this growth? Obviously, the quality of the 'factors of production' was an important element. Also, the factor triad of land, capital and labour identified basic preconditioning elements of an efficient economy (just as liberal and radical theories claim). However, neither exchange nor production on any scale will result without a high degree of social cohesion. The economists Theodore Schultz (1961) and Gary Becker (1975) approached this notion when they argued that to the traditional concept of tangible 'physical capital' must be added a concept of 'human capital' which they defined broadly as the knowledge and skills of human beings. The sociologist James Coleman (1990), pursuing this logic further, argued that neither 'physical capital' nor 'human capital' were sufficient in themselves. He argued that it is necessary to also include a concept of 'social capital' – i.e., an all-important ability to associate. This ability, Coleman continued, would depend on the degree to which individual people belong to societies with common norms and values.

Coleman shifted focus from the knowledge of humans to the values of society, and therefore preferred the term 'social capital'. He defined this as a people's ability to work together for common purposes in groups and organizations. Coleman, then, distinguishes between *three* types of capital: physical, human and social. He explains:

> Physical capital is wholly tangible, being embodied in observable material form; human capital is less tangible, being embodied in the skills and knowledge acquired by an individual; social capital is even less tangible, for it is embodied in *relations* among persons. Physical capital and human capital facilitate productive activity, and social capital does so as well. For example, a group whose members manifest trustworthiness and place extensive trust

in one another will be able to accomplish much more than a comparative group lacking that trustworthiness and trust. (Coleman 1990, p. 304)

Social capital, Coleman submitted, is critical not only to economic life, but to virtually any aspect of social enterprise.[1] Francis Fukuyama (1992, p. 26) pinned Coleman's core point down to a question of 'trust' – i.e., to the habitual, common 'expectation that arises within a community of regular, honest and cooperative behaviour, based on commonly shared norms, on the part of other members of that community'. Gambetta (1988) sees trust 'as a social lubricant which makes possible production and exchange' and extols it as a basic precondition for effective social order.

This point is, in fact, a basic argument in social studies. It is embraced in one way or another by conservatives (Burke 1988[1790]), radicals (Rousseau 1971[1762]) and liberals (Smith 1982[1759]) alike. In the present study of great powers, it provides theoretical support for a set of basic propositions. Most importantly, that the emergence of Spain, Holland and England towards hegemony was attended by a rapid rate of economic development and by a notable consolidation of social and political institutions, and that this development occurred in a social environment primed by a high degree of cohesion and trust.

'Trust' reflects the degree of confidence which people have in the reliability of undertakings made in the course of social interaction. This confidence is inscribed in a common frame of moral reference which encases society in a common, collective identity and in a consensual code of values, norms and rules of social behaviour. Trust is an important asset in any society. It is a decisive asset in periods of social development – which are always attended by change, turbulence and uncertainties. It constitutes a form of social capital which differs from other forms of capital in that it is an organic heritage of the past. It ensures that the individual members of society entertain fairly similar values, norms and outlooks. And, since individual liberty will produce little deviation from central norms in such a consensual community, such societies can allow their inhabitants relatively high degrees of individual freedom.

Social trust – or rather, the social cohesion and consensus which such trust signifies – can be considered an important precondition for the development of liberties and rights in modern society. Trust, cohesion and consensus are qualities which undergird those activities which spur economic growth and political development. Trust allows individuals to form (and spontaneously reform) social associations and partnerships. In the economic realm, it allows the development of a complex social division of labour which may, in turn, enable society as a whole to mobilize and coordinate its productive energies in fair and efficient ways. In the political realm, it allows the growth of a public sphere – an open, complex arena of communication of literary, social, economic and political matters.

An evolving division of labour in society and increasing efficiency in social transactions signal the integration of society into a functioning unit. Development in the sectors of production, trade, communication and education contribute to what Émile Durkheim referred to as society's 'organic solidarity'. Societies which display a high degree of organic solidarity may not only enable their inhabitants to form complex associations and efficient partnerships; they will also contribute to the material conditions which strengthen a larger, collective identity, Durkheim argued. This is done at the expense of extant, traditional identities – family, clan, locality, region. And, as this integrating development proceeds, it produces a functioning, modern society.

Durkheim's pupil, Marcel Mauss, added that during the course of this evolution the modern state unfolds. The modern state, according to Mauss, possesses four essential features: a clearly demarcated territory, a stable government which controls that territory, a high degree of integration between the economic system and domestic culture and a certain degree of moral and cultural homogeneity in a public sphere which can sustain conscious adherence to the government and its laws (Schnapper and Mendras 1990). By this definition, Spain, the United Provinces and England have consistently been the most modern states of their times. Furthermore, since they were hegemonic states, they influenced others. They did so partly by pushing other states to abide by standards they had evolved, and partly by offering other states an attractive blueprint for their own future. Hegemons have, in a word, been modernizing agents in modern international history.

One of Mauss's core properties of modern statehood is a population which is unified by a distinct narrative that informs their moral code and undergirds their collective identity and their support for the government and its laws. At the core of this property lies a common, affective element. This is expressed in a mythological narrative. It envelops social action. Citizens voluntarily obey the law and productively contribute to the community when they feel that, in so doing, they participate in a credible story of who they are and why their fates are inextricably linked. This common affective narrative intertwines political, economic and cultural institutions. It contributes to the consensus and cohesion of the community because it instils in every citizen a common understanding which is above individual vanity, presumption and rapacity. This common affective narrative consolidates social trust and supports civil order. If it were to unravel, civil society would become unstitched. If the common myth should fracture, material incentive structures and the enforcement of law would remain the only guarantees of authority and order. Politics would shift from consensus to coercion.

In every society, an affective mythology sustains common notions of justice and sobriety; it exerts a controlling power upon individual will and appetite and contributes to an orderly community in which efficient social transactions can evolve. In the four cases discussed here, a tight moral consensus provided a measure of identity, cohesion, stability and security in an uncertain world. In all cases, soon after the collective identity was formed, the ascendant state found itself involved in a large-scale interstate war. Also in all cases, this involvement in war strengthened domestic cohesion – it intensified patriotism; it mobilized domestic resources in order to further the safety and the interests of the state; it consolidated the legitimacy of domestic institutions. As a result, political development, economic growth, the evolution of social consensus and the advent of conscious nationhood all tied into one another in a positive feedback loop.

In addition, war offered the ascendant states opportunities to project their power and their code of values and norms on to the world outside. First, Spain, Holland and England pursued opportunistic strategies of easy economic gain. At the outbreak of extensive wars, the ascending hegemons tended to sell contraband to the warring parties. While most great powers were preoccupied with fighting each other, the ascendant hegemons projected their power far and wide. They expanded into neglected colonial areas. They acquired economic footholds in forgotten regions.

Later, when the war was well under way, the ascending states chose sides. They joined the war. They joined late, but two things followed when they did. First, they invested their considerable energies into a multistate coalition and they thereby tipped the constellation of forces in favour of their own coalition. Second, their intervention consolidated the wartime coalition and in the process infused it with their own values and norms. The ascending hegemons soon emerged as leading coalition members. And more than any other single factor, these coalitions provided the mechanisms by means of which the ascending states gained the trust of their coalition partners that allowed them to design a hegemonic order.

During the wave of great wars, the members of great-power coalitions increasingly came to assume, as a matter of habit, a propensity to cooperate in common ventures and comply with common rules. This cooperation was not limited to the level of monarchs, ministers and military commanders; as the war continued, it often also involved lower rungs of military command and, perhaps more importantly, sectors of civil society. The coalition partners opened up, tentative strands of cooperation developed into informal webs of civil interaction and interdependence across boundaries. The cooperating states and societies grew more similar in the process.

Most particularly, the cooperating coalition members adopted some of the ways and values of the ascendant hegemon. This also meant that the coalition members became more similar to each other. It also meant that the ascending hegemon exerted a significant influence on the conditions of postwar peace. If a moment needs to be identified at which this hegemonic pre-eminence came into its own, the most obvious candidate is the peace conferences which formally concluded the wave of great wars. To put it boldly, pre-eminent great powers become hegemons just as the waves of great war formally give way to the postwar era. Habsburg Spain, the United Provinces, England I and England II all influenced their respective wartime coalitions greatly – especially during the final phase of the wave of great wars. Furthermore, they exerted an important influence on the negotiations which formally ended the wars – the treaties of Cambrai (1529), Westphalia (1648), Utrecht (1713) and Vienna (1815), respectively. These treaties serve as convenient marks of transition from a condition of world war to one of postwar hegemony. They indicate the rise of the Iberian, the Dutch, the first British and the second British world orders, respectively.

On the phase of hegemony

'Hegemon' refers to the pre-eminent great power in the hegemonic international system; a hegemon is a strong core state, and it contributes decisively to the formation of a new, orderly system during the endgame of a wave of great wars. 'Hegemony' refers to a systems feature – it is a property which characterized the international system in the immediate aftermath of each wave of great wars.

During the first phase of a world order, the international system was 'managed' by a hegemon. This was a great power which was militarily strong, materially wealthy, and normatively influential. In domestic affairs, the hegemon possessed a stable government, social cohesion and a high degree of integration between a free and flexible economic system and a tolerant domestic culture. In international affairs, it was unopposed. It had no competitors.

This lack of international opposition is a peculiar feature of the hegemonic phase of world order. The interstate constellation was, for all practical purposes, unipolar. Realist theory would expect such a unipolar constellation to be inherently unstable and to quickly produce an alliance of states bent on counterbalancing and containing the pre-eminent power. Such policies of balance and containment were, however, not the most characteristic feature of the postwar world scene. The immediate postwar period was an era not of balance, but of bandwagoning. Bandwagoning, explains Walt (1991, pp. 53, 69) requires a high degree of trust in the non-malevolent intentions of the pre-eminent state. The orders which evolved after waves of great wars were, in fact, marked by extraordinary amounts of cooperation, cohesion, consensus and trust. This (for the realists, quite counter-intuitive) feature contains important clues to the nature of the hegemonic condition.

But we are getting ahead of the story. A better entry into the features of this unipolar constellation is to address the domestic properties of the ascending hegemon and then to work the argument towards the realm of international interaction. These properties were marked by high degrees of consensus and cohesion. Thus, an obvious question to pose is: what accounts for this high degree of cohesion? The answer can be hinted at, as Mauss suggests, by the presence of a strong, affective mythology which is historically grounded in traumatic collective experiences and which embodies a distinct code of values, norms and rules for social conduct. This common mythology undergirds a collective notion of identity, nationhood and the national interest. It contributes to making the hegemon a strong state, and it allows its inhabitants to communicate and cooperate with ease and trust. It ensures that the public sphere is informed by a common moral frame of reference. It helps socialize new generations into a common code of conduct – a code which is an organic heritage of the past and which is created and transmitted through the public sphere by tradition and historical habit, by institutions of education and participation in ritual public ceremonies of remembrance. This common moral framework, collective identity, sense of common interests, and the high degree of social trust it supports, helps explain why strong powers emerge as cohesive and consensual strong states during the endgame of a wave of great wars.

But why do strong powers emerge pre-eminent in the interstate system? The hegemonic condition is characterized by the presence of a great power which is economically dominant, militarily pre-eminent and morally influential. The first characteristic of the hegemonic condition is the pre-eminence of a strong power (with a strong state) and a uniquely productive economy. The economic and the military pre-eminence can be illuminated by the reference to a common moral framework. It is widely accepted that power is derived from resources – material as well as human. But history contains many examples of how large armies (or navies) have been defeated by smaller and more determined ones.[2] Dutch and English history provides several instances: during the waves of great wars, the United Provinces and England often had smaller armies than their adversaries, yet they showed themselves to be more disciplined and efficient on the battlefield. The unifying and motivating effect of their vivid political mythology goes a long way to explain the superior discipline and the string of military successes of their forces.

Under the stress of war, the general consensus reinforced social discipline and organization. In the 'fog of war', military performance was enhanced by considerable initiative. The communal spirit was expressed in a clear cause – at least among the officers, but often also among the men – to fulfil 'God's will', to preserve the honour of King and Country, to pave the way for the rule of justice and reason. The threat of war steeled the political determination of the Iberians, Dutch and English alike. It gave the soldiers a common cause to fight for. It unified the people around common war aims, motivated them with abstract ideals and cultivated grand visions of wholesale civic unity. It created a distinct identity, expressed in a common patriotism which defined politics in terms that went beyond the mere concepts of power and interests. This patriotic attitude involved a self-identity that courted arrogance through its identification with the wealth of society and the awesome force of the state. It exerted a strong unifying force in civil society. And the stronger it was, the more it displayed its excesses in oversimplified terms of congratulation and denigration, classifying whole peoples as 'good' or 'bad'. High-trust societies tend to draw clearer distinctions between 'us' and 'them'. They are likely to have weaker bonds with outside actors. And the internal consensus and confidence which mark the internal affairs of a hegemon are easily perceived from the outside as arrogance, Podsnappery and downright hypocrisy.

This military superiority was not exclusively the result of a high degree of social consensus; it was also the outcome of sophisticated industries capable of producing state-of-the art weapons systems which placed unrivalled military capabilities at the disposal of its men. But this industrial superiority was, in turn, related to the same tight social consensus which contributed to the soldiers' exceptional *esprit de corps*. This implies that strong states are productive states. But doesn't that fly in the face of established claims of economic theory? Isn't it rather generally accepted that individual liberty (rather than state strength) goes hand in hand with productivity? Doesn't this purported connection between state strength and economic productivity flatly contradict the key axiom of liberal social theory: that those societies which allow the greatest freedom for its inhabitants will also tend to be the most productive and, given enough time, also the most wealthy and powerful?

Sceptical questions like these are brushed aside by two responses. First, 'strong states' must not be confused with 'big government'. Rather 'state strength' refers to the robust nature of domestic institutions, e.g. to a high degree of socio-economic consensus and cohesion.[3] Second, the emphasis on 'strong states' does not dispute the axiom that a high degree of social liberty is associated with a high degree of economic productivity – indeed, this correlation is substantiated by the portrayal of Dutch and English societies as among the freest societies of their time as well as the wealthiest. However, this study suggests that the liberal argument which is most commonly used to explain this association between liberty and wealth – that free societies are most efficient because they unleash most effectively the talents of rationally self-interested entrepreneurs – is spurious. For the economically most efficient societies may not necessarily be those which award the greatest liberties to the most rationally self-interested individuals; rather, the most efficient societies may be those which are most cohesive and consensual.

On the phase of challenge

The second phase of world order begins with a sudden international conflict which erupts in war. In all cases this conflict took the hegemons by surprise. None of them had expected war, and none was prepared to fight one. They were caught unprepared, and they lost the initial battle. Cases in point are the Spanish defeats at Turkish hands in 1559, Dutch losses to England's Royal Navy in 1652, and the English defeats by Spain and Russia in 1739 and 1854, respectively.

In all cases, the hegemons quickly regained their composure. They rearmed, struck back and trounced the enemy. And in most cases their victory was so convincing that it restored their international prestige and national pride. The best example is Spain's victory at Lepanto (1571) which chased the Turks out of the western Mediterranean. This victory initiated a new phase of Iberian pride which expressed itself in a new wave of expansionism.

However, the optimism and expansionism which followed in the wake of victory were fairly brief affairs. Like Indian summers, they were temporary reminders of quietude and balminess. But they could not last. The deeper, general trend of unequal development described a longer-term autumnal setting. The Spanish soon discovered that the victory at Lepanto was purchased at a high cost. It was the result of a costly campaign to reorganize and modernize the armed forces and it had, in effect, saddled the nation with a heavy economic burden. This burden may be measured in concrete terms – e.g. by way of a substantial defence budget which the hegemon would ulti-mately have to pay somehow (or go bankrupt, as Spain in fact did). In addition, the burden must be assessed in more abstract, political terms – in terms of lost prestige and legitimacy.

When challenged to battle, none of the hegemons performed as commonly expected; they all suffered immediate losses in prestige as a result. In inter-national relations it is prestige (rather than power) which is the currency of day-to-day diplomacy. War reflects capabilities and power directly in battle-field tests – the fortunes of war are generally assumed to reflect the capabilities of the belligerent parties and to be a reliable indicator of their power. But war is not a routine occurrence in international relations. And in the absence of war, prestige is the common indicator of the system members' assumptions about the distribution of power in the system. So, when war *does* break out after a long period of relative peace, all states monitor the battles closely and assess the capabilities of the participants. In all cases discussed here, the international hierarchy of prestige was quickly redefined in light of the first fortunes of the unexpected wars. These reassessments were invariably to the disadvantage of the hegemons – respectively reflecting the Spanish defeats by Turkey (around 1560), the Dutch losses to England (1652), and the English defeats by Spain (1739) and Russia (1854). The hegemon's prestige plummeted in all four cases. The relative prestige of other powers increased by comparison.

All hegemons quickly compensated for their surprisingly poor initial showing by initiating costly crash programmes of reform and rearmament. However, prestige was not the only immediate casualty of war. The battle also involved an additional corrosive, which would prove much harder for the hegemons to combat: during the war of challenge, it became obvious that the hegemons were fighting to preserve their own state interests and to protect their own national security. As the hegemons struggled to recapture their falling prestige, they did great damage to their legitimacy as world leaders. For as each hegemon was forced to defend its own national interest, it acted as any ordinary power. And such action contradicted the common perception that the hegemon was an *extra*ordinary state – a protector of the common cause, a world leader and a representative of order and the common interest. Thus, in their attempts to re-gain their prestige, the hegemons all weakened the confidence which other states had invested in their leadership. This struck at the very core of the hegemonic condition. It affected the trust in and the legitimacy of its pre-eminence.

The erosion of prestige and legitimate leadership was the first, subtle signal of a weakening hegemon and an eroding world order. It adumbrated a new international configuration. The prestige of the hegemon suffered a fall, and – since 'power' is a relational concept – that of other powers enjoyed a relative rise. The result was that the international hierarchy of prestige lost some of its former steepness – as the great powers appeared more equal, the interna-tional hierarchy appeared 'squatter'. This adjustment, it turned out, caused conflicts in their own right: it introduced uncertainties as to the ranking order of the great powers. These uncertainties, in turn, fuelled competition. They also enhanced the possibilities of diplomatic misunderstandings.

In addition, subtle changes in the structure of order were at work in the internal affairs of the hegemon. Most conspicuously, the unexpected loss of an international contest was a blow not only to the international prestige of the state, but also to the patriotic pride of the nation. It triggered heated debate about the causes of the failure and about who was to blame. This was later followed by discussions about doctrines of defence, about the nature and size of armed forces and about how to pay for them. The government was subjected to increasing criticism. Dissent flowed more freely from various groups of the population and filled the public sphere with quarrels and rancour. One of the common causes of dissatisfaction concerned questions of fiscal fairness. One of its common consequences was a debate which reactivated old lines of domestic conflict – as in the case of Spain, where ripple effects of the Turkish attacks caused a great schism in the Spanish court and fiscal protests in the provinces.

On the phase of competitive disruption

During the third phase of world order, the old hegemons continued to decline relative to other great powers. After a period of relative calm, the hegemons became more engaged in foreign conflict and war. They spent increasing amounts of money on security and defence. Also, they lost their competitive edge – they fell behind other powers in their rates of productivity and economic growth and, it increasingly appeared, in military capabilities.

The orthodox argument of decline – expressed most succinctly by liberal Scottish and English theorists like Smith, Bentham, Cobden and Bright – holds that increasing defence costs siphon off capital from the sectors of productive investment; over time this causes the nation's economic performance to stagnate. This orthodox view does not express the full complexity of the issue. For an increase in defence expenditure is not always followed by a decrease in economic performance. Indeed, every case of hegemonic ascent represents an instance where increasing defence expenditure was attended by *in*creasing economic productivity. Three conclusions can be drawn from these observations. First, that the effects of defence expenditure are relative to some greater socio-economic context – for example, the effects of rearmament will vary according to which world order phase it occurs in. If defence costs increase in a phase of economic stagnation, then this may indeed exacerbate the situation; but if defence costs increase in a phase marked by economic upswing, it may have a tonic effect on the economy.

Furthermore, one factor which invariably attends a decrease in economic performance is decreasing socio-political cohesion. Phases of severe economic stagnation are regularly accompanied by a deepening of old cleavages of domestic conflict – often cleavages of a regional or ethnic/religious nature.

Finally, increasing competition and unrest within the hegemon are paralleled by greater unrest on the world scene. One reason for this increase in international conflict is structural in nature. As the old hegemon declines (relative to other great powers), the capabilities of power become more evenly distributed among the great powers. The principle of unequal development of states helps explain this process. Some powers develop more rapidly, others more slowly. Those powers that develop at a slower rate will suffer a relative decline. During the third phase of world order the old hegemon will be among these declining powers.

There are two main reasons why an old hegemon declines during the third phase of world order. First, because its best and most productive institutions have by now been emulated by others, stimulated their development and allowed them to catch up in terms of economic productivity. This emulation affects the structure of the international system. It makes the steep structure of the immediate postwar years slowly give way to a flatter and wider interstate structure. It replaces the 'hierarchical' properties of the first phase of world order with a structure which possesses more 'anarchic' features. This development prepares one of the basic preconditions for a balance-of-power system.

Second, new sovereign states emerge during the third phase of world order. Thus, the final phase of the Spanish order saw the emergence of England and Russia; the final phase of the Dutch order witnessed the rise of Sweden and Austria; the British orders experienced the rise of new states first in America and Prussia, then in Germany and Italy. This third-phase development contributed greatly to the complication of the international scene. For as a greater number of powers are introduced to the interstate system, a greater number of political permutations are made possible. A more numerous international scene allows for a greater range of diplomatic relationships and for more complex alliance dynamics. And as this development comes in addition to a more equal distribution of capabilities among the great powers, the result is a more complicated international scene in whose anarchic setting order is increasingly preserved not by concert and consensus but by balance-of-power dynamics.

One way to explain the increasing unrest of the world scene during the third phase of world order is by reference to changes in the international structure. Another way to explain this increase in unrest is in terms of a general erosion of values, norms and rules of international behaviour. The structural argument assumes that the norms and rules of international conduct are largely defined and enforced by the great powers. During the first phase of world order, the main rules were defined by a single, pre-eminent great power – the hegemon.

At this point must it be recalled that a hegemon is more than just a great power. During the first phase of world order, the hegemon enjoyed a remarkable measure of legitimacy as world leader. However, during the second and third phases, this legitimacy was spent. One reason for this lay in the old hegemon's new-found international activism: the more the old hegemon engaged itself in international conflicts and foreign wars, the more it hurt its image – it was perceived as just another great power set on furthering its own narrow advantages and protecting its own prosaic interests. This perception acted as a strong solvent on the hegemon's old, universalist claims to world leadership. It eroded the legitimacy which once supported this claim. States ceased to habitually comply with hegemonic rules and initiatives.

Another reason for this falling legitimacy lay in the hegemon's economic decline. As the old hegemon lost its competitive edge in the world economy, it also lost its attractiveness as an idol and an example. It could no longer credibly offer its own society as a 'blueprint' for others to emulate. Its social visions and political mythologies carried neither as much conviction nor as strong an appeal as before. This, too, acted as a solvent on the hegemon's universalist claims to leadership.

This erosion of the international moral order was paralleled by similar developments within the declining hegemon. The domestic consensus which once ensured the smooth working of society unravelled. And as this happened the old, efficient system based on solidarity and trust was replaced by a more costly system based on formal contract – a system whose smooth operation involved higher transaction costs.

Transaction costs and public spheres

The neo-institutional concept of transaction costs is a useful entry into the nature of a consensual, smooth-working, efficient and strong hegemonic state. The concept hinges on the notion that a civil society consists of a complex web of innumerable individual operations. In the economic sphere, a complex web of transactions link an enormous number of economic actors who make exchanges (of goods, services, favours and symbols) and contribute to the weaving of a tight web of social relations – a system of economic interaction which liberal economists commonly refer to as 'the market'.

In economic theory, a market comprises an incalculable number of single transactions; each such transaction can be seen as an individual, voluntary act in which one product or service is exchanged willingly for something else (usually money). A market is a meeting place for the purpose of barter and buying and selling.

In political practice, market transactions occur within a larger socio-historical context. The economy is embedded in social relations (Polanyi 1957; Ruggie 1982). These relations take place within a framework of rules and laws. And if the market is to operate smoothly, the social conditions which surround it and the basic rules which govern its myriads of operations must be constantly maintained, adjusted and enforced.

Transaction costs and the fall of great powers

On the basis of this concept of transaction costs, it is possible to amend the orthodox liberal argument of decline. The liberal theorists, who holds that increasing defence costs siphon off capital from the sectors of productive investment, could easily be criticized for forgetting a substantial expense which all societies pay for a smoothly functioning market economy: that is, the expenses which are required to ensure the workings of a modern market-based society. A quick backtrack to Paul Kennedy's argument may help substantiate the point.

Kennedy (1987) explains that the resources of a state are always allocated between two key purposes: protection and productive investments. Allocation to purposes of protection means investment in the armed forces to maintain the state's ability to protect the state's territory, its core institutions and its citizens. Allocation to productive investment ensures continued wealth creation – it means that some part of the state's wealth must be ploughed back into the productive sectors of the national economy in order to enhance its efficiency. The core claim, on which Kennedy's argument hinges, is that if 'too large a proportion of the state's resources is diverted from wealth creation and allocated instead to military purposes, then that is likely to lead to a weakening of national power over the long term' (Kennedy 1987, p. xvi).

Robert Gilpin (1981) maintains a more elaborate version of this argument. He claims that the resources of a state are allocated not between two, but among three, general purposes: protection, production and consumption. Gilpin and Kennedy agree that allocation to protection refers to 'the costs of national security and the costs of protecting the property rights of citizens' (Gilpin 1981, p. 158). They also agree that productive investment refers to 'that part of the national product that is returned to the productive sector of the economy to increase the efficiency and productivity of land, labour, and, in the modern world, industrial plant' (ibid.). However to Kennedy's two purposes of production and protection, Gilpin adds 'consumption' – a type of state expenditure which includes 'private and public consumption of goods and services' (ibid.) This inclusion of consumption as a third category of state expenditure allows for richer and more complex arguments about the political economy of rise and decline. Yet, Gilpin's basic point is constructed on the same last as Kennedy's: it flows from the same basic zero-sum distinction between productive and unproductive investments. Thus, Gilpin argues that, if substantial proportions of the state's resources are expended on military affairs or on private and public consumption (or on both), then resources are drawn away from wealth creation and are likely to weaken the national power base over the long term.

From Kennedy's notion of two socio-economic arenas, through Gilpin's notion of three arenas, it is easy to extend the liberal logic into the notion that modern societies are divided into four socio-economic arenas: the sectors of production, protection, consumption and transactions. The notion that transactions represent social expenditures hinges on the claim that activities which maintain the social order, adjust and enforce rules and laws are rarely really free; that it takes money to run a smooth, wealth-engendering market.

This point has often been forgotten by orthodox free-market advocates who put their faith in the self-adjusting magic of the invisible hand. However, as Adam Smith clearly recognized, it takes money to protect the private property of the market actors from thieves and swindlers. It also takes money to protect the transacting parties from the paralysing effects of ambiguities, misunderstandings and honest quarrels. In short, it takes money to run a system of justice that defines and enforces the property rights upon which a modern market economy hinges. In addition, it takes money to run a wide variety of activities which need to be ceaselessly performed if the basic processes of a modern, wealth-creating economy are to be smoothly maintained – some of the most important of which are related to the collection of taxes, the collection (and dissemination) of information about the goods and services available on the market, and to the measuring and metering of goods and activities.[4] The bottom line is that it is expensive to run an efficient, modern economy. It takes money to make money.

The costs involved in this sector of transactions are near-impossible to define with any precision. But Wallis and North (1986) present two arguments to suggest that transaction costs represent sizeable sums for a modern state. First, they claim that in the United States between 1870 and 1970 an annual average of about forty-five per cent of the national income was devoted to transacting. Second, they found that the percentage increased steadily over time – it amounted to well below half of the US national income in 1870 and to well above half a century later.

A hypothesis about the decline of hegemonic great powers could be inferred from this argument: that is, that the transaction costs of hegemons would be relatively low during the phase of hegemony, for this phase is characterized by social consensus and harmony. However, transaction costs would be comparatively higher during the phases of challenge and competitive disruption, for these phases are characterized by long-term increases in diversity, strife and social conflict so that more social wealth would have to be expended to ensure social order.

Transaction costs, cosmopolitan spheres and interstate peace

From one point of view, this argument is consistent with the basic zero-sum distinction which Kennedy and Gilpin draw between productive and unproductive investment. Thus, an orthodox liberal claim could be made that if substantial proportions of the state's resources are expended on military affairs, on consumption or on transactions (or on all three), then resources are drawn away from wealth creation and are likely to weaken the national power base over the longer term.

From another point of view, the concept of 'transaction costs' could give rise to a more complex argument. For transaction costs are intimately associated with the elusive qualities of social consensus and public trust. First, in economic theory – as noted above – a modern market is a meeting place for the purposes of barter and buying and selling; it is the product of an incalculable number of single transactions, each of which is an individual, voluntary act. In political practice, however, market transactions are embedded in social relations. The significance of this larger social context becomes obvious when one realizes that transactions only rarely consist of the simultaneous exchange of items of known equivalent value. In modern markets, the operations involved in exchange are often separated in time; this implies that whoever hands over his assets first must somehow trust the recipient to reciprocate in due course. In addition, advanced markets are usually opaque, so that economic activities include transactions in goods and services of uncertain value; this means that each transacting party must trust other parties to tell the truth about the quality of that which is offered.

Second, intimately associated with this complex economic interaction which describes a civil economy is the complex web of cultural and political interactions of civil society. These interactions constitute the core of a society's public sphere. Citizens of hegemonic states – knowledgeable and trusting members of relatively open and tolerant societies marked by a dynamic market economy – enjoy the greatest extent of freedom that the age can offer. They discuss the cultural and literary scene of the day. They debate social issues. They assess the performance of the economy. They criticize the practice of the state. And during the course of these activities, they constitute the most elaborate public sphere of the age through their sustained communicative interaction.

The point which needs to be stressed here is that the hegemon is the most open society of its day. This point helps illuminate several aspects of hegemony. First, openness tends to reduce the effects of established cliques and special-interest groups; it allows some measure of élite circulation, advancement for meritorious personnel and better political leadership. Second, more open societies allow a freer flow of information to citizens and decision-makers alike. Third, openness (together with the generally accepted notions of rights, liberties and tolerance which sustain it) is a main condition for the advent of a public sphere. Finally, this (by definition open) public sphere cannot be confined within the physical boundaries of a single open society. Hence, the public sphere of one open country will overlap with the public spheres of others. Together, several (adjacent) open societies will contribute to the formation of a transnational *publicum*. Citizens of open societies who interact across the boundaries of their respective states will contribute to the formation of a larger transnational or cosmopolitan public sphere. This notion of a cosmopolitan sphere of public communication helps explain the cultural influences which are peculiar to hegemons.

This cosmopolitan public sphere is a creation of open and tolerant societies, and the hegemon is the most open and tolerant society of its age. The enlightened citizens of open societies enjoy (comparatively high levels of) freedom of speech, association and movement. They interact routinely with foreigners. They read each others' books, magazines, journals and papers. They trade and travel. They exchange information on business and share knowledge in matters of scholarship and science. They discuss and argue. And among open societies, these activities can be maintained across state boundaries – as exemplified by the remarkably free stream of books and papers from Spain to the New World throughout the sixteenth century (Leonard 1992) or by the early seventeenth-century English-language newssheets which were printed in Amsterdam (and based on news from Dutch *corantos*) and sold in England.[5]

With this notion of a cosmopolitan *publicum* as their vantage point, several social philosophers developed valuable theories of democratic politics and international interaction. During the 1600s, Mathias de Saint Jean argued that common secular concerns unified the commercial classes of Europe into a distinct transnational force, and Pierre Bayle developed his notion of an 'international republic of letters'. Today, the most famous of these early cosmopolitan arguments is undoubtedly Immanuel Kant's vision of a 'universal community' and of 'cosmopolitan rights'. Kant (1991a[1784], 1991b[1793]) claimed most forcefully that the informed interaction between citizens across the boundaries of open states would produce an intersubjective consensus that would bind the citizens of these states together in a common programme embodied in a shared respect for international and cosmopolitan law. As several such states developed tight relations with each other, they would come to share a common public sphere informed by a self-sustaining, cosmopolitan code of norms.[6] Even Kant seems to assume that such a code is to a significant degree initiated and shaped by some pre-eminent state or hegemon.

The hegemonic phase of world order, then, is characterized by a concentration of power in the hands of a pre-eminent strong state/great power. In theory, the hegemonic constellation constitutes an anarchic system of states. But in practice, hegemony lacks some of the characteristic features of the anarchic condition. The hegemonic condition is a unipolar configuration, and may thus have more in common with a hierarchical than with an anarchical structure.[7] It lacks balance-of-power properties, yet it displays a remarkably stable order. Why don't the other great powers in the system produce an alliance of states bent on counterbalancing the pre-eminence of the hegemon? The answer lies in the extraordinary cosmopolitan consensus about basic human rights and social freedoms. States which contribute to this common cosmopolitan sphere share values and norms. They share certain understandings and expectations regarding interstate behaviour. The existence of such common expectations is a force for peaceful interaction (Deutsch *et al.* 1957). Strong, cosmopolitan states do not submit to any common supreme authority. Yet it would be a misnomer to call their interaction anarchic (Jeppeson 1996). Strong states which are members of a cosmopolitan public sphere which allows their citizens freely to cultivate common sets of values and norms, and thus develop a common identity and common interests, do not wage war on each other.

Concluding remarks

The hegemonic condition is characterized by the absence of war between strong states which belong to the same cosmopolitan public sphere. It does not mean the absence of interstate competition. Clearly, competition occurs; but it does not assume the form of a balance-of-power system, and it does not erupt into war. Rather than engaging in a balance-of-power play, the members of the cosmopolitan sphere adopt a game of catch-up. The hegemon plays the central role in the game. It is the pre-eminence of the hegemon which stimulates other states to try to catch up (Taylor 1996). The climate of consensus, cohesion and trust allows the interstate system to assume a constructive rather than a destructive dynamic. Indeed, its competitive game of catch-up stimulates the weaker powers to emulate the institutions of the stronger. And this element of emulation greatly assists in disseminating the values, norms and institutions of the hegemon to new members of the system.

A clear instance of the hegemonic dynamic occurred in the wake of the Napoleonic Wars. Although some authors see the system which emerged in post-Napoleonic Europe as a balance-of-power system, it is more fruitful to see it as a hegemony. For when the many descriptions of this system are considered more closely, it becomes apparent that most balance-of-power authors agree that the post-Napoleonic system was based on a significant agreement as to the values, norms and rules of the interstate game (Gulick 1967, pp. 19ff; Schroeder 1996, pp. x, 578ff.). For this reason the system is commonly referred to as a 'concert'.

The consensual properties which characterized the post-Napoleonic concert are also found, in varying degrees, after other waves of great wars – they are found after the wars of Louis XIV (1672–1713), after the Thirty Years War (1618–48) and even, to some degree, after the Italian wars (1492–1529). All cases contain some traces of hegemony – but admittedly, to insist that the Iberian system was a good case of hegemony would stretch the term beyond endurance.

Several of the key preconditions for the postwar condition of hegemony were formed during wartime cooperation. The waves of great wars involved great powers with overlapping public spheres and shared knowledge, norms and expectations, who built coalitions against a common enemy. This effort involved

most of them in such close cooperation that common market institutions and a
shared (or cosmopolitan) public sphere emerged among them. These institutions
then allowed the consolidation of those common values, norms and rules for
international conduct that lie at the heart of the hegemonic condition.

The degree of postwar consensus – and hence the hegemonic condition –
grows more pronounced as modern history progresses. Thus, the Dutch world
order (which emerged from the Thirty Years War) was more pronounced than
the Spanish (which preceded it). The first British world order (which grew
from the wars of Louis XIV), was more pronounced than the Dutch; and the
second British world order (which developed out of the Napoleonic Wars) was
more pronounced than the first. As an extrapolation of this progressive trend,
it is tempting to propose that the world order which emerged in the twentieth
century (after the conclusion of World Wars I and II), would have to be the
most pronounced case of hegemony of all. Chapter 6, below, investigates this
proposition by discussing US military power, economic efficiency and American values, norms and mores after 1945.

It is tempting to conclude this section on a note of idealism. One of the
mechanisms which have disseminated the hegemon's norms to other open
actors on the world scene has been surprisingly overlooked in international
relations analysis. Hegemons have been respected and emulated not only for
their pre-eminent strength and their great wealth, but also for their high ideals
and their good example. Hegemons have stressed the universal application of
their values and striven to exemplify good and decent virtues – like freedom
of expression and association, collective security, honesty, fairness and
equality. The hegemons have articulated these values with great sincerity in
the immediate postwar years. And if it is an error of naïvety to assume that
hegemons strive to act in accordance with their ideals, then it is surely an error
of cynicism to dismiss this assumption out of hand and to attribute always
disingenuous motives to the Iberian rhetoric of Catholic morality, the Dutch
advocacy of free trade or the English justification of liberty.

This idealist argument is supported by the failure on the part of realist theory
to account for the absence of balance-of-power dynamics during the hegemonic
phase of world order. During the phase of hegemony, the international system
has been dominated by a hegemon – by a single great power which is militarily
strong, materially wealthy and normatively influential. In international affairs,
this great power has been unopposed; it has had no serious competitors. And
this lack of international opposition has been a peculiar feature of the hegemonic phase of world order. The interstate constellation during the phase
of hegemony has, for all practical purposes, been unipolar. Realist theory
would expect such a constellation to produce quickly an alliance of states bent
on counterbalancing such pre-eminence. This, however, has not materialized.

Instead, unipolar world orders have evolved which have been marked by extraordinary amounts of cooperation, cohesion, consensus and trust.

Secular trends in modern world history

This study has emphasized the similarities of the four complete modern world orders in order to identify some of the recurring patterns of international interaction. It should be noted that these four world orders also display striking differences, and that to overlook these may produce a distorted image of long-term world events. Any investigation of cyclical rhythms would be incomplete without an accompanying study of secular trends. For cyclical rhythms in history never occur in the same way twice. Historical events do not repeat themselves as identities but as analogies. To limber up the static cycle produced by a monotonous discussion of similarities among world orders, it is necessary to identify some of the systematic differences between them. Such an identification may flesh out some of the salient long-term structural trends that characterize modern history.

Remunerative trends

Two secular trends can easily be identified as blazing trails of modernity through the modern world economy: the expansion of commerce and the evolution of new economic institutions.

The first important trend can be noticed as early as the eleventh century and was associated with a fairly brisk rate of population increase (North and Thomas 1973). However, this medieval development was cut short by the Black Death around 1350. A more lasting development of trade and commerce began around 1450 and lasted through the 'long sixteenth century'. This sixteenth-century wave of commercial expansionism was stimulated by several factors. One of these was a demographic increase which led to a rise in agricultural prices and a decline in real wages. Another factor was the rapid growth in exploration, colonialism and long-distance trade and the growing interconnectedness in the world economy.

These factors were connected with new techniques and technologies – new shipbuilding techniques, the introduction of the lateen sail, new navigational techniques are among the most celebrated ones. The technological capabilities of states, then, are an important consideration in this expansion of commerce. As technologies of communications develop and spread, they greatly affect the conditions for interaction among states. A trade system which relies on small boats with broad sails will have a lower capacity for transport than one which uses flyboats (*fluiten*) or ocean steamers; a system which relies on horse-drawn carts will have a lower communication capacity than one which can employ railways for transport and wireless telegraphy for communications (Buzan *et al.* 1993, pp. 69ff.). Obviously, the world's interaction capacity has increased vastly during the course of modern history – a fact which has transformed global trade and world politics in fundamental ways.

The second important trend in the world economy was the proliferation of new institutions which served to reduce imperfections in trade and trans-actions and to cope with problems of financing and risk. Among the most commonly recognized of these institutions are the insurance companies, the joint stock companies, the finance networks and the national banks which emerged during the transition from the medieval to the modern world – first along the Mediterranean's northern shores and later along the Atlantic rim. These institutions emerged as the basic structures of feudal society were fading away and their emergence undoubtedly hastened the elimination of the vestiges of the feudal common-ownership structures (North 1990). The result of this growth was a more complex web of commodity chains, a more interconnected world and an increasing opaqueness of the world economy (Braudel 1977, pp. 52ff.).

Trading companies, banks, insurance firms and stock exchanges were the most conspicuous institutions of this modern world economy. However, there was also another decisive institution which attended this development: that is, the evolution of the modern territorial state. The state was the locus within whose protective boundaries these economic actors were allowed to grow and blossom. Indeed, in the beginning it was the state which was the most signifi-cant owner of capital and made the most significant investments in companies and banks. In the fragmented world of the feudal society, the manor or the walled city had been the major institution of defence, protection and order. But these social formations were vanquished by new military technology (the longbow, the crossbow, the pike and the gun) which steadily increased the optimal size of the most efficient military unit. During the course of the Italian wars, the city and the city-state were irrevocably superseded by the territorial state.

The advent of the territorial state was, in a backhanded way, another important stimulus to the expansion of long-distance trade. First, in order to survive the competition with increasingly efficient weapons systems, the head of state needed to obtain greater fiscal revenues than he could get from tradi-tional feudal sources. He turned to exploration, colonialism and long-distance trade which promised to bring new kinds of revenue. Second, whereas the feudal manor had been unable to provide much protection for overseas ventures and long-distance trade, the new territorial states were capable of creating navies which could shelter more effectively the profitable routes of overseas commerce.

During the long sixteenth century, an increase in long-distance trade became an overriding concern of every monarch along the Atlantic rim. Through their shifting intrigues, coalitions, agreements, betrayals and renegotiations, they wove a tangled web of interstate diplomacy. The pre-eminent state of the system was decided upon by the strength which its head of state could exert in claiming the monopoly powers of government – which in turn left an imprint on the structure of the developing economy. In the fifteenth and sixteenth centuries, in the emergent territorial state of Spain, the head of state was a powerful monarch who gradually wrested power away from feudal bodies and developed a system (and level) of taxation which promoted local and regional monopolies. Royal monopolies stifled Iberian innovation and factor mobility, and in the longer run this led to a relative decline in the productive activities of the country.

In the sixteenth and seventeenth centuries, institutions developed around the fog belt of the English Channel. The United Provinces developed political structures which were controlled by an oligarchy of merchants; and the con-solidated kingdom of England, after years of strife, developed structures in which Parliament gained ascendancy over the Crown. On both sides of the Channel, these developments were attended by the growth of economic institu-tions which helped reduce imperfections in product and capital markets. These institutions possessed a flexibility and an adaptive nature which ensured that productivity increases were built into the system of the United Provinces and England. By the eighteenth century, these institutions were transferred to the New World as well. And over the next century, these institutions would induce a revolution in technology which gradually spread from the Atlantic rim over much of the rest of Europe and North America and helped weave the world into a web of complex interdependence. This development was noted by Norman Angell (1909) who hailed it as a force of world order and peace. It was later probed during the 1920s and 1930s, e.g. by Ramsay Muir who noted (with a nod to Immanuel Kant):

> If the interdependence of all people can be rightly used, it can bring an unimagined prosperity to the whole human race ... On the other hand, if interdependence is not rightly understood and used, it threatens a ruin more terrible than could ever have befallen mankind in the days of isolated and self-sufficient social units. The peoples of the earth are like climbers roped together on a rock-face, struggling to reach a summit from which a glorious vista will be revealed. If any of them start playing the fool, or acting as if the rope did not exist, the whole train may be precipitated into the abyss. (Muir 1933, pp. 27f.)

Punitive trends

This long-term macro-economic trend has been attended by two trends which mark the development of modern macro-politics: the growth of armed forces and their increasing lethality. First, it can be observed that the size of armies and navies has grown from one great war to the next. The mercenary armies of the sixteenth century rarely exceeded 25,000 men. When armies began to be nationalized in the seventeenth century, they sometimes counted 50,000 men. The growth continued through the eighteenth century: Marlborough and Frederick the Great commanded armies of up to 90,000 men; and, around the turn of the century, Napoleon had as many as 200,000 men in certain battles – and at times he may have had a million men mobilized (or 5 per cent of the French population). After 1815, a long period of relative peace occasioned some diminution in the size of armies; but after 1870, there was a strong and steady growth in the size (and cost) of military forces.

Second, the lethality of war has risen dramatically during the course of modern history. Weapons systems have steadily increased in range, accuracy, penetrability, mobility and volume of fire. Assisted by the greater speed and efficiency of military transport and communications systems, warfare has grown steadily more destructive (and costly). The lethality has grown at a particularly rapid pace since the industrial revolutions of the nineteenth century.

These two punitive trends of modern interstate history – increasing size and lethality of weapons systems – have been balanced by a third trend: viz., that major wars have grown less and less frequent.[8] Thus, although the effects of weapons systems have been increasingly destructive, these systems have been used with declining frequency over time. These two trends may, if rightly understood and properly managed, bring about an unimagined era of order and peace to the human race. However, if misunderstood and ill-used, they may bring about ruin. Immanuel Kant sensed both scenarios already in the 1780s, and he opted for the more optimistic of the options. He argued that as the destructive capabilities of weapons grow, the costs of war increase and the belligerency of modern statesmen and generals becomes progressively restrained. In the end, he claimed, the distress produced by wars would finally lead the advanced states of the world to develop a common set of rules and laws intended to maintain a general peace (Kant 1991a[1784]).

Normative trends

Kant claimed that republics would not fight against each other. States which allowed free expression of the popular will would contribute to a zone of peace in the world, he argued (1991b[1793]). Here, Kant captured two normative trends which blaze through modern Western history: individuation and secularization.

The emergence of individuation in the Western world is expressed in expanding respect for individual liberty and tolerance. Although it is often claimed that sixteenth-century Iberia was a society marked by ethnic pluralism and a high degree of tolerance, it would amount to quite a challenge to find much evidence of modern liberties in Spain at the time of the Inquisition. The United Provinces, however, possessed a remarkable degree of individual freedom. It was first manifested in the religious realm, but was soon extended to other spheres – a firm faith in the Christian values of humility, equality and modesty sustained social practices of freedom and tolerance (Rowen 1972, pp. 47ff., 127ff.). Similar practices were instituted in England after the Glorious Revolution. In the seventeenth, eighteenth and nineteenth centuries, the United Provinces and England were tolerant havens for religious and ethnic minorities who were persecuted elsewhere.

The secularization of human thought and theorizing is expressed in a steady evolution away from religion as a reservoir of universal norms and rules of behaviour towards greater reliance on human reason. However, this change is not easy to assess since it always involves a change of form but not necessarily a change in content – i.e., the fade-out of religious argument may not necessarily lead to a decline in moral principles. The secularizing trend can be observed in rulers' efforts to justify their policies as well as in citizens' notions of the community to which they belong. Rulers have sought to legitimize their claim to world leadership by appealing to universal values. In the early modern ages, these appeals were predominantly religious in nature – as when Charles V and Philip II regularly justified Habsburg foreign-policy actions by reference to Christian norms and the will of God. Such justifications reverberate through the foreign-policy discourse of the Dutch and the English as well. However, theological references have steadily declined in importance over time. Christian norms and values never entirely left the political discourse of the great powers, but they were, in the course of time, overtaken by more secular doctrines of power, wealth and universal rights.

The secularizing trend is also reflected in the development of new, more general narratives of identity. In the early modern period, religion was an important aspect of social identity; in later times, secular arguments grew more pervasive. As religion slowly relaxed its grip during the course of modern history (and as appeals to secular rights and liberties increased), the identity of citizens was increasingly attached to the territory and to the institutions of the state. The presence of religion was evident in the collective identity of sixteenth-century Spain – the loyalty of Charles V was tied to universal Christendom and to the Habsburg dynasty. In the seventeenth century, the United Provinces expressed a very different kind of collective identity where individual liberties, Protestant ideals and provincial autonomy were intertwined into one pervasive patriotic package. Similarly, in the eighteenth and nineteenth centuries, England's identity was tied to principles of personal dignity, individual liberty and political equality. 'These notions were primary in the definition of English nationhood. The casting away of the religious idiom did not change the principles, but only laid them bare', writes Liah Greenfeld (1992):

> Men were still believed to have reason because they were created in the image of God; the requirements of their equality and liberty, therefore, derived from the act of creation. But it was the pride in man's reason and not reverence for its source which inspired people like Milton after the Civil War; the right of the individual conscience, the liberty of man, the autonomy of a rational being were advocated for their own sake, as supreme values. These ideas were in no way peculiarly English and did not originate in England. Yet in England they were able to become the content of the people's very identity, and therefore rooted so firmly in the consciousness, both individual and collective, and the culture as to transform the social terrain which nurtured them itself. (Greenfeld 1992, p. 86)

With the comparative discussion of great powers *in mente*, it is tempting to agree with Greenfeld that the growth of a secular, collective identity is the most consequential normative trend in modern international history.[9] For, as noted above, the hegemons discussed here are strong, well functioning states – as well as strong powers (Buzan 1991, p. 98). Each possessed a territorial base and an efficient government which maintained order within its territory; in addition, each hegemon enjoyed a high degree of integration between government and society and a certain degree of moral cohesion – two factors which are institutional expressions of an affective idea of a national community. This idea of a community can be seen as a precondition for a collective identity and cohesion, for social trust, economic productivity and a strong state – which, in turn, constitutes the protective framework within which all the essential institutions of modernity can emerge and evolve.

In addition, this idea of a national identity is intimately associated with one of the most important concepts of the modern political world: that is, the notion of democracy. The core idea of nationalism (that every nation must find its proper expression as a sovereign state) lies very close to the core idea of democracy (that the will of the nation must be reflected in the will and the behaviour of the state). National identity and democracy are twins of modernity. Furthermore, both of them presuppose a public sphere. They presuppose a realm of social life within which a common identity – an 'imagined community' (Anderson 1983) – and a public opinion can be formed.

A collective national identity, embedded in society's 'public sphere', is an important feature of every modern hegemon discussed here. Unmistakable foreshadowings of a public sphere can be observed in urban centres of sixteenth-century Iberia. However, a more extensive, elaborate and characteristically modern sphere evolved in the civil society of the United Provinces. The rational attitudes, the individualist spirit, the high level of literacy and the high rate of political participation which are associated with the modern bourgeoisie were conspicuously present in seventeenth-century Dutch society (Smith 1984; Taylor 1996). This development came into its own in England where the values which sustained the smooth working of the public sphere – personal dignity, individual liberty and political equality – became tied to the definition of English nationhood (Greenfeld 1992). From there, these values, and the public sphere within which they thrived, were exported to the rest of the world.

Cycles, trends and the future of international relations

Four world orders can be distinguished through the history of modern international relations. Each order emerged from a wave of great wars. Each order evolved through a three-phase cycle – hegemony, challenge and competitive disruption. Historical cycles, however, do not repeat mechanically. Historical cycles are not mechanical in the sense that they return to an equilibrium point.

Historical cycles repeat themselves as analogies rather than identities. And the major reason for that is that historical rhythms occur within a larger setting which moves along secular trends. These trends affect the historical rhythms in ways which allow variations on the core themes of the world order cycle. And over time, these variations are removed from the characteristic themes of the rhythms.

Does this long-term effect of secular trends mean that the periodicities of world order cycles should be envisioned as a spiral movement rather than a repeating cycle? Or does it mean that the sustained forces of secular trends sooner or later push the historical rhythms beyond the core characteristics of the world order cycle and thereby break it? A discussion of the twentieth-century world order may help to illuminate these questions.

The twentieth-century world order has been championed by the United States – a single great power which has also been the predominant military power of the postwar world, the primary architect of the international economic order and the pre-eminent normative influence of the age. Has the United States, by virtue of its pre-eminence in punitive, remunerative and normative capabilities, been the hegemon of a fifth world order cycle? Or have the secular trends of modern history – most notably the increasing lethality of weapons systems, the growing interdependence of states and the internationalization of the public sphere – bent the rhythms of world order so far out of shape that they are no longer recognizable as characteristic phases of a world order cycle? Is the United States the ultimate hegemon? Or is the modern world order cycle broken?

Notes

1 The importance of social capital has been reiterated in studies of regional development in urban Europe in the 1970s and 1980s (see e.g. the celebrated study by Putnam 1993) and by development in rural Tanzania in the 1990s (cf. World Bank 1997, p. 115).

2 One clear discussion of this is found in Knorr (1973) who set out to identify all the constituent resources conferring power on states in international relations. In the end, he had to acknowledge that possession of resources was only part of the story; that even the most generous endowment of resources does not automatically translate into power and influence. Similar discussions are found e.g. in Hoffmann (1968), who likened the United States to a tied-up Gulliver rather than a master with free hands, and in Waltz (1979), who warned against confusing the use of power with its usefulness.

3 This point is elaborated by Barry Buzan (1991) who distinguishes between strong states and strong powers. The notion of a strong *state* refers to the degree of socio-economic cohesion which a state enjoys; the notion of a strong *power*, by contrast, refers to a state's material capabilities (to its means of military force and its wealth-creating abilities). 'Strength as a state neither depends on, nor correlates with, power', writes Buzan (1991, p. 98). Thus, there are many weak powers which are strong states – he mentions the late twentieth-century examples of Austria, Norway and Singapore. Conversely, there are many strong powers which have serious weaknesses as states – the Soviet Union during the 1980s may serve as a notorious example. As my study argues, and as the simple taxonomy below in Figure 3 suggests, hegemons are invariably strong powers as well as strong states.

		Power	
		strong	weak
States	strong	Spain, United Provinces and England as hegemons	[1750s Geneva] [1850s Iceland] [1950s Norway]
	weak	[1770s France] [1980s USSR]	[1980s Yugoslavia] [1990s Somalia]

Figure 3   *Hegemons as strong powers and strong states*

4 Several authors have contributed to this argument since Ronald Coase raised the issue in 1960. The present account draws heavily on the works of Douglass C. North – see e.g. North (1981, pp. 18f.; 1990, pp. 55ff.).

5 For a fascinating discussion of the freedom of the press in sixteenth-century Spain, see e.g. Leonard (1992, especially ch. 7). For an exploration of the influence of Dutch *corantos* on early English newspapers, see e.g. Dahl (1949), who shows that, even when printed in London, the English news-sheets drew heavily upon Dutch *coranto* material – as was recognized in a Ben Johnson play, Amsterdam was the Staple of News for the English public. By Dahl's account, some 60 per cent to 70 per cent of the news material in the English periodical press originated from the Netherlands, especially from Amsterdam, between 1622 and 1632.

6 Three points are worth mentioning. First, that Kant's argument includes a notion fairly similar to the concept of hegemonic power expressed here: cf., e.g., the following claim in Kant's famous essay on 'Perpetual Peace':

> if by good fortune one powerful and enlightened nation can form a republic (which is by nature inclined to seek perpetual peace), this will provide a focal point for federal association among other states. These will join up with the first one, thus securing the freedom of each state in accordance with the idea of international right, and the whole will gradually spread further and further by a series of alliances of this kind. (Kant 1991b[1793], p. 104)

Also, Kant's argument is complex, and only one facet of it is represented here. A fuller presentation of his argument must at the very least include a discussion of his 'Definitive Articles of a Perpetual Peace' (which, in addition to embracing a common code of cosmopolitan rights, also include factors like republican systems of political representation, freedom of travel, universal hospitality and transnational interdependence (see e.g. Kant 1991b[1793], pp. 98ff.).

Finally, arguments of a comparable thrust are more recently expressed e.g. by Kratochwil (1989), Ruggie (1993), Wendt (1994), Rengger (1997) and others.

7 It is a key claim in the neo-realist approach to international relations that the organizing principle of an international system is *either* an anarchical *or* a hierarchical structure. This dichotomous insistence has met opposition e.g. from Adam Watson, who develops an argument which resembles the claim submitted here. Watson (1992, pp. 14ff.) proposes that international history has ranged across a broad range of organizing structures with anarchy at one end, empire at the other and hegemony, suzerainty and dominion in between. It should be added that Buzan and Little (1996, p. 424) use the neo-realist dichotomy, but are open to the inclusion of other structures of organization. Deudney (1995) identifies what he calls a 'Philadelphian System' – an allusion to the concert created in America when the thirteen colonies broke away from Britain.

8 This development is reflected in Table 18 below, which shows that the average frequency of great-power wars in the nineteenth century was less than one-fifth of the average frequency in the sixteenth:

Table 18 *Average frequency of great-power wars*
in modern history, 1500–1900

Century	Average frequency of wars per decade
sixteenth	2.6
seventeenth	1.7
eighteenth	1.0
nineteenth	0.5

Source: Wright (1965, p. 651)

9 However, yielding to this temptation would stand the common understanding of nationalism on its head – it would replace the orthodox view of 'nationalism' as an outcome of modernity with the claim that modernity is better seen as a consequence of nationality.

Part Two
Déjà vu

6

Wars to end all wars

'Toto, I have the feeling we are not in Kansas any more'.
(Dorothy in *The Wizard of Oz*)

Industrialism, nationalism and imperialism undermined the old nineteenth-century order. These forces fuelled state rivalries and contributed to the nervous great power relations of turn-of-the-century diplomacy. These restless forces had a peculiar effect in the American hemisphere. They were chipping away at America's traditional isolationism and setting the nation on the road to global greatness.

The United States was the power with the fastest pace and the greatest possibilities for expansion. No other power could rival the United States in terms of vastness of territories, richness of natural resources and popular energies. Also, no other power could show such rapid demographic growth as the United States.[1] This remarkable rate of demographic growth did not undermine the American economy; it stimulated it. The industrial growth profited from unique circumstances: unlimited land, cheap labour and the absence of traditional privileges and impediments – the United States had no quaint aristocracy, no medieval guild system and no strong, modern union system. The enormous resources available, the steady supply of labour, the vast domestic market, no labour parties to affect capitalists' dispositions, contributed to a rapid economic growth.

The demographic growth also fuelled a remarkable territorial expansion. The Alleghenies were an initial barrier. But once they had been crossed in the early 1800s, adventurers and settlers swept across the great western plains. More than any other single power, the USA was destined to become not only a great power, but the greatest power of all. However, the United States neither understood nor accepted this destiny. Its foreign policy wobbled between the principle of isolation on the one hand and the dream of empire on the other.

Domestic upheavals

In the past, the expansion of great powers and their rise to hegemony have been preceded by domestic upheavals – by great revolts or revolutions which effected profound economic and political transformations of the rising nation. For Spain, it was the completion of the *reconquista*. In the United Provinces, it was the wars of liberation – the long, violent rebellion against Habsburg domination. For England, it was first the Civil War and the Glorious Revolution, and then the Industrial Revolution. The United States had its own great upheaval which occasioned a peculiar great, domestic transformation: the American Civil War.

The origins of the Civil War lie partly in northern industrialism and partly in western expansionism. Almost from the first decades of the American union these two great, irrevocable movements produced regular crises among the newest territories and states over the issue of slavery. Political bargains were repeatedly struck to balance slave states and free states, but all of them became unstuck after a short while. In the end, the slave-based plantation system of the south saw only one way to preserve its distinct socio-economic system and its cultural identity: to leave the Union. This act was justified in terms of traditional, British social contract philosophy: each state, it was argued in the south, had originally entered into the American Confederation on a voluntary basis; each state should therefore also be allowed to leave the Union voluntarily. The north disagreed! And President Lincoln observed that the USA was divided into states of liberty and states of slavery and, as he put it (echoing Mark 3:23–7), that a house so divided cannot stand. Lincoln was prepared to side with liberty against slavery, to defend the liberal policies of the northern states and to preserve the Union by armed force. The result of this conflict exploded in one of the bloodiest conflicts of modern history up to that time.

In the end, the industrial states in the north won the contest. And the victory was followed by significant economic and political reconstruction. After the Civil War, American industrial capital grew by leaps and bounds. It is this rapid economic development that Beard (1929) had in mind when he referred to it as 'the Second American Revolution'. But there is also a political side to the term: the Civil War was revolutionary also because it destroyed the confederate principles of Union and because the victorious north imposed upon the entire republic a new, federal structure informed by a new interpretation of the US Constitution. This decisive reform was largely the work of Abraham Lincoln. He left the old US Constitution unaltered. But he added amendments, and he encased it in a new interpretation.

Simply put, Lincoln taught the Americans to read the Constitution in light of Jefferson's preamble to the Declaration of Independence. This change may appear too subtle to be called a revolution. However, it effected a decisive conceptual change in American politics. First, Lincoln's reinterpretation introduced into constitutional argument a new emphasis on human equality.[2] It stated bluntly that no man is born a slave; it emphasized that negroes and whites are equally endowed by the Creator with inalienable Rights to Life, Liberty and the Pursuit of Happiness.

Second, Lincoln's reinterpretation destroyed the slave-based plantation system of the southern states and transformed the political economy of a substantial number of American states from the principles of plantation economy to that of agrobusiness. This transformation was carried out on northern premises. And the assassination of President Lincoln towards the end of the war contributed to its being carried out in a thorough and hard-handed fashion. Lincoln's sudden death on the eve of the southern surrender afforded the radical northern Republicans a chance to redesign the entire American republic in their own image.[3] During the course of a few fateful years, the northern reconstruction imposed upon the ruins of the vanquished south a liberal political economy based on wage labour, industrial growth and the vision of a self-regulating market. It created a new political structure which involved a more powerful and more decisive federal government whose main task was to guarantee the liberty and equality of all. It required a firmer, more modern and dynamic political structure based on the principle of federalism.

The effect of the northern victory was that the American states were forged into a greater federal unity. The Civil War created the *United* States. This unification had a mental aspect; during the reconstruction a northern, liberal–democratic, industrial culture was laid as a unifying veneer upon the regional differences of the new, great Union. During the final decades of the nineteenth century, this common culture was consolidated by several factors – among them were the rapid rise of standardized processes of production and the development of mass-produced consumer goods.

One important aspect of the emerging industrial culture was the growth of an urban, north-western mythology which produced an image of a common immigrant heritage and a common American destiny. This mythology was rooted in a great influx of 'new immigrants' from Southern and Eastern Europe (Italians, Poles, Hungarians, Czechs, Slovaks, Russians and Jews) to America's great industrial cities. The mythology, then, was predominantly a product of the great north-eastern cities. Here, society was portrayed as a 'colossal cauldron, a *pot-au-feu* or a melting pot' (Zangwill 1909) which efficiently converted the children of immigrants into Americans. In the north-eastern cities, waves of new immigrants arrived and blended into an increasingly complex multi-ethnic society. In the less urbanized, formerly confederate states of the south-east, the foundation myth of the 'melting pot' was far less applicable – here society remained ethnically segregated for nearly another century.

Foreign wars

In the cases of the Spanish, the Dutch and (twice) the English, domestic upheaval was followed by global wars. And rather than exhausting these countries, the wars appeared to aid their consolidation and stimulate their growth. The United States is no exception. International wars stimulated the processes of American state-building after the Civil War and the reconstruction.

The first sign of serious foreign conflicts had already emerged in 1848, in the war against Mexico, and was followed by several armed incidents in both Central and South America. However, the Americans did not seem to count the conflicts with Central and South America as foreign entanglements – even though the Spanish–American war pulled both Cuba and Hawaii into the US sphere of influence and also saddled the United States with a commitment to defend the Philippines seven thousand miles off the Californian coast. The foreign affairs in Asia did not really count as foreign entanglements either.[4] But this isolationist attitude was dealt a fatal blow by World War I.

To most of Europe, war came as no surprise in 1914. To America, it came as a bolt from the blue. President Woodrow Wilson responded instinctively by pledging neutrality in the conflict. This stance reflected the popular sentiment of the nation – and during the presidential elections of 1916 he campaigned as the president who 'kept us out of war' and was re-elected to a second term.

But when Germany resumed its indiscriminate submarine warfare in the spring of 1917, Wilson saw no option but war. On 2 April 1917, he made a speech before Congress to ask for a declaration of war. In this speech, Wilson explained that Germany's unrestricted naval war was more than a crime against the United States, it violated the natural rights of all men and destroyed the very laws which civilized humanity lives by. It was an assault on liberty. His address was rewarded with tumultuous cheers from the audience.

Once committed to the Allied cause, the Americans went to work with their usual enormous energy. US industries began to build warships and weapons at a rapid rate. The US government began to register and draft young men and to train them for service. American sailors managed to rid the Atlantic of the German U-boat menace. US soldiers arrived in Europe at a time when the static horror of trench warfare was broken and a war of manoeuvre began – and the Americans began to arrive in March 1917, just in time to compensate for Russia's leaving the war. In April, 120,000 American 'doughboys' were shipped overseas; in May 250,000. By October, the American Expeditionary Force in France numbered over 1,750,000 men. The Americans comprised a jolly, singing army compared with the morose and mutinous troops of Europe. Their arrival strengthened the military might of the Allies and boosted their morale.

The war effort forced President Wilson to expand significantly the US foreign-policy establishment. He appointed talented outsiders to oversee the war effort and to advise him on foreign-policy problems. Some of these were business people of proven capacity. Others were intellectuals. All of them subscribed, like the president, to the ideals of free trade and the advancement of democracy, foreign aid, arms control and multinational cooperation for peace.

These liberal ideals informed the 'fourteen points' which Wilson announced in January 1918. It was the key document for the peace conference at Versailles and the basis for a new world order. The European delegates were not particularly receptive to Wilson's demands for open diplomacy, freedom of the seas, free movement of capital, disarmament and a general association of nations. Clemenceau, Lloyd George, Orlando and others raised objections which stalled the discussions and forced Wilson either to pull out of the negotiations or to compromise. To reach a settlement at all, Wilson felt compelled to give ground on his fourteen points. His demands for open covenants, increased freedom of the seas and reduced economic barriers were all diluted by the demands of European state leaders.

Many members of Congress argued that the conference and the treaty it produced were flawed. They resented the fact that Wilson's fourteen points were not acceptable to European leaders and they deplored the compromise Wilson had made. But this disagreement between state leaders merely reflected a deeper problem: i.e., that there existed no consensus between the great powers as to the basic rules of the postwar international game. Wilson's liberal ideals of free trade and multilateral cooperation may not have been appropriate for the postwar world. But neither were the realist recipes of the European statesmen: the traditional conditions of Europe's great-power equilibrium had been shattered by the War. Germany was smarting from defeat and infamy; the nation was bitter and unpredictable. Russia had been seized by an anti-systemic, Bolshevik regime which refused to help shore up the capitalist powers of Europe; Russia could no longer be counted on to counterbalance Germany.

The problems of the Versailles conference did not merely flow from the fact that a fundamental disagreement separated America from Europe; they also lay in the basic agreement of the two camps. American idealists and European realists, both, excluded Germany and Russia from the Versailles conference. As a result, neither Russia nor Germany was given any incentive to support a peace agreement which was made over their heads. Both nations were abundantly infused with anti-liberal sentiments. Both became anti-*status quo* powers. Both were among the most powerful states in Europe. And if war should break out again, one of them could be contained or defeated only if the other joined a liberal-democratic alliance with England and France as key members. And here, in this lack of consensus of the Versailles conference, lies the cruel dilemma of the postwar world order: in any war in which one of these two excluded powers joined, the liberal-democratic side could scarcely be fought to a complete and successful finish without placing this collaborating power in occupation of large parts of Eastern Europe. For Austria-Hungary and the Ottoman Empire had both been dissolved by World War I; and between Russia and Germany lay a motley collection of weak and wobbly states that had slim traditions in democratic politics, domestic stability and foreign-policy statesmanship.

The Versailles treaty was unviable. Indeed, it had all the tragedies of the future written into it. Some analysts identified its basic flaws spot-on. Keynes (1919) and Bainville (1920), for example, immediately captured the peculiar logic which flowed from World War I; and by drawing the economic and political consequences of this logic, they predicted with amazing accuracy the general course of the events which led up to World War II. And unless the United States was prepared to involve itself deeply and alter the entire postwar logic, US membership of the League would have made little difference. In the final account, the failure of the Versailles peace conference lies in the fact that it produced neither consensus nor equilibrium among the great powers.

Franklin D. Roosevelt was elected president in 1933. It is unclear whether he saw the Versailles conference in this critical light. However, it is abundantly obvious that he was aware early on of the storm clouds which gathered over Europe during his first term. He also realized that war in Europe was a serious threat to American interests and that, if war broke out among the great powers, then the United States could not avoid involvement. During his second term, an increasing number of Americans arrived at the same conclusion – by the spring of 1940, fifty per cent of Americans anticipated US involvement before long (Stein 1978, p. 31). As a result, a large share of American industry was quietly geared towards production of war material during the late 1930s. The US Air Force was created in 1939. A two-ocean navy was created in 1940. Peacetime conscription was enacted in 1940 and produced a trained army of 1.5 million soldiers before the end of the year. The United States and Britain cooperated secretly on radar and atomic research. The Lend–Lease policy, by which America aided the allies with war materials, began long before the USA entered the war – aid to Britain was authorized in March 1941; it was extended to China in April and to the USSR in September. Also, the United States occupied Iceland and Greenland in the summer of 1941, thus acquiring air and naval bases half-way across the Atlantic – half a year before the United States entered the war.

The Japanese attack on Pearl Harbor on 7 December 1941 blew away all remaining doubt about the US stance. The American nation united behind President Roosevelt and immediately declared war on Japan and Germany.

The declaration of war did not require any radical changes in America's economy, as in 1917. It merely required an acceleration of what was already under way. The draft was extended to include all men between 18 and 45 years of age; about ten million were thus induced into service. Four million men were transported to battlefields all over the globe.

The task which Wilson had tackled earlier, without success, was resumed by Roosevelt. Drawing on mistakes made in the interwar era, his administration laid the foundations of a new world order while the war was still in progress. The plans for a United Nations Organization were completed in San Francisco shortly before the capitulation of Hitler. Also, plans for an international economic regime were drawn up at a conference in Bretton Woods, New Hampshire, before the Japanese gave in.

War and material might

World wars hastened industrial expansion. Also, they breathed new life into the foundational mythology of the pre-eminent power and consolidated the patriotic pride and consensus of the nation. Like Spain, the United Provinces and (twice) England, the USA entered the waves of great wars with great dynamism and emerged from them some years later with a relative preponderance of punitive and remunerative power.

The outlook of the nation was changed by the wars. Its political institutions were greatly altered and its military capabilities had become second to none – this became particularly obvious in August 1945, when the United States ended World War II in Asia by dropping two atomic bombs on Japan. If World War I ended America's isolationism, World War II created the American hegemony. Much as the War of the Spanish Succession (1702–13) occasioned the rise of the first British hegemony, and the Napoleonic Wars fuelled the rise of the second, World Wars I and II made the United States a hegemonic actor in world politics.

Over 50,000 American lives were lost in World War I; nearly 300,000 were lost in World War II. These were light losses when compared with those of other states.[5] They were also light when considering the number of Americans who served in the wars. Nearly 5 million Americans served in World War I and about 15 million in World War II – or about 10 per cent of the entire US population.[6]

War and US economic growth

World War II was the costliest American war of the twentieth century. It cost the United States nearly $300 billion. The average annual cost of waging war was 93 per cent of the entire national income for 1940 – whereas the average annual cost of World War I was 44 per cent of the average national income of the years 1912–16. The two World Wars unleashed powers of unprecedented destruction and inflicted great damage on human lives and on material wealth. But since the United States joined late and since no battles were fought on American soil, the wars imposed fewer costs on the United States than on most other great powers. And when the momentous human sorrow of war is excepted from the equation, the wars brought great economic benefits to American society.

All the resources of the vast and diverse American society were mobilized for the purpose of victory. The mobilization for war suspended the market mechanisms on which the USA had traditionally relied. The market was replaced by principles of command for the duration of the war. The government became dictator over agriculture, industry and labour and harnessed the country's forced production by wartime central planning. In World War I, for example, an emergency fleet corporation was given unlimited powers to order, build, buy and operate ships. Similarly, a war industries board co-ordinated the entire field of American manufacturing; a labour administration regulated relations between capital and labour, fixed hours and wages in certain industries and banned strikes; a war finance corporation supervised the floating of security and underwrote loans to industries engaged in the production of war materials. During World War II, farming, mining, manufacturing, transport, finances and even science and education were brought under government controls. Old industries were enormously expanded, such as shipbuilding and aircraft manufacturing; and great new enterprises were created virtually overnight – notably in the manufacture of magnesium and synthetic rubber.

The extensive measures of state planning and government intervention which were effected during World War II were attended by full employment for the first time in years – indeed, the demand for labour was so high that women were integrated into the workforce for the duration of the war. Government intervention often stimulated private business. On the one hand, many of the tasks performed by this expanding federal structure depended on deliveries from private enterprises. Federal purchases of goods and services exploded during the wars.[7] On the other, mobilization for war involved the US government in the actual production of goods needed for the war effort. Huge sums of federal money were poured into the enlargement and construction of plants for war purposes. The country kept the gold standard. Inflation was kept at a minimum.

War and government growth

The increased rate of federal activity during the two World Wars reflected an expansion in the number of tasks undertaken by the government. The more tasks a government undertook, the more funds it needed to cover the expenditures associated with the greater scope of its activities. And the more employees it needed to make plans and decisions and to carry out its policies and programmes. During the two world wars, America's federal sector expanded immensely in size. Following the war, the federal sector contracted; but it always remained larger than it was before the war.

This pattern of expansion, contraction and expansion again is borne out by US budgetary statistics and by federal employment records. First of all, both World Wars were attended by significant increases in US government expenditures. During the years which preceded World War I, federal expenditures amounted to an annual average of less than 3 per cent of the country's GNP. During the course of World War I, the US federal budget increased to over 20 per cent of the GNP. As soon as the war was over, federal expenditure was reduced. However, it never dropped below an annual average of 6–7 per cent for the interwar years – which was twice the share of the pre-war period.

The reason why the federal expenditures did not drop to a lower level than this could be attributed to Roosevelt's efforts to combat the recession of the early 1930s.[8] But there is another phenomenon at work as well: preparations for war. For when the economic recession subsided, World War II was on its way. First, federal expenditures soared from the interwar average of 6–7 per cent of the GNP, via 22 per cent of the GNP in 1942, to 47 per cent in 1944. Then, when federal expenditure was cut after the war, it never dropped below 12–13 per cent of the GNP – twice the share before the war.

Second, the wartime growth of the American government is indicated by the increase in the number of federal employees. This increase was, obviously, most pronounced in the armed services. Before World War I, the United States entertained a remarkably small military force – it amounted to less than 200,000 men in 1914. But this doubled by 1917, and rose steeply to nearly 3 million men in 1918. This number was reduced by nine-tenths after the war, and counted less than 350,000 in 1938. When World War II broke out in Europe in 1939, the number increased. Slowly at first. Then it exploded to 5 million in 1942, reached 11 million men in 1944 with a climax of over 12 million in early 1945. When the war was over, military manpower was again reduced by nearly nine-tenths. However, the number rose again at the onset of the cold war, and fluctuated between 2 million and 4 million men during the 1950s and 1960s.[9]

Third, the wartime growth of the American state is indicated by a rapid growth in the size and the power of the executive branch of the US government. It is well known that during its period of isolationism, the United States had a minuscule military establishment. It is less appreciated that this vast nation had foreign-policy institutions of comparable modesty. When President Wilson declared war on Germany in 1917, the USA not only lacked experience in foreign affairs; it lacked the capacity! It is tempting to refer to prehistory for a suitable parallel to America's capacity for foreign-policy decision-making: to the giant dinosaur which possessed only a walnut-size brain.

The US Constitution is not specific on foreign-policy matters. Article I notes that Congress, among other functions, has the power to 'define and punish piracies and felonies committed on the high seas, and offences against the law of nations; to declare war ...; to raise and support armies ...; to provide and maintain a navy ...'. However, it does not specify the authority to proclaim neutrality, and it is silent on procedures concerning recognition of foreign governments. Article II of the Constitution states that 'the President shall be the Commander-in-Chief of the Army and Navy of the United States ... He shall have the power, by and with the advice and consent of the Senate, to make treaties ...'. However, it says nothing about the control of information and intelligence relevant to foreign-policy decision-making; nor does it mention the role of executive agreements in foreign affairs.

In previous wars the president had, as commander-in-chief, tended to take matters into his own hands and disposed of military resources to the extent that Congress's powers of appropriation would allow. Woodrow Wilson referred to precedents set by Abraham Lincoln and Theodore Roosevelt when he subsumed great foreign-policy-making powers during World War I.[10] For example, Wilson took it upon himself to declare that the USA would remain neutral in the war.

Roosevelt, too, usurped the authority he had as commander-in-chief, thus continuing the rapid twentieth-century growth of a strong executive power. After World War II, the growth of the president's powers continued, fed by cold war emergencies. During the 1950s and 1960s, the executive power of the United States would evolve into a bloated 'imperial presidency' (Schlesinger 1974).

Wars and nation-building

The United States was initially a reluctant member of a *status quo* alliance in the World Wars. America was, as in comparable cases in the past, situated at some distance from the battlefields; it joined the war effort late and only after great domestic debate.

Once a member of the *status quo* alliance, it tended to participate lightly in the warfare; instead it assumed a decisive economic role in the alliance. But when its wartime role was defined, the United States rapidly evolved into an important member of the wartime coalition by supplying its partners with moneys and materiel. This role allowed the United States – like the United Provinces and (twice) England in the past – to convert relatively few of its citizens into soldiers destined for death on faraway fields; instead, it set its citizens to work at home as labourers and engineers.

Like comparable cases in the past, the United States did not expend state funds on the purchase or manufacturing of arms; rather, the Americans converted their moneys into capital. The moneys were converted into industrial capital on the one hand – the investments in which served to improve tools and machinery, build appropriate infrastructure and systems of communications and to educate the workers. They were converted into finance capital on the other – they were given as loans to America's coalition partners in the expectation that they would be repaid when the war was over.

The World Wars also stimulated the growth of global infrastructures – international industries, international finance and communications – and of a postwar debt structure which allowed one distinct actor to dominate and shape the postwar world. By the end of World War II, the United States was wealthy and powerful. It had been welded into greater political unity. The war effort had stimulated an American world view which cast them in terms of a conflictual relationship between just and decent liberal democracies on the one hand and evil, belligerent totalitarian dictatorships on the other. The World Wars thus consolidated an American vision of a mortal struggle between 'us' and 'them' and unified the American nation in a common discourse of world affairs.

Also like previous cases, the World Wars created patriots. The mass mobilization of national resources enhanced the cultural and political consciousness of the victorious actors' citizenry. The protracted struggle against foreign enemies contributed in decisive ways to the spiritual unity of the victorious countries. This was complemented in the secular sphere by the war efforts' tendency to improve the national structures of administration and decision-making.

Forging a new world order

Wartime cooperation had infected America's democratic coalition partners with similar values and attitudes. At the very outset of the war, Roosevelt had sought to stimulate a coalition consensus; not just to smooth wartime cooperation, but also with a view to the postwar world order. Roosevelt wanted, like Wilson, to establish an international organization within which the various countries of the coalition could resolve their disagreements and grievances before they erupted in conflict and war. But, unlike Wilson, Roosevelt insisted on establishing this organization during the war.

According to Roosevelt, Wilson had made a big mistake by making the League of Nations part of the peace conference at Versailles in 1919. To avoid Wilson's failure, Roosevelt argued that his international organization should be firmly in place before the war ended and before any peace conference agenda was set up. Indeed, Roosevelt was so determined to avoid a repetition of Wilson's failure that he started to plan a new postwar organization even before the USA joined the war in December 1941. During the war he informed the members of his wartime coalition – which was formally referred to as 'the United Nations' – of his evolving plans. In autumn 1944, the US Department of State presented a plan for a United Nations Organization (UNO) at a meeting of diplomatic experts of the big four (the USA, the USSR, Great Britain and China) at Dumbarton Oaks. Discussions about the UNO continued at the Yalta conference between Roosevelt, Stalin and Churchill in February 1945. It was finalized at the United Nations Conference on International Organization which convened in San Francisco a few weeks after Roosevelt's death in the spring of 1945. The convention counted twenty-six states which drafted a UNO Charter. Its stated purpose was ambitious: to maintain international peace and security, to develop friendly relations among nations on the principle of equal rights and self-determination, and to encourage international cooperation in solving international economic, social, cultural and humanitarian problems (US Department of State 1985a[1945]).

Roosevelt also recognized another of Wilson's shortcomings: the former president had neglected the economic aspects of world affairs. World War I had been followed by a paralysing economic crisis. And part of the reason was, by Roosevelt's reckoning, that Wilson had failed to understand fully how the world economy, no less than the interstate system, needed to be managed by international organizations. Roosevelt maintained that a postwar regime which would prevent economic nationalism by fostering free international trade must be an integral part of a postwar regime designed to guarantee a lasting peace. With memories of the interwar recession, and the New Deal freshly in mind, they had already begun to draw up detailed blueprints for a stable, postwar economy during the first years of the war.

The US Department of the Treasury, in close cooperation with English diplomats and economists, drew up the design for a postwar regime of international finance in 1943 and 1944. The Americans and the English agreed that, in order to set the world economy on a sound footing after the war, it was essential to design a system of loans for postwar reconstruction and development that could replace the wartime Lend–Lease agreement. In July 1944, the United States arranged a United Nations Monetary and Financial Conference at Bretton Woods, New Hampshire. Here, representatives from forty-four nations met and drew up the final plans for an International Bank for Reconstruction and

Development (IBRD or 'World Bank') and an International Monetary Fund (IMF). The World Bank was conceived as a UNO agency which would help the war-torn states of Western Europe rebuild their economies. It would make long-term capital available to states which urgently needed loans for reconstruction and restructuring. The IMF was designed to facilitate international finance and trade; it would guarantee the convertibility of currencies, and fix and stabilize exchange rates; it would also finance short-order imbalances in international payments and thus stabilize the finances (and the currencies) of member states (US Department of State 1985b).

The American initiatives to establish the Bretton Woods system and the UNO were paralleled by US efforts to establish an international trade regime. In 1943 the Americans obtained from their allies support for a postwar commercial order based on the principles of free international trade. The US Department of State drew up a blueprint for an International Trade Organization (ITO) and hosted international conferences to assure agreement on the details. But the trade regime proved more controversial than the UNO and the Bretton Woods system. Negotiations were tortuous. No charter for a commercial regime was agreed upon before the war's end.

Conclusion

In 1945, the United States was more of a modern, unified state than at any other time in its independent history. Its economic system was highly informed by and integrated with its dominant domestic culture. Its government was stable and sustained by a degree of moral and cultural homogeneity which was remarkably high for such a diverse nation. Also, the United States was wealthy and strong. By the end of World War II, the United States was the strong leader of a victorious wartime coalition.

More than any other single factor, this coalition of the United Nations provided the mechanisms by means of which the United States evolved into a postwar hegemon. During wartime coalition diplomacy, the Americans gained the trust of their allies through cooperation and coordination. And in the process the Americans exerted a significant influence on the conditions of the postwar peace. If a moment needs to be identified at which the US pre-eminence formally came into its own, it was around the time of President Roosevelt's death.

First, Roosevelt had sponsored the development of the atomic bomb. For a handful of postwar years, the United States would have a monopoly of the most powerful weapon ever devised by humankind. And for nearly a quarter of a century after World War II, the United States would have nuclear stockpiles so much larger than anyone else's that the international order for all practical purposes described a unipolar system marked by a hierarchical structure.

Second, Roosevelt had, together with his primary allies, eagerly made preparations for a series of conferences which were designed to yield three sets of
institutions which would provide the bases for a liberal postwar world order.
First, there was the UNO – an updated and efficient League of Nations in which
the world's states could meet to present grievances, resolve conflicts and cooperate to isolate and punish aggressive states. Second there was an international
finance regime, with the International Monetary Fund and the International
Bank for Reconstruction and Development at its core. It would ensure loans to
rebuild Europe after the war, and ensure the convertibility of its currencies and
stabilize their exchange rates. Third, there was an international commercial
regime, with the International Trade Organization (ITO) as its centrepiece. It
was designed to encourage free trade among the nations of the world.

When President Roosevelt died, the UNO and the Bretton Woods system
were established. The ITO, however, was heading towards a more uncertain
future. By the end of the war, negotiations were still tortuous. A year after the
war, negotiations were grinding to a halt. Yet, all in all, two out of three was
no mean record. And they allowed the United States, like previous cases of
hegemony, to consolidate its pre-eminence just as the wave of great wars gave
way to the postwar era. When World War II was concluded, the Americans
enjoyed a monopoly of the most powerful weapons ever invented. They had
created an organizational framework within which international diplomacy
would play itself out in the postwar era. They wielded a significant authority
which cast world affairs in terms of a conflictual relationship between just and
decent democracies on the one hand and evil, belligerent totalitarian dictatorships on the other. After Roosevelt's death, the Soviet Union began to withdraw
from the United Nations coalition of anti-fascist states and to follow its own
course under the iron rule of Josef Stalin. Roosevelt's successors quickly consolidated a general perception of a mortal struggle between the just and decent
liberal democracies of the world on the one hand, and the evil, repressive
Communist dictatorships on the other. For nearly half a century, this vision
of a struggle between 'us' and 'them', between free states and slave states,
remained the basic definition of world affairs.

Notes

1 Stimulated partly by a relatively high birth rate, and partly by massive immigration, the number of inhabitants doubled from about 4 million in 1790 to just over
   8 million in 1814. It tripled from over 10 million in 1830 to over 30 million in
   1860. By 1880, the US counted 50 million inhabitants. By the end of the century
   this number had nearly doubled.
2 This *coup* is most famously apparent in Lincoln's Emancipation Proclamation (23
   July 1863) – 'an event more revolutionary in human relationships than any event

in American history since 1776' (Morison 1974, p. 435) – and in the Thirteenth
Constitutional Amendment (18 December 1865). Nowhere is this 'very American
coup' expressed more clearly than in Lincoln's Gettysburg Address – as is brilliantly advocated in Wills (1993).

3 The radical Republican Congressman Thaddeus Stevens exercised great power
   during a few fateful years after the war. He demanded a thorough reconstruction
   of the South. 'The foundations of their institutions both political, municipal, and
   social, *must* be broken up and *relaid*, or all our blood and treasure have been
   spent in vain. This can only be done by treating and holding them as a conquered
   people', Stevens maintained (Moore 1969, p. 144). Stevens was a skilful politician
   who cleverly exploited his chairmanship of the Ways and Means Committee and,
   later, the Appropriations Committee to further his stern cause. When he died in
   1868, enough of his radical agenda was implemented to dramatically alter the
   socio-economic structure of the South.

4 As Morison (1972, p. 53) notes, relations with the various Native American nations
   were more important to the government in Washington than relations with the
   nations of Europe. This is a priority which is reflected in the US defence budgets
   of the time.

5 Table 19 below allows one to compare the losses of the great Western powers in
   the two World Wars.

Table 19   Casualties in World Wars I and II

Country	WW I	(% of total)	WW II	(% of total)
Russia	1,800,000	9.0	20,000,000	50.0
Germany	1,700,000	8.5	3,500,000	8.7
France	1,400,000	7.0	200,000	0.5
UK	1,000,000	7.0	350,000	8.7
USA	53,000	0.3	291,000	0.7

Source: Morison 1972, p. 199; Palmer and Colton 1971, p. 907

6 Table 20 below shows the costs the two World Wars inflicted on the USA:

Table 20   Duration and cost of World Wars I and II for the USA

World War	Duration (months)	Casualties (deaths)	Personnel in svc	Casualty rate (in %)	Cost (bn $)
I	19	53,402	4,734,991	1.1	26
II	46	291,557	14,903,213	1.9	288

Sources: Stein (1978, pp. 34ff.); LaFeber (1989, p. 298)

7 Federal purchases of goods and services increased during the 1930s, but did not
   exceed 10 per cent of America's GNP before 1940. When the United States entered
   the war, federal purchases skyrocketed to over 40 per cent of GNP. After the war,
   the figure dropped steeply to well below 10%. For figures and sources, see Stein
   (1978, p. 58).

8 The crisis decreased the productivity of the nation (thus lowering the GNP in
   absolute terms) while government efforts to combat it expanded government
   action (and hiked federal budgets in absolute terms).

9 It deserves notice that the non-military sector of the US federal government shows a comparable pattern – although the fluctuations are not nearly as dramatic. During World War I, the number of civilian employees doubled – it grew from about 1 per cent of the total US labour force before the war to over 2 per cent during it. After 1918, the federal sector was reduced, and its share of the US labour force contracted to an average of 1.2 per cent for the years 1920–33. The next seven years saw a steady increase in the federal employment rate, reflecting the establishment of make-work programmes during the recession. In 1940 World War II brought a massive increase in the number of federal employees; it reached over 7 per cent of the civilian US labour force towards the end of the war. After 1945, the number of federal employees was, again, reduced. But it never again reached its old low level; it fluctuated between 3 and 4 per cent during the 1950s and 1960s (Stein p. 59, Figure 6-2).

10 Wilson was a professor of law and politics. He knew that the founding fathers were well acquainted with Locke's discussion 'Of Prerogative' – the critical exception to the democratic tone of his social contract.

7

Pax Americana

First we got the bomb and that was good,
'Cause we love peace and motherhood

Tom Lehrer

The United States emerged victorious from both World War I and World War II. Each victory gave fresh impetus to a distinct code of American values, tufted on the twin visions of free-market economics and of liberal democracy. And each victory improved the conditions under which American values, norms, rules and laws could take root. World War I pushed the old, European empires into collapse, replacing them with successor states which found their self-definition by either emulating or combating liberal American principles. The Austro-Hungarian and the Ottoman empires were fragmented by the war and new states were carved out of the ruins of Eastern Europe – most of these were established by Wilson's encouragement and largely according to liberal, American principles. The tsarist empire tottered on the cusp of collapse for a few years, until Lenin's Bolshevik Party miraculously reconstructed it into a Soviet empire which had a sharp, potent anti-capitalist, anti-liberal and anti-American orientation.

World War II destroyed anti-liberal warrior cults in Japan and Europe. The postwar world was subjected to the leadership of the United States and deeply affected by America's values and lifestyles. Democratic regimes and liberal economies were installed in Japan, Germany and other states. Liberalism was encouraged as a vital force in the postwar world.

However, the Soviet Union, with its Stalinist version of Marxism–Leninism, was a hold-out from the earlier age. The USSR, an empire more than a modern nation-state, emerged from World War II as the primary anti-American force in the postwar world – as America's antithesis, as the 'un-American', fearful 'other'.

On military pre-eminence

The US pre-eminence in the interstate system is well documented and needs no elaborate explication. It is sufficient to note that the United States emerged from World War II as a military giant. This was a new experience for America. For, measured in military might, the USA had never before been a great power.

During the World Wars, America's armed forces expanded rapidly. The US Army counted well over 12 million men by 1945. The US Navy had evolved into the biggest naval force in the world. The US Air Force had become the world's leading aviation force – the United States produced 297,000 aeroplanes during World War II; production for the US Air Force reached 95,000 planes during 1945 alone (more than America's chief enemies, Germany and Japan, combined). Also, by the time Germany surrendered in May 1945, the United States had a technological monopoly of the atomic bomb, the most powerful weapon ever made.

This rapid development of US military power is undoubtedly the most striking political change associated with America's rise to global predominance. In 1938, the United States had a defence budget of about $1 billion. During World War II, this amount increased a hundredfold. After the war it dropped steeply – to below $13 billion. But in the early 1950s it quadrupled under the impact of the Korean War.

In 1938, the United States had committed itself to no military alliances and no US troops were stationed on territory outside the Americas. By 1965, the US defence budget exceeded $100 billion, and the nation had military obligations confirmed by treaty with forty-three countries and equipment at 375 major bases and some 3,000 minor installations spread around the world. This remarkable expansion occurred at a different pace in different parts of the world. South America noticed little difference from previous decades. The USA had long considered this area its own sphere of influence; it had sought to minimize the influence of other powers there – even if it meant active intervention. After World War II, this engagement was not significantly altered.

The United States also had a long-standing interest in the Middle East. In the early decades of the century this was largely defined by US oil companies and focused on the Arab peninsula. By the late 1940s, however, these interests were defined by the US government and cast in more comprehensive, geostrategic terms (Yergin 1991). In 1947, the United States took over England's traditional role of opposing Russian expansionism through Turkey and Iran; when the English also abandoned Palestine, the US moved in to fill England's role there as well. In North Africa, too, American interests expanded after the war.

The US position in Asia and the Pacific had already been visible before the war. After 1945, it was considerably expanded. The United States assumed control over Japan and wielded decisive influence in South Korea and the Philippines. The US engagement in China escalated so rapidly that by 1946, 100,000 US soldiers were stationed there. In 1950 the US paid a high price to retain its influence in South Korea; also, the United States was increasingly financing the colonial war in Indochina which France was fighting (but which it could no longer afford). It was also a significant reflection of America's new status that both Australia and New Zealand shifted their geostrategic orientation towards the USA after World War II – they began to rely more heavily on their membership of US-led alliances and to turn away from their traditional cooperation with England.

But it was in the relationship with Europe that America's foreign policies underwent the most dramatic changes. The United States had intervened in two World Wars to prevent Europe from falling under sway of a hostile power. In the late 1940s, after a brief and intense domestic debate, the United States established a permanent presence in Europe. Spurred by the rising Soviet threat, the Americans formalized their new geostrategic commitment in a massive economic-aid programme and in the US-controlled North Atlantic Treaty Organization (Nato).

On economic pre-eminence

Military pre-eminence requires a strong economic base. The USA had a base strong enough to carry such a global commitment. The nation was richly endowed with a wide variety of natural resources. And the two World Wars had greatly stimulated America's ability to convert these resources into economic wealth and military might. During World War II alone, America's annual GNP growth was around 10 per cent – or about 50 per cent for the duration of the war.[1]

Much of this growth was spurred by vast wartime federal purchases of goods and services and by government-initiated production projects. The federal government spent well over $30 billion dollars on construction facilities during World War II. Some of it was invested in infrastructure which vastly improved communications after the war. Almost 15 billion of these government dollars were spent on the construction of war plants (as opposed to military installations). These plants were usually quite large – nearly one-third of them exceeded $50 million in value and nearly two-thirds exceeded $10 million.

During the war, the US government became the owner of emergency shipyards and of facilities for the manufacture of rubber, aluminium and a multitude of other products. They represented a valuable and lasting addition to the nation's industrial base. And when the war was over, these plants were sold – often cheap – to private entrepreneurs.[2]

Also, the US government had invested great sums in improving America's infrastructure during the war – bridges, railroads and roads. In 1942, for example, the so-called Industrial Expressway was built along the Great Lakes. It was designed to transport men and materiel between Detroit and the new bomber factory at Willow Run. By 1943, the Willow Run factory was producing one new B–24 bomber every hour, and expressway traffic was substantial. When the war ended, the Industrial Expressway had become the main artery of the world's greatest centre of high-technology manufacturing.

By the same token, the US government called upon universities and industrial research laboratories to develop new techniques, gadgets and inventions and for research. Such activities resulted in the development of such things as radar, sonar, the proximity fuse and the atomic bomb. They also laid the bases of America's computer revolution. Mathematicians, physicists and engineers were funded by the US Department of Defense to develop machines which could compute firing tables and ballistic trajectories with super speed.[3] War contracts, then, greatly hastened the first steps taken on the electronic road which would lead to a micro-electronic revolution – first in intelligence, cryptography and military computations and, then, in business machines, civilian computers and a worldwide web of electronic communications (like the Internet). In the process, such military-funded projects would greatly stimulate the rapid growth of US universities and laboratories – a trend that would continue into the postwar world.

The US economy was greatly stimulated by the World War. Wartime production, central planning and government initiatives started an economic boom which continued when the war was over. And most Americans obtained a share in it. The millions of homecoming soldiers were integrated into the expanding economy. Rather than becoming a burden on the labour market, the veterans represented a vast new consumer market. They wanted houses, cars and education. Their demands were transmitted through various veterans' organizations to the federal government which, in turn, made funds and university slots available. The boom was reinforced by full employment during the war. Since few goods were available for consumer purchase, much cash went into workers' savings accounts. After the war, as industry returned to peacetime production and began to pour out civilian goods, people had the money to buy them. The result was industrial growth and a rapidly rising standard of living. American prosperity became the wonder of the world. Encouraged by the sustained boom, moneylenders grew confident and bold. In the early 1950s, they began to lend former GIs the entire purchase price of houses, and most cars were bought with $100 down on three years' credit.

America's economic boom also affected other countries. US corporations like Singer, Bell, Standard Oil and many others already had large investments

abroad at the turn of the century. By World War I, US direct foreign investments amounted to around 7 per cent of America's GNP. After World War II,
America's international business grew further. It also changed in nature. The
postwar world saw the growth of a new and powerful form of international
business venture: the multinational corporation (MNC). In the 1950s and 1960s,
the world's largest and most influential MNCs were American. By extending
their markets, increasing their sales and absorbing smaller companies, they
obtained holdings in many countries and extended America's economic
influence across the world.

Franklin Roosevelt, like Woodrow Wilson, saw America's engagement in the
World War as a struggle to contain European-style militarism, imperialism and
exclusive trade blocs. America's aim, in both wars, was to preserve the conditions for a liberal world order – for a democratic system of politics and an
economic system based on free-market principles. Wilson and Roosevelt both
sought to liberalize world trade. And they both sought to use America's leading
position in world politics to bring other countries into line with America's
policy.

In order to ensure the smooth working of the liberal system on a world
scale, Roosevelt took the initiative to create international institutionalized
liberal values, rules and laws. The International Monetary Fund (IMF) and the
International Bank for Reconstruction and Development (IBRD or 'World
Bank') were created in the summer of 1944 to ensure a smooth-working,
market-based finance and trade system. The United Nations Organization
(UNO) was created a few months later to ensure a forum where the nation-
states of the world could openly discuss and solve their grievances.

When Europe faced a severe, economic crisis in the winter of 1946 and spring
of 1947, the US secretary of state George Marshall repeated that it was an
important American foreign-policy goal to produce 'a revival of a working
economy in the world so as to permit the emergence of political and social
conditions in which free institutions can exist'. Accordingly, the USA initiated
a magnanimous European Recovery Program (ERP or 'Marshall Plan'), which
helped reconstruct the market economies of Western Europe.

On normative pre-eminence

Before these arrangements are discussed, it is necessary to understand that the
United States has always seen the furthering of freedom as its special assign-
ment within the community of nations. This was strongly emphasized by
President Wilson who committed America to 'fight a war to end all wars', to
champion trade and 'the freedom of the seas' and to 'make the world safe for
democracy'.

When Alexis de Tocqueville visited the United States in 1831, he immediately sensed that 'freedom' was a key concept in the belief system of the young nation. He observed that Americans greatly valued individual liberty and tolerance. But he also noted that these two precepts were balanced in complicated ways – that liberty was restricted by conformity and by a 'tyranny of the majority' on the one hand, and that tolerance was tempered by 'great standardization of opinion' and respect for authority on the other. Beneath this complex, composite ideal of liberty, de Tocqueville found two beliefs which he held to be deeply ingrained in the American people: a deep belief in human equality and in popular sovereignty. These beliefs were the central precepts of America's political mythology. A century later Gunnar Myrdal made very similar observations about 'the strong common heritage' which informed the political ideals of America. These ideals, argued Myrdal (1944, p. 3) contributed to 'a strong unity in this nation and a basic homogeneity and stability in its valuations'.

De Tocqueville and Myrdal are not the only observers who have noted that although Americans tend to think of themselves as insistent individualists, American social life has also been marked by a strong tendency to form voluntary associations, durable organizations and cohesive communities. There exists a foundation mythology in the United States which has provided a considerable unifying force to this great and disparate nation and which has wielded a major influence on the everyday lives of American citizens. Among the central precepts in this mythology are values like individual liberty, human equality, popular sovereignty and private property. Alongside these individualistic values, expressed in America's political mythology, there has also existed a strong, unifying political culture, the main precepts of which have been rooted partly in a colonial heritage of British political philosophy, and partly in a reconstruction of this heritage in light of America's own, unique set of historical experiences. At the core of this heritage lies a universalistic, rights-based, natural-law philosophy.

The double paternity

The first thing to note about America's historical experience is that it includes not one but two beginnings. The first was the arrival of the pilgrims in the New World; the second was the making of the American Revolution. The United States, then, has two foundation mythologies; America has a double paternity: the 'Pilgrim Fathers' and the 'Founding Fathers'.[4]

A great many 'founding tales' could have been developed into a foundation mythology by the early Americans – after all, several settlements already existed in America when the 'Pilgrim Fathers' arrived on board the *Mayflower* in December 1629. However, among the many possible tales, it was the story of the pilgrims of Massachusetts which obtained mythological status and which made the deepest and most lasting imprint on the collective self-image of the new nation. The pilgrims of Massachusetts were a self-selected group of deeply religious people who fled from persecution in Europe. Their idea of a stern, Christian God has marked America. The Pilgrims (or 'Puritans') were, in fact, dissenters of the Calvinist persuasion, and this provides an important clue to the culture and the social values which informed their new society. First, the Calvinist faith made an indelible imprint on the moral code of the emerging nation through its emphasis on individualism. As Weber (1930) explained, the Calvinist doctrine implied an intensive individualistic set of social values.[5]

Second, the Calvinist faith of the first settlers shaped a unique Anglo-American advocacy of religious tolerance. It must be recalled that the dissenters were a persecuted religious minority back in England, and that tolerance and freedom of expression are values and demands characteristically entertained by any persecuted minority group. When the Puritans left Europe for the 'New World', it was natural that they sought to build a society informed by the principles of equality, tolerance, reason and liberty – values which they had always advocated.

Finally, the Calvinists entertained a vociferous opposition to the secular state. For in their experience back in England, government did not only repress individuals. More importantly, the government forced its citizens into religious conformity; and by so doing, it prevented their proper execution of religious sacraments. State-enforced conformity, in a word, represented the greatest of all threats: it endangered the souls of the true believers. It imperilled their salvation. Puritan advocacy of individual liberty and scepticism towards big government have remained strong features in US politics – although the original, religiously based fear of eschatological condemnation has long been replaced by secular argument. Yet, America's political mythology rests, to a degree which is commonly underestimated, on a secular inheritance of Puritan values.

Sorel (1950) and others insist that at the core of every political myth lies the vision of an important difference between 'us' and 'the other'. In America that difference was originally drawn between the new, pure community of the Puritan settlers – 'the City upon a hill' – and the corrupt ways of old Europe. This distinction was drawn clearly during the Revolutionary wars (1776–1781). These wars consolidated the American nation. They transformed colonial frontiersmen, backwoodsmen and pioneers into American 'minutemen' – patriotic soldiers who defeated the disciplined troops of the world's greatest military power. The regimentation and discipline of the British army, symbolized in its origins in a bureaucratic and centralized state conceived in sinful Europe, were precisely those characteristics that made it vulnerable to American scouts and backwoods marksmen who knew how to exploit the natural assets afforded by the wilderness. The strong, capable individual operating beyond the authority of any state – and certainly without the need of its assistance – became a staple item of America's foundational mythology.[6] The intrepid scout, the hardy pioneer, the struggling settler: they became *Americans* through the struggle against English colonialism.[7]

On one level, the American revolution represented a break with England and Europe. But on another, it very much embodied a continuity of the political doctrines of seventeenth-century England. The goal of the American revolution was a peculiarly conservative one. Rather than reject the political values of English society, it sought to defend them and to maintain 'the rights of Englishmen'. Consider the Declaration of Independence. This text, largely written by Thomas Jefferson, is one of the foundational documents of American politics. It specifies the conditions of America's political system in clear and precise social contract terms. Indeed, its first few sentences distil the conclusions of centuries of English liberal theorizing into a string of crystal-clear philosophical axioms:

> We hold these Truths to be self-evident, that all Men are created equal, that they are endowed by the Creator with certain inalienable Rights, that among these are Life, Liberty, and the Pursuit of Happiness – That to secure these Rights, Governments are instituted among Men, deriving their just powers from the Consent of the Governed, that whenever any Form of Government becomes destructive of these Ends, it is the Right of the People to alter or to abolish it, and to institute a new Government, laying its Foundation on such Principles, and organizing its powers in such Form, as to them shall seem most likely to effect their Safety and Happiness.

As is obvious in these lines, one of the most central concepts is that of a social contract. The idea of a ruleless state of nature, which is the conceptual vantage point of all social contract theories, coloured the many tales of the first settlers. Furthermore, the idea of a deliberately established compact, which lies at the heart of all contractarian reasoning, also informed the foundational mythology of the American revolution. It portrayed the establishment of the United States in terms of a series of congresses during the course of which representatives from thirteen American colonies, through long and rational deliberations, established a political community by the will and determination of the majority of a free, equal and independent people. Once united, they made a constitution which was designed to protect and preserve mankind's natural rights and to spell out clearly the natural law people should live by.

Echoes of natural-law philosophy

The individuals who justified US independence and laid the rafters of America's foundational mythology were heavily influenced by British contract philosophy – especially in its Lockean version. During the 1770s, John Locke was known in America for his theories of perception and his philosophy of knowledge. His political theories grew more influential after the American revolution. Then the political history of the new nation was increasingly read in light of Locke's *Second Treatise of Government* (1960[1688]). Through the early nineteenth century, America's key political texts were increasingly expressed in Lockean imagery – the most elemental visions of which include a 'state of nature' and the rational forging of a 'social contract'.

Locke's *Treatise* developed the concept of a state of nature – i.e., the idea that people once existed in a primitive, stateless condition of full and natural liberty in which they lived 'without a common Superior on Earth with Authority to judge between them' (Locke 1960[1688], p. 321).

Also, Locke drew a sharp distinction between this 'state of nature' and a 'state of war'. He insisted that statelessness did not mean lawlessness. In an assertion that suited the Puritan mind of the first immigrants, Locke claimed that there exists a God-given natural law which regulates the state of nature. According to this law, all men are created free and equal. They are endowed with reason and with natural rights – among which are the rights to life, liberty and property. The God-given law of nature is governed by reason. It tells all men to respect one anothers' natural rights. And since most men are rational, equal and compassionate they will be content to enjoy their natural rights and not 'harm another in his Life, Health, Liberty, or Possessions' (Locke 1960[1688], p. 311).

Finally, Locke elaborates the notion of a social contract – i.e., a collective agreement (or 'compact') among all men wherein they denounce their full, natural freedoms, identify the basic dictates of natural law, build a civil society according to these dictates, and promise to obey them. The purpose of this contract, Locke explains, is to guarantee men's 'comfortable, safe, and peaceful living one amongst other, in a secure Enjoyment of their Properties and a greater Security against any that are not of it' (Locke 1960[1688], pp. 374f.).

Concepts of social contract and natural law were very relevant for early American politicians and lawyers. Through Lockean lenses, the early Americans recognized the contours of their own fragile communities. They observed in the everyday life of American frontier towns individual men who were deficient in reason or compassion; men who disregarded the law of nature and who knowingly violated the rights of others by theft, extortion and murder. Such men, argued Locke, forfeit their natural rights. By committing acts of theft and murder, such persons would, in effect, set themselves outside the law of nature (which is governed by reason). By their own actions, they make themselves 'outlaws'. And any innocent and reasonable man can pursue and punish them. By the same token, innocent and reasonable men who are threatened by violators have the right to self-protection – i.e., man is endowed not only with natural rights to life, liberty and property; he is also given the right to protect and defend these rights. Such inferences were uniquely relevant for the pioneers and settlers in the western states of the expanding American nation.

The social contract philosophy of Locke and his followers not only shaped the American attitude towards domestic affairs, it also informed the approach to international politics. It deserves to be dwelled upon some more: early Americans tended to view relations among states as analogous to Locke's description of human relations in the state of nature. They assumed that relations among sovereign states are governed by natural law, and that this law obligates all states to respect one another's rights. This Lockean logic was succinctly expressed by Emmeric Vattell, whose book on *The Law of Nations* ('Droit des gens', 1758) early became the standard text on international law in the United States.

Until around 1900, most Americans shunned interstate politics, and sought to limit their external relations to economic transactions. They wished to remain aloof from the world. Few men in power questioned the simplistic belief that the United States would actually be left alone if it just made its intentions sufficiently clear.

The end of isolationism

Before 1885, American politics stopped at the water's edge; America's foreign policy was to have no foreign policy. But at the turn of the century, this attitude was becoming increasingly difficult. Industrialism and trade were interweaving states into interdependent relationships. Expansionism, imperialism and rising patriotic self-consciousness were steadily chipping away at America's traditional isolationism. Also, the unravelling of the second British world order exposed the Americans to world politics: throughout the nineteenth century, English naval power had in fact sustained an Atlantic regime which guaranteed American isolation. As this power began to waver, the United States found itself faced with some very unpleasant foreign-policy choices.

The policy of American isolationism was eroding. This was apparent when the US stock-market crash in 1873 triggered a panic which immediately swept the capitals of Europe. It was evinced in the debates which attended Mahan's proposal for a two-ocean navy. In the election of 1900 the nation divided over the consequences of the Spanish–American war which involved actions in the Caribbean and the Pacific.

World War I marked a watershed. It caught the United States unprepared, and President Wilson initially responded with instinctive references to traditional isolationism. He pledged neutrality and imagined that the United States could play the role of a neutral broker in Europe's suicidal conflict. But when his appeals to reason and education failed, he saw no option but war. On 2 April 1917, he made a speech before a joint session of Congress to ask for a declaration of war on Germany. Wilson's speech was cut from the cloth of the natural-law philosophy of Locke and Vattell: Germany's unrestricted naval warfare not only violated American property and destroyed American lives; such reckless behaviour violated the natural rights of *all* men. Germany had violated the natural laws which all humanity lives by. In order to protect these common laws of humanity, Wilson argued that it was America's duty to declare war on the leaders of the German nation. For they had violated the rights of others, and thereby forfeited their own natural rights and set themselves outside the law of nature. Thus, any reasonable state could pursue and punish them.

Wilson's declaration of war had two immediate consequences. First of all, it dealt America's liberal isolationism a mortal blow. Congress bought his Lockean natural-law argument. They agreed that Germany could not safely be allowed to coexist with democratic nations; that by so flagrantly violating the elementary rules of international conduct, Germany had set itself outside civilized world society; that countries which dutifully obeyed the rules of civilized politics had to be protected; that Germany had to be punished for its reckless transgressions. Wilson set the United States on a new course in world affairs. Tellingly, national defence was not a good enough cause of war for him. He had to justify the war with universalist references: to human rights, to the common rules of the global community and to the rights of nation-states. He committed the American people to a war for the noble cause of democracy.

Second, Congress accepted Wilson's proposal for a new world order, the centrepiece of which was to be an international organization designed to guarantee the rights of all rational, law-abiding states. The guarantee would take the form of an arrangement of collective security – a confederacy of states established 'in order to humble and chastise' any delinquent state which, as Vattell put it, made open profession of trampling justice, reason and natural law under foot (Vattell 1863[1758], p. 161). For Wilson as for Vattell, an aggressor against any one state must be considered an aggressor against all states, which must act together to repeal the aggression. To facilitate a coordinated campaign against an aggressor state, Wilson proposed to establish a League of Nations – a general association of states 'for the purpose of affording mutual guarantees of political independence and territorial integrity to great and small states alike' (Walworth 1969, p. 148).

Finally, World War I laid the foundations of America's national security

establishment. President Wilson expanded US foreign-policy institutions significantly. Bypassing the regular Cabinet, he appointed talented outsiders to
oversee the war effort and to advise him on a wide variety of foreign-policy
problems. Many of the overseers were businessmen of proven capacity – like
Bernard Baruch, Herbert Hoover and John McCloy. A surprising number of
the foreign-policy advisers were young intellectuals – recent graduates from
the Ivy League schools; members of a privileged group of talented, well-
travelled individuals who often commanded two or three foreign languages.
Young men who embraced the ideals of free trade and the advancement of
democracy, foreign aid, arms control and multinational cooperation for peace.

A substantial number of these young advisers subscribed to the fashionable
doctrine of 'new liberalism'. They shared with the 'old liberals' a strong faith
in Locke's endowment theory of human rights and his doctrine of human
reason. They also entertained a natural-law philosophy which expressed itself
in a vision of a harmonious social order based on trade and commerce and a
meliorist faith that people could be made free by means of reason and new
knowledge about political and economic structures. But they broke new ground
in American liberalism by advocating that government intervention was necessary to guarantee the equality and freedom of individuals. In domestic politics,
the new liberals advocated protection for workers, income transfers and the
expansion of voting rights. In foreign affairs, they defended free trade and
investment while abhorring imperialism; they advocated the advancement of
democracy, foreign aid, arms control and multinational institutions. At the
pinnacle of liberal belief in domestic affairs stood the trade union movement;
in foreign affairs, the League of Nations.[8]

When Wilson declared war on Germany, the new liberals embraced him.
And when he announced his intention to establish a League of Nations to
maintain peace after the war, they responded with elation. Some of them –
young men like Adolf Berle, David Bruce, James Forrestal, Robert Lovett and
Sumner Welles – could not join the US armed forces fast enough. Others were
eager to move to Washington, DC and use government institutions to improve
society at home and better the world into the bargain. By 1918 young men like
William Bullitt and John F. Dulles shared their intimate knowledge of Europe
with secretary of state Robert Lansing and presidential adviser Edward House.
The twenty-eight-year-old Walter Lippmann even briefed the president on
foreign-policy issues (Taft 1989, p. 7; Steel 1981, pp. 107ff.).

The new liberals insisted that the war which had started as a clash of empires
in the Balkans would dissolve into democratic revolution the world over. They
sought to seize the democratic momentum and impose a new order and a
lasting peace upon the world. In January 1918, Wilson announced 'fourteen
points' as a basis for such a new world order. His demands for open diplomacy,

freedom of the seas, the free movement of capital, disarmament and a League of Nations were influenced by America's new liberals. No wonder they received his proposals with acclamation.

The old state leaders of Europe, by contrast, were not at all receptive to Wilson's 'articles of faith'. They raised objections. They stalled the discussion and forced Wilson to compromise. To reach a settlement at all, Wilson gave ground on his fourteen points. The members of his delegation reacted with shock and disbelief. Some of them, like Walter Lippmann, resigned in anger; others stayed on to salvage as much of the remains as possible – William Bullitt stayed because he saw a need to protect the League and John F. Dulles stayed in order to ensure an economic recovery plan for Europe (Taft 1989, p. 25).

When Wilson returned to the United States after the peace conference, the progressive, liberal mood which had dominated twenty years of American public life was gone. The extension and improvement of democracy, law, justice, morality and order which had been national articles of faith were spent. Lofty, liberal visions of selfless Americans pursuing shared national goals were replaced by special-interest politics – cities vied with small towns, workers with corporations, farmers with businessmen, intellectuals with fundamentalists, government with private enterprise, Protestants with Catholics, Wets with Drys. The entire country plunged into divisive debates about American foreign policy – debates in which the old sentiment of isolationism returned with a vengeance. Still, this sudden change did not entirely kill off reform. City workers, farmers, intellectuals, state and city officials sustained progressive liberalism through the 1920s and kept it alive until the Depression once more made reform and intervention the predominant national mood.

The global commitments

World War I gave the United States a foreign-policy establishment. World War II gave the country a foreign-policy consensus. In his effort to justify America's war aims, Roosevelt drew a sharp distinction between the values which Hitler represented and those that the United States stood for. He portrayed Hitler's Nazi regime as a diabolical other, as an evil antithesis of American ideals – German Nazism stood for militarism and autocracy whereas American democracy represented civil liberties and individual choice; Nazism exemplified a centrally directed one-party state, whereas liberalism stood for a multi-party democracy; Nazism meant a strong party which would plan sweeping reforms to be implemented by an omnipresent apparatus of compulsion, whereas liberalism meant openness and free-market fairness; Nazism respected only the precepts of a totalist ideology, whereas liberalism meant respect for human rights.

During World War II, the American foreign-policy establishment recast the

American ideals as an absolute negation of Hitler's Nazi ideology. They made America's belief system pronounced and relevant. Roosevelt's foreign-policy establishment portrayed the World War in terms which were identical to Lincoln's Civil War rhetoric: as a struggle between 'liberty' and 'slavery'. They revived and recast the nation's political mythology. The war against Nazism imposed upon the variegated American nation a unified, collective Lincolnian outlook which gave its members a sense of accomplishment, confidence and destiny. It resolved to protect the life, liberty, independence and religious freedom of all individuals. It promised to preserve human rights in all countries. It vowed to guarantee unimpeded trade and general security for the world.

This foreign-policy consensus was importantly shaped by the men who translated the initially vague aims of the war into the clear political proposi-tions of the immediate postwar era. These people, led by President Roosevelt and his immediate staff of secretaries, generals and advisers, laid the ground-work for a strong foreign-policy consensus which survived World War II by a quarter of a century or more.

This consensus was affected by the fact that America's foreign-policy-making establishment constituted a remarkably homogeneous group. Its members belonged to the same type of people: they were middle-aged men who shared the same privileged, north-eastern background from prep schools like Groton and universities like Harvard, Yale and Princeton. They belonged to the same generation and shared the same historical experiences. They recalled World War I and the rise and demise of Wilson's new world order. They remembered the collapse of the market economy, the Great Depression and the New Deal at home. They recollected the collapse of democratic government abroad. Most particularly, they recalled the rise of fascist dictatorships in Europe and the shameful way in which Czechoslovakia was divided and 'betrayed' by the Continental great powers at the Munich conference in 1938 (May 1976). It was of paramount importance for them to avoid the evident errors and the consequences of World War I.[9]

Roosevelt and his New Deal advisers hammered out this foreign-policy consensus according to a conscious design. They had all drawn useful lessons from the bitter debates which had stymied Wilson's postwar plans. They saw themselves as counterweights to the anticipated postwar resurgence of isolationism. They were determined to prevent a retreat to 'fortress America' once the war was over. They wanted to break with America's isolationist inheritance and make the United States play an active role in a new world order.

First, Roosevelt tried to muster broad, bipartisan support for his postwar visions. He began by working actively with Congressional leaders to ensure bipartisan support for his postwar designs – he involved Democrats as well as

Republicans, senators as well as influential private citizens, in the planning process. Later, he launched public relations campaigns and worked with the bipartisan movement to win the support of the remainder of Congress and the broader public. Finally, when it was apparent that the public backed his postwar plans, Roosevelt pushed to get Congressional approval in a joint resolution which endorsed the proposed course of action. This three-step process lay at the core of Roosevelt's domestic wartime policies. It performed two decisive roles. It evolved into an effective consensus-building mechanism; and it added to the strength and authority of the presidency. And because it performed these two roles successfully, it was utilized by subsequent US presidents for the next quarter of a century as a standard consensus-building method in foreign-policy matters.

Second, Roosevelt agreed wholeheartedly with Wilson's attempts to establish a League of Nations and to try to saddle the USA with an active, stabilizing role in world affairs. Roosevelt had been assistant secretary of the navy in Wilson's cabinet and was deeply affected by the US rejection of the League and by the subsequent paralysis of the organization. He was so determined to avoid a repetition of this failure that he had started to plan a United Nations Organization even before Pearl Harbor, and he brought it almost to fruition before his death in the spring of 1945. Furthermore, by Roosevelt's reckoning, Wilson had failed to understand fully how the world economy, no less than the interstate system, needed to be managed by international organizations. Roosevelt's cabinet agreed that a postwar regime which would prevent economic nationalism by fostering free international trade must be an integral part of a postwar regime designed to guarantee a lasting peace. With memories of the interwar recession and the New Deal freshly in mind, already, in the first years of the war they began to design stabilizing postwar institutions of international finance and trade – the IBRD, the IMF and the ITO.

Third, the Roosevelt administration divorced the establishment of organizations designed to preserve a postwar world order from negotiations towards a peace treaty. They wanted to avoid the all-or-nothing choice which Wilson had presented to the American people in 1919. So, they sought to set up the most important postwar institutions before the conditions of peace were even raised. They rushed the conferences on the UN, IBRD, IMF and ITO into session before Germany and Japan surrendered.

American hegemony

Roosevelt died suddenly of a cerebral haemorrhage in April 1945, in the final weeks of the war. But the work he had begun was completed by his successor, Harry Truman.

The new president had no experience in foreign affairs – indeed, Roosevelt had never kept Truman informed of America's wartime diplomacy – and his first actions in office were dictated by plans already laid. During the last half of July, he was in Potsdam to meet with Stalin and Churchill (who was replaced as British Prime Minister by Clement Attlee during the conference). Here he told Stalin about a 'new weapon' which America intended to use against Japan. And a week after returning home, the USA did just this. The dropping of the atomic bombs on Hiroshima and Nagasaki sent shock waves through all great powers. The United States had demonstrated a frightful new weapon, the technology of which was an American monopoly.

The atomic blasts over Hiroshima and Nagasaki, caused Great Britain, the Soviet Union and other great powers to suspend their own postwar plans. They immediately looked to Washington and waited for an American foreign-policy directive. Truman, who suddenly found at his disposal the capacity to dictate the terms of a new world order, did not know what to do. However, after some hesitation, he took the initiative.

Interstate initiatives

Truman's initiative came in an unexpected form in a Navy Day speech (27 October 1945) in New York City. The president outlined America's foreign policy goals in a twelve-point programme. Echoing Wilson's fourteen points from 1919, Truman pledged to support the freedoms of commerce, of expression and of religion; he defended the principle of national self-determination and vowed never to recognize governments imposed by foreign powers; and he promised to support the United Nations (Department of State 1985d).

In Washington and other Western capitals Truman's speech triggered confusion. The liberal scheme for world order that the president proposed would obviously be countered by Stalin at every point. How did Truman intend to implement these ideals in league with Communist Russia? The short answer was that he had no intention of cooperating with the USSR. He did not trust Stalin. He did not think it was possible to negotiate the values and rules of postwar international relations with the Soviet leader. He had decided that if the world were to be peaceful and secure, Communist dictators must be disclosed as outlaws and enemies of the fundamental principles of human interaction, combated and contained. Truman's Navy Day speech, then, was not meant to assuage the Soviet Union. It had two other purposes. It was intended to spell out the criteria according to which the United States would build a new world order, and it was meant to play the ball into the Soviet court – it left it up to Stalin to accept or, more likely, reject the American criteria (and thus reveal himself, in American eyes, as an international outlaw).

Truman's analysis was soon supported by a succession of events. The first of these was Stalin's announcement of 9 February 1946 that the Marxist–Leninist analysis of world affairs remained correct! The world was divided into a Communist and a capitalist camp and the Communists were surrounded by implacable, capitalist enemies. No stable peace could be established between the two camps, Stalin explained. The Soviets must therefore prepare themselves for a replay of the 1930s. Three or more five-year plans would be necessary to develop Soviet heavy industry and collective agriculture to adequately prepare the USSR for the future capitalist onslaught. This message was received by Western observers with incredulity – some went as far as to characterise it as 'The Declaration of World War III' (Forrestal 1951, pp. 134f.).

The second formative event came four weeks later in the form of a speech which Churchill gave at Fulton, Missouri, on 5 March 1946. After an introduction by President Truman himself, Britain's former Prime Minister claimed that Europe was now divided into two hostile camps: 'From Stettin in the Baltic to Trieste in the Adriatic, an iron curtain has descended across the Continent', said Churchill. He recommended that the United States should guarantee, with its nuclear weapons, an effort to create a united Europe which could withstand the Soviet threat (Harbutt 1986).

Churchill's message met with anger in Moscow. Stalin saw it as a set-up for war; a call for a showdown with the Soviet Union. Yet the USSR remained a passive international actor in the summer and autumn of 1946. Stalin concentrated on securing his position at home and on consolidating his power in newly acquired territories. He tightened his grip on eastern Europe; and he pushed hard to get control over the oil wells in Azerbaidjan – indeed, he pushed so hard that Truman felt the need to show American force by sending the powerful aircraft carrier the *Franklin D. Roosevelt* into the eastern Mediterranean in August 1946.

A third, formative event occurred on 21 February 1947. The British ambassador in Washington informed Truman that England, plagued by a failing economy, felt forced to retreat from the eastern Mediterranean – an area which had been England's traditional buffer against Russian expansionism for centuries. Truman understood that if the United States did not take over Britain's traditional role of containing Russian expansion in this area, then Greece (where a Communist-inspired civil war was raging) and Turkey would be left to the mercy of the Soviets. He worked out a detailed proposal for $400 million to aid Greece and Turkey in a hurry. And to ensure that the request was accepted by Congress, he worked intensely with important Congressmen to explain the extent of the Soviet threat. When he thought the time was ripe, Truman appeared dramatically before a joint session of Congress (12 March) intent to 'scare the hell out of the American people'.

The president prefaced his request for aid to Greece and Turkey with a dark and frightening geostrategic scenario. He drew a sharp distinction between 'us' and 'them' – on the one hand were 'the free peoples of the world' who obeyed Law and Reason; on the other were 'totalitarian regimes' which relied on terror and oppression. This Manichean model scared the American people all right, and it shocked Congress into appropriating the $400 million that the president requested. From then on, US foreign policy was encased in the new, purposeful discourse of the cold war.

World economic designs

Truman's new-found political activism included economic initiatives. The two most important ones were designed to remedy the Bretton Woods system (which did not operate as intended) and the ITO negotiations (which were grinding to a halt). The main source of the world economic difficulties, Washington believed, was that Europe suffered from shortages of capital goods, fuel and foodstuffs. And although the United States could supply these goods in abundance, Europe had no money to buy them with. The liberal economies of the West were facing a deep payments crisis. Many US analysts recalled the deep recession that followed World War I and called for immediate and decisive measures.

In May, the US State Department was devising a plan of action. In June, secretary of state George Marshall invited all European countries to make a list of the capital goods they needed, and pledged that the United States would give Europe the needed capital. He imposed only one condition: that the goods must be used by the Europeans in a coordinated way and not individually by different countries for different purposes.[10] The states of western Europe responded enthusiastically – especially Great Britain, where foreign minister Bevin seized the American offer and immediately began to organize a European response. Between July and October 1947, sixteen European nations established a European Recovery Programme (ERP). Within its confines, each participating country defined a goal as to recovery, along with an assessment of the imports necessary to sustain progress towards that goal. The resulting balance of payments deficit was then covered by the United States through the ERP.

At this time, the Americans tried to save the International Trade Organization (ITO) by a two-track strategy. On the one hand, they arranged a meeting in Geneva which produced a preliminary General Agreement on Tariffs and Trade (GATT) among twenty-three states in October 1947; it was intended as a temporary arrangement until an ITO was established. On the other hand, the Americans arranged a conference in Havana in the hope of producing a charter for the elusive ITO. This conference did produce a charter (Department of State 1985e[1948]), but this was a complex compromise which embodied the wishes of everyone but satisfied no one. It was never enacted. The Americans realized that an agreement on an international trade regime was impossible as long as the European economies were in ruins. Instead of pursuing the ITO, they sought to make the most of GATT. They worked to amplify and enlarge the lists of tariff concessions and the elementary code of trade behaviour specified by the treaty. So, although GATT was intended to be a temporary treaty, it came to serve by default the role of a world's trading organization.

Uniting 'us' by containing 'the other'

The capital infusion of the Marshall Plan harnessed by the Bretton Woods system and the GATT rounds helped reconstruct and liberalize the market economies in Western Europe. World trade grew faster than production during the first postwar years. The Soviet Union, committed to combating free-market capitalism, condemned the Western ventures and sought to establish an alternative, socialist order, the Council for Mutual Economic Assistance (CMEA or Comecon). And as Western Europe grew more tightly linked to the US economy, Eastern Europe grew more tightly integrated into the Soviet design. The main ideological opponents of world politics consolidated into rival industrial and military blocs.

The division between East and West deepened. In February 1947, Truman had scared Congress with a model which portrayed the postwar world as divided between two ways of life:

> One way of life [Truman said] is based upon the will of the majority, and is distinguished by free institutions, representative government, free elections, guaranties of individual liberties, freedom of speech and religion, and freedom from political repression.
>
> The second way of life is based upon the will of a minority forcibly imposed upon the majority. It relies upon terror and oppression, a controlled press and radio, fixed elections, and the suppression of personal freedoms. (Department of State 1985c[1947], p. 533)

Truman's speech repeats the stark distinction drawn by Lincoln, Wilson, Roosevelt and others between 'liberty' and 'slavery'. Truman echoes the Manichean vision of natural law between a way of life led according to reason and law, and another which trampled law, rights and reason underfoot. When a law-abiding state is faced with an opponent which 'regards no right as sacred', Truman reasoned, then the safety of the human race requires that this state must be repressed (Vattell 1863[1758], p. 161). Truman's analysis was quickly elevated to foreign-policy doctrine and expressed in a policy of 'containment' (Gaddis 1982).

In order to carry out the new policy, the Americans redesigned their entire defence structure. In June they proposed that the UN Security Council establish an armed UN force (Department of State 1985f [1947]). In July, the Congress passed the 'National Security Act' which called for the development of a comprehensive national security structure (Department of State 1985g[1947]) – which included a new Department of Defense to be overseen by a National Security Council (NSC) and informed by a Central Intelligence Agency (CIA). Also, they enacted an elaborate Federal Employee Loyalty Program.

Then a series of rapid events finally froze the fronts of the cold war. In February 1948, the Czech coalition government collapsed and the Communist Party, tightly guided by the USSR, assumed complete control. The American public rapidly evolved a pronounced anti-Communist stance. In March, the Truman administration decided to unify the three Western occupation zones of Germany and rebuild it into a pillar of strength in Europe. By June, Britain and France supported the idea. Stalin countered immediately by blocking all surface routes into the Western occupation zones of Berlin. The Americans responded rapidly by initiating a massive airlift which supplied the isolated sectors of Berlin.

With the Czech *coup* fresh in mind and in the shadow of the steady traffic of US planes which brought a daily average of 13,000 tons of supplies to blockaded Berlin, Truman's new activist foreign policy was endorsed by Congress. In the so-called Vandenberg resolution, Congress pledged the President to pursue a progressive development of regional and other collective arrangements for individual and collective self-defence in accordance with the purposes, principles and provisions of the UN Charter. With reference to the Vandenberg resolution, Truman's negotiators invited representatives from friendly European allies with a view to establishing a collective security arrangement for the Atlantic states – much like Churchill had called for in the conclusion of his Fulton speech (Harbutt 1986). The negotiations were concluded during the following spring, and the North Atlantic Treaty Organization (Nato) was established in April 1949.

Always attuned to the deepening division of the West, the Policy Planning Staff of the US State Department began to work on a new long-term strategic vision. The initiative gained momentum after the 'loss' of China and the Soviet atomic-bomb tests in 1949, and was completed during the spring of 1950. It was presented as a policy directive before the National Security Council (NSC) in April. This top-secret directive, written under the leadership of Paul Nitze and simply referred to as NSC–68, began with a reminder of the object of defence. NSC–68 first presented the values extolled by the Declaration of Independence and the US Constitution – individual liberty, free institutions, representative government and so on; in short, the American way of life. Then it identified the threat: Soviet Communism as a coordinated global movement. In order to fend off this threat, the NSC directive recommended a massive military mobilization of American society with the intention of righting the power balance, and in the hope that through means other than all-out war changes could be induced in the nature of the Soviet system. The directive discouraged any negotiation with the Soviet Union. Instead it mandated three courses of action: the development of the hydrogen bomb to counter the Soviet atomic threat, a rapid build-up of conventional forces for the United States as well as its allies, and the forging of strong alliances worldwide under US leadership. The directive recognized that these recommendations would be immensely expensive, but concluded that they were necessary courses of action and that the government should increase the federal tax rate in order to pay for it all.

Several readers of the NSC–68 were shocked by the dark and gloomy scenario displayed in the document. President Truman, a determined fiscal conservative, recoiled before the prospect of a defence-driven tax increase. In April and May, the US national security establishment was stirred by an intense, internal discussion about NSC–68. In June, the discussion was suddenly silenced: as a bolt from the blue, Communist North Korea launched a massive military attack on South Korea. Truman acted immediately. Within a week he had dispatched US troops to Korea and he had approved the NSC–68. As Dean Acheson (1969, p. 420) recalled it, with one stroke Korea 'removed the recommendations of NSC–68 from the realm of theory and made them immediate budget issues'.[11]

Hegemony and Podsnappery

Four factors help explain the nature of the first phase of the postwar world order. First, there was the determination of American leaders to break out of their nation's traditional isolation, create a new world order and accept a role of leadership in it. Having drawn lessons from World War I, the American leaders did not want a replay of the isolationism of the 1920s and the recession of the 1930s.

Second, there was the development of nuclear weapons. The nature of the postwar order was affected by the fact that scientists who worked for the US armed forces were the first to produce an atomic bomb and use it in war, and also by the fact that the Soviet Union within a handful of years had developed its own atomic bomb. Their possession of nuclear weapons set the USA and the USSR apart from the great powers of the past. They became greater than great; they became 'super'. And as superpowers they had it within their capability to effect unimaginable destruction on the planet and the people who lived on it.

In 1945, the United States had demonstrated over Hiroshima the horrible lethality of a 12 kiloton A-bomb (whose blast equalled that of 12,500 tons of trinitrotoluene (TNT)). In 1954, the USA tested a 15 megaton H-bomb (yielding an effect equal to 15 million tons of TNT). In 1964, the Soviet Union tested an H-bomb of 57 megatons – the largest bomb that has ever exploded. The effect of the superpowers' imponderable capabilities was a security dilemma of an entirely new order. The conventional concept of counterpoise had involved a balance between the costs and benefits of war – if the probable benefits of war were lower than its probable costs, then states would be deterred from going to war; if the probable benefits exceeded the probable costs, then the situation was uncertain and unstable. In the nuclear concept of counterpoise, by contrast, the probable benefits of war would *never* exceed the probable costs. Since the costs of a nuclear war could be considered unlimited, no assessment of probable gains could exceed it. The result of this way of thinking was that nuclear weapons contributed greatly to the geostrategic stability of great power politics – a condition which John Gaddis (1987) has termed 'the long peace'.

The third factor which illuminates the nature of international relations in the postwar era is the different qualities of the two superpowers. The USA stressed the value of civil society and market dynamics while minimizing the amount of government; the USSR insisted on the necessity of government control over society and economy to such a degree as to almost stifle individual will and liberty. Intimately related to this difference was the fact that the two superpowers were never really equal players in the early postwar world order. In spite of a common denotation of 'bipolarity', the United States was always the pre-eminent actor. The reason for this pre-eminence lay in all three dimensions of international power: force, wealth and norms. America's military superiority was clear and obvious in the immediate aftermath of World War II – in terms of punitive capabilities the world was far from bipolar; it was *uni*polar for more than twenty years after World War II. In addition, the US economy was vibrant and dynamic when compared with the Soviet economy which was bled white by the war. The key to America's pre-eminence, however, lies in the normative dimension of America's power. For it is an astonishing fact about America's postwar pre-eminence that it enjoyed massive support abroad – notably from the great powers of Western Europe. In a word, whereas the United States enjoyed substantial trust and legitimacy in the aftermath of World War II, and was a strong power as well as a strong state, the Soviet Union was 'merely' a strong power.

The fourth and final factor which helps explain the nature of the postwar world order is the communications revolution. The medium of printed text, which had been a characteristic feature of the entire modern age, was, during the twentieth century, complemented by the advent of the screen – first by the movies, which had grown to become a popular medium by the beginning of World War II; then emerged television and, later, videos and personal computers (PCs). New microelectronic technologies have revolutionized the ways in which humanity communicates messages and stores knowledge. One important effect of this revolution was to expand greatly and transform the public sphere to cosmopolitan proportions. Another effect was to diversify it. The worldwide spread of new means of mass communication would sustain public spheres on various levels (local, regional, national and global) and for different segments of the postwar *publicum* (generational, subcultural, political and religious applications as well as by class, race and gender). The commercial applications of new communications technologies contributed greatly to consolidate a cosmopolitan public sphere which included the USA and the allies which pledged to uphold the ideals of natural law, the values of the Enlightenment tradition and the norms of Western, liberal-democratic societies.

In the normative realm the postwar influence of the United States contrasts sharply with that of the Soviet Union. The cosmopolitan public sphere was dominated by the United States, whose culture industries confidently broadcast their messages, norms and values across the world. These values were not only embraced by America's own inhabitants; they were substantially supported by America's allies and trading partners as well. By contrast, the Marxist–Leninist ideas of the Soviet Union did not have nearly as much support – either domestically or among the USSR's foreign allies and trading partners. The Soviet values were more abstract and distant. They did not even constitute a genuine public sphere. They tended to appeal to the poor and the weak states of the world. They were sterile and static and sustained by naked propaganda. They grew doctrinaire and stale over time.

The different status of the two superpowers was most obvious in the old divided Europe. For whereas American ideas and values were voluntarily embraced by the inhabitants of Western Europe, Soviet ideas were largely secured by the presence of the Red Army and consolidated by intelligence agencies and the secret police. Although obvious and significant exceptions can be cited, most Western Europeans saw the USA as a legitimate great power, whereas most Eastern Europeans saw the USSR as a conqueror and an oppressor. It was this normative difference between the two superpowers which sustained America's postwar authority. Like other pre-eminent great powers, the postwar hegemony of the United States was ultimately anchored in a pervasive, legitimizing 'political mythology'.

Empire by invitation

Lundestad (1986) argues that America's expansion after World War II must be understood as a case of 'empire by invitation'. 'Occasionally', he writes, 'the United States did thrust itself into the affairs of other countries. Yet, the basic pattern, particularly in the early postwar years, was ... that the United States was invited in' (Lundestad 1990, p. 56). Gaddis (1997, pp. 285) agrees.

In 1945 the United States emerged as the most powerful country in the postwar world. During a few, short, postwar years the USA became the pre-eminent great power in a hegemonic world order. During the early 1950s, the Americans signed, in a flurry of diplomatic activity, treaty alliances and established military bases all over the globe. This military pre-eminence cannot be explained in terms of force capabilities alone. The expansion must also be viewed in light of economic and normative factors.

The United States expanded its productivity and its earnings greatly during the war. The USA could muster an immense wealth after World War II, and this was undoubtedly an inducement which significantly enhanced America's appeal as a postwar ally. Countries hurt by the war were clearly attracted by America's generosity, and their leading politicians flocked around the United States to sponge off its wealth.

The United States greatly fortified its normative influence during the war. This, too, helps explain America's postwar pre-eminence. It cannot be fully accounted for as a function of economic inducement. It must be seen as a political force in its own right. It cannot be appreciated fully in terms of domestic American concerns; it can only be comprehended as a coalition phenomenon – as the outcome of an interactive relationship among equal participants in a greater project. Military omnipotence and economic expansion were indispensable preconditions for America's postwar pre-eminence. But they do not alone explain why other great powers so easily accepted US leadership in the postwar period.

Why did the nations of Western Europe allow the USA in effect to define the rules of the postwar international game? One answer is that America's leading role and normative influence were prepared by wartime diplomacy – by a process of political socialization which attended the building of a tight, anti-fascist coalition under American leadership. Initially, other Western countries embraced the United States in order to get assistance in their struggle against the Nazi threat. But war-time cooperation quickly occasioned a significant harmonization in political goals and values among the liberal-democratic coalition members.

This answer, however, cannot stand alone. Such a process of rapid socialization could hardly have occurred were it not for the fact that America's distinct set of ideas were rooted in ideals which were European in the first place; America's liberal-democratic vision was informed by Enlightenment concepts of social contract and natural law which had strongly appealed to the nations of Western Europe for over two hundred years. When the USA announced a new international order which was informed by these known and cherished ideas, the nations of Western Europe took to it like ducks to water. This early acceptance of America's liberal vision of a new world order is suggested by the allied reception of President Roosevelt's proposal to host a series of wartime conferences to establish postwar organizations for political as well as economic activities on a global scale.

Finally, Europe's acceptance of America's influence may be seen as making a virtue of political necessity in the face of a common external threat. During World War II, the momentous threat of Nazi Germany created the sentiment of an Atlantic community. After the war, the weakened states of Europe were unified by a common fear of an expansionist Soviet Union on the one hand and of a revived Germany on the other. Initially, Western countries may have embraced the United States in order to get assistance in their struggle against the German threat. But wartime cooperation soon fuelled a significant *rapprochement* among the coalition members; and the resultant solidarity was later maintained by the cold war – when Germany was defeated, Hitler was quickly replaced by Stalin as the incarnation of a common, evil enemy; the old totalitarian threat of the Nazi party was replaced by the threat of a Communist totalitarianism. Liberal-democratic countries rallied around the United States in order to get protection from the Soviet 'other'. President Truman, too, hosted conferences which consolidated this cold war consensus among liberal-democratic states. With reference to the Soviet threat, old institutions were first fine-tuned (UN, Bretton Woods, GATT), then new institutions were added – first the Organisation for European Economic Cooperation the OEEC (later the Organisation for Economic Cooperation and Development (OECD)) in 1948 and then a string of treaty organizations and alliance systems (Nato in 1949, and then the Australian, New Zealand and US Defence Pact (ANZUS), South East Asia Treaty Organisation (SEATO), Central Treaty Organisation (CENTO) and others). All were designed to preserve individual liberties, free institutions and representative government against the Soviet threat.

The perils of Podsnappery

There was more to the American appeal than a simple promise of protection against a totalitarian threat. There was also the independent appeal of America's social values – a factor which has often been underestimated in international relations scholarship. American values had a Western European root and were built into the organizational arrangements within which important postwar interaction occurred. In hindsight, it may appear as if this was done by design and calculation. For during the endgame of World War II, the United States consciously established a system of international organizations which laid down distinct rules for international behaviour. But more likely this infusion of American values occurred informally and unconsciously.

The United States did not force these organizations upon other Western nations. Rather, Americans planned them, and took the initiative to get them established – they arranged broad conferences which would, through multi-national negotiations, arrive at a basic document or founding charter for a specific multinational organization. They laid the premises of the political processes, and they guaranteed the solvency of the operation. But the decisive, multinational process was essentially a cooperative effort. Its success did not rest upon American pressure alone – to which the failure to establish an international trade organization testifies. Rather, the Americans succeeded by their ability to define the key rules and laws for a worldwide community of like-minded, liberal-democratic states and for their comfortable, safe, and peaceable existence – 'in a secure Enjoyment of their properties, and a greater Security against any that are not of it' as Locke (1960[1689], p. 375) put it.

It is tempting to explore further the subtle mechanisms by which non-American nations were conditioned to embrace American values through concepts like 'habitus' or 'discourse'. But such an exploration would require an analysis of more depth and substance than the present historical sketch allows. Awaiting a more satisfactory explanation, it is warranted to view the Americans' behaviour as a simple function of Podsnappery. American diplomats, generals, soldiers and businessmen simply did their jobs abroad as well as circumstances would allow, but they were all the time confident in the virtues of their own society and in the values which informed them. Animated by these values and norms, their actions would invariably impart some of them to the organizations they left behind – respect for human rights, equality, liberty, property, popular sovereignty and free trade. The Americans in Europe, like the British in India a century earlier, never for a moment doubted the superiority of their own institutions. They abided by them. Americans who were sent on foreign missions after the war may have been boisterously patriotic beyond the point of arrogance; American forces in Germany did not behave impeccably – the initial level of looting was outrageous, and the American treatment of prisoners was bad enough to evoke subsequent accusations of genocide. But, on balance, the Americans behaved formally and fairly in their zones of occupation. They sought consent and cooperation, writes Gaddis (1997, p. 288), but adding that they did so less from intention or ideology than from instinct, for 'when otherwise unsure what to do, Americans tended to revert to their democratic habits and encourage others to adopt them as well'. With little direction from above, they were driven by cultural instincts to create democratic institutions in both Germany and Japan. Soviet soldiers did nothing of the kind. The Soviets, too, replicated their domestic habits wherever they went, but as these were of a coarse and autocratic nature – and included the rape of an estimated two million women in the Soviet zone of Germany – they made few friends.[12] In a word, the unbridgeable division which emerged across Europe in the wake of World War II was a division between societies of coercion in the East and societies of consent in the West.

Gaddis (1997) intriguingly invokes a principle from chaos theory, 'self-similarity across scale' to account for the decent behaviour of Americans abroad. However, this approach fails to account for a curious facet of the confident, self-congratulatory American society: amid its power and plenty, American society was also racked by suspicion and intolerance. At the very peak of its international pre-eminence, the United States was marked by a curious duality. On the one hand, society exhibited a self-confident cultivation of liberty, wealth and personal freedoms. On the other hand, it was haunted by a deep insecurity – indeed, a fear – that these freedoms would not last. In the immediate postwar period, this was a fear based on the historical experience that after World Wars come deep recessions; later, it became a fear of Soviet expansionism.[13]

Hegemons have regularly been the wealthiest, freest and most progressive societies of their age; and the United States is no exception. But hegemons have also experienced gloomier aspects of collective uncertainties and even fear. As the Iberians feared Islam, and the Dutch and British feared Catholicism, so the Americans feared monolithic Communism. In all cases of hegemony, this fear of the other worked to constrain the liberties which the hegemons, in their fits of self-congratulatory arrogance, flaunted to the world – and which the world after a while interpreted as inconsistency at best or hypocrisy at worst.

During its age of hegemony, the USA was a good, stable and affluent society. American real disposable income rose by 16 per cent in the 1950s and by another 16 per cent between 1960 and 1965. American life extolled a simple, wholesome happiness – which is still preserved in the innocent situation comedies of the age and in Disneyland (which opened in 1955). On the other hand, aspects of American life were pervaded by deep uncertainties and fears. It is difficult in hindsight to appreciate the pervasiveness of this fear and the atmosphere of suspicion and intolerance that it bred. It is reflected in some of the scary mass entertainments of the age – such as Jack Finney's *Invasion of the Body Snatchers* which Don Siegel made into a classic horror movie in 1956. It is easy to dismiss these as adolescent 'hysterics' and twisted reactions to excessive reruns of 'Leave it to Beaver'. But the attentive reader may find similar echoes of such deep and morbid attitudes in Forrestal's diaries and in the fact that some American parents sent their children to school with nametags around their necks, so that in case the heathen Communists attacked, the children's bodies could be easily identified in the debris and given a Christian burial.

The cold war consensus which undergirded America's pre-eminence was, just like earlier cases of consensus and hegemony, purchased at a price. In the American case, this price included the imposition of limits on the very values and norms which America held most dear. For example, a basic human right like freedom of expression, which was the very precondition for America's public sphere and for the self-regulating processes of civil society, was eroded by political practices. In postwar America political debate was reduced to a question of method, of the means of implementing the goals of policy. What was American was defined more sharply by explicitly contrasting it with what was un-American – a one-party dictatorship, a planned economy, state-run systems of education and unionization – and it was assumed that if you wavered in your support of the one, then you supported the other.[14]

Towards the end of the 1950s, several critical observers noted this odd combination of innocence, confidence and fear which marked American culture. Some of them noted the growing intolerance of cold war America and feared the loyalty oaths and the McCarthyism which made their mark upon American society. Others (Riesman, Packard, Whyte, Goodman) ridiculed the materialism and the conformity of American life and asked what had happened to America's traditional values. Such criticisms and ridicule would, in turn, fuel an introverted, self-examining sentiment which would work as a solvent on the consensual American creed during the 1960s – a solvent which attained self-destructive proportions during the Vietnam War. Then America's own critical voices would be exported abroad and, in turn, take root in the younger, rebellious generations of America's primary allies.

Notes

1 Measured in constant 1958 dollars, the US GNP grew from about $200 billion in 1939 to more than $300 billion in 1945 – the latter figure representing about half of the world's goods and services at the time. The value of US exports increased from $2.4 billion in 1936 to $4 billion in 1940 to $15 billion in 1944.

2 It is worth noting that when Congress passed the Surplus Property Act (1944), which regulated the transfer of federal plants into private hands, it was decided to avoid turning them over to big, established companies which had built them or operated them during the war. The plants were instead turned over to smaller companies or new ventures.

3 One notably important contribution to the growth of the modern computer was sponsored by the US Navy: Howard Aikin of Harvard University, in association with engineers from the International Business Machines Corporation (IBM), developed a superfast electromechanical calculator – the Harvard Mark I – which could be fed data encoded on punch cards.

Another important development was sponsored by the US Army: two scientists from the University of Pennsylvania, John P. Eckert and John W. Mauchly, won a contract during the war to build a digital computer which stored data on magnetic tape. In 1946 they completed what they called an Electronic Numerical Integrator and Calculator (ENIAC). It was a thousand times faster than its electromechanical predecessors, could execute up to five thousand arithmetic operations per second and was used by the army for ballistic calculations. In 1948, the two scientists established a computer firm which also catered to civilian customers. In 1950, the Eckert-Mauchly Computer Corporation was acquired by Remington Rand. In 1955, Remington Rand merged into the Sperry Rand Corporation.

4 The 'founding fathers' primarily include the men who met at the Continental Congress (1776) and who passed the Declaration of Independence. A more generous definition would also include the members of the Constitution Convention (1787) who produced the Constitution of the United States. It can be noted that each set of fathers is considered important enough to be commemorated by separate national holidays – the ritual celebration of which contributes importantly to the self-definition of the nation and which introduces new generations into its values, norms and rules: 'Thanksgiving' and 'the 4th of July'.

5 The purity and virtue of the individual, Calvinist souls were reflected in this world by success in secular activities. Wealth was a mark of God's favour. It flowed from adherence to virtues of hard work, faith and simple living. This idea instilled in the Pilgrims an acute attention to hard work and material success. It is worth recalling that Weber (1930) used the late eighteenth-century American colonies to illustrate his proposition that there is a causal relationship between the Calvinist ethic and the spirit of capitalism. Indeed, Weber refers to Benjamin Franklin as the quintessential capitalist.

6 The choice of holiday selected to commemorate the American revolution is telling: Americans celebrate 4 July to commemorate the Declaration of Independence (of 1776), and not the passing of the Constitution (of February 1789). In a word, the Americans celebrate the *de*struction rather than the *con*struction of state power.

7 George Washington, more than any other single individual, emerged from the American revolution as the first and best among a 'new race of men'. He remains the greatest hero in American political mythology. Beneath him, two individuals occupy high places of distinction. Benjamin Franklin is one – he is first of all portrayed as a common man, a practical patriot who rose to fortune, wisdom and prominence by his own hard work. Thomas Jefferson is the other. He is portrayed as an aristocrat, a thinker who embodied the peculiarly American revolutionary spirit and who gave final form to the ideas and the ideals it embodied. Below Franklin and Jefferson, America's mythological panopticon is crowded with tertiary heroes: Samuel Adams, Alexander Hamilton, Patrick Henry, James Madison, the Marquis de Lafayette, Nathan Hale and others – about whom American schoolchildren have traditionally been told patriotic tales and stories.

8 The new liberals had no clear links with either of the main political parties. They were dominated by upper middle-class professionals and intellectuals – some of whom founded the *New Republic* magazine in 1914. And although the *New Republic* applauded President Wilson's policies of centralized reforms to help workers and farmers at home, it castigated his isolationist stance in foreign affairs and urged him to enter the war on England's side to contain the German empire and destroy its aggressive military machine (Steel 1981, pp. 74ff., Acheson 1969).

9 Indeed, the US consensus was marked by the fact that several members of

Roosevelt's foreign-policy establishment were personal acquaintances. They had gathered around President Wilson and Colonel House in 1917, and been members of the US delegation to Versailles in 1919. Thus, they had the same personal experiences. During the 1930s, some of the old, liberal moguls of finance (such as Adolf Berle, James Forrestal, Averell Harriman and Robert Lovett) had been recruited by President Roosevelt to preside over his efforts to combat the recession. When the threat of new international conflicts was looming in the late 1930s, these men transferred to top-level, foreign-policy positions. They accompanied lawyers and academics who had belonged to President Wilson's entourage in World War I, who had participated in meetings and seminars at the Council of Foreign Relations and written articles for *Foreign Affairs* in the interwar years. These men constituted an influential, invisible élite whose members shared a distinct set of cultural attitudes, social aspirations and political instincts.

10 The Europeans first requested $28,000 millions from the United States; the Truman administration reduced the amount to $17,000 million; and Congress in turn appropriated about $13,000 million (Lundestad 1990, p. 57).

11 The outbreak of war in Korea was such a propitious saviour of the recommendations of NSC–68 that several historians have suspected Truman of somehow setting the whole thing up. This has been a popular chestnut among left-wing cold war historians – and a far-fetched (but nevertheless influential) scenario is submitted by Kolko and Kolko (1972, pp. 565–99); a more elusive conspiracy theory informs the massive (and also influential) account of Cumings (1981, pp. 379–567). As to the right-wing historians who are still preoccupied with Stalin's mastery of a grand cold war design, it is tempting to note the sobering thought that Stalin, by instigating the Korean War, in effect was the real saviour of NSC–68. Indeed, from this perspective, Stalin's involvement in Korea is a strong candidate in a very large field of contenders for the stupidest foreign-policy move of the twentieth century.

12 Gaddis's application of the same principle of cultural habit to account for the behaviour of both American and Soviet soldiers implies an unflattering portrait of Russian culture and society. Comparing the 'occupying styles' of the two superpowers, Gaddis notes that whereas the Americans brought new capital to their occupied territories, the Soviets stole capital from theirs. Also, where American soldiers acted with comparative fairness, Soviet soldiers behaved with gratuitous brutality. By Gaddis's account, Stalin empathized with the classic attitude of victorious officers, that troops who had risked their lives 'deserved a little fun' for their trouble (Gaddis 1997, p. 286). According to Norman Naimark (1995, pp. 69ff.), the result of this attitude was a semi-sanctioned wave of soldierly abuse during which as many as two million German women may have been assaulted and raped in 1945–46.

13 Perhaps the United Provinces provides the best parallel to this American oddity, for in the Dutch case, too, this fear was expressed in religious terms – it manifested itself as a fear of retribution (Schama 1987).

14 The debate which swept US social sciences in the 1950s about the nature of 'totalitarianism' is greatly enlightening in this regard. For in hindsight it is tempting to conclude that what was then branded as 'totalitarian' and was used as an analytical term in mainstream political science was a simple negation of the American ideal (consider for example the classic definition of 'totalitarian' in Friedrich and Brzezinski 1965).

8

Challenges, responses and nuclear weapons

I ain't gonna work on Maggie's farm no more
Bob Dylan

The second phase of world order is marked by increasing international instability. In previous cases of order, this change was attended by a sudden eruption of conflict which militarily challenged the hegemon. This challenge invariably took the hegemon by surprise. It responded. But in doing so, it displayed such unexpected ineptitude that its prestige was hurt. And as it sought to re-establish its prestige, it undermined its legitimacy. There was also a second factor at work which complicated the hegemon's task: the principle of unequal development of states. Some states evolved at a more rapid pace than the hegemon. As a result, the international system began to lose the unipolar feature which characterizes the hegemonic phase. The great powers grew more equal in power. The old hegemon lost its legitimacy and the old world order appeared to unravel.

A comparable chain of events can be recognized in twentieth-century international history. The second phase of the American world order was initiated by a substantial and serious challenge. The American state leaders responded to it. But as they did so (in controversial and costly ways), they brought about an erosion of America's prestige. American presidents like Lyndon Johnson and Richard Nixon found themselves facing some of the same problems that previous leaders of hegemons had faced in comparable circumstances. Johnson and Nixon faced street demonstrations, racial unrest and anti-war protests at home. Their troubles were exacerbated by splits in their foreign coalitions and alienation among their allies. Also, their situation was made worse by a relative weakening of the US economy.

World economic challenges

During the 1960s the burden of global leadership was weighing heavily on the US economy. The Johnson administration intensified Kennedy's anti-insurrection policies, and proudly refused to put a price tag on the security policy goals they chose to pursue. Increasing defence costs and increasing balance-of-payments deficits weakened the dollar. The economic downturn, which had troubled Kennedy during his last year in office, spun out of control in 1964. So did the Vietnam War. The costs of the war skyrocketed, from $8 billion in 1966 to $21 billion in 1967 – large portions of which were used abroad. It was becoming apparent that the United States could not afford both a war on Communism abroad and a war on poverty at home. When the Johnson government printed more dollars to pay for its imperial activities, they sharply increased the rate of inflation.

One consequence of this inflation was to constrain the domestic economy. US goods, priced in inflated dollars, were priced out of international markets. Dollars fled the USA in the form of private investments abroad. In 1971, the United States ran its first trade deficit of the twentieth century. In subsequent years, US foreign trade figures ran increasingly in the red.

Another consequence was to export inflationary pressures to America's allies and trading partners. French President De Gaulle had warned as early as 1965, that America's militarist policies created inflationary pressures, and that the USA used its dominant position in the world to export its problems. De Gaulle demanded that the dollars held by France be converted into gold. This shook the Bretton Woods system. It also sounded the klaxon for a lengthy monetary crisis, for in 1970 the British and the German governments began to echo French concern and to object to US practices. The Bretton Woods system had limped through the 1960s. But in 1971 it was dealt a paralysing blow. Increasingly worried about trade deficits and the steady outflow of gold, the Nixon administration decided to end the status of the dollar as reserve currency. The president announced in August 1971 that the United States would abandon the gold standard. In 1973, Nixon's men decided to let the dollar float. Suddenly the Organization of Petroleum Exporting Countries (OPEC) countries, in a rare display of united policy action, quadrupled the world's oil prices. This dealt the Bretton Woods system a final blow.

Many of the economic problems which faced the world around 1970 would have existed without America's Third World adventurism. Also, the relative decline of the United States was, to some degree, a natural case of other countries recovering from the World War and catching up with the United States – several countries in Europe and Asia had recovered during the 1950s and gone through spurts of rapid growth in the 1960s (notably West Germany and Japan). However, these alterations were clearly exacerbated by the billions spent on idle ventures like the disastrous war in Vietnam. Such militarism spurred many US allies to voice dissatisfaction with collecting inflated US dollars in return for protection against the Soviet threat (which they perceived as steadily diminishing), and for supporting American Third World wars (which most Europeans increasingly disapproved of). The members of the IMF and the World Bank complained about America's self-serving leadership of organizations which were designed to serve the common good of the Western world. Tension grew as currency issues began to compete with security concerns in the politics of American allies. In the words of Robert Gilpin,

> for both foreign policy and domestic reasons, successive American administrations pursued expansionary and inflationary monetary policies that eventually undermined the dollar and destabilized the monetary system. [The United States had become] the rogue elephant of the global economy. (Gilpin 1987, pp. 149, 153)

Interstate challenges

America's opponents observed how foreign and domestic conflicts engulfed American presidents. The Soviet leaders in the Kremlin imagined that events confirmed their Marxist–Leninist analyses of world affairs: capitalism was paralysed by crisis. The American social economy was unravelling. The United States was in decline. The Brezhnev Politburo did not sit idly by waiting for the Americans to self-destruct. They did what they could to hasten the process. They expanded their own military capabilities enormously, and gave large-scale aid to anti-American movements around the world.

Presidents Lyndon B. Johnson and Richard M. Nixon faced some of the same challenges as Queen Victoria, King George III, Grand Pensionary Johan de Witt and King Philip II had done. But if there are striking similarities between their situations, there are also conspicuous differences. One of the most important was that Johnson and Nixon faced a more elusive challenge. The United States was not presented with as clear-cut and focused an international conflict in its second phase as their predecessors were in theirs. The USA faced a more subtle and elusive challenge. It was more difficult to address directly, and the containment policy of the United States did not immediately manifest itself in the characteristic features of earlier hegemons.

The main reason for this American variation on a common modern theme must be sought in a unique element of twentieth-century international relations: that is, with the advent of atomic weapons. Nuclear means of mass destruction intruded upon the interstate sphere at the tail end of the twentieth-century wave of great wars, and they quickly altered the logic of geostrategy. In the hegemonic phase of previous world orders, most statesmen agreed on which the pre-eminent state was. In the wake of great wars, power capabilities were distributed unequally among the states in the system. And if great power relations were fairly stable, this was partly because no one wished to challenge the pre-eminent state and risk a war which they knew they would lose. The advent of nuclear weapons altered this. It added to the great power mode of reasoning the notion that *everyone* might lose in a war which involved nuclear weapons – including the hegemon.

The Americans were the first to appreciate this. During the early 1950s, Presidents Truman and Eisenhower realized that military superiority in the nuclear age did not necessarily guarantee national security; and that nuclear weapons had made great power wars unwinnable. Soon after Stalin's death, Soviet leaders reached the same conclusion.[1] This basic agreement among American and Soviet leaders about the limited usefulness of nuclear weapons, had a profound effect on great power politics. It created a common understanding between the two rivals that nuclear war was so dangerous that it must be avoided at all cost. Thus emerged a common, tacit doctrine of war avoidance which transcended the enmity of the superpowers and which, in turn, added a unique element of basic cooperation to the absolute antagonism which otherwise marked their interaction.

From the mid-1950s, the common realization of mutual vulnerability pushed both superpowers towards negotiations that produced agreements about a growing set of rules for superpower conduct. It was a unique feature of the American world order that challenges to American leadership were posed within such an ultimate framework of rules for superpower conduct. By the mid-1970s, this set of rules had evolved into a relatively robust, stable and peaceful bipolar system – at least as far as direct superpower relations went.

Strategic challenges and nuclear condominium

In order to deter and contain the Soviet Union cheaply and efficiently, the Americans launched a massive nuclear weapons programme in the 1940s. This programme gathered speed in the 1950s, fuelled by the fears and frustrations created by the Korean War. President Eisenhower feared that more conventional efforts to contain Communist expansionism would be prohibitively expensive. He was frustrated by the inconclusive fighting of the conventional war in Korea, and thought that by building a sizeable nuclear arsenal, he could hit two birds with one stone. Nuclear weapons would be relatively cheap to build and maintain; also, nuclear weapons would represent a far greater deterrent than conventional forces.

In addition, there was a more subtle aspect of the president's reasoning.

Eisenhower was a military man. He realized quickly that nuclear weapons represented something more than simply bigger and better bombs; they implied a qualitative change in great power warfare. Nuclear weapons could result in such monumental destruction that it might imperil humanity itself. Eisenhower was deeply convinced that nuclear war must never occur, that any war would carry with it the possibility of escalating into a nuclear conflagration and that *all* wars must consequently be avoided. The best way to avoid war, according to the logic of the old general, was to prepare for war. And in the nuclear age, he insisted, such preparations must be made credible while the prospect of war must be made appalling.

Some of the president's own advisers recoiled before this reasoning – secretary of state John Foster Dulles argued that a credible nuclear build-up would frighten the allies. The national security staff produced reports to the effect that if war should occur, the United States might be left with only two courses of action: full capitulation or all-out nuclear war. Several outside critics protested the wisdom of Eisenhower's argument – among them Dean Acheson, Adlai Stevenson, Paul Nitze, John F. Kennedy and Henry Kissinger. But Eisenhower was adamant. He stuck to his argument. He wanted to convince *all* adversaries that *any* war might escalate to a nuclear level from which *no one* would emerge victorious. Although this logic of 'massive retaliation' met with strong criticism, Eisenhower was convinced that it was the key to survival in the nuclear age.

To contain and deter the Soviet Union, the Eisenhower administration designed new bomber and missile programmes. It dispersed the Air Force units more widely and placed them on permanent alert; it built more missiles – tripling US nuclear stockpiles from 6,000 weapons in 1958 to 18,000 in 1960. Most of the missiles were deployed in underground silos; many of them were deployed on a fleet of fourteen Polaris nuclear submarines (the first of which went into service in 1960 and carried sixteen missiles each); a few were deployed abroad in places like Italy and Turkey.

However, this build-up did not make the United States feel more secure. Rather, it fuelled the fear that the Soviet Union, too, was building an indomitable nuclear arsenal. This fear first erupted in 1949 when the USSR detonated its first 'nuclear device'. It was intensified by the revolution in China, the war in Korea (1950) and by the first Soviet hydrogen bomb (1954). In 1957, when the USSR successfully brought an artificial satellite into orbit around the earth, many Americans believed they were lagging dangerously behind the Soviet Union in military technology; they discovered 'gaps' in everything from missile production to science education.[2]

The fear reached a climax in October 1962, when the Americans discovered that the Soviet Union had installed nuclear missiles in Cuba – only some ninety miles from America's own shores. The resulting 'missile crisis' altered the strategic outlook of the two superpowers. In the United States, the crisis dealt the final blow to Eisenhower's doctrine of massive retaliation and stimulated new ways of thinking about nuclear diplomacy. In the Soviet Union, the crisis irreparably weakened the leadership of Nikita Khrushchev and contributed to the rise of a new group of Kremlin leaders. The Soviets felt humiliated by the way the United States had called Khrushchev's bluff, and fortified their resolve of launching a rapid build-up programme of their own, so that a sizeable nuclear arsenal would prevent the USSR from ever being humiliated again. After Khrushchev was ousted (in October 1964) the Soviet nuclear stockpiles increased considerably – from less than 100 strategic carriers in 1962 to nearly 2,000 a decade later.

By 1970, the two superpowers had about the same number of strategic carriers and a comparable number of nuclear warheads. This presented the United States with an entirely new foreign-policy situation. The world was dominated by equipollent superpowers and the global balance of forces described a condition of 'parity'.

As in previous phases of challenge, the interstate system had thus evolved towards bipolarity and a logic of counterpoise was introduced into great power politics. However, the fact that this development occurred in the nuclear age added an unprecedented factor to the situation: it pushed the leading powers towards risk-averse behaviour. It made both superpowers realize that the outbreak of war between them would have catastrophic implications for them both – and in the worst-case scenario destroy life on earth. The distinct possibility of a nuclear Armageddon altered the ways in which statesmen of earlier ages had calculated counterpoise. It made American and Soviet leaders more careful and conservative in their geostrategic relations than Philip II and George III had been. It gave both superpowers a common interest in reducing direct conflicts to a minimum and in avoiding war altogether.

Nuclear weapons enhanced the common interests of the primary cold war adversaries and made them both into *status quo* powers. The prospect of a nuclear Armageddon suggested to both of them that a smooth operation of the nuclear balance of terror could best be ensured if the two superpowers regulated their adversarial relations by certain elements of cooperation. Thus, under the twisted logic of nuclear strategy, interstate competition was harnessed by risk-averse conduct and by the superpowers' common interest in peace. From a combination of this common interest and the reality of nuclear parity emerged the unprecedented condition of ordered rivalry known as *détente*. It included a set of agreements among the nuclear rivals about the basic rules of geo-strategic conduct. The most visible indication of this was the Limited Nuclear Test Ban Treaty (1963) the Non-proliferation Treaty (1968) and the Strategic Arms Limitation Treaty (1972).

In a sense, the advent of nuclear weapons gave the Soviet Union a comparative advantage. For nuclear weapons focused superpower relations on the only dimension of international competition in which the Soviet Union could compete: that is, on the production of military hardware. By implication, cold war diplomacy drew attention away from the many other dimensions of politics where the Soviet Union was abysmally inferior – such as the economic productivity of the nation and the ethical aspects of society and politics. It privileged the military dimension of power and it marginalized the others.

The Cuban crisis

In theory, the Soviet Union was the primary threat to the American world order. In practice, the Soviet Union had in some respects become a *status quo* power in the international system. Thus, the main systemic challenges did not come from the Second World, but from the Third World. The most consequential assaults on the American world order came from China and Cuba – i.e., from those areas of the globe where the Second and the Third Worlds overlapped. American decision-makers initially assumed that the regimes of Mao and Castro were controlled from Moscow. They did not immediately understand the degree to which Beijing and Havana, although allied with Moscow, entertained ambitions on their own.

It ought to come as no surprise that American analysts never really understood Mao Zedong – who, ever since he assumed power in 1949, viewed the United States as his chief adversary and committed his vast nation to an intense anti-American foreign policy. It is more surprising that they did not understand Castro either. After he took power in 1959, Castro quickly developed a policy of such an intense anti-American tenor that it took US policy-makers aback. The Americans attributed Castro's bellicose behaviour to Soviet machinations. They were slow to discover that Cuban foreign policies were more complicated than they allowed for. The Cuban revolution was informed by a genuine anti-American *ressentiment* – a new collective identity based on xenophobia, a sense of moral superiority and a thirst for revenge (Scheler 1961; Greenfeld 1992, pp. 15ff.). And the Soviet leaders quickly learned to shape and exploit it. With Soviet collusion, the Cubans challenged the entire US-led world order in the 1960s. Between them, Khrushchev, Mao and Castro pushed the United States into the impossible position of having to balance its old anti-colonial theories against its new anti-Communist practice. They forced the Americans into an untenable cold war dilemma: on the one hand, if the Americans were to conduct a convincing anti-colonial policy, they would have to break up colonial empires, alienate old allies like England and France, release droves of post-colonial states on to the cold war world scene where they might drift into radical and revolutionary alliances. On the other hand, if the Americans were going to maintain a global policy of containment, they would have to depend on the cooperation of old European colonial powers to build their anti-Communist coalitions with.

By 1960, the contours of a geostrategic condominium were emerging between the superpowers. At the same time, Cuba and China were challenging US interests in regional and local politics in Latin America and Asia. Soviet policies towards these regions had long reflected Stalin's attitudes. Stalin viewed the Third World from a Eurocentric perspective; he had tended to brush off indigenous Third World leaders as petty bourgeois nationalists – and as such he refused to support the Indochinese Communist leader Ho Chi Minh because he feared that might split the French Communist party. Stalin's death brought into power Soviet leaders with other attitudes. After a period of internal uncertainties and strife, the reins of Soviet power were in 1955 concentrated in the hands of Nikita Khrushchev. He approached Third World leaders in a very different way. Besides, as Khrushchev was neither respected nor trusted by Mao, his ascension to the Soviet premiership meant that the old Sino-Soviet policy of cooperation was replaced by quarrels and rivalries. During the late 1950s, Sino-Soviet relations turned sour and Khrushchev began to outbid Peking in the appeal to revolutionary movements in the Third World. In 1959, his eyes fell on Cuba.

In 1959, Fidel Castro, Ernesto 'Che' Guevara, Camilo Cienfuegos and their guerrilla rebels vanquished the corrupt regime of US-supported dictator Fulgencio Batista. Castro had scarcely assumed power before it became obvious that he aimed at greater things than merely replacing a corrupt *caudillo*. He intended to end the system of imperialistic dominance which Batista represented and which had so long condemned Cuba to dependence and poverty. Only in this way would it be possible to rectify the social injustices which the island had suffered in American bondage, Castro claimed. As soon as he had installed himself in power, Castro demonstrated that the Cuban revolution was propelled by more than empty rhetoric. In the spring of 1959, Castro carried out sweeping agrarian reforms. During the summer he confiscated American properties.

Castro's rhetoric was sweet music to the ageing Communists in the Kremlin.[3] They offered Castro support. He accepted, and quickly began to instigate Soviet-style reforms – such as converting his own revolutionary party into the Cuban Communist Party. In a stunningly short time, Cuba was transformed from a prized member of the American family of nations to a prime symbol of Soviet design to win the hearts and minds of the Third World.

In April 1961, the United States responded by allowing the US Central Intelligence Agency (CIA) to support a plot to kill Castro and sponsor an invasion of exiled Cubans at the Bay of Pigs. But the plot failed and the invasion was an embarrassing failure. It amounted to a loss of diplomatic face which greatly undermined American prestige in the world and eroded the credibility and the legitimacy of the United States in its own hemisphere. The Soviets exploited the American embarrassment for all it was worth and strengthened Cuba's dependence on the USSR into the bargain. The Bay of Pigs fiasco and Cuba's sudden defection to the Soviet camp made American policy-makers realize that they had failed to understand the problems of Central and South America. So they began to design a variety of programmes which would prevent Castro-like revolutions in Latin America. They established propaganda campaigns and programmes which would work as political antidotes to the revolutionary threat.

Castro had violated a hemispheric code of conduct which went back to Theodore Roosevelt and James Monroe when he signed agreements with the Soviet Union. He caused the United States to retaliate, first with economic and political pressures and then with invasion. Khrushchev, in turn, took the unprecedented step of offering to defend the Cuban revolution against US aggression. Indeed, he proposed to deter the United States by deploying medium-range nuclear missiles on the island. Castro leaped at the offer. And the rest, as they say, is history. US intelligence services discovered the missiles and demanded that the Soviets remove them. The Soviets complied. They thereby avoided a superpower confrontation; but they also lost prestige.

Third World revolutions

As the Americans dealt with Castro and perceived world affairs in light of their Cuban (mis)adventures, they increasingly saw in Castro an ominous representative of anti-American dictators in poor states in the cold war world. Castro charged the United States with being an imperialist great power. During the early 1960s, the Americans suddenly found themselves faced by this charge being repeated from all corners of the earth. Castro was not alone. He expressed a point of view which he had in common with impoverished nations all across the world. And once this point of view was introduced into America's public sphere and seriously discussed, it immediately tarnished America's old self-image. It fuelled a disturbing, even destructive, dilemma in US politics: Castro's left-wing criticism of the United States portrayed in colonialist terms a nation which had always perceived itself as an anti-colonial power!

The struggle against colonialism had always been an important aspect of US foreign policy. Wilson had tried to make the great powers dissolve their colonial empires after World War I, and Roosevelt had pressured England and France to dismantle their colonial empires after World War II. By the 1960s, the world's former colonies were close to self-determination and nationhood. They began to oppose the old, liberal ideas of free trade and a capitalist world market and to embrace socialist-sounding doctrines of liberation politics and command economies.

In Africa, radical liberation movements were on the rise. Along its northern, Muslim rim, the Algerian National Liberation Front enjoyed great progress in its war against French colonialism. South of the equator, armed resistance emerged in the Congo and in Portugal's colonies (primarily in Angola, Mozambique and Guinea Bissau). At the southern tip, the African National Congress (ANC) added sabotage and guerrilla warfare to its verbal campaigns for greater civil rights and political liberties. In other places these radical, anti-Western movements were repeated with increasing volume – e.g. by Egypt's president Nasser who challenged the West with his radical pan-Arabic rhetoric. In Asia similar developments were inspired by the apparent successes of the Vietnam's National Liberation Movement (FNL or Vietminh) led by Ho Chi Minh.

Policy-makers in Washington witnessed the emergence of an apparent worldwide challenge from anti-imperialist revolutionary movements represented by figureheads and ideologues like Ernesto 'Che' Guevara, Ho Chi Minh, Frantz Fanon, Amilcar Cabral and others. The Americans saw the hand of the Soviet Union behind this development. They knew that these movements were encouraged by the USSR. They understood that Soviet Premier Nikita Khrushchev had suddenly perceived the national liberation movements of the Third World as a great revolutionary promise. The Americans knew that Khrushchev had approached these movements with offers of Soviet military and economic support. They were convinced that many movements had accepted Soviet aid. But what should they do?

The first attempt to deal with a radical Third World revolution had been a terrible fiasco. The Bay of Pigs invasion had been counterproductive. In the wake of this embarrassing failure, the Kennedy administration began to design carefully a variety of programmes which would expand the containment doctrine to the Third World. On the one hand the administration established propaganda campaigns and programmes which would work as political antidotes to the revolutionary threat. President Kennedy inaugurated the Peace Corps in 1961; and, under the cover of a large-scale development scheme, the Alliance for Progress was designed as a counter-insurgency tool in Latin America.

On the other hand, the Kennedy administration also developed special forces which were trained to counter revolutionary threats in the Third World. President Kennedy had a special fascination with the military power that his office gave him and was infatuated with these new counter-insurgency forces. In 1961, the Kennedy administration doubled the number of combat-ready divisions in the US Army's strategic reserves, expanded the Marine Corps, established special counter-insurgency forces (such as the so-called 'Green

Berets') and jungle warfare schools at Fort Bragg, North Carolina and in the Panama Canal Zone. Also, the administration added seventy vessels to the USA's active fleet and a dozen wings to its tactical air forces. And a special office was established in the US Department of Defense to sell US arms to foreign (but friendly) nations. These efforts were costly. But they paid off. In 1965 American operators foiled a left-wing *coup* in the Dominican Republic. In 1967 they hunted down and killed Cuban revolutionary Ernesto 'Che' Guevara in Bolivia. In 1973 they helped overthrow the socialist regime of Salvador Allende in Chile.

A similar application of the containment doctrine took place in Africa. In 1961, Congo's revolutionary leader Patrice Lumumba was slain; after a few years of upheaval Belgian paratroopers with English and American support intervened, crushed the self-proclaimed government of Pierre Mulele in 1964 and transferred power to CIA-financed Desiré Mobutu. From the mid-1960s, the USA supported Portuguese efforts to crush black independence movements in Angola (FNLA: National Front for the Liberation of Angola), Mozambique (FRELIMO: Mozambique Liberation Front) and Guinea Bissau (PAIGC: African Independence Party for Guinea and Cape Verde). Right-wing *coups* removed nationalist leaders in Ghana (1966) and Mali (1968).

In the Middle East, the effects of Egypt's pan-Arabic movement were contained; radical Palestinians were crushed by King Hussein's Bedouin Legion (1970); when Nasser died, Egypt moved rapidly rightward under its new president Anwar Sadat. Indeed, the entire Arab world swung markedly rightwards in this period. Further east, guerrilla movements in India (the Naxalites) and Ceylon (the JVP) were contained by confident post-colonial regimes. In Indonesia a right-wing *coup* opened up the systematic killing of radicals – up to 300,000 people may have been massacred during the second half of the 1960s.

Thus the Western world under US leadership managed to block the left-wing wave of anti-imperialist revolutions which had threatened to sweep the Third World. Between 1962 and 1974, there was only one case of revolutionary seizure of power anywhere in the Third World (South Yemen). 'Che' Guevara was dead and Castro's revolution was securely bottled up on its island; its followers on the Latin American mainland were routed by severe repression. The Portuguese were holding on to their colonial empire in Africa. The growing power of Sadat in Egypt and the Shah in Iran were major bulwarks against revolution and change; the rise of the Arab oil states appeared to add to the stability of the region.

Only in one region was US foreign policy courting catastrophe: in Indochina. Although Mao was fading into senile seclusion, Chinese foreign policy was still conducted within the framework of his old pledge to combat American imperialism in Asia. American engagements in Laos and Vietnam mushroomed during the 1960s – from around 500 US 'advisers' in 1960 to 10,000 by 1962, to 23,000 by 1964, to 183,000 by 1966 and nearly 500,000 by 1968 (Cohen 1995, pp. 167ff.).

Normative challenges

As in previous phases of challenge, the international engagements and the relative economic despondency of the hegemon were accompanied by greater uncertainties and unrest at home. And, as in previous cases, the growth of uncertainties was intimately connected with challenges from distant regions that eroded its political mythology.

During the 1940s and 1950s, US policies were justified by a political mythology based on the concepts of liberty and democracy. But during the 1960s, America's foreign-policy practice was increasingly expressed in military interventions in the Third World. Towards the end of the 1960s, the conflict between idealistic theory and militant practice disastrously undermined the credibility of America's political rhetoric. US appeals to democracy and freedom were increasingly perceived as disingenuous. The USA was seen as just another great power trying to protect its own national interests. The United States was increasingly portrayed in the same terms as the Soviet Union; both were described as superpowers and the American discourse of democracy was compared to the propaganda of the USSR.

This development amounted to a deep and fundamental deflation of America's political mythology. The old liberal rhetoric could no longer sustain the legitimacy of US policies. The United States lost its legitimacy as world leader. For as the American foreign-policy élite claimed that it was necessary to use military means to protect a world order based on democracy and freedom, their arguments were increasingly countered by groans of disbelief. How could democracy be secured by carpet-bombing the primitive infrastructure of distant and poor countries? How could the cause of liberty be protected by dropping napalm and defoliants on the meagre crops of Asian peasants? The US government did not further democracy, it was argued; it destroyed it! Belligerent behaviour in the Third World was revealing the worst aspects of US government – secrecy, conspiracy, state-sponsored terrorism. It was destroying democracy and liberty both abroad and at home.

The public opposition to the Vietnam War was greatly enhanced in the early months of 1968. First, by a North Vietnamese offensive on 30 January 1968. While most Vietnamese relaxed during the Tet (or lunar) new year holiday, the North Vietnamese staged well coordinated attacks on a vast number of targets in South Vietnam – including a suicide attack on the US mission in Saigon. The operations weakened America's positions in cities and villages all over the South, and they shattered public confidence in government assurances at home. General Westmoreland argued (correctly, as it turned out) that the offensive had cost the North Vietnamese irreparable losses, and that their military capabilities were exhausted to the point of collapse. But Westmoreland undermined his own case when he also repeated the official line that victory was close at hand. His credibility was destroyed by a news leak which revealed that the general had secretly asked the president for 206,000 more US troops.

Second, the war effort was weakened by the defection of US public figures. It received an irreparable blow in February 1968 when Walter Cronkite, America's most respected newsman, openly questioned whether the USA would ever win the Vietnam War. And President Johnson's resolve was shaken when several senior officials, led by Dean Acheson and McGeorge Bundy, privately told him that he was being misled by his advisers; they argued that the costs of the war had soared so high that it had long rendered victory a meaningless term, and that the burden of the war was endangering America's own domestic economy – arguments with which Johnson's own secretary of defence, Clark Clifford, strongly agreed. In March, the president announced that he would not run for re-election in the fall.

Eroding the cold war consensus at home

America's foreign-policy consensus was defined by Franklin D. Roosevelt under the impact of world war. Harry Truman and Dwight D. Eisenhower consolidated it during the early phase of the cold war. John F. Kennedy pressed it to its fullest limits. Then Lyndon B. Johnson pushed it beyond endurance. From the mid-1960s, American politics drowned in a bitter debate about the ends and means of American foreign policy. When Nixon took office, the consensus, which had been the ballast of US foreign policy from Truman to Johnson, was at an end. On 20 January 1969, there was no basic foreign policy to be handed over intact to the new administration. Nixon's national security adviser observed this and insisted that the main challenge to US foreign policy no longer came from the growth of a foreign military threat, but from the erosion of a domestic consensus. At the threshold of the 1970s, the main threat to US security was neither military nor economic, reiterated Henry Kissinger (1969, pp. 79, 199). It was normative and philosophical.

There were several reasons for this change of affairs. One of them involved a generational change in America's foreign-policy leadership. The old-time framers of America's foreign-policy precepts were retiring. This departing group of foreign-policy veterans constituted a generation who were forged into a cohesive group by the same traumatic experiences of the 1920s and 1930s – Dean Acheson, Charles Bohlen, John McCloy and Averell Harriman, Robert Lovett. They were replaced by men who were unschooled in the old pre-World

War II dogmas and pre-Depression doctrines. They were the 'best and the brightest' of their generation – George Ball, McGeorge and William Bundy, Robert McNamara, Maxwell Taylor (Halberstam 1969; Hodgeson 1973) – but they brought to their jobs different experiences from those of their predecessors.

Another reason for the change in American affairs pertains to the changing attitudes of the population – to changes in perceptions and the will to contain Communism by military means. These changes were notably expressed in the rapidly growing resistance to the Vietnam War. This war had indubitably destroyed Vietnamese society – the fighting destroyed the agriculture and moved the farmers, defoliants triggered an ecological catastrophe, urban terror destroyed city life and unravelled the very fibre of civil society. In addition, the Vietnam War had also contributed to the destruction of American society. The palliatives which attend any war had a direct effect on the US military – drug abuse, venereal disease, petty crimes and violence were plentiful in Saigon and commonplace among frustrated US soldiers. Morale and discipline were low. The war had become a growing cancer which drained the United States of its foreign-policy energies at home and eroded its prestige abroad. The debate about this war ruthlessly exposed the major flaws in American foreign policy.

Also, the war undermined respect for America's political institutions. An anti-war movement was growing in American society. A 'new left' emerged which thrived on the opposition to war and on the counter-culture which critically scrutinized claims which were long taken for granted by established members of American society. Some aspects of the movements were iterations of a traditional American scepticism towards big government. But others went further. Applying radical analyses to American society, some activists rejected the creeds and codes of the establishment. They portrayed America's entire political system as crooked. They saw the Vietnam War as a logical outcome of a corrupt system.

Comparable connections between wars in distant provinces and the emergence of radical, counter-cultural movements at home can be found in all challenged hegemons. However, in the American case this phenomenon was particularly significant. The reason for this must be sought in two kinds of changes which were unique to the 1960s and contributed to rapid changes in American social life. First, there was a rapid expansion in higher education. The 1960s saw a dramatic increase in the number of young Americans who attended colleges and universities. Second, American society went through a veritable media revolution. This development was partly driven by advances in communications technology – transistors and microelectronics occasioned rapid progress in miniaturization and in wireless transmission of sound and images. The development was also driven by the speed with which such innovations were commercially applied. The development of popular music played an important role in the cultural transformations of the 1960s – especially the development of rock. Compared with the handsome representations of the pop idols of the 1940s, the pioneers of rock were freaks and malcontents. They rejected the white and wholesome suburban ideals of the 1950s, and drew their lyricism and emotional power from the gritty rural traditions of Anglo-Irish riff and folk music and African-American gospel and blues. Their dark poetry and insistent beat recalled the archetypes of energy and passion, and they were informed by the *ressentiment* of radicalism and romantic rebellion. Their influence was immediate, international and momentous. And it only increased as the media industry replaced the singles of the 1950s with the albums of the 1960s. This shift facilitated the marketing not only of music, but of concepts, personalities and lifestyles.

Rock exploited the opportunities afforded by the new media – portable gramophones and tape decks, car radio programmes, TV shows, movies, etc. It helped open up a public sphere for a new generation of suburban youth trapped in the comforts of second-hand experiences and with money to burn. Many rebels turned out to be imaginative and ambitious commercial entrepreneurs, with an uncanny ability to convert counter-cultural themes into successful industries – trademark clothes, boutiques, discotheques, night clubs, art galleries, photo and model agencies, record labels, head shops, pornographic magazines, etc. In the 1960s, rock became the dominant musical form in America and a major carrier of counter-cultural values and norms. It 'permanently altered the sensoriums of two generations of Americans born after World War Two' (Paglia 1992, p. 20). Indeed, it transformed the entire American sphere of influence on to a global scale. The new communications technologies allowed the values and norms of the US rock culture to be disseminated internationally and reproduce America's commercialized postwar generation in other countries which were marked by increasing openness, welfare, and revolutions in mass media and higher education.

Western Europe followed the American example most closely; here, too, expanding universities created a segment of budding academics who, in the prime of life, were no longer children, but not yet participating in the remunerative processes of the economy nor integrated into stabilizing norms and roles of society. They had time and money but few socio-economic duties and routines to attend to. And they had an urge to distance themselves from established values, norms and rules.

Erosion of the cold war consensus abroad

The criticisms which began in the 1960s against America's war in Vietnam were carried over into the 1970s. Then they were more sharply honed, included in the American youth culture and exported to audiences abroad.

The US dominated the world media after World War II. In the 1940s and 1950s, this dominance eased the spread of liberal democratic values and fortified US leadership around the world. In the 1960s and 1970s, the US dominance of the world media was greater than ever; but the media content had become more diverse. The US mass media were increasingly filled by reactions to the old, straight-laced *status quo*. They expressed civil rights arguments and anti-militarism. They also catered to younger audiences. Through the US youth culture, critical messages spread through the US-dominated, cosmopolitan public sphere. These messages were often most pronounced in those countries with which the United States had evolved its tightest postwar connections and where American culture had the strongest hold on the population.

In addition, the cosmopolitan sphere was intruded upon by America's enemies. The radical one-party regimes in Cuba, Vietnam, China and the Soviet Union had always recognized that culture played an important role in politics. In their domestic affairs, they sought to maintain a tight monopoly of information. In foreign affairs they devised media and propaganda techniques as anti-imperialist weapons in the cold war. For the leaders in Havana, Hanoi, Peiping and Moscow, the cold war was fought on two levels: in the jungles of the Third World and in global public sphere. Accordingly, the purpose of the North Vietnamese Tet offensive of 1968 was to win decisive victories on two fronts: on the battlefield and in global public opinion. The North Vietnamese were ultimately defeated on the battlefield – after weeks of close combat, US soldiers managed to contain and defeat their offensives on the ground. However, the North Vietnamese won the war in the public sphere. Thus, in spite of the fact that the North Vietnamese were defeated militarily, the Tet offensive must be counted as a decisive turning point in the Vietnam War. It turned American opinion around towards opposition to the war; also, the offensive drove the thin end of a wedge between the United States and many of its Western allies.

America's rivals systematically sought to influence the populations of the rest of the world. They often scored victories. Notably along the margins of Western societies, e.g., in segments of the young, rebellious generations. These generations rejected the stiff moralism and the *status quo* attitudes of the 1950s. This rejection was magnified by the international public sphere and intensified by conflicts like the Vietnam War. In some sectors it yielded a wholesale rejection of US values and policies, and an embrace of the rhetoric and values of the established 'other'. It was predominantly a US generation struggle, but it was broadcast globally by the modern media of the counter-culture and swelled into a global anti-American tidal wave. Politically it tied in with sympathies for anti-colonial struggles in the non-Western world. If the counter-culture was affected by Elvis, the political youth movement was informed by

'Che'. The distance from Sinatra to Lennon was far greater than that from Lennon to Lenin. If Hendrix and Fanon became symbols of similar causes, it may have been for no other reason than the superficial fact that they were both famous. If nothing else, they were united by 'fame' and included in a public sphere which was increasingly cosmopolitan in scope and commercial in nature.

Conclusions: challenges

As the second phase of the twentieth-century world order evolved, the United States and the Soviet Union were perceived as more equal players on the world scene. First because the second half of the 1960s saw a rapid build-up of the Soviet strategic capabilities, so that by 1970 the Soviet Union had achieved nuclear parity with the USA. At the same time, a rapidly increasing number of nations came to view the two superpowers in terms of moral equivalence.

This change in moral perception reflected to some degree the development of the superpowers' nuclear capabilities. But more importantly it reflected a steep decline in America's international prestige. This decline was an effect of America's interventionist responses to Third World challenges – most particularly, it was an effect of America's warfare in Vietnam. The US intervention in South East Asia was nothing less than a catastrophe. In a surprisingly short time America had squandered a substantial part of its wartime goodwill and legitimacy through its small and dirty Third World wars.

The most visible challenge to US hegemony was expressed by the socialist bloc and by the Soviet Union most conspicuously. However, as Soviet power grew, the US–Soviet relationship became encased in a common set of risk-averse cold war norms and rules. This softened the sharp edges of the superpower rivalry. An absolute antagonism still existed between the two, yet as an adjustment to nuclear realities the Soviets altered the Leninist doctrine of absolute antagonism between capitalist and socialist societies to a doctrine of peaceful competition. The Americans, on their side, suspended their initial cold war doctrine concerning the 'rollback' of Communism.

Although the policy-makers in Washington routinely portrayed the Soviet Union as their chief rival in world affairs, they often considered China the more dangerous opponent. In practical politics, the most consequential challenges increasingly came from those post-colonial nations in the Third World which had adopted a Chinese-style foreign-policy discourse. North Vietnam presented a notably noxious challenge to the United States. This underdeveloped, far-way country managed, with substantial aid from China, to lock the United States into a senseless war which cost over 50,000 young American lives and untold billions of dollars, and which sowed deep dissent in American society.

Vietnam, then, was a most consequential challenger to the US hegemony. But the Vietnamese must share this dubious honour with the Cubans. The reason is that it was Cuba which staged the most significant mythogenic Third World revolution of the postwar era, and Castro became for many Americans the first close embodiment of the 'Other'. The Cuban revolution was not obviously Communist at the outset; rather, it was expressed in a general, humanitarian discourse – not unlike that which the American minutemen had used some hundred and fifty years earlier. However, the revolution was radicalized partly by America's inability to understand its nature, and partly by its pragmatic collaboration with the Soviet Union. And in the process, Fidel Castro alerted the USA to a horrible possibility: that as Western, democratic values spread to the Third World, they might undermine Western interests rather than reinforce them.

The Cuban revolution was in many respects a 'dress rehearsal' (Bailey 1990) for subsequent anti-colonial struggles which occurred in other regions of the Third World. It put the United States in an excruciating dilemma. On the one hand, anti-imperialism had always been an important girder in America's foreign policy platform. The USA had itself been a colony. Anti-colonialism had been an important political stance since the days of Washington; and anti-imperialism had been a characteristic stance in America's economic policy at least since the days of Wilson. Long before the twentieth century, America's foreign policy had consistently expressed sympathy with those who were oppressed by colonialism and exploited by imperialism. On the other hand, once the USA assumed responsibilities for policing a brittle cold war order, it suddenly realized that America's traditional discourse of anti-colonialism dovetailed with that of the Soviet Union; that during the cold war, a worldwide policy of decolonization might, in fact, serve the expansionist interests of the USSR.

Notes

1 In 1953, President Eisenhower developed a steely conviction that nuclear weapons were useless in war. The old general, who had studied Carl von Clausewitz carefully, served as a junior officer in the 1920s, and may have relied on the Clausewitzian notion of 'absolute war' when he warned the world, in his December 1953 speech to the United Nations, that a nuclear war would mean

> the probability of civilization destroyed – the annihilation of the irreplaceable heritage of mankind handed down to us generation from generation – and the condemnation of mankind to begin all over again the age-old struggle upward from savagery towards decency, and right, and justice. (Quoted in Gaddis 1997, p. 227)

After Stalin's death, similar notions surfaced among Soviet leaders. In March 1954,

Georgi Malenkov unexpectedly announced that humanity no longer faced a choice between 'cold' and 'hot' war. Rather, owing to the advent of all-destructive nuclear weapons, the choice was between 'cold' war and 'the end of world civilization' – an announcement which amounted to the first acknowledgement by a Soviet leader of what Truman and Eisenhower had already recognized: that nuclear weapons were making great-power war obsolete. When Nikita Khrushchev replaced Malenkov in February 1955, the new Soviet leader entertained the same attitude towards nuclear weapons as his predecessor. And in February 1956, Khrushchev announced to the Twentieth Party Congress that nuclear weapons had made it necessary to jettison Lenin's (and Stalin's) doctrine of the inevitability of war with capitalist powers. Khrushchev instead introduced a new doctrine of 'peaceful coexistence'.

2 In 1957 President Eisenhower ordered a top-secret investigation of America's nuclear posture to update the seven-year-old NSC–68. The final report, written by Rowland Gaither and reverberant with reactions to the Soviet 'Sputnik', recommended that the US increase its military spending by 50 per cent in order to meet the 'expansionist' Soviet threat. Eisenhower dismissed the Gaither report as misguided – correctly, as it turned out: in 1957 the Soviet leadership decided not to build a first generation of intercontinental ballistic missiles (ICBMs), but to wait for further developments in missile technology. Instead, Premier Khrushchev slyly encouraged the false US perceptions of a Soviet build-up (Horelick and Rush 1966, pp. 36–8).

3 Khrushchev sent a KGB representative to Havana. His reports were so intriguing that Anastas Mikoyan, deputy chairman of the Soviet council of ministers, soon went to assess the situation for himself. Mikoyan immediately found that in Cuba the Soviets had been handed on a silver platter an unexpected opportunity to unsettle the Americans. But he also found more: the Cuban revolution affected the ageing Communist as if it were an ideological fountain of youth. 'I have been told', Eisenhower noted some months later, 'that Mikoyan on returning to Moscow from Cuba, was exuberantly rejuvenated, finding that what was going on in the youthful and disorganized Cuban revolution brought him back to the early years of the Russian Revolution'. Mikoyan subsequently confirmed this in a conversation with Dean Rusk: 'You Americans must realize what Cuba means to us old Bolsheviks. We have been waiting all of our lives for a country to go Communist without the Red Army. It has happened in Cuba, and it makes us feel like boys again' (Eisenhower to Harold Macmillan, 11 July 1960, FRUS: 1958–60, vi. p. 1,003; quoted in Gaddis 1997, p. 181).

9

The end of US hegemony?

Reason will be replaced by Revelation. Instead of Rational Law,
objective truths perceptible to any who will undergo the necessary
intellectual discipline, Knowledge will degenerate into a riot of
subjective visions ... Whose cosmogonies will be created out of
some forgotten personal resentment, complete epics written in private languages, the daubs of schoolchildren ranked above the
greatest masterpieces. Idealism will be replaced by Materialism.
Life after death will be an eternal dinner party where all the guests
are twenty years old ... Justice will be replaced by Pity as the
cardinal human virtue, and all fear of retribution will vanish.
(Auden 1945)

In the late 1970s, the United States showed several signs of being a declining
hegemon. Like Spain, the United Provinces and England, the United States
continued to decline during the third phase of its world order. Its military
capabilities fell relative to those of other powers – that, at least, was the
common perception of the time. Also, the United States increasingly engaged
in foreign conflicts and wars. These engagements were reflected in a steady
increase in the US defence budgets. After several years of stable or decreasing
budgets, the United States began to increase its expenditures on security and
defence substantially after 1978.

Second, the United States clearly suffered from conspicuous adverse economic trends during the late 1970s and early 1980s. Productivity slowed down
and American products were increasingly defeated in foreign market competition. These trends were reflected in a wave of bankruptcies which washed
across America's industrial heartland. It was also reflected in yearly deficits in
America's foreign trade and in a rapidly mounting foreign debt.

In addition, as in previous cases of hegemonic decline, these trends of
military and economic deterioration were observed by historians and social
theorists. The trends were so plentifully recorded that Samuel Huntington
coined the term 'declinism' to mark the discussions which they engendered
as a distinct approach to the study of US foreign policy. As in previous cases

of decline, the commentators tended to interpret the events in light of a liberally grounded overstretch hypothesis. The most famous overstretch de-clinist was Paul Kennedy (1987), whose book on the *Rise and Fall of the Great Powers* was a bestseller during the late 1980s. However, by the early 1990s, it was apparent that Kennedy's forecasts were mistaken. His warnings that the audible creaking in the joints of America's political system might presage a political crisis proved groundless; it was not the United States but, rather, the Soviet Union that spun out of political control. Also, his fear of America's imminent economic decline proved groundless; during the 1990s, the American economy visibly recovered from its slump and re-emerged on the world scene as the pre-eminent economy. Also, as a function of the Soviet Union's collapse and of America's economic revival, the United States re-emerged in the 1990s as the world's pre-eminent great power.

Changes in the world economy and US stagnation

The 1970s and 1980s saw a rapid growth of what Samuel Huntington termed 'declinist' literature – i.e., social-science arguments which showed how the United States was losing its pre-eminence in world affairs. The declinists regularly appealed to change in the world economy. It was a common argument in the declinist case that the US share of the global product fell from over 30 per cent in 1955, via 28 per cent in 1975, to about 23 per cent in 1979 (Block 1981, pp. 74–7, 86f.). Among the many concerns addressed in this vast lit-erature, two major events of the 1970s were commonly portrayed as watersheds in international economic relations: the breakdown of the Bretton Woods system and the Organization of Petroleum Exporting Countries (OPEC) oil embargo.

The first event followed President Nixon's 1971 announcement that the United States would no longer exchange dollars for gold. This decision meant that the United States could no longer guarantee the convertibility and the stability of the world's major currencies. And since no other single country could assume America's old role as guarantor, Nixon's announcement in effect caused the old Bretton Woods arrangement to unravel. As the fluctuations of the world economy were no longer harnessed by enforceable rules, the ex-change rates of great power currencies began to float and the world economy suddenly became more uncertain and unpredictable.

The second event was caused by the oil-producing nations temporarily restricting the gush of petroleum to the Western world. The first time this happened was in 1973, triggered by the Yom Kippur War in the Middle East. Arab members of OPEC reduced the flow of oil to Europe to a trickle in order to show that they had the power to paralyse the economy of any Western country which supported Israel's campaigns against its Muslim neighbours. The OPEC action caused the world price of petroleum to leap fourfold – from less than $3 a barrel to over $11. A second oil shock occurred in the wake of the revolution in Iran (1979). This time, the world price of oil made an unprecedented jump to over $40 a barrel.

These two events contributed to alter the world economy of the 1980s. The collapse of the Bretton Woods system meant that the United States lost control of the world economy – and if the United States lost control, then there was no other single country which could take up the slack. The world economy began to follow complex market principles to a greater degree than at any other time in the postwar world. The petroleum price hikes played havoc with the world market.

The immediate effect of these price hikes was to depress the economies of oil-importing countries while significantly increasing the earnings of the world's oil-exporting countries. At one extreme, many oil-importing countries found themselves unable to foot skyrocketing energy bills, their industries quickly grinding to a halt and their populations sinking into destitution. At the other extreme, many oil-exporting states accumulated petrodollars at such a rapid rate that they did not know what to do with their new-found fortunes. In effect, they channelled their vast fortunes into the Western world – they spent them on Western products, invested them in Western companies or deposited them in Western banks.

The United States was directly affected by these market changes. For example, as the value of the dollar was undermined by inflation and uncertainty, the United States attracted vast amounts of foreign capital. US real estate and many of America's core corporations were purchased by foreign investors during the 1980s. By 1990, several landmark US institutions had fallen into foreign hands – RCA, CBS Records, Columbia Pictures, Doubleday, Firestone, Goodyear, Giant Food, Grand Union, Bloomingdale's, Pillsbury, National Steel, among others. As the list grew longer, more Americans saw it as a reflection of the nation's economic decline. They grew increasingly concerned, and demanded that their politicians 'do something' to stop the Germans and the Japanese from 'buying up' America.[1]

The United States was also indirectly affected. For example, many *nouveau-riches* oil-exporting countries deposited their petrodollars in American banks – and many banks set up offshore affiliates in order to manage the new deposits, thereby exempting substantial financial assets from governmental control. The banks, then, sought to unload these massive deposits on an increasingly glutted market and began to dump cheap loans to needy customers – foremost among whom were poor, oil-importing countries whose economies were pushed towards bankruptcy by the massive rise in oil prices. In the absence of any political regime to regulate these new world economic trends and financial dynamics, the world market rapidly responded with a severe case of inflation. Those poor states which had borrowed heavily on cheap terms to stave off mounting energy bills were suddenly faced with escalating interest rates. Soon they faced interest payments which vastly exceeded the principal. The debt of many Third World countries quickly spun out of control. They could no longer service their banks, which in many cases were American conglomerates. Several major US banks suddenly saw their very existence threatened by customers' inability to pay back their loans.

During the 1980s, several US banks balanced on the cusp of solvency. They appealed to the US government to bail them out. But the Reagan administration was committed to a free-market doctrine of competition, and was reluctant to come to their aid. Besides, the administration were facing substantial economic problems of its own. The federal outlays increased substantially during Reagan's first term. The federal revenues hardly increased at all (due e.g. to Reagan's pledge to cut taxes). The result was a rapid doubling of America's national debt – from nearly $1,000 billion when Reagan entered the White House in 1981 to nearly $2,000 billion when he began his second term in 1985.[2]

What could account for this state of affairs? The short answer offered by most contemporary observers was an appeal, in some way or another, to the principle of unequal growth. The US economy suffered a period of slow and uncertain expansion, whereas other states enjoyed a higher rate. According to the president's advisers, this was a natural development. The US share of world production had long been artificially high – during the aftermath of World War II, the United States had few if any serious competitors, since most other industrialized states were exhausted by war. But as these states recovered during the 1950s and modernized during the 1960s, they presented increasingly stiffer competition to American producers of goods and services. Clearly, during the 1970s several fully recovered nations re-entered the world market in full force and contributed to a steadily tougher world economic climate.

Countries in Europe and Asia emerged as strong competitors to American producers. Europe had developed greater economic strength and greater political cohesion during the postwar era; West Germany was emerging as a particularly strong challenger to the American lead in the world market. Japan and several other Asian Pacific states launched export-driven development strategies. While shielding their own economies from competition, and benefiting from the open international economic order (which was created and long protected by the United States), several Asian economies identified a suitable niche in the world market and sought to fill it with specialized products of competitive price and quality.

By the 1980s, the western Pacific could boast the highest regional growth rate in the world.[3] Many American producers were losing the competitive battle to Asian rivals. Demand for the products of America's old-line manufacturing industries, such as metals, declined markedly during the 1970s. And as American consumers increasingly preferred foreign products to domestic brands, imports of cheaper foreign goods into America increased. As a result, the United States developed an unprecedented deficit in its balance of trade.

During the 1950s and 1960s, the United States had large surpluses on its merchandise trade and current accounts. But since 1971 – when the USA recorded its first merchandise trade deficit in over a century – Americans have consistently imported more goods than they have exported. Troubled by this trend, US business leaders demanded that President Reagan initiate measures which would shield American industries from foreign competition. But Reagan refused. The president was wedded to a free-market doctrine. His administration began, in fact, to deregulate the American economy. The vulnerable sectors were thus more exposed to world market forces. The US trade deficit skyrocketed from $24 billion in 1980 via $132 billion in 1985 to a staggering $171 billion in 1987.[4] The national economy reeled from the impact of the largest wave of business failures since the Great Depression.[5] Reagan's policies involved a globalization of competition which increased pressure on US businesses. But he was convinced that this would force US managers to restructure, slim down, toughen up and become more competitive in the longer run.

Interstate challenges and increasing defence costs

In the 1970s, the United States was facing more problems than those presented by a rapidly changing world economy; it also faced a changing interstate system. During the 1960s, the United States had increased its punitive capabilities, but it had done so at a slower rate than the Soviet Union. Consequently, the interstate system changed from the unipolar configuration of the 1950s towards a bipolar structure. By the late 1960s, a more equal distribution of nuclear weapons had produced an equipollent balance of terror between the two superpowers.

In addition, growing tensions within the Communist world erupted in armed clashes between the Soviet Union and China along the Amur river border in 1969. This added a complicating element to the bipolar view of interstate politics. During the 1970s, world politics were increasingly cast as a triangular constellation with the USA, the USSR and China as the major powers. In this environment, interstate affairs came to be conducted along the lines of Realpolitik.

Towards a multipolar order

President Richard Nixon and his security adviser Henry Kissinger saw it as their role to manage these changes in ways which maintained the national interests of the United States. They singled out for special attention what they saw as the decisive change of the age: that the United States was falling behind in the geostrategic context of the international system. The spread of nuclear weapons to new powers – such as China (in 1964), India (in 1974), Israel (1979?) and Pakistan; and possibly also Argentina, Brazil, Iraq and South Korea – contributed somewhat to the relative decline of American power. However, it was the Soviet military build-up which affected the global balance of forces the most.

The Soviet Union expanded its nuclear capabilities greatly after the mid-1960s. The United States also expanded its nuclear capabilities, but at a much slower rate. Consequently, by 1970 a rough equivalence of nuclear power – or 'parity' – existed between the two superpowers. During the 1970s, the USA maintained a constant number of 1,252 nuclear launch platforms, whereas the USSR steadily increased its number. Soon the Soviet number of launchers surpassed that of the US by a wide margin. As a consequence, the relative power of the United States appeared to be diminishing. In the face of this development, the United States replaced its traditional goal of 'nuclear superiority' with the concept of 'nuclear sufficiency'.[6]

In the 1950s, the Americans had vastly overestimated the Soviet rate of nuclear procurement; in the 1970s, they underestimated it. By 1980 great uncertainties existed about the relative capabilities of the two superpowers. In the early 1980s, most Americans believed that the United States was the militarily weaker of the two superpowers.[7] Doubts about America's conventional capabilities were added to these uncertainties as several new states emerged in the international system and challenged old notions of international order. China was the most significant newcomer. The Chinese leaders broke irrevocably with the Soviet Union in the 1960s and engaged in clear rivalry with their former mentor. By the 1970s, Chinese leaders were willing to cooperate with the USA. Henry Kissinger's 'secret trip' to Beijing in July 1971 was a watershed in postwar international relations because it introduced elements of balance-of-power politics into the bipolar world of the cold war. Presidents Nixon and Carter sometimes referred to their 'China card', by which they meant their new-found ability to press the Soviet leaders into compliance by drafting China into an anti-Soviet initiative. The international scene still described a bipolar system by the 1980s; however, it had become a system with fewer and fewer alliance handicaps, thus providing opportunities for a degree of balance-of-power manipulation (at which Nixon and Kissinger were true masters).

Nixon and Kissinger exploited the Sino-Soviet rift to shape a new global balance of power in which the United States could retreat from Vietnam with minimal damage to US international prestige. Their achievement was to manage the transition from a period dominated by the cold war to a new phase in which the elements of the cold war were brought into balance with the new elements of *détente*. Kissinger's design was essentially a balance-of-power system. It survived him. But his successors were not nearly as adept at managing this new global balance as its author. The design deteriorated. And the reasons for its deterioration are found in two major internal weaknesses. The first was that Kissinger was unwilling to understand fully and respect the liberal tenets of America's political mythology and to give his system indigenous roots – as a result, US public opinion did not adequately support his policies and Congress did not provide the resources needed for their implementation. The second weakness was that Kissinger allowed no independent role for the Third World. Kissinger always perceived Third World issues as a reflection of the superpower confrontation, and the United States appeared unprepared when a second wave of global revolution erupted in the spring of 1974 and triggered a major challenge to the US world order.

In addition to China, a great number of smaller states emerged as actors in the international system. This was largely the effect of the postwar great power policy of decolonization. The unravelling of the old colonial empires was attended by turbulence and unrest. Several of the new states had won their independence through long wars of liberation which had contributed to the wave of revolutions which washed across the Third World during the late 1960s – a wave which the administrations of Kennedy, Johnson and Nixon had managed to contain. In the mid-1970s, a second and more substantial revolutionary wave washed across the world. It caught Presidents Ford and Carter by surprise.

Internal and external challenges

President Carter was badly equipped to deal with this new global challenge. First, it erupted shortly after America's inglorious withdrawal from Vietnam. Carter had run for president in 1975/76 on an anti-establishment ticket. He had exploited the popular outrage at corruption and skulduggery which erupted in the wake of Vietnam and Watergate. He vowed to bring honesty back into Washington politics. Thus, he had a domestic policy focus and no clear foreign policy platform – other than to preserve détente and guard human rights.

Second, Carter faced a revived US Congress. As a reaction to the Vietnam War, Congress had sought to reduce military spending in the early 1970s, and to delay or cancel procurement of new weapons. In the wake of the Watergate scandal, Congress had passed measures like the War Powers Act, which were designed to control and constrain the office of the presidency.

Third, America's conventional forces had deteriorated. Even if the president should decide to implement a new containment effort, and even if Congress should decide to fund it, the United States might not have military forces that were up to the job. The US military establishment was shaken and divided by the defeat in Vietnam. Officers and soldiers were frustrated by repeated budget cuts. Morale and discipline were stretched to breaking point. The United States faced the second wave of revolutionary challenges with a 'hollow army'.

While the United States thus writhed in its own frustrations, external threats multiplied. In addition to the complication of the revolutionary threats, great power relations grew increasingly complex. Two important revolutions erupted on Carter's watch: in Ethiopia (February 1974) and in Portugal (April 1974). The first toppled Ethiopia's emperor Haile Selassie; the second toppled the last avowedly colonial regime in Europe and gave, overnight, power to radical liberation movements in half a dozen African colonies. Ethiopia was at the time the third most populous state in Africa. Selassie had provided one of America's most important bridgeheads on the African continent – and had in return been the recipient of two-thirds of America's postwar military aid to the sub-Saharan region. His fall initiated a political deterioration which would end, in 1977, with Ethiopia's severing of military ties with the United States – and the Soviet Union moving into the vacuum.

The revolution in Portugal opened the door to immediate revolution in no fewer than six African countries – five Portuguese colonies (Angola, Mozambique, Guinea Bissau, Cape Verde and São Tomé) and Zimbabwe. In October 1975, Cuba, the Soviet Union's primary ally in the Third World, sent thousands of troops to Angola. Their mission was to defend the besieged socialist government of Angola's new president Agostino Neto against opponents (FNLA and MPLA) backed by South Africa, Zaïre, China and the CIA. Such outside interference increased the level of conflict in Africa. This increase suddenly belied the American perception of a 'manageable' Third World. The extant conflicts in Namibia and South Africa flared up. The government of Lt-Col. Mathieu Kerekou in Benin suddenly (November 1974) proclaimed that 'Marxism–Leninism' was the country's official ideology; he was echoed (in June 1975) by Madagascar's Didier Ratsiraka. Nationalists attempted to take over the copper-producing region of Zaïre (1977 and 1978) and Western troops intervened to repel them. POLISARIO guerrillas intensified their opposition to Moroccan forces. Liberia and Libya showed signs of turning against the West.

Comparable complications erupted in Asia. The wars in Vietnam, Laos and Cambodia all came to a head when their pro-American governments simultaneously collapsed in 1975. In Afghanistan a left-wing military *coup* (1978) brought to power a regime which was determined to forge close ties with the Soviet Union. In neighbouring Iran, America's old anti-Communist ally, Shah Reza Pahlavi, fell from power in 1979; he was ousted by a mass insurrection and replaced by the leadership of an anti-American orthodox Shiite clergy.

To these troubles was added a series of upheavals in Central America. The most significant occurred in Nicaragua, where radical Sandinista guerrillas toppled the US-supported dictator Somoza in a Cuban-style revolution. Politicians in Washington tried very hard to contain the Sandinista revolution – they sought to block its spread to nearby areas and to prevent the Soviet leaders exploiting it for their own sinister purposes.

This spate of Third World upheavals amounted to the most massive revolutionary wave that the United States had faced in the postwar period. US policy-makers perceived it as a major Soviet offensive. This was hardly an accurate perception. However, the radical wave which suddenly swept the Third World attracted the attention of the Soviet leadership. The many anti-Western *coups* and overthrows in Africa, Asia and the Middle East quickly convinced the ageing leaders in the Kremlin that history favoured revolution after all. They saw their old, ideal precepts confirmed and decided to support several radical anti-capitalist revolutions. However, this commitment caused great strains on the subtle web of superpower norms and rules which had been established during the 1960s and 1970s. The Soviet decision to support friendly Communists in Afghanistan by an invasion (December 1979) was the final straw. It destroyed the brittle trust which sustained the rules of superpower *détente*. It ended any pretence of superpower cooperation and reinvigorated America's traditional concept of Communist containment.

The Carter administration immediately adopted more forceful security and defence policies. But it was too late. Carter had lost the confidence of a nervous nation. In 1980 he also lost the presidential elections to California governor Ronald Reagan who combined a distaste for Communism which was reminiscent of the early 1950s with a fundamentalist faith in a free-market economic doctrine.

Reagan's first years in the White House coincided with Brezhnev's last years in the Kremlin. There were disturbing superficial similarities between these two leaders. Both were old men steeped in the imagery of the cold war. Their conceptual directives were vague and largely driven by tradition and ideology. Both of them were primarily absorbed with pressing domestic concerns. Neither exerted strong and purposeful foreign-policy leadership – protective circles of long-time friends saw to it that the two heads of state were not unnecessarily bothered by day-to-day decisions.

In the USSR, top-level interaction deteriorated to crisis proportions after

1982 as the removal of old leaders fuelled the fires of factionalism.[8] In the USA, by contrast, the situation improved greatly. The foreign-policy makers began to agree on a single approach; the cabinet became more engaged in foreign-policy decision-making; the president's statements became less rhetorical and more informed. In 1983 the administration defined clear and articulate strategies to counter the Soviet Union. In March 1983, Reagan announced that he had a plan to counter the Soviet Union's nuclear threat: a Strategic Defence Initiative (SDI). And in February 1985, at the beginning of his second term in office, he launched a strategy designed to meet the Soviet expansion in the Third World: the so-called 'Reagan doctrine'.

The SDI was conceived as a high-tech shield which could intercept incoming nuclear missiles. It was designed to have many purposes. The most important was to address certain emotional needs in the population for certainty and safety. President Reagan never accepted that the doctrine of mutual assured destruction (MAD) contributed enough to the nation's security – 'it was like having two westerners standing in a saloon aiming their guns at each others' head' (Reagan 1990, p. 547). The president thought of the SDI as a replacement for MAD. Some of his advisers conceived of the SDI as a tonic which would invigorate research in microelectronic technologies and push the US computer industries into unquestionable world leadership in the field. Still another group saw the SDI as a way to challenge the Soviet Union to a hi-tech, high-cost arms race – a contest which would represent a far heavier burden for the technologically backward USSR than for the advanced United States.

The 'Reagan doctrine' began as a presidential pledge to support anti-Soviet rebel groups wherever they existed in the world. This pledge was, like previous presidential doctrines, a response to a foreign-policy crisis. It addressed the widespread sentiment that the global balance of forces had shifted to the advantage of the Soviet Union.[9] And it intended not only to contain this new wave of Soviet expansionism but to 'roll back Communism'. Reagan insisted that the proper way to do this was to nourish and defend freedom and democracy, and to communicate these ideals everywhere he could. This pledge to support anti-Soviet forces on every continent proclaimed a new US readiness to support indigenous anti-Marxist rebels – 'freedom fighters' as the president consistently called them – in an active effort to roll back Soviet influence in the Third World (Knutsen 1992).

American overstretch?

While President Reagan was assuming steadily greater global commitments, Paul Kennedy was preparing his weighty *Rise and Fall of the Great Powers*, and the concerns of the times carry strong echoes on its pages. As when he discusses the American predicament from a historical perspective:

Simply because [the United States] is *the* global superpower, with far more
extensive military commitments than a regional Power like Japan or West
Germany, it requires much larger defense forces – in just the same way as
imperial Spain felt it needed a far larger army than its contemporaries and
Victorian Britain insisted upon a much bigger navy than any other country.
... [Yet] a very heavy investment in armaments, while bringing greater
security in the short term, may so erode the commercial competitiveness of
the American economy that the nation will be *less* secure in the long term.
(Kennedy 1987, p. 523f.)

Kennedy was not the only observer who was troubled by Reagan's belligerent
foreign policies and by the economic controversies which marked his
presidency. Neither was he the only one who sensed a connection between
the two phenomena. Many observers embraced the old notion that a zero-
sum relationship exists between wealth and force. And they noted, first,
that US military expenditures had been on the rise since the late 1970s – that
twelve years of Republican government under Reagan and Bush had tripled
the US defence budget (from nearly $90 billion in 1975, via $130 billion in
1980 and $250 billion in 1985, to nearly $290 billion in 1990). Then they
observed that this rise in military costs coincided with the advent of a mushrooming national debt. Finally, they concluded that the first somehow caused
the second.

This argument, which lies at the core of the overstretch hypothesis, would
lead one to expect that a sustained increase in defence expenditures would be
followed by economic downturn. This expectation is, however, hardly borne
out by US budget statistics. The early 1980s – when the United States suffered
its most marked period of economic stagnation – were not attended by particularly high defence expenditures. In fact, the defence burden of the 1970s
was lighter than at any other time in America's postwar history. Reagan's
critics noted correctly that America's arms expenditures increased conspicuously in absolute terms – from $85 billion in 1975 to $130 billion in 1980.
However, they neglected to note that this increase occurred in an atmosphere
of inflation. And, as Table 21 shows, the increase in the defence budget was
largely offset by comparable increases in the federal budget and in America's
gross national product (GNP).

The overstretch hypothesis would lead one to expect that America's period
of economic decline would be preceded by a steady increase in military expenditures. The budget figures presented in Table 21 do not confirm this
expectation. The table rather shows that the period of economic decline was
preceded by a long and steady decline in military expenditures. Since the Korean
War, America's defence expenditure has declined steadily as a percentage of the

nation's GNP – except for the period of global challenge in the late 1960s and early 1970s.

Table 21   *US military expenditure and national debt, 1965–95 (in US$ billions)*

Year	Defence budget	Federal budget	Percentage of federal budget to defence	Accumulated national debt	GNP	Defence as % of GNP	Debt as % of GNP
1940	1.5	9.1	16.0	42.9	100.6	4.8	50.9
1945	81.6	95.2	85.7	258.6	211.9	38.5	122.8
1950	13.1	43.1	30.4	257.4	284.8	4.6	90.2
1955	40.2	68.5	58.7	274.4	398.0	10.1	68.9
1960	45.9	92.2	49.8	286.3	503.7	9.1	57.8
1965	49.6	118.4	41.9	317.3	684.9	7.2	47.2
1970	80.3	196.6	40.8	370.9	977.1	8.2	39.2
1975	85.6	326.2	26.2	541.9	1,528.8	5.6	35.7
1980	130.4	590.9	22.1	909.1	2,518.0	5.2	36.1
1985	252.2	946.4	26.7	1,817.5	4,012.1	6.3	45.3
1990	289.7	1,252.7	27.8	3,206.6	5,509.6	5.3	58.2
1995	272.1	1,538.9	17.7	4,961.5			

Sources: Gaddis (1982, p. 359); US Census Bureau (1996)

When calculated as a percentage of America's federal budget, the US defence expenditures fell during the 1970s, from nearly 40.8 per cent in 1970 through 26.2 per cent in 1975 to 22.1 per cent in 1980. It then increased during the 1980s – via 26.7 per cent in 1985 to 27.8 per cent of the budget in 1990. A similar fall is evident when the US budget is calculated as a share of America's GNP – defence expenditures amounted to 8.2 per cent of America's GNP in 1970 and fell via 5.6 per cent in 1975 to 5.2 per cent in 1980 before it increased to 6.3 per cent in 1985. As Table 21 also shows, the US military budget never exceeded 10 per cent of the country's GNP after 1955. There does not seem to be any direct and obvious connection between America's defence expenditures and its economic stagnation. However, if lessons from previous cases of decline are anything to go by, it may be worth investigating whether America's economic and military fall may somehow be connected with the final, normative aspect of power: was the United States in addition to military threats and relative economic stagnation also faced with a crisis in moral philosophy?

Moral fragmentation

Evidence from several sources suggests that the answer is in the affirmative. By the time the United States renounced world leadership, America's stock of social capital had been shrinking for more than a quarter of a century (Putnam 1995, p. 666). The trust which adult Americans have in their political authorities and in many social institutions declined sharply during the 1970s.[10] This is evident from American opinion polls,[11] and reflected in the increasing incidence of social unrest and crime.

It is tempting to interpret this evidence of declining cohesion and trust in light of the findings from Part One of this study. Gibbon was not the only one to observe that people unite in the face of a convincing threat. Philip II undoubtedly noted that the strong cohesion of Iberian society in important ways was a function of the long struggle against a sustained Muslim threat. Similarly, several US presidents sought to unite Congress behind their foreign-policy plans by appealing to a vast, looming Soviet threat (Department of State 1985c; Campbell 1992, pp. 153ff.). After World War II, the United States found in the Soviet Union a potent image of a nefarious enemy. Among America's many foreign-policy goals during the cold war, the overriding national purpose was to contain and defeat Communism. For forty postwar years, 'virtually all the great American initiatives in foreign policy, as well as many in domestic policy, were justified by this overriding priority' (Huntington 1997b, p. 30). The threat of a powerful, Communist 'other' sustained the cohesion of American society – in spite of postwar shocks to the system, such as the rise of the women's rights movement and the civil rights revolution of the early 1960s. By repeated reference to the sinister, alien 'them', the geographically vast and culturally diverse American society was welded tightly together into a reassuring postwar 'us'. This common identity sustained the high level of adult social trust during the 1940s and 1950s.

A major change occurred with the moral challenge from the Third World during the 1960s. This change coincided with the assassination of John F. Kennedy. It was compounded by the deaths of Robert Kennedy and Martin Luther King and several thousand US soldiers in the Tet offensive in 1968. The Vietnam War was a decisive solvent on America's unifying cold war mythology among Americans who were born during the 1940s and later. The moral challenge from Third World conflicts battered that liberal consensus which was superimposed over an array of considerable internal differences. The conflicts spilled over into America's ethnically diverse population and exacerbated the situation. By 1970, the cold war mythology had grown less credible, and its legitimizing force had weakened considerably. Members of the American élite increasingly questioned the 'Soviet threat' explanation which was

designed to justify America's interventions in Third World nations. Soon élite
dissent affected virtually every facet of America's political culture – academic
circles, business, the federal bureaucracy, Congress, organized labour, and
even the military itself. Some disaffections were spectacular (like that of
J. William Fulbright who chaired the Senate Foreign Relations Committee);
others were more quiescent (like that of Robert McNamara, President
Johnson's secretary of defense).

The disintegration of America's postwar foreign-policy consensus and the
decline in social trust among America's young adults can partly be seen as a
public revulsion triggered by the governmental deception and abuse of power
which surfaced during the contentious cases of Vietnam and Watergate. But it
can also be seen in a larger social context; it may be interpreted as symptomatic
of declining social cohesion and a more general rise in asocial behaviour. By
the mid-1970s, the popular mood had assumed a clear scepticism towards
politics in general – from 1975, polls clearly identified domestic economic issues
as the most salient concerns of the public.[12] By 1985, the chief concerns of the
American public were law and order. This is reflected e.g. in the number of
prison inmates in US prisons tripling in fifteen years from around 500,000 in
1980 to nearly 1.5 million in 1995.

American decline?

Among Gibbon's four causes of decline – injuries of time and nature, hostile
attacks, abuse of materials and domestic quarrels – the second has been a
perennial favourite of great powers. In the case of the United States, whose
collective scenario of fear-as-attack was shaped by Pearl Harbor and sustained
during the cold war by nuclear rivalry, decline has been synonymous with a
sudden outside attack on a massive scale. The best way to prevent decline has,
in the American mind, therefore been to deter potential attackers by a vast
military establishment with a potent, invulnerable nuclear arsenal at its core.
However, this great power notion, that a military establishment is necessary
to protect the American way of life, has coexisted uneasily alongside a traditional liberal fear that such an establishment may itself threaten the way of
life it is set to protect. At the beginning of the cold war this liberal paradox
affected Walter Lippmann (1944). At its end it informed Paul Kennedy (1987).

For Edward Gibbon, the most formidable cause of imperial destruction was
not hostile attack but domestic quarrels. And after the decline of the USSR, a
new generation of doomsayers had emerged to explain America's decay in
terms of internal conflict and contention. What is striking about the these new
diagnoses is the anxiety about the ills of American society. This anxiety is
fuelled by visible, and seemingly unhealable, wounds in the very fabric of

American community life (Schlesinger 1992; Hughes 1993). During Ronald Reagan's second term, the most-cited threats to American society were, according to public opinion polls, drug dealing, indiscriminate gunfire, rising rates of violent crime and the disintegration and disorganization of the family.

In the late 1980s, the United States displayed several of the characteristic symptoms of decline. Like England in the late 1880s, the United States suffered from rising concern about losing order and law at home and competitiveness abroad. Several authors noted the historical parallels with declining late nineteenth-century England. Far fewer noted the similarities between the United States and Spain in the 1580s – the United States suffered the loss of a major rival in the late 1980s, and after a brief period of celebration, the United States suffered (like its Iberian predecessor) a decline in national identity, political purpose and sense of national interest.[13] Hardly anyone noted that the growth in the United States of an egotistical 'culture of contentment' (Galbraith 1992) had clear parallels with comparable developments in the United Provinces in the 1670s. Few commentators, if any, noted the most uncanny parallel of them all: with late eighteenth-century England.

The United States was, like England in the 1780s and the 1890s, profoundly concerned about the loss of international competitiveness; President Reagan, just like the government of King George III, sought to revitalize the nation's productive economy by lowering taxes. In both cases, the measures were highly controversial, especially since they were accompanied by expensive military build-ups. Both were aloof leaders about whom everyone seemed to have a strong opinion – both were revered by some and maliciously lampooned by others. Both escalated a global struggle with a long-standing rival. Both experienced the collapse of the rival (in 1789 and 1989–91, respectively). Both experienced an economic revival of notable proportions that wrought great changes in the socio-political structure of society – the United Kingdom was propelled by a veritable industrial revolution from a society which relied on manufacturing to one which pioneered machinofacture; the United States made the transition from the industry-based society of the 1950s and 1960s to the post-industrial, service-based society of the twenty-first century. Both societies regained some of their former confidence, order and cohesion. Both emerged, once more, as leading powers in the international system.

With hindsight, the signs of the Soviet collapse [14] and the foreshadowings of America's revival were present all through the 1980s. Just like the English case of the late 1700s, trends of economic decline could be found alongside the trends of revival.

Notes

1 Based on the dollar value of the purchases, investments by the Europeans exceeded those of the Japanese. By 1990, the British possessed the largest US holdings. In the first half of 1990 alone, the British purchased $7.9 billion worth of American assets, the French $5.7 billion worth and the Japanese $3.8 billion (as reported by *The New York Times*, 17 July 1990, p. D2).

2 Since the exact numbers are surrounded by a good deal of political contention, the official figures (from the *Statistical Abstract of the United States*) are presented in Table 22.

Table 22   *Federal revenue, expenditure and national debt, 1975–95*
(in US$ billions)

[Year]	Federal revenue	Federal outlay	Annual surplus/deficit	Accumulated national debt
1977	355.5	409.2	−53.7	706.4
1978	399.6	458.7	−59.1	776.6
1979	463.3	504.0	−40.7	829.5
1980	517.1	590.9	−73.8	909.1
1981	599.3	678.2	−79.0	994.9
1982	617.8	745.8	−128.0	1,137.3
1983	600.5	808.4	−207.8	1,371.7
1984	666.5	851.8	−185.4	1,564.7
1985	734.1	946.4	−212.3	1,817.5
1986	769.1	990.3	−221.2	2,120.6
1987	854.1	1,003.9	−149.8	2,346.1
1988	909.0	1,064.1	−155.2	2,601.3
1989	990.7	1,143.2	−152.5	2,868.0
1990	1,031.3	1,252.7	−221.4	3,206.6
1991	1,054.3	1,323.4	−269.2	3,598.5
1992	1,090.5	1,380.9	−290.4	4,002.1
1993	1,153.5	1,408.7	−255.1	4,351.4
1994	1,257.7	1,460.9	−203.2	4,643.7
1995	1,346.4	1,538.9	−192.5	4,961.5

Sources: Gordon (1997, p. 204); US Bureau of the Census (1996, Table 512, p. 330)

3 In 1962, the western Pacific region accounted for around 9 per cent of the world's GNP; twenty years later, its share had climbed to more than 15 per cent. Comparable figures for the United States were 30 per cent and 28 per cent respectively.

4 The following rough numbers in Table 23 show that the ballooning US deficit in merchandise trade was partly the result of an increase in imports and partly a stagnation of US exports.

Table 23   *US exports, imports and merchandise trade balance, 1975–95*
(in US$ millions)

[Year]	Value of exports	Value of imports	Merchandise balance
1975	107,652	98,503	9,149
1980	220,626	244,871	−24,245
1985	213,133	345,276	−132,143
1990	394,030	495,042	−101,012

Source: US Bureau of the Census (1996, Table 512, p. 330)

5 During the 1980s, American businesses filed on average an annual number of 63,500 bankruptcies. That was an increase of 155 per cent over the 24,900 annual petitions filed during the 1970s, and up 302 per cent over the 15,800 filed in the 1960s.

6 It was in connection with this development that the notion of Mutual Assured Destruction (MAD) became America's strategic doctrine.

7 Even after President Reagan's military build-up in the early 1980s, only about one-fifth of the American people believed that the United States was ahead of the Soviet Union in overall military strength. About a third of the American public believed that the country's nuclear arsenal was weaker than that of the Soviet Union, and half believed that the United States was behind in conventional military strength (Nye 1991, p. 2).

8 Brezhnev's death in November 1982 was followed by the brief and bewildering interregnums of Yuri Andropov (who died in February 1984) and Konstantin Chernenko (who died in March 1985).

9 Reagan built his justification for this doctrine on three assumptions. First, he re-iterated the orthodox cold war view that the revolutionary upheavals of the Third World were everywhere stoked by the Soviet Union. Second, he assumed that if regimes in the Third World embraced Marxism–Leninism, they would fall irreversibly into the Soviet camp. Finally, he believed that the Soviet Union had succeeded in defeating America's traditional containment policy; it had become strong and adventurous enough to expand beyond its Eurasian confines and encourage revolutionary insurgencies in the Third World in a 'third wave of expansionism'.

10 The decline in trust is evident from Table 24, which identifies American age cohorts according to their year of birth – beginning with those born at the very beginning of the century and continuing downwards to their grandchildren who were born in the 1960s. As we move down the first column, we note that people who were born in the 1910s (who reached early adulthood during the 'Roaring Twenties' and most of whom became established citizens during the 1950s) entertain levels of social trust which are twice as high as their grandchildren (most of whom can be assumed to have been born in the 1950s and 1960s and to have reached adulthood during the final decade of the cold war). Education and social trust are tightly correlated – indeed, Putnam (1995b, p. 667) explains that education is by far the strongest correlate that anyone has discovered 'of civic engagement in all its forms, including social trust'. This observation suggests an obvious question which deserves to be addressed immediately: can the evident decline of social trust in American society since the 1970s be explained by increasing levels

Table 24 *Social trust as reflected in generations of US adults, 1910–65*
(percentage of adult population who say they trust the system)

Year of birth	Social trust (%)	Turned 20 during the:	Turned 40 during the:
1910	51	1930s	1950s
1920	48	1940s	1960s
1930	49	cold war	1970s
1940	43	1960s	end of the cold war
1950	33	1970s	post-cold war era
1960	28	1980s	year 2000
1965	23	mid-1980s	—

Source: Putnam (1995b, p. 675)

of education? The short answer is a resounding no! Research has repeatedly shown that education and social trust are *positively* correlated – i.e., that more highly educated people are more trusting. Americans in the 1970s and 1980s were far better educated than their parents and grandparents, and this trend of rising education should dispose newer generations of Americans to be a good deal *more* trusting than their forebears, not less. When studies show an obvious decline in social trust since the early 1970s, this decline must have occurred *in spite of* the rapid rise in education during the 1950s, 1960 and 1970s, not because of it.

11 Evidence from the General Social Survey (GSS) demonstrates that the level of social trust dropped by roughly 30 per cent between 1972 and 1991. The GSS builds on annual surveys of the adult American population since 1972 by the National Opinion Research Centre, under the direction of James A. Davis and Tom W. Smith. See also Putnam (1995b, p. 681, n3).

12 The gap between the rich and the poor widened during the 1980s. This development was reflected in the conspicuous changes which occurred in the US wage structure which began in the mid-1970s and would assume dramatic proportions during the 1980s. People who earned between $20,000 and $50,000 experienced an annual salary increase of 4 per cent during the 1980s – or about 44 per cent during the course of the decade. People who earned between $200,000 and $1 million experienced an increase in their earnings during the decade of 697 per cent. For people who earned more than $1 million the ten-year increase was even more dramatic: 2,184 per cent. This lopsided development was accompanied by highly publicized Wall Street scandals and by one of the largest financial scandals in US history: the so-called savings-and-loan scandal. It testifies to a degree of blind greed and social cynicism that thoroughly alienated many Americans.

13 Georgiy Arbatov, Gorbachev's adviser in the late 1980s, hit the nail on the head when he commented: 'We are doing something really terrible to you – we are depriving you of an enemy' (Huntington 1997b, p. 30).

14 American policy-makers were greatly concerned by the geostrategic and military situation of the 1980s. However, their concerns were minor compared with the troubles which visited the Soviet leaders. For whereas the United States was also experiencing signs of economic recovery, the Soviet Union was suffering a progressive paralysis which forced its leaders to radically rethink its role in world

affairs. By the late 1980s, the Soviet Union (rather than the United States) was showing increasing signs of overstretch and decline.

The Achilles heel of the Soviet system was always its inability to devise a smooth and legitimate system of succession. By the 1980s, this problem was becoming acute – as evinced by the deterioration of its ageing leadership. Brezhnev's death in November 1982 was followed by the brief interregnums of Yuri Andropov (who died in February 1984) and the doddering Konstantin Chernenko (who died in March 1985). The progressive illness of the Soviet bosses had fuelled the fires of factional strife in Kremlin politics. The election of Mikail Gorbachev promised to settle the problem of succession for some time. The new leader – by Soviet standards a spry youth at fifty-five – had ambitions to get his country 'out of the quagmire of conservatism, and to break the inertia of stagnation' (Gorbachev 1987, p. 51). His ambitions were indicated at the time by the much-used concepts of *glasnost* and *perestroika* ('openness' and 'restructuring').

Gorbachev's policies can be discussed in a variety of ways. The way in which he handled the long-standing superpower competition in the Third World captures very well that facet of his policies which is most germane to the present discussion: i.e., the changing nature of the US–Soviet relationship. Gorbachev's immediate concern as General Secretary of the Communist Party of the Soviet Union pertained to domestic affairs. He needed to prepare a firm foundation for reform. And he did this by stacking the central organs of the Soviet system with adherents, thus consolidating his own power base. President Reagan's primary concerns, by contrast, included foreign affairs. Reagan wanted to impress on the Soviet leaders that America would contain all Brezhnev-style adventurism in the Third World. In his fifth State of the Union address (February 1985) Reagan pledged to assist anti-Soviet rebel groups in the Third World. During the subsequent months, the United States began to escalate its assistance to Son Sann and Norodom Sihanouk in Cambodia, the Unita movement in Angola, the *contras* in Nicaragua and the *mujaheddin* in Afghanistan.

The Soviets immediately countered the US initiative. Gorbachev's regime prodded the radical governments in Pnom Penh, Luanda, Managua and Kabul to launch military offensives against the US-supported rebels. During the autumn of 1985, the rebels suffered heavier casualties and setbacks. Committed to the tit-for-tat logic of the cold war, the Reagan administration responded by upping the ante. Reagan's men worked intensely to increase US aid to the anti-Communist forces in Cambodia, Angola, Nicaragua and Afghanistan.

Some time in 1986, Gorbachev got Reagan's message: the Americans were willing to match the Soviet escalation in the Third World and capable of raising the war costs to levels which the Soviet Union would find unacceptable. In 1987, Gorbachev announced his intention to withdraw all Soviet troops from Afghanistan. This was followed (in 1988) by Cuba's resolve to begin a phased pull-out from Angola, by Vietnam's decision to withdraw its occupation forces from Cambodia, and by the commitment of the Sandinista government (in 1989) to stage presidential, legislative and municipal elections in Nicaragua.

In 1986, the Soviet leaders not only yielded to American pressure in the Third World. They also began to yield to increasing pressure on other cold war fronts as well. There is no doubt, for example, that they took Reagan's Strategic Defence Initiative (SDI) seriously. It troubled them that the SDI was a conscious American violation of the anti-ballistic missile (ABM) Treaty of 1972 (and therefore, strictly, an illegal act). But what concerned them more was that the SDI threatened to make obsolete an entire generation of Soviet nuclear weapons. And if the Soviets were to keep up with America's SDI technology, they would have to commit vast resources to a research programme of enormous proportions and with uncertain results. Gorbachev was willing to go to great lengths in order to stop the American SDI project. At a bizarre summit meeting in Reykjavik (October 1986), he even proposed to remove *all* nuclear weapons within the decade if the United States would cancel its SDI programme.

More consequentially, the Soviets yielded to mounting pressures in their own sphere of influence in Eastern Europe. These pressures were largely created by Gorbachev's ambitious programme of domestic reform. For the better part of twenty years, relations between the Soviet Union and its Eastern European allies had been governed by the Brezhnev doctrine, by which the Kremlin arrogated to itself the right to determine the acceptable limits of socialism. Gorbachev's initiatives broke with the old line. *Glasnost* and *perestroika* gave Eastern European regimes greater liberty to experiment with new forms of government. The Kremlin's limits of tolerance were left ambiguous; however, the Soviet decision to withdraw from Afghanistan was widely read as a signal that military intervention in Eastern Europe was far less likely than before.

As the implications of Gorbachev's reforms sank in, Eastern European groups began to reconsider their form of government and to redefine their role in the 'socialist family of nations'. The diversity and strength of these groups varied greatly from one country to the next. They were generally most advanced in Poland and Hungary. Here intellectuals had long criticized Communist dogma and policy. In the late 1980s, such criticisms began to find expression in public media and to spill over into street demonstrations. In Poland, the strikes of 1988 greatly swelled that part of the population that listened neither to the government nor to the independent Solidarity labour movement. Caught between the threat of political chaos on the one hand and Soviet intervention on the other, Polish president Jaruzelski began to negotiate with Solidarity early in 1989.

The Kremlin leaders were keenly aware of the dangers of the situation. A collapse of Communist authority in any Eastern European country would present them with two uncomfortable scenarios: either to intervene militarily and try to re-establish order by force and repression, or to leave the countries alone and run the risk that a collapse in one country would spread, like a row of falling dominoes, to other countries in the region.

Gorbachev wanted to avoid intervention at any cost. It would mean the end of *glasnost, perestroika* and Gorbachev's entire reform project – it would confirm the Brezhnev doctrine. Gorbachev calculated that not only was the Soviet Union unstable without reform; he also reasoned that the countries of Eastern Europe were unstable without reform as well, but that the old Communist bosses there would launch no reform voluntarily. He thought that Soviet interests would be better served by stable though friendly governments in the area – even if these governments were non-Communist ones. As Gorbachev had seized every opportunity to voice support for reform in the USSR, he could not deny it to Eastern Europe. He did not lift a finger to prevent the downfall of the old Communist leaders in Eastern Europe.

The uninterrupted negotiations in Poland between the Communist government and Solidarity meant, in effect, that the days of Communist monopoly were numbered and that the introduction of a multiparty system could no longer be avoided. The events in Poland were followed by mass demonstrations in Hungary, East Germany, Czechoslovakia and Bulgaria. In all countries, the surface unanimity of the political system was broken during the spring and summer of 1989 – as was the nerve of extant governments. In the autumn, virtually all Eastern European countries developed interconnecting public spheres the dynamics of which swept the old Communist élites from power (Ash 1990).

By 1989, the Soviet Union behaved in ways characteristic of states which suffer defeat in major wars. It surrendered its most recent conquests and retreated to its old, pre-war boundaries. Also, it shifted leadership – first toppling the old leaders, then denouncing them and finally blaming them for mistaken policies which had inflicted such harmful casualties on their own nation as well as on the world outside. In a final indignity, the country suffered a deep economic crisis which drove the new leaders to beg their old enemies for economic help to stave off hunger and chaos.

In December 1991, following a botched *coup* by the old power élite, Soviet president Gorbachev saw no alternative but to officially dissolve the USSR. But by dissolving the social formation which he presided over, Gorbachev also destroyed the institutions whose representative he was and which gave him his political stature and power. But before he officially dissolved the USSR, Gorbachev gave the codes of the Soviet Union's nuclear forces to the President of Russia – i.e., to Boris Yeltsin who led the largest republic of the old Union of Soviet Socialist Republics. Yeltsin quickly assured the world that the weapons were in safe hands. His assurance was echoed by the presidents of the Ukraine, Belorussia and Kazakhstan – three other republics which had gained autonomy by the dissolution of the USSR and on whose soil nuclear weapons from the old Soviet Union were stationed.

Epilogue:
and then there was one ...

The parade began with great hoopla. As the emperor marched his pale, bloated, patriarchal carcass down the street, everyone loudly oohed and ahed at his beautiful new clothes. All except one small boy, who shouted:

— 'The emperor is naked!'

The parade stopped. The emperor paused. A hush fell over the crowd, until one quick-thinking peasant shouted:

— 'No he isn't. The emperor is merely endorsing a clothing optional lifestyle!'. (Garner 1994)

The first part of this study identified five world orders in the history of modern international relations: the Iberian, the Dutch, the First and Second British and, finally, the American. It has identified a wave-like pattern of war, hegemony, challenge and competition that helps illuminate the nature of each world order and analyse the behaviour of great powers within it. The second part of the study has discussed the American world order and has re-read US cold war history in the light of this wave-like pattern. This conceptualization of international relations history gives rise to a series of questions about post-cold war world affairs. Where are we now? Is the United States still the pre-eminent great power of the world order? Which phase of the world order cycle are we in upon the threshold of the twenty-first century? The phase of hegemony, challenge or competitive disruption?

Other questions flow from the claim that all of the five world orders have displayed distinct cyclical rhythms and that these have been influenced by secular trends during the course of modern history. Some of them concern the observation that although the evolution of each world order has largely followed the cyclical rhythms of previous orders, there have also been deviations. Which deviations are these? Which deviations have been notably evident during the course of the twentieth century?

The first section of this epilogue argues that the USA is, in spite of the declinist forecasts of the 1980s, the pre-eminent actor of the post-cold war order. The second section discusses the singular fact that the United States has retained its international pre-eminence while escaping the convulsions of large-scale war which marked previous ages. This observation gives rise to a few final questions about contemporary world affairs. Does the absence of large-scale war presage the advent of a lasting great power peace? Does it imply the rise of 'one world' – as so many state leaders and scholars have claimed after the collapse of the cold war? Or are such arguments merely hegemonic hyperbole?

The contemporary world order cycle

The twentieth-century (American) world order emerged from the debris of the old, nineteenth-century (British) order – and the United States was in some ways groomed for its leadership task (as England had once been groomed by Holland, and Holland by Habsburg Spain). Most concretely, the American world order was, like previous orders, prepared during the course of a wave of great wars: during the endgame of World Wars I and II, the United States imposed its principles of order upon the world.

After World War II, the United States was the pre-eminent military power on the international scene as well as the primary architect of the international economic order. Also, the United States was the pre-eminent moral actor of the age, presiding over a world order whose governing principles were derived from the Western traditions of social contract theory and natural law philosophy. These Western values and norms have been disseminated across the globe during the twentieth century, and the process has been assisted by a communications revolution which has greatly affected the societies of the world. The American values were to a substantial degree European in origin and were already present in the countries of postwar Europe. This presence ensured a normative commonality which unified the Atlantic community (Deutsch *et al*. 1957) – a unity which was accentuated during the cold war by a common fear of the Soviet Union.

After some twenty postwar years of American hegemony, the USA was – like previous hegemons – challenged at home and abroad. However, unlike previous cases, this challenge was not accompanied by a great power war. It was a unique feature of the American world order that the most consequential challenges to the hegemon came from outside the great power system. Indeed, it was the tragic irony of the American world order that the USA, which had always considered itself a defender of the downtrodden and oppressed and a champion of the anti-colonial cause, found its most immediate military challengers in the postcolonial world. Although America's primary rival was the Soviet Union, America's military engagements were with poor countries in the Third World – although many of them were allied with or aided by the Soviet Union, American soldiers did not directly fight Soviet troops.

As with previous cases of challenge, it was not the hegemon which eventually sank back into prostration; rather, it was the hegemon's primary rival that declined. Furthermore, after this rival's demise, the old hegemon experienced a revival of fortune and self-confidence – again, like previous cases. Upon the threshold of the twenty-first century America is the preponderant power in world affairs. How solid is this American leadership? Does it signify a brief interlude? Or does it represent a solid, longer-lasting phenomenon? Is it an Indian summer or a new hegemony?

America's pre-eminence became clear during the early 1990s. No other country had the ability in 1991 to coordinate and supply as vast a military operation as that against Saddam Hussein's invasion of Kuwait. Later, the intervention of Nato in Bosnia would hardly have occurred if it were not for the US decision to act. The United States also played a leading role in converting Nato from the leading military alliance of the cold war to a collective security organization of the post-cold war era with a broad mandate for maintaining democracy and order in Europe (Nato 1997). Also, America's *sense* of pre-eminence grew during the 1990s. This was expressed by President Clinton in his 1998 State of the Union address. These 'are good times for America,' the president began. Then he boasted:

> We have more than 14 million new jobs. The lowest unemployment in 24 years. The lowest core inflation in 30 years. Incomes are rising, and we have the highest home ownership in history. The welfare rolls are the lowest in 27 years, and crime has dropped for a record five years in a row. Our leadership in the world is unrivalled. The state of our union is strong ...
>
> For three decades, six presidents have come before you to warn of the damage deficits pose to the nation. Tonight, I come before you to announce that the federal deficit – once so incomprehensingly large that it had eleven zeros – will be, simply zero. I will submit to Congress for 1999 the first balanced budget in 30 years.

Clinton's message was that America was back, and that its revival is not merely a brief Indian summer. Rather, the United States is again the pre-eminent great power and the leader of the world. But how could that be? Previous hegemons have emerged from waves of great wars; Clinton's America has not. How can the USA re-emerge as the world's pre-eminent power in the absence of large-scale war?

It could easily be argued that Clinton's statement was political hyperbole and that America's resurgence merely expressed a brief respite – such as has occurred in all previous cases of hegemony and marked a transition between the second and third phases of the world order. It could be claimed that the US resurgence merely was an Indian summer, a final flash of hegemonic energies presaging a final phase of demise. Some authors have, indeed, intimated this. Paul Kennedy (1993, 1997), for example, claims that the United States may keep up its global pre-eminence for a few more years – until around the year 2000, perhaps – but not very much longer. This forecast seems unlikely. Indications are that rather than facing an imminent demise, the United States has consolidated its position as the world's leading power for another world order cycle. At the threshold of the twenty-first century America's military capabilities are unrivalled. Its economic dynamism is conspicuous – while states which were America's primary challengers in the 1970s and 1980s (notably Germany and Japan) stagnated during the 1990s, US industries defined new frontiers in important sectors of industry. Observers agree that America's moral consensus tightened during the 1990s and have sought to substantiate the claim in various ways. Some refer to the conspicuous drop in crime rates, others to a dramatic decrease in pregnancies among unmarried women, and still others to a clear rise in church attendance. Also, the values and norms which the United States has consistently sought to represent are accepted by more people in the world than ever before – since the 1980s, vast public assets have been wrested away from government hands in world-sweeping waves of privatization and deregulation which have redrawn the map of the global economy along liberal, American lines (Yergin and Stanislaw 1998). In a word, America's resource base is too comprehensive, its material capabilities are too vast and its moral authority is too strong to allow it to suffer a crippling collapse within the coming decade.

It could also be argued that the second American hegemony emerged not from a hot war but from a cold one. It could be claimed that the final phase of the cold war, during which the United States countered and contained a renewed wave of Soviet expansionism, was the functional equivalent of a great war. Some authors emphasize that the 1980s constituted a particularly tense contest – a 'Second Cold War' in Halliday's (1983) term. It may be recalled that the costly superpower struggle which marked these years caused Kennedy (1987) to fear the exhaustion of the United States. This was partly due to an Augean proxy struggle for influence in the Third World and to a hi-tech race towards a new missile defence system deployed in space.

With the benefit of hindsight, it can now be seen that the momentous expenditures associated with these events shook the United States and contributed significantly to the collapse of the Soviet Union. However, even if this second cold war was tense and costly, it can hardly compare with any of the waves of great wars of modern international history. The cold war never occasioned the physical destruction or the scope and cost that the wars against Louis XIV, Napoleon or Hitler did. Clearly, if the United States has re-emerged as a pre-eminent world power during the 1990s, this has occurred in the absence of great wars. How could that be?

The absence of great power war can be understood against the background of certain secular trends which have long been visible in modern international affairs. Chapter 5, for example, argued that the lethality of war has risen dramatically during the course of modern history – that weapons systems have increased their range, speed, accuracy, penetrability, mobility and volume of fire. The chapter also shows that the frequency of great power war has steadily declined during recent centuries.[1]

On the one hand, then, great power wars have broken out with steadily diminishing frequency during the course of modern history; on the other, *when* such wars have erupted, they have caused increasing destruction and death. *Pax Americana* expressed an extrapolation of both of these two secular trends: the distinguishing mark of the American hegemony was a remarkably long great power peace coexisting with the ever-present threat of an all-destructive nuclear war. During the course of the American hegemony, then, the advent of new technologies and new means of destruction created unprecedented constraints against military escalation. As a result, crises which in other ages would have caused great wars did not. The new, nuclear-based means of mass destruction kept the cold war from getting hot.[2]

Nuclear weapons exchanged destructiveness for great power stability. This was intimated in Chapter 8, which argued that the advent of nuclear weapons marked a watershed in international history. For as one great power after the other obtained nuclear capabilities during the 1940s and 1950s, a sense of mutual vulnerability spread throughout the diplomatic community of the world, pushing the USA, the USSR and their allies into a common under-standing of some basic rules of interstate conduct. By the 1970s, this set of rudimentary rules had evolved into a relatively robust, stable and peaceful bipolar system which differed from previous international systems in one de-cisive respect: its great powers were unified by a common interest in avoiding nuclear war, and assumed risk-averse ways of conduct.

This reasoning does not explain why the United States re-emerged pre-emi-nent during the 1990s. However, it does explain the absence of great power wars in the postwar (nuclear) era. And it does more: it indicates a larger, significant point: that is, that secular trends may affect the periodic rhythms of history. For if a steadily increasing trend in weapons systems' destructive capabilities can produce, through the paradoxical logic of Mutual Assured Destruction (or MAD), an unprecedented period of great power peace, then it is established that long-term, large-scale secular trends may modify established rhythms of world order. This, in turn, raises the question of whether *other* secular trends exist which may also affect established rhythms of world order.

Chapter 5 identifies two additional trends – the growing interdependence of states and the steady globalization of the public sphere. These two trends have, together with the growing capabilities of military force, exerted decisive influences on the cycles of world order in recent decades. Before the second American hegemony is explored more closely, it will be helpful to recall these secular trends and their effects on the cycles of world order.

Secular trends of modern world politics

No social cycle involves a simple repetition of events. No historical cycle repeats itself mechanically in the sense that it eventually returns to an equilibrium point. Such cycles repeat themselves not as identities but as analogies. Historical rhythms occur within shifting circumstances.

Some of these shifts may be captured in terms of specific secular trends. Some of the trends can be captured through analyses of technological development and innovation. For technology and innovation affect economic means of production as well as military means of destruction in direct ways. They also affect transport and communications and decisively determine the interaction capacity of international society (Buzan *et al.* 1993, pp. 69ff.). A world which relies on horse power as its main form of overland transport will produce different forms of economic interaction than a world where jumbo-jets and high-speed trains are commonplace. A world in which knights in armour are the pre-eminent weapons system will produce different modes of warfare than a world of nuclear missiles. A world in which texts are set in lead type will develop different modes of intellectual interaction than one in which most households have access to worldwide websites and satellite dishes. Sooner or later, the momentum of technological progress affects secular trends. Sooner or later such momentum pushes the historical rhythms so far away from the characteristic themes of the world order cycle that new variations cease to reflect the characteristic properties of the original pattern. The continued development of secular trends may eventually break the cycle.

Secular trends in the twentieth century

Some of the secular trends of the century suggest that the world is becoming more integrated, unified and peaceful. It was noted in the concluding section of Chapter 5 that three trends are of particular importance for the modern world order cycles: the steady rise in the destructive capabilities of weapons, the increased interdependence of nations and the steady evolution of a cosmopolitan public sphere. Are these trends fuelling a development towards global integration and unification?

On punitive trends

The increase in the destructive capabilities of states is the most obvious long-term trend and, perhaps, the most generally accepted one. This trend was greatly enhanced by the advent of industrialization and science-fuelled arms races. During World War II, weapons-systems engineers began to draw on nuclear physics to produce the most destructive devices humanity had ever possessed. Immediately after the war, state leaders of the great powers recognized that as new and more destructive weapons systems were developed, the potential costs of war increased to such a magnitude that they could, for all practical purposes, be considered incalculable. And as the potential costs increased, the belligerency of state leaders and generals was progressively restrained.

The looming danger of nuclear war has tormented great power leaders since the late 1940s to become increasingly risk-averse and driven them to develop rudimentary norms and rules so as to avoid any accidental outbreak of a nuclear holocaust. Strategists understood early that as the lethality of the weapons systems grew, their suitability for warfare decreased. Indeed, as more states acquired nuclear weapons, bombs and rockets rapidly became more than tools of war; they also became deterrents against unleashing the horrors of war. Paradoxically, then, as science and technology evolved and were capable of producing more massive means of destruction, mankind increasingly realized the pressing need to keep order and peace.

This development was foreshadowed by arguments which Immanuel Kant (1991b[1793], p. 90) developed some hundred and fifty years earlier: that as the lethality of their weapons increased, the most technologically advanced states in the world would tend to avoid wars with each other.[3]

On remunerative trends

The increase in interdependence among national economies is a second conspicuous secular trend. Modern social institutions which occasioned great progress in communications, transport and trade in the West spread to other regions during the twentieth century and helped weave the nations of the world into a web of complex interdependence. Again, Kant (1991a[1784], p. 51) captured some of the key elements of this process and gauged some of its effects upon world affairs. During the 1780s and 1790s he imagined that a world which was increasingly 'linked by trade' would also be an increasingly orderly and peaceful world.

Kant's argument hinged on the traditional assumption that God had endowed different nations with different resources; since no nation possessed all the necessities of life, trade and exchange will almost always lead to welfare gains for all nations that engage in it.[4] A few decades later, Anglo-American liberals added a new, seductive dimension to the peace-through-trade argument. They removed God and the unequal distribution of resources from their purview, and claimed, simply, that trade would always lead to welfare gains for all who engaged in it. Their argument was anchored in David Ricardo's doctrine of comparative advantage, which held that trade would lead to welfare gains even in circumstances where one trading partner could produce all goods at a lower cost than any other. This claim – which has expressed the enduring liberal view that trade, interdependence and 'the spirit of commerce' are important forces for peace among states – has been a founding argument in twentieth-century interdependence theories.

A rough sketch of the history of international relations may help put this liberal argument in a proper perspective. During modern history, great powers have pursued two different kinds of international activities. On the one hand they have participated in a territorially based interstate system which has its origins in the late Middle Ages but found its modern form in the 'long sixteenth century' world of absolutist states. These interstate activities occurred between territorial actors which were homogeneous in form and strove for autonomy. On the other hand, great powers have been part of an oceanic, trade-based world economy which also harks back to the long sixteenth century, but which today occurs between a variety of actors who have differentiated objectives and perform a variety of functions.

These two spheres of great power activity are governed by very different principles of order – for example, whereas the sphere of interstate politics has long obeyed balance-of-power principles, the world economy has worked according to principles afforded by an international division of labour. All modern states have had to balance the demands of the interstate system against those of the world economy (Rosecrance 1986, pp. 22ff.; Knutsen 1996, p. 41). Great powers have regularly faced the choice of whether to pursue their national advancement through the interstate system or through the world economy. Modern hegemons have preferred the possibilities offered by the world economy and trade over those offered by interstate competition and war. During the course of the modern ages, there has been a growing tendency for other states to follow suit.

After World War II, an unprecedented number of states chose to pursue their national advancement through specialized production and trade. Although this development can hardly be isolated from the advent of nuclear weapons, the evolution of interdependence is a distinct historical process. It was well under way before the nuclear age (Muir 1933) – and therefore cannot be seen exclusively as an effect of nuclear weapons (Mueller 1989). During the cold war, it was encouraged by the establishment of the Bretton Woods system and by measures of European integration. Since the cold war it has been stimulated by the unravelling of Communism – partly because this paved the way for 1.9 billion people of the old Communist bloc to link up with the global market economy.

The advent of global interdependence in the nineteenth and twentieth centuries has represented a secular trend which has affected the rhythms of world order. It has greatly reduced the incentive for developed countries to wage war: the members of an evolving global trading system have understood that war disrupts the web of interdependence on which trade is based and from which wealth derives – as Kant (1991c[1795], p. 114) had noted already in the 1790s. The result of this development has been that, in the age of (nuclear weapons and) economic interdependence, open trading states have tended to avoid war with each other.

On trends of cosmopolitan interaction
A final major long-term, large-scale secular trend concerns the development of unprecedented interaction capacities. Not only in terms of new and rapid modes of transport and travel, but also by virtue of new modes of mass communication.

In the early years of modernity, mass communication was revolutionized by movable type and by techniques of mass printing. In the final years of the modern age, the modes of mass communication have been revolutionized by technologies of electromagnetism and miniaturization. During the twentieth century, means of mass communication have developed beyond the printed page to the screen. This transition from pages to screens – first movie screens, then TV screens and, more recently, PC screens – occurred with accelerating speed. It contributed significantly to the consolidation of an American hegemony in the 1940s and 1950s; but it also helped spread the anti-hegemonic messages of the 1960s and 1970s.

On the threshold of the twenty-first century, the global proliferation of interconnected PCs has made it near-impossible for any single state to maintain anything approaching an editorial monopoly of texts conveying information and argument. The twentieth-century communications revolution has greatly expanded the *publicum* of informed and concerned citizens who confer about matters of general interest. The growth of cyberspace and the rapid spread of interconnecting microcomputers have created a public sphere of unprecedented cosmopolitan scope. In the twentieth century, this development has, to a substantial degree, been driven by technologies and organizations of US origin, and it has been dominated by American values and norms. However, this evolution has been highly path-dependent. US pre-eminence has been grafted on to trends which can be traced back through the centuries.

It can for example be traced back to the sixteenth century and to the visions of the many authors who described a spiritually unified Europe – a Christian republic or, in the felicitous phrase of Pierre Bayle, a 'republic of letters'. In Bayle's time, nascent public spheres evolved in a few urban centres in the wealthy core of the Western world. In the seventeenth century, the public spheres were increasingly embedded in the civil societies of open, liberal, tolerant, strong and well-functioning trading states. The citizens of these states grew interconnected through innumerable transactions. And increasingly, these citizens cultivated connections with citizens of other states, thus contributing to the evolution of an international culture and a cosmopolitan public sphere. Several seventeenth-century authors argued that many common factors encouraged a growing sense of similitude and unity among the states of Europe and to a collective commitment to maintaining interstate order. Edmund Burke (1772, p. 2), for example, emphasized the Christian religion, the Roman-law heritage and monarchical principles of government as common factors of interstate order in the West.

In the seventeenth and eighteenth centuries, this cosmopolitan sphere had shallow roots in most societies. It represented little more than a thin veneer of common norms and values among the élites of Western states. Yet this normative veneer was significant because it involved some of the most respected and powerful individuals of their respective societies – merchants, bankers, scholars, officers, diplomats, princes and kings. The nations of Europe were connected at the top. At the élite level, the states of Europe 'shared a common culture and maintained extensive contacts via an active network of trade, a constant movement of persons, and a tremendous interlocking of royal families' (Tilly 1975, p. 18). Shared norms were defined by diplomats and increasingly expressed in international law (Buzan 1993, pp. 335ff.).

In the eighteenth and nineteenth centuries, the advent of literacy, education and modern mass media and of mass mobilization in general caused the public spheres of Western states to overlap to an increasing degree. Through continued interaction among citizens across boundaries of open societies, a common understanding of values, norms and rules evolved. There developed, on the one hand, common Western notions of right and wrong. On the other, there evolved a common respect for different faiths and mores. This development gathered momentum during the nineteenth and twentieth centuries and was stimulated by two developments. First, by the growth of international organizations (the Central Commission for the Navigation of the Rhine, the League of Nations, the United Nations (UN), Organization of American States (OAS), North Atlantic Treaty Organisation (Nato), European Union (EU), Organization for Security and Cooperation in Europe (OSCE) among others), multinational corporations (Standard Oil, GM, IBM, etc.) and a variety of political movements of international scope (the Red Cross, Amnesty International, Greenpeace, and so on).

Second, the development was encouraged by the new technologies of com-munication – steamships, telegraph, telephone, fax and electronic mail – which wove the citizens of the world closer together in global webs of information and interdependence. Innovation in technology, economic relations and social institutions exerted global as well as local pressures on the old territorial states. The more developed a state has been, the more it has allowed a growing number of its citizens to interact and communicate across boundaries, installing in each a sense of shared destiny with people of other states.

This development has stimulated the growth of a modern cosmopolitan public sphere – which was conceptually foreshadowed by a development which Immanuel Kant referred to as the growth of a 'pacific union' based on a common moral foundation. The public spheres of open societies evolved methods designed to solve conflicts among free citizens. These methods, which Kant saw as morally superior to violent behaviour, were increasingly trans-ferred from the sphere of domestic politics to diplomatic relations among open commercial societies.

This development marked the beginning of a virtuous circle in Western (world) politics. And as Kant noted, as 'culture grows and men gradually move towards greater agreement over their principles, they lead to mutual under-standing and peace' (Kant 1991c[1795], p. 114). Kant's argument was recaptured after World War II by Karl Deutsch's studies of international (and transnational) communities. Especially relevant is his concept of a security community – i.e., a group of people who have developed common values and norms to sustain a considerable degree of transnational trust. These people, write Deutsch *et al.* (1957, p. 5), have become integrated to the point where there is a 'real assurance that the members of that community will not fight each other physically, but will settle their disputes in some other way'.

Towards a unified world?

Three secular trends – punitive, remunerative and normative in nature – have modified the cyclical rhythms of world order. On the face of it, they have affected the traditional patterns of interstate interaction in the same distinct direction: towards a more interdependent, integrated global community.

After the end of the cold war, it has often been claimed that universal norms and values will triumph over those based on local, national or regional social formations. The most widely discussed formulation of this claim has been the 'end of history' thesis advanced by Francis Fukuyama. According to Fukuyama (1989, p. 4), post-cold war observers may be witnessing 'the end of history as such: that is the end point of mankind's ideological evolution and the univer-salization of Western liberal democracy as the final form of human government'. The war of ideas is a thing of the past. The age of global conflict is over. The future will be devoted not to great, exhilarating ideological struggles but rather to resolving mundane economic and technical problems. And, Fukuyama concluded rather sadly, it will all be quite boring.

Are these kinds of universalist claims simply hegemonic hyperbole? This is an appropriate question, for the argument that the world is rapidly moving in the direction of a vast, global community (albeit with a faltering step because of the contest between forces representing common interests and those representing the old, particularistic order) have been voiced by the power élite of every hegemon since the dawn of the modern age. Of course, it is hard to dispute that secular trends like these have brought about a more integrated world. However, interdependence alone does not occasion a moral society.

It is a distinctively ideological argument which submits that this overall trend towards greater integration also signifies the emergence of 'one world' and of a larger, international *community*. Liberal writers often make this connection. Radical writers do not – indeed, it is one of the characteristic claims of radical analysis that the evolution of an interdependent world system is based on a fundamental clash of interests between the peoples of its component core, semi-periphery and periphery (Wallerstein 1994). Conservative authors do not readily make this connection either – Brzezinski (1993) and Moynihan (1993), for example, see no sign of any integrating trend in the post-cold war world; rather, they see a fragmenting tendency. They see breakdown of governmental authority, intensification of tribal and religious conflict, the spread of terrorism and of ethnic cleansing. Samuel Huntington has made this kind of argument notably famous – first in a direct response to Fukuyama's end-of-history thesis, later in a *Foreign Affairs* article and a book with the telling title *The Clash of Civilizations and the Remaking of World Order*. In the post-cold war world, explains Huntington, a new style of politics is emerging based on cultural consciousness and ethnic loyalties. The 'most pervasive, important, and dangerous conflicts will not be between social classes, rich and poor, or other economically defined groups, but between peoples belonging to different cultural entities' (Huntington 1997a, p. 28). The greatest threat to order and peace will emerge from conflicts between different civilizations. Such conflicts will carry with them dangerous potential for escalation as other states and groups from these civilizations rally to the support of their 'kin countries'.

Which argument is best sustained by the secular trends of the twentieth century? That of Fukuyama (1989, 1992) who anticipates a homogenization of global politics along Western, liberal-democratic lines? Or that of Huntington (1997a) who, echoing older arguments about *Kulturkampf* and *Lebensraum* (Schmitthenner 1938), foresees increasing cultural variety and renewed civilizational conflict?[5] As a vantage point, three observations can be levied against Fukuyama's vision of a unified world. First, punitive trends alone are unlikely to cause any international agreement on values and norms. During the cold war, Soviet and American leaders were unified in their efforts to avoid large-scale nuclear war, yet this hardly indicated deeper agreement on social values, moral norms and political ideologies.

Second, remunerative trends alone will hardly produce harmony and peace. One of the most apparent trends in modern economic history has been the worldwide dissemination of Western-made products – guns and liquor since the sixteenth century; trains, trucks, tractors, tapes and T-shirts in the twentieth. Is there any reason to expect that this development should also produce normative consensus, harmony and peace? [6]

Third, as hegemonic norms and values have spread around the world during the course of modern history, they have been eagerly emulated in some societies (as when Japan and Germany adapted to American-style democracy and capitalism after World War II), while they have been resisted and combated in others (as when fundamentalist groups in Iran, Iraq and Afganistan have vowed to rid the world of 'the American Satan'). The fact that 'contemporary technology seems to work better when based on Western science rather than, say, Hindu scriptures is, obviously, something that is useful to know about the world', writes Chris Brown (1995, p. 94). However, he adds, 'something further is needed if an essential *empirical* account of an increasingly unified world is to be accompanied by an essentially *normative* account of the emergence of a world community'.

It is a basic insight of the social sciences that when people receive new information, they interpret it in terms of their existing perspectives. Thus, one particular message will be interpreted differently by different people in different contexts. For example, whereas North Americans might see the advent of global communications as a step towards a unified world, non-Americans might view it as a manifestation of US power. What Americans see as 'globalization' non-Americans often see as 'Americanisation', and those who perceive the increasingly interdependent and liberalised world as inimical to their identity and their interests, may vent their rage on the United States. Nowhere have US foreign policy-makers had to balance their new hegemonic status more delicately than in their relations with Afghanistan. During Reagan's presidency, they secretly aided the Afghan *mujaheddin*, who mounted a truly remarkable struggle against Soviet invasion forces. This aid, which amounted to over $3 billion as well as modern missile technology, played a decisive role in pushing Soviet forces out of Afghanistan in 1988. The aid earned the US sentiments of gratitude from several groups in the region. However, it also fuelled complex processes of *ressentiment* among fundamentalist groups in the area. No sooner had their *jihad* against the USSR been crowned with success than groups in the *mujaheddin* turned their xenophobic thirst for revenge against the US. Rebel centres in Afghanistan and Pakistan have been teeming with anti-American activities – such as those coordinated by the 'Muslim Brotherhood' who have funded terrorists and anti-American agitators in several countries (Lohbeck 1993; Roy 1994).

The larger point is that as long as significant populations of the world perceive themselves as threatened by the spread of US values – as long as they see the US as the 'other' – the US will fuel resentment in those populations. In this way, even anti-Americanism of the violent terrorist type, may be seen as a side effect of America's domination of global communications. In a divided world, American pre-eminence will produce not agreement and harmony but resentment and conflict. If a new world order is to be established under American aegis, then the United States must appear as a just and trustworthy leader.

Towards a peaceful world order?

The future international scene will be multi-ethnic. But will it be conflictual or will it be peaceful? It has been argued above that when people define their allegiances and identities, they do so in contrast to what they are not. It may be inferred from this that, if identity and unity are dependent on the existence of an 'other', then a truly universal cosmopolitanism will never evolve – unless one is willing to concede that the earth may some day be mortally endangered from outer space.

It has also been argued above that three important secular trends of modern history all contribute to reducing conflict and war; and emphasis has been put on how a cosmopolitan, pacific public sphere has emerged among open, neighbouring societies of the world. The little adjective 'open' plays an important role in the argument, for it intimates that this pacific trend is not global in scope. Most open and strong states are found in the developed, Western world, which indicates that the cosmopolitan public sphere is primarily a Western phenomenon. Here, in the West, the pacific trend has been unmistakable – indeed, even periods of setbacks and wars have, on further inspection, been affected by the trends in ways which are revealed in telling international patterns. After Westphalia, constitutional states have increasingly tended to band together. Since the eighteenth century, the open trading states of Western Europe have tended to end up on the same side in major wars. Since the nineteenth century, the open and strong states of the Western world have tended to avoid war with each other.[7]

During the twentieth century, the regular diplomatic relations among open and strong states have produced a steadily widening cosmopolitan public sphere, a security community or a 'zone of peace'. This is indicated by Table 25. This table suggests the extent of the cosmopolitan sphere. It indicates a tendency for liberal, democratic, Western states to avoid wars with each other – where 'war' is defined as interstate violence with more than 1,000 battle deaths (Small and Singer 1982).

Table 25   *Distribution of international wars, 1945–89*

	Fought in		
Fought by	*OECD countries*	*Communist countries*	*Less developed countries*
OECD countries	0	1	7
Communist countries	0	3	3
Less developed countries	0	1	19

Source: Russett (1990, p. 120) who has updated Small and Singer (1982, pp. 78ff.).

Table 25 shows that no wars were fought in the West by Western countries between 1945 and 1989 – i.e. during the course of the *Pax Americana*. It reveals that Western countries were not entirely peaceful during this period; they did fight wars, but they fought them outside the Western region – they fought one war in the Second (or Communist) World and seven wars in the Third World. But Western countries fought no war among themselves. How does this apparent advent of a cosmopolitan zone of peace in the West affect the arguments of Fukuyama and Huntington? Which of the two arguments does the pacific trend more readily support?

The immediate answer is that it supports Fukuyama. The existence of a Western zone of pacific relations dovetails nicely with Fukuyama's end-of-history argument. Huntington's argument, by contrast, receives no such support from the table. At the core of Huntington's argument lies the claim that the end of the cold war implies a watershed in international relations: before 1990 interstate wars tended to be *intra*civilizational, whereas after 1990 such wars have increasingly tended to occur across civilizational lines. Unfortunately, Table 25 does not contain the right kind of civilization-specific data to evaluate these claims.

Conflicts, wars and Fukuyama's claims

Table 25 above supports Fukuyama's claim that large-scale conflicts among great powers are passing from the scene – and, by extension, it also indicates that a security community, or a cosmopolitan zone of peace, has developed in the Western core of the world system. But can the claim be universalized? Will the ideals of an open, liberal-democratic society triumph in *all* areas of the globe? By Fukuyama's own account, it will. But Table 25 lends no support to his universal claim – and, by extension, it lends no support to the claim that the Western zone of cosmopolitan peace is expanding to the rest of the globe. The table only indicates that peace and order were unequally distributed across the globe during the 'first' American world order.

There may be three reasons why Fukuyama's universal claim does not find any support in Table 25. The first and most obvious reason is that the universal claim is wrong. This is the verdict of many of Fukuyama's critics. Some of them intimate that Fukuyama's sweeping macro-historical argument may be seen as a Soviet expert's hyperbolic reaction to the fall of the Soviet empire. His claim really reflects a surprisingly narrow historical perspective. It is a long idealistic leap of liberal faith to infer from the collapse of Soviet Communism the global victory of American liberalism.

The second reason why Fukuyama's universal argument finds no support in Table 25 is that the table is based on obsolete information: Fukuyama's universal argument needs to be confronted by post-cold war data; it cannot be tested on cold war data alone (which are the basis of Table 25). Such a post-cold war dataset has been collected by Wallensteen and Sollenberg (1997) who have recorded forty wars (interstate wars as well as civil wars) for the eight post-cold war years 1989–96. Their record is tabulated in Table 26. Table 26 supports, just like Table 25, Fukuyama's moderate argument by confirming that no wars have occurred in the West; but it lends no support (like Table 25) to his universal claim, as several wars have occurred in the extra-Western regions of the world after the end of the cold war.

Table 26   *Distribution of wars (including civil wars), 1989–96*

	Fought in		
Fought by	*The West – i.e. the First* World	*The former Second World*	*The Middle East and the (former) Third World*
The West	0	0	1
The former Second World	0	6	0
The less developed countries	0	0	33

Source: Wallensteen and Sollenberg (1997)

The third reason why Fukuyama's universal claim finds no support in existing datasets for war is that it is meant as a forecast and that any empirical test is therefore premature. Fukuyama does not really maintain that democratic rule is actually spreading across the post-cold war globe. His claim is more modest than that, and more ideational. He claims that at the end of the twentieth century, the political values and norms which are associated with the Western form of liberal democracy no longer face any serious ideological competitors.

It is on the level of ideas, norms and values, then, that the West has won. Fukuyama posits the total triumph of one ideology and the consequent end of ideological conflict. He claims that the Western liberal-democratic ideal has emerged as 'the final form of human government' after the fall of the Marxist–Leninist creed. However, here his argument is, again, faced with critics who claim that only traditional cold war shortsightedness can induce Fukuyama to interpret the fall of Soviet Communism as tantamount to the victory of US liberalism. The scepticism of his critics is also fuelled by the curious fact that Fukuyama's liberal, neo-Wilsonian message is founded on illiberal, Continental authors like Hegel and Nietzsche (Knutsen 1991; Aoudijt 1993).

Although Fukuyama argues that open, Western societies will triumph in other areas of the globe, he concedes that this triumph will not occur immediately. Anti-liberal creeds may long survive in pockets of atavistic politics around the globe – believers in the totalitarian ideas of Marxism–Leninism may for example linger 'in places like Managua, Pyongyang, and Cambridge Massachusetts'. Thus, the triumph of the West 'does not by any means' imply the immediate end of international conflict. Indeed, 'there would still be a high and perhaps rising level of ethnic and nationalist violence', for these are impulses which are still incompletely played out in many parts of the world (including parts of the Western world). 'Palestinians and Kurds, Sikhs and Tamils, Irish Catholics and Walloons, Armenians and Azeris, will continue to have their unresolved grievances' (Fukuyama 1989, p. 18). On this point Fukuyama and Huntington agree. But the numbers expressed in Tables 25 and 26 harmonize best with Fukuyama's argument. The tables show that although no wars occurred in the West during or after the cold war, several wars were fought in extra-Western regions – these have either been wars between the West and Third World countries, wars between Third World countries themselves or wars among successor states along the rim of the former Second World.

Conflicts, wars and Huntington's thesis

Table 26 does not support Huntington's argument. If his claim is true – if interstate wars have increasingly broken out across civilizational lines after the end of the cold war – then we should expect to see an increase in the number of wars between the First, the (formerly) Second and the (formerly) Third Worlds. Table 26 suggests the exact opposite. The cells which would most readily indicate the presence of intracivilizational wars are all empty, except for one cell in the table's upper right-hand corner – which indicates an action launched by the USA in 1989 when American forces went into Panama and captured strongman Manuel Noriega. When Table 26 is compared with Table 25, it is suggested that wars increasingly occur *within* civilizations rather than across civilizational lines.

It could be argued that this failure to substantiate Huntington's claim is due to the fact that the tables miss the core of his argument. Table 25 only reflects wars between sovereign states during the cold war, whereas Huntington primarily addresses conflicts and war between civilizations in the post-cold war era. Table 26 includes post-cold war wars but it does not capture conflicts short of war.

However, when more suitable datasets are procured, they do not support Huntington's argument either. Wallensteen and Sollenberg's (1997) data, for example, are an exhaustive record of 101 armed conflicts in the world for the eight post-cold war years 1989–96 – six of these were conflicts between states;[8] the remaining ninety-five were conflicts within states. Their data are tabulated in Table 27 in a format which shows that post-cold war conflicts have over-whelmingly occurred outside the open strong states of the West. It does not substantiate Huntington's universal claim that violent civilizational conflicts have intruded upon the politics of Western states. In fact, Table 27 rather supports Fukuyama's argument – and, by implication, the argument of the cosmopolitan peace.

Table 27   *Distribution of violent conflicts, 1989–1996*

	Fought in		
Fought by	The West – i.e. the First World	The former Second World	The Middle East and the (former) Third World
The West	2[a]	0	1
The former Second World	0	17	0
The less developed countries	0	0	81

Source: Wallensteen and Sollenberg (1997)
Note: a. These two conflicts are the 'minor armed conflict' in the Basque territories of Spain and the 'intermediate armed conflict' in Northern Ireland

To sum up: the hub of Huntington's argument is that the end of the cold war represents a historical watershed in interstate relations, because it involves the transition from an old age in which great-power conflict was largely *intra*civilizational to a new epoch in which great-power conflict will be *inter*-civilizational. Huntington does not contend that states will cease to be key actors in world affairs after the cold war; rather, he argues that states will begin to behave differently. 'The key issues of the international agenda involve differences among civilizations', claims Huntington (1997a, p. 29). But his claim suffers from several problems. One of the more crippling of them is that it isn't true.

There is no evidence to support Huntington's claim that interstate conflict *after* the cold war has been largely *inter*civilizational. First, the data which have been systematically collected about post-cold war conflict suggest – as indicated by Tables 25–7 – that there may, in fact, be a *de*creasing tendency for interstate conflict to occur across civilizational lines. Second, case study data (which Huntington draws heavily on) may be construed to support a conclusion precisely the opposite of Huntington's. One case in point is the Gulf War (which Huntington uses as his prime example of a 'civilizational war'). The cause of its outbreak lies squarely within the Islamic civilization: the war was triggered by Iraq attacking another Islamic state (and the war is found in Table 27 in the lower right-hand cell as one of eighty-one non-Western cases). Once the war was a fact, Iraq's attack was repulsed by a multi-civilizational coalition. The coalition was organized and led by the United States. But several Western and Muslim states participated on America's side (and with tacit support from Israel!). Another example is the war in Bosnia (which Huntington uses as a prime example of a 'fault-line' war). Quite contrary to what Huntington's thesis would lead us to believe, Western soldiers did not assist fellow Westerners (in this case Croats) in Bosnia. Rather, they largely protected Muslims. Indeed, Western countries may have given far more military aid to the Bosnian Muslims than have the Islamic countries of the world. And Russia has, by the way, offered little substantial support to its Orthodox brethren. The Gulf War and the Bosnian conflict may, in effect, be seen as cases of intercivilizational cooperation rather than intercivilizational conflict.

Furthermore, it is a bold exaggeration for Huntington to claim that interstate conflicts *before* the cold war were largely *intra*civilizational. The discussion above of the Iberian, Dutch and English world orders indicate that non-Western states have regularly intruded in great-power wars. This is most clearly the case during the Iberian order (up to the battle of Lepanto in 1571), when the Muslim presence was a constant element in interstate affairs. Non-Western states also participated in conflicts and war during the Dutch and British world orders. One such state is Japan (which Huntington defines as a civilization in its own right). Japan has competed and fought wars with Western states since the final quarter of the nineteenth century and through World War II. Another such country is Russia (which Huntington also sees as a civilization in its own right). Throughout modern history, Russia has interacted and competed with Western as well as Eastern states (Braudel 1994, p. 535ff.). During the British world orders, Russia was part and parcel of two waves of great wars – the Napoleonic Wars and World Wars I and II (and it could be argued that Russia's participation repeatedly affected the outcome of these great-power conflicts). During the American world order, Russia, in its Communist incarnation, constituted the very image of the diabolical 'other' in Western world affairs. Certainly, with the Soviet Union, China and large sections of the Third World involved in conflicts with the United States, the cold war was no *intra*civilizational conflict.

So, if pre-cold war world conflicts were not *intra*civilizational, and if post-cold war conflicts have not been *inter*civilizational, severe doubt is cast on Huntington's claim that the end of the cold war represents a civilizational watershed. What remains of his argument is the observation that states with different civilizational backgrounds sometimes fight one another. But this is hardly a new insight.

Concluding comments

This discussion about conflicts and order in the post-cold war world strengthens Fukuyama's case whereas it weakens Huntington's. Also, it suggests three questions: first, it raises the question of whether punitive trends may be accompanied by trends of behavioural and moral convergence. Previous chapters have argued that societies which ally against a common enemy tend to grow more alike as they emulate the social and military institutions of the most efficient alliance member. Some degree of convergence, then, occurs within lasting alliances. But can convergence also occur across alliances? Can military rivals come to behave more similarly? Military rivalry may, on the face of it, seem an unlikely vehicle for disseminating values, norms and rules. Yet, such rivalries have been known to prevent functional differentiation among states (Waltz 1979, pp. 87ff.) and to cause some convergence among states. Arms races have been known to drive states to develop similar weapons, similar systems of communications, command, control and intelligence, and similar military strategy. For example, the arms race ignited by the French *levée en masse* in 1791 drove other great powers to emulate revolutionary France and thus evolve comparable military structures all over Europe. By a similar token, the nuclear arms rivalry after World War II drove the two superpowers to develop strikingly similar weapons systems – a technological convergence on the basis of which it was possible to engage in diplomatic dialogue and arrive at arms limitation agreements and mutual inspection regimes during the cold war.

Second, it raises the issue of whether remunerative trends are accompanied by trends of moral convergence? Huntington is undoubtedly correct when he argues that trade alone is unlikely to produce convergence in norms and values. However, trade hardly ever occurs alone. It takes place in larger commercial and social contexts – as has been observed by social-science thinkers for centuries (Knutsen 1997, pp. 122ff.). Montesquieu, Kant, Hume and many others have explained how commerce among a number of neighbouring and independent states is accompanied by emulation, improvement and the 'rise of politeness and learning' (Hume 1985). Nineteenth-century theorists narrowed the analytical perspective of this argument, and argued that commerce caused peace. But late twentieth-century authors have expanded the argument again, and claimed that commercial interaction between states tends to reproduce in participating states the institutions of the pre-eminent economies (Mitrany 1933; Carr 1945; Deutsch 1970; Krasner 1983; North 1990), complete with Western-type goods, consumer habits, consumption patterns, ways of life and systems of payment, cash and credit.

Third, if late twentieth-century wars are not caused by civilizational clashes, what, then, has caused them? Now, as in the past, wars are waged between (and within) nationalities and ethnicities. The causes of war today are as varied, complex and inscrutable as they ever were – conflict over territory, religion, strategic or commercial advantage remain potent causes of war. Neither economic nor military conflicts can be properly understood when viewed mainly through the lens of clashing civilizations.

The studies of hegemonic decline suggest that wars are a particular problem of weak states – not of weak powers or of strong states but of weak states; i.e., states with a low capacity to command the loyalty necessary to extract resources needed to provide services and to rule. This is confirmed by Tables 25–7 which indicate that since 1945 most wars have occurred in the Third World and, more recently, in areas which were formerly situated within the Second World. It is also confirmed by Holsti, who claims that since 1945 the great powers of the West have not initiated war. Rather:

> They have primarily *responded* to the problem of war in and between weak states. They have not themselves been the sources of war, as they had been between the seventeenth century and 1945. To study war, then, the new focus will have to be on states other than the 'powers'. Theories of international relations will have to veer away from Rousseau's insights and recognize that anarchy within states rather than between states is the fundamental condition that explains the prevalence of war since 1945. (Holsti 1996, p. 82)

It was suggested in Chapter 4 that conflict breaks out when consensus unravels; that wars occur when social cohesion, imposed or maintained by some traditional authority, disintegrates. Society's various constituent groups then turn to their primary sources of solidarity for sustenance and protection – to their basic 'markers of identity', whether these are political, economic, local, ethnic, religious or otherwise constructed (Martin 1998). The conflicts which Huntington discusses in light of his macro-cosmic paradigm of clashing civilizations may be better explained in a micro-cosmic perspective of unravelling identity and consensus. Croats don't kill Serbians simply because they belong to a different civilization; the killings occur in (and are themselves fuelling) a greater context of unravelling cohesion and disintegrating trust in a distinct region and of its population's increasing retrenchment into more elementary collective selves which carry with them enormous weights of local historical consciousness.

Huntington's macro-cosmic analysis leads to a portrayal of the West as besieged by enemies who reject Western civilization in general and the American creed in particular. He claims, in terms reminiscent of earlier and colder times, that the West must defend itself. Western states must begin by unifying to contain the tide of multiculturalist pressures. 'Europe and America will hang together or hang separately', concludes Huntington (1997a, p. 321). Against his macro-cosmic claim could be levied a micro-cosmic argument which would depict the West as the besieger rather than the besieged. It would see the West as consisting of strong and wealthy states whose liberal–capitalist practices are eroding traditional authority in extra-Western regions. It would see the many conflicts and wars outside the West as fuelled by regional anarchy and local *ressentiment*.

There are, of course other dynamics at work behind extra-Western conflicts. And the forces of change may vary in nature and speed from one extra-Western case to the next. But when this is said, it must be added that liberal ideas, capitalist practices and modern Western institutions may, in fact, add uncertainty, pressure, change and tension to extra-Western societies. It has been argued in earlier chapters that states are communities which are sustained by mythologies and by common beliefs about good and evil, about the sacred and the profane. Such communities are constituted by more than rules, laws and formal institutions; they are also anchored in culture, in religion, in family networks, in daily habits, in 'structures of everyday life' (Braudel 1981; Fukuyama 1992, p. 213). In most societies, modernization – including the introduction of democracy – means change; it involves the fading of established habits, the unravelling of formal and informal institutions and the marginalization of established identities, interests and groups. Such change is, in turn, attended by uncertainties, conflicts, *ressentiment* and violent modes of resistance.

Huntington acknowledges this point. And he draws on Joseph Nye's distinction between 'hard' and 'soft' power to drive the point home. 'Hard power' refers to the ability to punish or reward and flows from material resources like economic wealth and military strength; 'soft power' is the ability of a state to get '"other countries to *want* what it wants" through the appeal of its culture and ideology' (Nye 1990, quoted in Huntington 1997a, p. 92). If the culture and ideology of a state are attractive, then other states will be more disposed to follow its leadership. But what makes one particular national culture so attractive to other nations that they decide to follow its lead? To a large degree, a state becomes attractive when it can demonstrate material success.

'Soft power is power only when it rests on a foundation of hard power', explains Huntington (1997a, p. 92). But here he is surely mistaken. For if he is right, then poor and weak states which possess no hard power can possess no soft power either. Consequently they pose no credible civilizational challenge to the wealthy states of the West. Huntington's major point is, in fact, precisely the opposite: that is, that materially poor states *do*, at times, challenge the wealthy states of the West.[9] And their challenges indicate that values, norms and ideas do exert some influence of their own accord.

The efficacy of hard power depends on the level of trust and the political context within which it exists. Thus 500 British nuclear missiles are usually perceived as less threatening to the United States than five North Korean or Iraqi ones; by the same token, the nuclear arsenal of a chaotic (but post-Communist) Russia appears less scary than that of the Soviet Union. The same point applies to the efficacy of soft power. If the general atmosphere is characterized by mistrust, then normative power may trigger *ressentiment* and conflict. If a great power consciously activates normative resources for political effect in conjunction with force and wealth, it may fuel ugly, even violent, modes of resistance. In the first hegemonic case discussed here, Philip II was met with such resistance when he invested his high religious ideals in an intense effort to Catholicize the Spanish Netherlands (thus debasing the ideals to propaganda and causing the Dutch to unify in a long and violent war of liberation). In the last hegemonic case discussed here, Lyndon B. Johnson was met with such resistance when he sought to democratize and pacify Vietnam with the aid of dollars and arms.[10] However, if the general atmosphere is marked by openness, tolerance and trust, normative power may prove irresistible. Thus, it is argued in previous chapters, the values, norms, ideas, ideologies and political mythologies of pre-eminent states are influential when exercised in an atmosphere of trust and openness in which citizens are free to converse upon the general arrangements of society.

The uncertain revival

A main *motif* of all the cases of hegemony discussed above is the remarkable accumulation of material wealth and power which their peoples achieved during certain phases of their histories. The discussion has examined how this wealth and power were accumulated, whence they derived, how they were used and how they eventually diminished. During the phases of hegemony, many Dutch and English people were unconscious of the very foundations of this power. The worldwide power of the City of London, for example, was 'as discreetly veiled from public view as the legs of Mid-Victorian pianos; the supremacy of the British Navy was normally as silent as footsteps upon the layers of drawing-room carpets', writes David Thomson. He concludes that because the nakedness of power was withheld from view, for long periods people forgot how necessary this basis of power was to the whole structure of British greatness. It was, paradoxically, when this power was crumbling that the British began to talk about it – and even to brandish it – most (Thomson 1978, p. 10).

Thomson's comment on nineteenth-century England applies equally well to twentieth-century America. The foreign-policy initiatives of the United States met with greatest success when most Americans were unconscious of the very foundations of US power. During the 1950s, when the mechanisms of power were withheld from view, Americans and their allies forgot how necessary this basis of power was to their greatness. And when least fully aware of whence their power came, the Americans usually used it well, for they used it in the cause of freedom. It was only during the late 1960s, when the power was beginning to crumble, that they began to talk about it, analyse it and understand its nature. One effect of this new-found consciousness of national power (and of its diminishing base) was to try to use it with greater efficiency. But this was never a success. For the effort was offset by another effect, which was to uncover the bases and the mechanisms of American power and to reject its workings as wicked and immoral.

During the 1950s American values, norms and ideas reached global levels of influence. During the 1990s, American norms and values were again embraced worldwide in ways reminiscent of the heyday years of American hegemony – this occurred after the cold war, and was attended by an unprecedented dismantling of America's cold war military structures. How tight was this embrace? Does the re-emergence of American power amount to a brief Indian summer? Or does it signal the first, hegemonic phase of a re-established US world order? Which effect does increased attention to civilization, culture and multi-ethnicity have on America's role in post-cold war world affairs?

America's hard power

The American economy expanded rapidly after the end of the cold war. The superpower rivalry weighed heavily on the economies of both the USA and the USSR for nearly half a century. During its final decade, following the final breakdown of *détente* in 1979, the cold war grew more intense. It became more focused on conflicts in the Third World and on new rounds of expensive hi-tech arms races. Both arenas – the Third World arena as well as the arena of technological competition – saddled the two superpowers with great costs. Both reeled under the impact. Yet some sectors of America's domestic economy experienced a veritable industrial revolution during these years. This was accompanied by a sustained economic expansion and is reflected, on the one hand, in mounting rates of business capital spending, increasing household demand for goods and services and resurgent export sales and, on the other, in falling rates of unemployment and inflation. Most of all, this expansion is reflected in the 1990s development of the US stock market.[11] The expansion was most notable in the fields of electromagnetic and microelectronic manufacturing. And, best of all, in contrast to the growth of the 1980s, the growth of the 1990s was not attended by mounting government deficits.

On balance, the United States emerged in the 1990s as the only plausible leader of the post-cold war world economy.[12] How long can it last? The most likely answer is that it can last a long time. First, the United States possesses a vast domestic resource base – which includes material resources (like minerals, oil and good soil for food production) as well as leadership talents and cheap immigrant labour. Few great powers are, in fact, as self-sufficient in basic factors of production as the USA. Second, America's major businesses are informed by teams of social scientists and technologists who do research on change. They know about socio-economic theories (such as Kennedy's uneven-development thesis or North's neo-institutionalism). They are familiar with the trajectories of secular trends and ready to adapt to new historical circumstances. American firms do not only have at their disposal the old quantitative, static models of neoclassical analysis; they have also embraced more qualitative and evolutionary arguments. They have long seen production and growth as activity-specific and technology-dependent (Nelson and Winter 1982; Porter 1990); they increasingly view trade and transactions as institutionally informed (North 1990). They see economic activity as embedded in a world of constantly changing societies (Drucker 1998).

Business leaders are not the only Americans who are fully aware of the secular trends of world affairs. The same can be said of members of the US foreign-policy élite. After all, Huntington has long been adviser to the US government and Fukuyama has been deputy director at the Policy Planning Staff with the US State Department. US policy-makers include large-scale, long-term perspectives in their foreign-policy assessments. This was evident in departmental discussions which preceded the US decision to include new members in Nato and thus expand the peace zone of liberal-democratic Europe further east. (Such awareness has, however, not been equally evident in the US Congress. Nor has it been apparent in Western Europe, whose governments have been more preoccupied with refurbishing the European Union after the end of the cold war than with expanding its liberal-democratic institutions eastward.) But do US policy-makers have at their disposal the resources necessary to deal with the contingencies which the assessors sketch? Do they command a force that is both economically sustainable and easily deployed far afield? Yes, they do. It is not the same kind of force they had during the cold war. But it is still the best military force in the world.

American military efforts no longer focus on Russia and Europe, but on extra-European areas, where US policy-makers deem the chances of war to be far greater. This reorientation is reflected in two changes in America's military doctrine. The first change is the scrapping of the old geostrategic principle of cold war military planning – i.e., to fight and win 'one and a half' major wars.[13] Instead, the USA has adopted a new, less ambitious strategic premise: that US armed forces must be able to engage in 'two medium-sized wars' simultaneously and win them. The second change is a replacement of the old strategy of 'forward defence' (which dominated the 1980s) with a new strategy of 'forward presence' – which must be understood to mean US presence in strategically important extra-Western areas, notably in the oil-rich regions of the Middle East and in conflict-prone areas of the Third World.

Are these wise changes, many observers ask? Are not the reductions in US military budgets likely to endanger US pre-eminence at a time when the number of conventional weapons is steadily growing in the non-Western world? More and more non-Western states have acquired nuclear weapons (Russia, Khazakhstan, China, India, Pakistan) or have made strenuous efforts to acquire them (Iran, Iraq, Libya, North Korea and, possibly, Algeria) at the same time as the United States is cutting many arms programmes and withdrawing from several bases around the world.[14] How long can the doctrine of 'one and a half' major wars be maintained under such circumstances? The most likely answer is: a long time. What the United States loses in quantity, through arms reductions, it seeks to recapture in quality through modernization and the development of new weapons systems. During the 1990s, the US armed forces have consciously pursued the modernization of the country's force structure – they have developed new military units (smaller, quicker and more independent and flexible units designed to perform new rapid deployment tasks). They have also adopted new weapons systems based on sophisticated new technologies – including 'smart' bombs and cruise missiles, 'stealth'-type systems for delivery and new modes of communication, command, control and intelligence. In spite of its vast military reductions, the USA is, on the threshold of the twenty-first century, the most powerful nation on earth. It possesses a global military force which can be used far afield. It possesses a nuclear armoury of intercontinental range, large enough and well protected enough to survive a surprise attack by any other nuclear power. Even without its nuclear weapons, the US arsenal is irresistible when used in a focused and surgical way.

America's soft power

Does the USA have a government capable of running a vigorous foreign policy? Does it have a people who can tolerate a vigorous and active foreign policy? These are difficult questions to address because the answers vary with the winds of political fortunes. The first question can generally be answered in the affirmative. The second question is more difficult. But on the whole, the American people are unlikely to tolerate just any foreign-policy activism – people still remember the infamous intervention in Vietnam which still casts dark shadows on US armed engagements in other regions of the world.

The domestic base of US hegemony

Huntington fears that the US identity is dissolving. He fears that this dissolution is disturbingly clear; in his collected assessments of America's national interest he precludes the nation from conducting a firm foreign policy. He argues that America's identity has disintegrated since the cold war, because the United States no longer has an enemy to define itself against. He adds that this disintegration has been exacerbated by changing immigration patterns, the rise of multiculturalism and the ebbing of assimilation (Huntington 1997a, pp. 305ff.; 1997b, p. 29ff.).

Huntington pinpoints a serious weakness in the American hegemony. It is worth recalling that previous hegemons have emerged from waves of great wars and that such wars have regularly strengthened the hegemonic state by causing its inhabitants to unify more tightly around a set of common values and norms. Furthermore, wars have contributed to the relative superiority of the hegemon: they have created a broad economic gap between the hegemon (which gained from the war) and other powers (which were exhausted by it). Finally, great wars have forged interstate coalitions united by a consensus as to the rules of the international game. They have accentuated the common identity of the wartime coalition in general and that of the hegemon in particular. None of these formative functions was performed by the 'second cold war' which preceded the re-emergence of the United States as a pre-eminent power.

First, the second cold war did not exhaust any other great power than America's primary rival – the Soviet Union. Other great powers of the international system retained their wealth and stature, so that no great gap separates America's hegemonic economy from the economies of the other great powers. Thus, America's economy may be pre-eminent, but its pre-eminence is uncertain and may, in the new and volatile post-cold war world economy, quickly be challenged by competing economies – e.g. by a coordinated EU.

Second, the 'second cold war' forged no tight coalitions united by a common consensus as to the rules of the international game. If such a consensus has nevertheless evolved, this must be explained by other factors – e.g. by the presence of nuclear weapons and by the development of interdependence and a cosmopolitan public sphere.

Third, the 'second cold war' did not forge any new common identity among the members of the 'victorious' (Western) coalition of states. Neither did it accentuate the common identity and the social cohesion and trust within the hegemon itself. As a result, on the threshold of the twenty-first century, the international pre-eminence of the United States is precarious. America's foreign-policy stance appears more fickle and uncertain than that of any previous hegemonic power.

The United States reduced its military capabilities during the 1990s (as it did during the late 1940s). Yet, as the twenty-first century approaches, its military capabilities are second to none (as they also were during the late 1940s). However, America's pre-eminence relies not on military power alone, but also on prestige, economic efficiency – from a reputation for efficiency derived from technological and economic pre-eminence – and from its cultural pre-eminence and moral example. It is a chink in America's hegemonic armour that its moral example is marred by an absence of the high patriotic unity and the massive sense of social cohesion which marked previous hegemons. The United States has neither dispelled its reputation for hedonism and moral laxity (indeed, it may have been accentuated by the highly publicized sex scandals of President Clinton) nor solved the problem of ethnic diversity – issues which emerged in the 1960s and tormented its domestic affairs during the unruly 1970s. The socio-ethnic contests which characterize the third phase of world order have been carried across America's revival and into its new phase of hegemony. Against this background, it is reasonable to ask whether the weak socio-ethnic cohesion in US society may, in the final account, prove to be America's Achilles heel in the twenty-first century? In all previous cases, a solid sense of communal identity was a precondition for the hegemon's definition of the national interest. For without a clear sense of identity a nation has neither a clear sense of national interest nor a clear set of foreign-policy maxims.

Huntington puts his finger on an important weakness in America's ability to play the hegemon of the early twenty-first century. However, he exaggerates it. He stretches the point too far. First, his historical perspective is too short. He treats the 1950s and 1960s as normal years of civil consensus in the United States, whereas these years rather were clear exceptions to the norm. For most of its history the United States has been diverse and conflictual. The immediate postwar decades were years of exceptional harmony in US history. They were years of hegemony, and, as such, characterized by a high degree of domestic consensus. Before this hegemonic phase, the United States was a fragmented, turbulent society; and as hegemony started to wane in the late 1960s, US society again splintered the cold war consensus into a kaleidoscope of multiple competing identities (Bell 1992). In the 1990s, the United States may be more conflictual than in the 1950s. However, it is more consensual than in the turbulent 1970s. Also, its consensus must be considered remarkably high when compared with the 1870s, the 1890s, the late 1910s or the 1920s (Dallek 1983, pp. 92–4; Carnochan 1993). This assessment finds support in recent theories as well as in survey data. American society is something far more than a mere container of different cultural and ethno-racial communities; America's is a society whose many ethnic groups share values, norms and ideals. Among the most characteristic American ideas are openness and tolerance.[15] These ideals are deeply anchored in a nationality that is based on the principle of consent and which is ostensibly open to persons of different ethno-racial affiliations (Hollinger 1995, pp. 14, 134). Survey data suggest that the American people have never really lost these ideals. They still lie at the core of an American sense of identity, and 'cosmopolitan liberalism remains the dominant outlook' in the United States (Citrin *et al.*, 1994, p. 20).

Second, Huntington's spatial perspective is too narrow. He skates too easily over the important fact that multi-ethnicity is a *global* phenomenon today. *All* great powers are currently multi-ethnic. The United States is not the only great power which is troubled by ethnic strife. Other great powers are in the same situation, including the old hegemons like England and the Netherlands.

Projecting American values and norms
The historical chapters of this analysis suggest that trade, openness, mass immigration and multi-cultural urbanization are sources of social energy and economic innovation; however, they also suggest that multi-cultural societies are vulnerable to political strife. All late twentieth-century Western states are to some degree multi-cultural societies, and they all are searching for the best balance between dynamism and strife. The United States may be in a better position to find this balance than other Western states. Indeed, of all the large multi-cultural countries in the world, the United States may, in fact, be the one society which has managed its cultural and ethnic tensions best. The USA has a tradition of ideals and agencies of assimilation. Its ideals are still strong and the agencies are still effective. Thus, rather than being adrift in a multi-cultural sea, America is able to deal sensibly with the multi-ethnic challenge of the twenty-first century, thus fuelling the social energies and the economic vibrancy of its multi-ethnic society.

America's ideals of openness and tolerance seem to be respected and embraced by an increasing number of domestic groups – in spite of these ideals being criticized, even rejected, by radicals and ethnic ideologues. Furthermore, America's values and norms are embraced abroad. US-type agencies of assimilation are emulated by other Western states. Bussing schemes (from the American 1960s) are discussed by European politicians who wish to avoid ethnically segregated schools (in the 1990s). American-type, contractarian citizenship oaths are proposed to ensure that extra-Western immigrants will obey the rules and laws of their new European homelands. Other states, including the states of Western Europe, are emulating America's multi-cultural, 'politically correct' discourse. America's allies are more frequently appealing to traditional American ideals in their efforts to find solutions to the problems of multi-cultural societies – such as minority rights, voluntary affiliation, dialogue and tolerance of multiple identities, all of which are hinging on the basic values of an open, market-based, liberal democracy.

It is a significant indication of America's soft power that its domestic concerns are universalized, echoed and repeated by other great powers. This indication was apparent in the late 1960s when America's own normative crisis, complete with divisive debates about civil rights and warfare in Vietnam, deeply affected the politics of America's allies. It has been repeated, *sotto voce*, in the 1980s and 1990s, as liberal ideals of privatization, deregulation and fiscal conservatism transformed the political economies of industrial and industrializing nations around the world. President Reagan, together with Britain's Prime Minister Margaret Thatcher, wielded a remarkable influence on this transformation. Reagan's presidential campaign was a catalyst of change – first in the United States, then in other countries around the world.[16]

Many of the ideas which Reagan expressed during his presidential campaign in 1980 were products of American decline. His campaign was driven by deep, patriotic concerns about America's impotence – the Soviet Union was acting aggressively, Iran was holding US citizens hostage and the country suffered the worst economic slump since the 1930s. To raise America's international prestige, Reagan proposed an orthodox build-up of military power. To mend America's sorry state of domestic affairs, he proposed unorthodox solutions: above all else, he was intent on reducing the size and power of government. He replaced the interventionist doctrines of Keynes with the neo-liberal philosophy of Hayek. In a clear break with past American policies, he intended to cut both taxes and government spending. He wanted to deregulate the many industries of public service, break the power of labour and, in effect, dismantle the vast, regulatory structure created by Roosevelt's New Deal. He wanted to turn federal, state and city activities over to private actors in a free market. In 1980, Reagan's policies were intensely controversial. By 1985 crisis-ridden welfare states in Western Europe had begun to follow suit. By 1990, after the collapse of the Soviet Union, even socialists were embracing free-market capitalism, calling back multinational corporations which they had earlier expelled and selling off public assets which they had previously nationalized. The 1990s offered the greatest global jumble sale on record:

Governments are getting out of businesses by disposing of what amounts to trillions of dollars of assets. Everything is going – from steel plants and phone companies and electric utilities to airlines and railroads to hotels, restaurants, and nightclubs. It is happening not only in the former Soviet Union, Eastern Europe and China but also in Western Europe, Asia, Latin America, and Africa ... The objective is to move away from government control as a substitute for the market and toward reliance on competition in the marketplace as a more efficient way to protect the public. (Yergin and Stanislaw 1998, p. 13)

This liberal policy of privatization created critics and opponents. It is a telling indicator of America's soft power that not only are the new, liberal (free-market) doctrines of the post-cold war age significantly shaped by American thought and practice, the new critique of these doctrines is *also* primarily American in origin. The so-called communitarian project began in the USA and has since spread to many other states. Communitarianism began in the 1980s (apparently as a reaction against Reagan's emphasis on free-market social ideals). It departs from the classical argument that the individual self is constituted through the community, and it is concerned with how a unifying consensus and solidaric trust can be instilled in the plural, market-based, liberal democracies of our age.[17]

The debate is not restricted to American academia. It has engendered a network with important political connections. One such connection is the White House and the Democratic administration of Bill Clinton. Another connection is Downing Street and Tony Blair's new Labour Party – and through Tony Blair in England (and Jacques Delors in France), the communitarian idea has influenced the debate and the political agenda of the EU.

On a less academic and élitist level, US concerns also affect the premises of popular public discussions around the world. This occurs through America's vast export of books, magazines, newspapers, films (on TV, video or in cinemas) and entertainments. America's 'cultural exports' account for about 3 per cent of its export earnings. Thus, they are economically significant, but not overwhelmingly so. But because these exports dominate the world of entertainment and information they are carriers of soft power. Their impact is far greater than their economic export value suggests. First, they have a greater economic impact than mere export figures suggest because they underpin the trade of many other commodities – for example, the licensing arrangements of MacDonald's, Coca-Cola, Levi's, Walt Disney and other brand names add value to other goods.

Second, they have a significant normative impact because they reach virtually every city on the globe and there stimulate increasing awareness of American fashions, tastes and norms. In most cases they subtly familiarize their audiences with the political mythologies which underpin US ways of life. The thousands of pumpkins which the inhabitants of Paris found on the Champs Elysées on the morning of 31 October 1997 may illustrate the point. For the French capital is only one of several foreign communities which in recent years have been introduced to Hallowe'en in its most American (and for the French fairly unfamiliar) incarnation. Hallowe'en has long been familiar to international consumers of US comic strips and children's TV shows. But only in recent years has this peculiarly American pumpkin cult been practised outside the United States – undoubtedly encouraged by an unholy alliance of children who crave candy and cool costumes, of parents who seek to amuse their children and of commercial entrepreneurs who want to fill the lull between autumn sales and Christmas with novel pretexts for theme shopping. The point to note is that an innocent 'cultural export' may channel the social imagination of its audiences – it may limit it in some ways while enlarging it in others, thereby affecting the construction of distinct world views which may, in turn, broaden their political horizons. Popular tellers of tall tales (like Michael Crichton or Tom Wolfe) may thus have broadened the political views of more people than the analyses of famous academics (like Kenneth Waltz or Robert Keohane). The conservative outlook of Tom Clancy must surely have had as much channelling impact on the film-viewing mass audiences of the 1990s as did Anthony Hope on the reading public of the 1890s (Goldsworthy 1998, pp. 43ff.).

The influence of the US film industry has been substantial since the days of World War I. During the 1950s and 1980s America's cultural hegemony reached unprecedented proportions. Several factors encouraged this cultural expansion. The most basic have been wealth and technology. First, the countries of the world grew richer during these decades. The new-found worldwide prosperity increased the disposable income (and perhaps also the leisure) of thousands of millions of consumers around the world. Second, this economic growth was attended by the rapid development of new communications technologies and their commercial exploitation on a global scale. This is evinced in the proliferation of commercial news and entertainment institutions around the world. One example is the privately owned television stations which have replaced state-owned monopolies in Finland, Israel, Malaysia, Russia and several other countries. Another is the rapid growth of satellite and cable systems, which allow most countries to watch the world news on CNN. This development is also evident in a worldwide surge in sales of TV sets, satellite dishes, video cassette recorders and personal computers – and in the fact that by the end of 1997 America's leading video hire chain had 2,000 outlets in twenty-six foreign countries.

By 1990, American film companies controlled 85 per cent of the world's film market (excluding India and China). On the European continent, eight out of the weekly top-ten films have regularly been of US origin during the 1990s –

in Scandinavia and the UK the share is even higher. Table 28 indicates the global pre-eminence of US-made films. It shows that not only does the USA dominate the world movie market; the *same* US films are top-grossing moves in virtually every corner of the capitalist world; a worldwide audience –

Table 28   *The three top-grossing movies in 1994 in twenty-one countries worldwide*

Countries	Film no. 1	Film no. 2	Film no. 3
Europe			
Austria	The Lion King	The Flintstones	Forrest Gump
Denmark	House of Spirits[a]	The Lion King	Nightwatch[b]
Finland	Forrest Gump	Schindler's List	Naked Gun 33
France	The Lion King	Un indien dans la ville[b]	Forrest Gump
Germany	The Lion King	The Flintstones	Schindler's List
Hungary	The Flintstones	The Lion King	True Lies
Iceland	Four Weddings and a Funeral	True Lies	Forrest Gump
Italy	Il mostro[b]	The Lion King	Forrest Gump
Luxembourg	The Lion King	The Flintstones	Schindler's List
The Netherlands	Schindler's List	The Lion King	Aladdin
Norway	Forrest Gump	Schindler's List	The Flintstones
Poland	The Fintstones	The Lion King	Schindler's List
Spain	The Flintstones	Schindler's List	Philadelphia
Sweden	Sune's Summer[b]	Aladdin	Four Weddings …
Switzerland	The Lion King	Mrs Doubtfire	Four Weddings …
UK	Four Weddings …[b]	Mrs Doubtfire	The Flintstones
Other			
Argentina	The Lion King	The Flintstones	House of Spirits
Brazil	The Lion King	Mrs Doubtfire	The Flintstones
Chile	The Lion King	The Flintstones	Schindler's List
Egypt	Baby's Day's Out	Mrs Doubtfire	Speed
Japan	Cliffhanger	True Lies	Pon Poko[b]
Mexico	The Lion King	The Flintstones	The Specialist
Turkey	The Flintstones	Mrs Doubtfire	Speed

Source: Variety International Film Guide, 1996
Notes: a.   Partly Danish
       b.   Domestic production

including moviegoers in Argentina, Brazil, Chile, Denmark, Egypt, France, Germany, Hungary, Iceland and Japan – watch the same American movies at the same time. As this pre-eminence persists, US cultural products contribute to building a cultural public sphere of international scope.

Table 28 indicates the global scope of this sphere as the twenty-first century approaches. The movies which were top-grossing in the mid-1990s were dominated by innocent entertainments (*The Lion King, Forrest Gump* or *Aladdin*) or tales of compassion (*Schindler's List* and *Philadelphia*) which may all be termed 'politically correct'.

The global dissemination of US-made movies is matched by US-made TV shows – either in their original US-made version (such as *Baywatch*, the world's most watched TV series [18]), or in some natively adapted emulation (which has the been the fate of *Wheel of Fortune, Jeopardy* and countless other American game shows). America's lead in the important software industry has in recent years approached a clear pre-eminence among the world's computer programs. However, the most significant indication of America's cultural influence may, when push comes to shove, not be technological at all; it may be discursive and linguistic. It may lie in the fact that the basic concepts with which businessmen, researchers and writers grasp their worlds are increasingly of English origin. Untold millions around the globe have English as their first foreign language – and as a consequence the first non-native culture they have access to is the Anglo-American commercial culture. When millions of people all over the world boot up their PCs in their offices or in the privacy of their homes, they switch to English as a matter of course. For the language of the 1990s is overwhelmingly English (Crystal 1997). We may be approaching a multi-ethnic world. However, English is its *lingua franca*. It is through English that the world is increasingly communicating interculturally – and then not in the Queen's English but in the President's.

The dangers of democratic peace

The Achilles heel of America's hegemony is hardly the multi-ethnic nature of the American nation. For the USA has developed ways of dealing with its multi-ethnicity so successful that other Western states are emulating them and parroting their underlying ideals. Indeed, in the post-cold war world order, America's communitarian brand of liberal multi-culturalism is probably its most influential ideology.

The transition from the first American world order to the second occurred without an intervening wave of large-scale war. The transition was relatively smooth. The line of demarcation remains relatively thin and unclear. The post-cold war world does imply new international norms and rules. However, the absence of a clear line of demarcation may represent a foreign-policy

problem for all states and their populations. This problem is more than anything a philosophical challenge. And the most vulnerable spot for America's
post-cold war hegemony may lie in the inability of the entrenched élites to
quickly master the transition to a new set of post-cold war attitudes. America's
weak seam may be the many leftover precepts from an ancient liberalism
(which e.g. constructivist, communitarian and multi-ethnic movements have
sought to make clear).

The old foreign-policy precepts contain materials which may still lead post-
cold war US foreign policy back into its pre-cold war ways – either back into
an era of isolationism or into fits of messianic actionism. On the whole, the
American people are unlikely to tolerate an activist foreign policy – as is most
apparent among many young Republican members of the US House of
Representatives. However, in the post-cold war era substantial segments of the
American people may nevertheless revert to the traditional belief that their
country stands for some splendid idea that other nations should be helped to
have a share of. The American people will not tolerate any brand of foreign-
policy activism; however, they may accept a vigorous foreign policy in the
name of democracy and peace. Many Americans are confident that their own
liberal norms and ideals resonate in many extra-American regions. The foreign-
policy élite is eager to define a new (and leading) role for the United States in
world affairs. Powerful groups lobby Congress and pressure the president for
overseas engagements.

Recent US presidents have tapped into America's political mythology and
forged a foreign-policy doctrine tailored to the needs of the post-cold war world
order: the doctrine of democratic peace. At the core of this new foreign-policy
doctrine lies the old idea that democracy and peace are causally connected.
This has been one of the few consistent themes in President Clinton's foreign-
policy rhetoric, and one of the few elements of continuity between the
administrations of Reagan, Bush and Clinton.[19] Indeed, the idea that democracies are predisposed to peace is an old standby in America's foreign-policy
rhetoric. It was maintained by Thomas Paine and other liberal activists of the
1770s. The pledge to 'make the world safe for democracy' has long been a
forceful item in America's foreign-policy discourse. It was a strong motivating
force in the foreign policy of Woodrow Wilson in the 1910s when the USA
broke out of its traditional policy of isolationism. It was a significant factor
in the international relations thinking of Franklin Roosevelt during the ascendance of America's hegemony in the 1940s. It informed American state leaders
and academics alike during the 1950s.

The democratic peace idea largely faded from view during the phase of
challenge in the 1960s and 1970s. A great many academics then embraced the
rival idea that liberal democracy was attended by capitalist practices. These

were seen as expansionist, and liberal democracy was tainted by association and portrayed as a conquering and oppressive, if not downright warlike, force in world politics. However, this view faded during the late 1980s, and the idea that democracy was a peaceful regime type was restored during the 1980s and 1990s.

On the threshold of the twenty-first century, a new enthusiasm for liberal views is shared by populations all across the world. Liberal views include the ideas that individuals are endowed with rights and that the purpose of the state is to facilitate the project (or 'happiness') of its individual members. They also include the idea of democratic rule – i.e., that the most powerful decision-makers of the state are brought to power through fair, honestly contested and periodic elections in which candidates freely compete for the votes of virtually all the adult population. Liberal views such as these lie at the core of America's political tradition. And intimately intertwined with this tradition is the idea that democracies are not only morally superior as a regime or type, but that democracies are also more peaceful than other regimes. This basic idea informs President Clinton's policy of bringing 'the world close together around basic principles of democracy, open markets, law and commitment to peace' (Albright 1998).

The claim that democracies do not fight each other is in perfect harmony with America's foreign-policy tradition. It provided the same guiding role for Reagan, Bush and Clinton as the idea of the inherently peaceful nature of democracies did for Wilson. It permeates the post-cold war policies of Nato because it also informs the foreign policies of America's Nato allies (Nato 1997). But can it last? And can it break away from the tight grasp of idealist liberalism?

If liberal democracy indeed is the best bulwark against war, many seemingly hard choices between realism and idealism can be vastly simplified and all good things can be made to go together. However, if democracy turns out to be an unlikely cause of peace, then an active US foreign policy based on the simple formula of democratic expansionism may prove disastrous. The American advocates of the democratic peace thesis should consider more carefully how their advocacy might be affected by three claims.

First, they need to consider that democratization means institutional change; it entails a transition from one type of rule to another, and such changes are regularly attended by uncertainties, resistance, conflict and violence. It was noted above that regimes are rooted in communities which are sustained by common values, norms and beliefs about good and evil. They are anchored in mythologies, religion, family structures, daily habits and in ways of life (Braudel 1981). For traditional societies, democracy involves more than the introduction of new institutions, it also means the displacement of old ones – of historical norms, extant forms of solidarity and traditional markers of identity. Here, the introduction of democracy may thus erode traditional authority, unravel local consensus and undermine social cohesion. So although established democracies may be peaceful and orderly both internally and in relation to other democracies, democratization may be destabilizing, disorderly and conflictual in countries with non-liberal rule (O'Donnell *et al.* 1988). Almost every democratization between 1974 and 1990 involved some violence. Admittedly, democratization seems to involve lower levels of violence than transitions between other regime types (Huntington 1991, p. 192). But this does not invalidate the larger point. Democratization involves *ressentiment* and resistance. It may be a destabilizing process. It may weaken states and, as demonstrated in Chapter 4, foment conflict, violence and war.

Second, the advocates of democratic peace need to consider the fact that the traditional notion of 'democracy' has always quietly been assumed to be encased in sovereign territorial states. It is therefore a problem that the notion of sovereignty has become untenable as states everywhere have been vastly weakened in recent decades. Among the major solvents of territorial sovereignty are the rapid growth of complex interconnections among states and societies which are commonly referred to as the process of 'globalization'. In this development lies a paradox of our age. Liberal democracy has emerged as 'the final form of human government' (Fukuyama 1989, p. 18) at the moment when substantial areas of human activity are increasingly organized on a global level, thus throwing the very efficacy of democratic government open to question. David Held (1995, p. ix) warns:

> If democratic theory is concerned with 'what is going on' in the political world and, thereby, with the nature and prospects of democracy, then a theory of democratic politics today must take account of the place of the polity within geopolitical and market processes, that is, within the system of nation-states, international legal regulation and world political economy. The pursuit of political knowledge on old disciplinary grounds is not adequate to this task.

Nowhere is Held's warning more urgently needed than in the popular area of the democratic peace, whose participants have long sought to explain an essentially international phenomenon on the basis of the internal properties of sovereign states.

Third, the advocate of democratic peace might consider the claim that democratic processes are not an internationalizing force. Democratic politicians win elections not by demonstrating how internationalist they can be, but by convincing local voters that they can represent them well in some central national assembly. In this process lies a second paradox of our age. Democratic elections include campaign processes which stimulate each candidate to fashion what he believes will be the most popular appeals within the relevant electoral district. Today such appeals are often ethnic, nationalist and religious in character. In the extra-Western world, democracy has been known to further a paradoxical indigenization: here the adoption of democratic institutions and processes of popular participation may give political power to anti-Western movements. The most obvious case in point is Algeria, where the introduction of democratic elections would have ensured the electoral victory of fundamentalist Islamic groups if the military had not intervened to cancel the second round of elections in 1992. A more subtle case is India, where the elections of 1998 brought to power a minority coalition government led by a party of populist patriots, the Bharatiya Janata Party (or BJP), whose pro-nuclear foreign-policy platform represents a dramatic break with India's pacific past and threatens to trigger a troublesome thermonuclear arms race on the subcontinent.

US policy-makers ought to consider carefully the differences between their own traditional democratic peace thesis and the 'cosmopolitan peace thesis' – they ought, most notably, to consider the different foreign-policy consequences of the two theses. First, there is a decisive difference in level of analysis. The democratic peace thesis is state-focused; it discusses the domestic attributes of territorial states. The cosmopolitan peace thesis is system-focused; it sees peace as an attribute of a system of open and strong states.

Second, the democratic peace thesis tends to lead to ahistorical and mechanistic arguments. It sees the international system as a function of its parts – and in its recent incarnation, as a function of *pairs* of states. The cosmopolitan peace thesis is, by contrast, historical and organic; it sees the world as composed of regional civilizations, and it sees the West as a region whose civilization has 'matured' through time. It sees Western international relations as having developed from the contentious, 'immature anarchy' of the seventeenth and eighteenth centuries, towards a more orderly 'mature anarchy' (Buzan *et al.* 1993) and a complex, cosmopolitan society unified by sustained interaction in the military, political, economic and cultural sectors (Deutsch *et al.* 1957).

Third, the democratic peace thesis treats 'peace' as an effect of democratic government. It envisions 'democracy' as the independent and 'peace' as the dependent variables in a simple, statistical association. It treats 'democracy' as an operative peace-causing factor. It infers that because democracy causes peace, then more democracies must cause more peace.[20] The obvious foreign-policy implication derived from this argument is the Wilsonian stance that the spread of democracy will diminish the frequency of war in the world; that peace can be promoted by an activist policy of democratization. For if more democracies mean less war, then it is a logical peace policy to try to overturn authoritarian regimes in the name of democracy and world order. The cosmopolitan peace thesis, on the other hand, treats 'peace' as an attribute of order and sees order as a complex, region-based composite of political, economic and cultural factors. Also, the cosmopolitan peace thesis would not succumb to activist temptations. First, because it sees peace as historically conditioned and regionally specific; second, because it acknowledges that all social change – democratic included – may challenge established identities and foment *ressentiment* and movements of resistance.

The cosmopolitan peace thesis flows from the observation that a 'zone of peace' has emerged slowly from the interaction among the open and strong states of the Western world. It draws on American theories of international regimes (Krasner 1983; Haas 1992; Rittberger 1995), on English theories of international society (Bull 1977; Vincent 1986; Watson 1992; Held 1995), on communitarian concerns with the anomic and disorderly consequences of liberal idealism (Etzioni 1997) on the neo-institutional arguments about the impact of norms and rules in social life (North 1990) and on the evolving constructivist notion that 'ideas matter' in international relations (Katzenstein 1996; Finnemore 1996; Adler 1997). It sees the Western zone of peace as an expression of a growing community of states (Deutsch 1970; Buzan 1993) which has been formed through modern history by a succession of leading powers (or hegemons) whose promulgation of principles like openness, tolerance and self-determination facilitated their pursuit of national interests. In this perspective, peace is a syndrome rather than a simple effect. It augurs the evolution of a transnational *civic culture* which engenders mutual trust and legitimacy. It is an attribute of a (regionally concrete, civilizationally specific and historically constructed) order secured by a complex, interactive web (rather than a simple bi-variate, unidirectional relationship). Democracy is certainly an important element in this ordering web. However, the web also involves other important elements. It involves a common, historically based understanding as to the rules which govern the interaction among sovereign states. And it involves the regional evolution of an intersubjective, liberal identity whose common norms and values – social openness, pluralism and dialogue, natural law, individual and equal rights, representative political bodies of freedom of trade and possession – operate as identity markers and common indicators of reciprocal peaceful intentions.

The reason why no war has broken out among Western states, then, lies not primarily in the national make-up of individual Western states, but in an *inter*national (cosmopolitan) public sphere which sustains the development of a shared set of values and norms that transcend the cultural characteristics of individual states. In the twentieth century, the United States has been the pre-eminent guarantor of this cosmopolitan sphere and the defender of the peaceful community of states which it inscribes. The USA has sustained a cosmopolitan peace in the Western world by arguing for its liberal ideals in an open international debate and by demonstrating how a society founded on these ideals can remain orderly, wealthy, strong and just. The United States has existed, like any other society, in a perpetual tension between a moral pressure for equality and the functional necessity of hierarchy. Thus, the ideals were not realized during the first American hegemony, and they are unlikely to be fully realized in the second. Yet they cannot be discarded. The United States has always been a diverse and polyglot country, and as the world is becoming increasingly polyglot, US ideals will have steadily greater appeal – at least in other strong and wealthy countries of the West. The ideals which the United States brings to the new post-cold war world order involve equal rights to multi-cultural variation, to construct one's life as one sees fit, to choose one's travelling companions.

The core of US society does not lie in a distinct ethnic history, but in its myth-enveloped, hallowed texts – most notably in the Declaration of Independence and in the US Constitution. America is an immigrant country. Its citizens do not constitute an *ethnos* but a *demos*. It is a construction of mind, not of race or inherited class. The American nation is not built around a unifying ethnic core according to which everyone must look the same, speak the same language and worship the same gods. America's unifying core is its Constitution, to which all citizens pledge allegiance – as if to repeat individually the original contract which is quietly assumed in the nation's political mythology and thus collectively renew the legitimacy of its government.

The norms and values contained in America's hallowed texts are deeply rooted in the Western traditions of Enlightenment optimism and in natural law. But their application is moulded by America's own historical experience. They are unceasingly reread in light of waves of new immigrants (which pledge allegiance to them) and of the jostling of scores of tribes which became American to the extent to which they could negotiate accommodations with one another. Such negotiations succeeded unevenly. Indeed, they often failed – as is abundantly obvious from the history of American race relations. Yet, the most recent chapters of that history also include chronicles of reform and civil-liberty legislation which indicate a secular trend towards a more equitable realization of American ideals. They indicate more than unilinear progress; they indicate that the American nation is ever-changing; that America is a collective act of the imagination whose making never ends.

This image of a multi-ethnic and nervous change is reflected in America's culture and in the cultural exports which it inflicts upon the rest of the world. As the twenty-first century is upon us, this world is itself marked by multi-ethnicity and change and peculiarly receptive to messages which, in turn, help sustain America's pre-eminence. As the twenty-first century approaches, the United States has the ability to influence debates and agendas in vast areas of the globe. It possesses the authority to establish the shared meaning of key concepts and the terms used in them – the ability to define authoritatively 'democracy' and 'dictatorship', 'freedom-fighter' and 'terrorist'. This leadership (*hegeisthai*) involves a possibility of establishing norms of international behaviour which may lead towards a world order which may resemble Kant's peaceful confederation more closely than any order hitherto established.

Kant's scheme for perpetual peace has, for two hundred years, been regularly brushed aside with the argument that his analysis is a pipe dream. Commentators have found it unrealistic. Peace is not an end which can be achieved in the present age. However, such protests are clearly beside the point for Kant. In Kant's philosophy, moral norms – be they individual or international – are unrelated to empirical fact or probability. Norms of human behaviour belong to the realm of reason, not of empirical fact. They flow from the demand of practical reason which informs all rational agents. And by this demand, Kant concludes with a maxim which is, if nothing else, a sensible rule of international conduct in the nuclear age:

> It is no longer a question of whether perpetual peace is really possible or not, or whether we are not perhaps mistaken in our theoretical judgement if we assume that it is. On the contrary, we must simply act as if it could really come about (which is perhaps impossible), and turn our efforts towards realizing it and towards establishing that constitution which seems most suitable for this purpose. (Kant 1991e[1797], p. 174)

Notes

1 Table 18 shows that the frequency of war has fallen from an average of 2.6 wars per decade during the sixteenth century, via 1.7 wars during the seventeenth and 1 war during the eighteenth to 0.5 wars per decade during the nineteenth century.

2 See Gaddis (1997) for an elaboration. This argument is still not universally accepted – as indicated e.g. by Mueller (1995).

3 Many realists justify doctrines of deterrence with reference to Kant's argument – as when Winston Churchill and Henry Kissinger claimed that in the atomic age peace has been the sturdy child of nuclear terror. See also Gaddis (1997).

4 This was a common assumption in eighteenth-century international relations theory – it informs Rousseau's writings on war and peace and, perhaps, also Hegel (Brown 1996, p. 34) and Montesquieu. The assumption can be traced far back – it is for example found at the core of Grotius's famous doctrine of *mare librum* (Knutsen 1997, p. 100).

5 It should be noted that the dichotomy between Fukuyama and Huntington is artificial. However, it is a convenient dichotomy because they can be said to represent extreme positions on a continuum along which there is room for a variety

of intermediate scenarios. Near Fukuyama there is room to envisage a new era of transcultural dialogue from which a genuine universal consensus about moral and political principles may emerge (Vincent 1986; Watson 1987); near Huntington there is room to envisage the demise of all but the most rudimentary principles of international coexistence (Brown 1988; 1996). This concluding chapter is not the occasion to range these intermediate positions nor to explore them in any detail – however, several good explorations are found in Fawn and Larkins (1996).

6 This question has regularly received affirmative answers; since the Age of Enlightenment and through the Industrial Revolution authors have argued that economic interdependence is a stronger force than national passions. Unfortunately, several historical cases from the nineteenth and twentieth centuries suggest differently. During the mid-1800s, 'moderates' argued convincingly that the American states were too economically intertwined for any war to occur among them; however this did not prevent the shots fired at Forth Sumpter exploding into one of the most vicious wars of that century. In 1913 international trade was at a record high, and the liberal peace movement claimed that the growth of interstate trade had made war unlikely and that the trading states of the West were creating a web of lasting peace. Yet, within a year industrialized states were tearing at each others' throats with unprecedented ferocity. The argument that trade alone does not create a normative convergence can be polemically pinpointed by the events of the 1970s and 1980s: in those decades American consumers bought millions of Japanese cameras, cars, TV sets and other electronic gadgets, but they hardly grew noticeably more 'Japanized' in the process. The fact that young people everywhere desire the same jeans, shoes, shirts and electronic games does not necessarily make them more disposed towards a common religion or ideology. 'Somewhere in the Middle East a half-dozen young men could well be dressed in jeans, drinking Coke, listening to rap, and, between their bows to Mecca, putting together a bomb to blow up an American airliner', writes Huntington (1997a, p. 58).

7 Among the four hundred interstate wars which have been recorded between 1816 and 1980, about ten were wars between democratic states – i.e., between strong, open and tolerant trading states of the Western world.

8 The six interstate conflicts were: Panama–USA (1989), India–Pakistan (on and off during the period), Mauritania–Senegal (1989–90), Iraq–Kuwait (1990–91), Equador–Peru (1995) and Cameroon–Nigeria (1996 to the present). Only two of these (Panama–USA and Iraq–Kuwait) were counted as interstate wars – i.e., they involved more than a thousand battle-related deaths during a particular year (Wallensteen and Sollenberg 1997, p. 339).

9 The appeal of Lenin and the Soviet revolution during the 1920s and 1930s is a case in point; the appeals of Mao, Ho and Che during the 1960s is another.

10 It could be added that, as the examples of Holland and Vietnam suggest, in a general atmosphere of distrust and antagonism, each suspicious participant tends to construct an other and defend itself against this other. This insight would be an important point in a more thorough evaluation of Huntington's *Clash of Civilizations*. For his is not the only American book of its kind, and it is tempting to portray this kind of book as a partisan effort to construct an alien, threatening other during a brief period of American transition from a known cold war world into a new unknown kind of world order. These books are 'orientalisms' in a Saidian sense.

11 It was discussed in Chapters 8 and 9 how the USA supported anti-Soviet guerilla
    movements in the Third World, and forced the USSR to assume the more difficult
    role of protecting unpopular *status quo* regimes – a reversal of roles from the late
    1960s and early 1970s. Also, it was noted how the superpower competition shifted
    into high-tech arenas in which the United States had the advantage over the Soviet
    Union. By challenging the Soviet leadership in these and other areas, the Reagan
    administration added to the pressures under which the Soviets found themselves
    and forced changes upon the American economy. By the late 1980s, the Soviet
    Union was (like France in the late 1770s) on the cusp of collapse. The United
    States showed signs of distress – for example, it was plagued by growing federal
    deficits as well as a sustained imbalance in foreign trade. But the United States
    under Reagan was also (like England under Pitt) marked by a new economic
    dynamism. In hindsight, it is tempting to conclude that the US difficulties of the
    1980s are best understood as problems of a historic transition. Clearly, this tran-
    sition could have been slowed down had US manufacturers been able to move
    upmarket more quickly. Also, the transition might have been less costly and
    controversial had the US leadership struck out against the most outrageous cases
    of abuse and corporate greed. Finally, the transition would have been less brutal
    had American politicians shown more compassion towards those people who most
    directly suffered its effects. But essentially, the United States went through major
    socio-economic adjustments in the 1980s. And this claim is strengthened by the
    fact that they involved adjustments which other mature industrial countries sub-
    sequently have sought to emulate.

12 In the early 1990s, the Clinton administration demonstrated this by finalizing the
    global agreement at the Uruguay round of GATT (1993/94) and by insisting that
    the new World Trade Organization (WTO) should begin renegotiations on agri-
    culture, services and other central issues by 2000. The USA reinforced this
    impression by concluding a North American Free Trade Association (NAFTA)
    (1993), and by leading the agreement of the thirty-four democracies in the Western
    hemisphere to create a Free Trade Area of the Americas (FTAA) (1994/95). The
    USA also turned the eighteen-member Asia Pacific Economic Cooperation forum
    (APEC) into a substantive organization – the Americans initiated annual summit
    meetings and supported its agreement to achieve free and open trade and invest-
    ment by 2010 (for its industrialized members) and 2020 (for the rest). Finally, the
    USA has taken the lead in the effort to achieve free trade in the western hemisphere
    and the Asian Pacific.

13 In practice, this concept meant that the United States must be strong enough to
    win a war against the USSR in Europe while still fending off one or more Soviet
    allies in Asia.

14 America's military forces have been markedly reduced since the fall of the Soviet
    Union and the end of the cold war. Under the plans of the Bush and Clinton
    administrations, US military spending was due to drop from $342 billion (1994
    dollars) in 1990 to $222 billion in 1998 – a 35 per cent cut in less than a decade.
    Total military personnel were scheduled to go down from 2.1 million to 1.4
    million. Several military programmes have been cancelled – between 1985 and
    1995, annual government purchases of ships went down from twenty-nine to six,
    of aircraft from 943 to 125, of tanks from 720 to none, and annual purchases of
    strategic missiles declined from forty-eight to eighteen. Also, the force structure

in 1998 will be reduced to between half and two-thirds of what it was at the end of the cold war

15 Or as Hollinger (1995, p. 84) puts it, the different groups share a 'profound suspicion of enclosures' and a 'recognition, acceptance and eager exploration of diversity'.

16 Reagan's arrival had been prepared by others. It had been prepared by liberal economists from the University of Chicago (who argued in the 1970s that government was not the solution to America's decline but part of the problem) and public choice theorists from the University of Virginia (who explained how special interests exploited government activities for their own benefit). It had been prepared by disillusioned liberals (including Nathan Glazer, James Q. Wilson, Norman Podhoretz, Peter Berger) who, under the banner of neo-conservatism argued that big government spawned laxity, decay and moral decline. It had been prepared by many people. Some of them had a radical past (like the former Trotskyist, Irving Kristol); many of them were Democrats (like Ben Wattenberg and Jeane Kirkpatrick) who deplored the radicalization of their party. In the early 1970s they were turned off by its peacenik foreign policy and the nomination of George McGovern as the party's presidential candidate. In the late 1970s they criticized its domestic government programmes for failing to deliver on its promises. By 1980, liberal economism fused with neo-conservatism and became an important force behind Reagan's presidential campaign.

17 Amitai Etzioni (1988; 1996), a key figure in the communitarian movement, claims that the liberal champions of individual freedoms have gone too far. Reagan and his supporters insisted on individual rights, but did this at the cost of communal values. They encouraged, in effect, a rampant egotism which threatened modern, liberal-democratic socities with relativism, atomism and, ultimately, the unravelling of social order. The most important task of contemporary social theory is to challenge this free-market opposition to the old concept of the 'common good', he writes. Many leading American academics share Etzioni's concerns, and have contributed to his reassessment of liberal ideas and to the new defence of the 'common good'. Benjamin Barber (1984), Robert Bellah (1991) and Michael Sandel (1996) are only some of the academic contributors to the debate (Daly 1994).

18 It is estimated that 2.4 billion viewers in 120 countries watch *Baywatch*, making it the most popular TV show on earth. For those who are quick to reject such shows as American vulgarity, it is worth noting that when *Baywatch* first aired in the US in 1990, it was cancelled after a single season. The producers then exported it to Europe, where it became an instant hit. The show was then reintroduced in the United States with foreign ratings and revenue as a springboard for syndication (http://www.baywatchtv.com/episodes/production/bayhist.html).

19 Clinton first advanced it during his 1992 presidential campaign. In 1993, President Clinton's national security adviser arranged a policy talk around the proposition that 'democracies don't tend to go to war with one another'. And in his 1994 State of the Union address, Clinton maintained that 'ultimately, the best strategy to ensure our security and to build a durable peace is to support the advance of democracy elsewhere. Democracies don't attack each other'.

20 It is simply assumed out of hand that 'democracy' is the independent variable in the association. Strictly, this assumption cannot be accepted without a convincing rejection of the obvious alternative: the claim that peace contributes to the growth

of democracy. This alternative notion of a causal relation is often noted in the international relations literature (Wright 1965, p. 841). Adam Smith, William Godwin and other liberals have long approached this argument from two angles. On the one hand, they have argued that less peace causes less democracy – i.e., that societies at war have often restricted citizens' rights and freedoms. On the other they have claimed, more interestingly, that a peaceful and stable society may encourage trade, investment and economic growth (see e.g. Smith 1965[1776], pp. 878f.; see also Gates *et al.* (1996)).

Bibliography

Acheson, D. (1969), *Present at the Creation*, New York: Norton

Adler, I. (1997), 'Seizing the Middle Ground: Constructivism in World Politics', *European Journal of International Relations*, 3(3):319–65

Albright, M. (1998), 'Secretary of State's Remarks to Bretton Woods Committee', Washington, DC, *USIA Daily Policy Update*, 13 February

Anderson, B. (1983), *Imagined Communities*, London: NLB

Anderson, P. (1979), *Lineages of the Absolutist State*, London: NLB

Aoudjit, A. (1993), 'The End of History and the Last Man', *Clio*, 22(4): 377–82

Aristotle (1941)[*c.* 300 BC], 'Politics', in *The Basic Works of Aristotle*, London: Random House

Ash, T. G. (1990), *We the People*, Cambridge: Granta Books

Auden, W. H. (1945), *For the Time Being*, London: Faber, pp. 115ff.

Bailey, J. L. (1990), 'Dependent Revolution: The United States and Radical Change in Bolivia and Cuba', Ph.D. dissertation. Denver: University of Denver

Bainville, J. (1920), *Les Conséquences Politiques de la Paix*, Paris: Nouvelle librairie nationale

Barber, B. (1984), *Strong Democracy*, Berkeley: University of California Press

Barbour, V. (1950), *Capitalism in Amsterdam in the 17th Century*, Ann Arbor: University of Michigan Press

Barker, J. E. (1906), *The Rise and Decline of the Netherlands*, London: Smith Elder

Barraclough, G. (1974), *An Introduction to Contemporary History*, Harmondsworth: Penguin

Barratt-Brown, M. (1970), *After Imperialism*, New York: Humanities Press

Barth, F. (1969), *Ethnic Groups and Boundaries*, Oslo: Universitetsforlaget

Beard, Charles A. (1929), *An Economic Interpretation of the Constitution of the United States*, New York: Macmillan

Becker, G. S. (1975), *Human Capital*, New York: National Bureau of Economic Research

Becker, K. L. (1932), *The Heavenly City of the Eighteenth-Century Philosophers*, New Haven: Yale University Press

Bell, D. (1992), 'The Culture Wars', *The Wilson Quarterly*, 16: 74–88

Bellah, R. N. (1991), *The Good Society*, New York: Knopf

Bendersky, J. W. (1983), *Carl Schmitt*, Princeton: Princeton University Press

Bentham, J. (1843), 'Principles of International Law', in *Works II*, Edinburgh: Tait, pp. 531–61

Best, G. (1982), *War and Society in Revolutionary Europe, 1770–1870*, London: Fontana

Bloch, M. (1961), *Feudal Society*, London: Routledge & Kegan Paul

Block, H. (1981), *The Planetary Product in 1980*, Washington, DC: US Department of State, Bureau of Public Affairs

Blok, P. J. (1907), *History of the People of the Netherlands*, London: Putnam

Booth, K. and S. Smith, eds (1995), *International Relations Theory Today*, Oxford: Polity Press

Bowle, J. (1977), *The Imperial Achievement*, Harmondsworth: Penguin

Boxer, C. R. (1973), *The Dutch Seabornes' Empire*, Harmondsworth: Penguin

Braudel, F. (1973), *The Mediterranean*, New York: Harper & Row

Braudel, F. (1977), *Afterthoughts on Material Civilization and Capitalism*, Baltimore: Johns Hopkins University Press

Braudel, F. (1981), *The Structures of Everyday Life*, New York: Harper & Row

Braudel, F. (1982), *The Wheels of Commerce*, New York: Harper & Row

Braudel, F. (1984), *Perspectives of the World*, New York: Harper & Row

Braudel, F. (1994), *A History of Civilizations*, New York: Allen Lane/The Penguin Press

Brinton, C. (1964)[1938], *An Anatomy of Revolution*, New York: Random House

Bromley, J. S., ed. (1971), *The Rise of Great Britain and Russia*, Cambridge: Cambridge University Press

Brown, C. (1988), 'The Modern Requirement', *Millennium*, 23: 339–448

Brown, C. (1995), 'International Political Theory and the Idea of World Community', in Booth and Smith, pp. 90–110

Brown, C. (1996), ' "Really Existing Liberalism", Peaceful Democracies and International Order', in Fawn and Larkins, pp. 29–47

Brzezinski, Z. (1993), *Out of Control*, New York: Scribner

Buchanan, J. (1991), *The Economics and the Ethics of Constitutional Order*, Ann Arbor: University of Michigan Press

Bull, H. (1977), *The Anarchical Society*, New York: Columbia University Press

Bull, H. (1990), 'The Importance of Grotius in the Study of International Relations', in Bull, Kingsbury and Roberts, pp. 65–95

Bull, H., B. Kingsbury and A. Roberts, eds (1990), *Hugo Grotius and International Relations*, Oxford: Clarendon

Burke, E. (1772), *The Annual Register*, XV, London: Dodsley

Burke, E. (1866)[1791], 'Letter to a Member of the National Assembly ...', in *Works III*, pp. 1–57. Boston: Little Brown

Burke, E. (1988)[1790], *Reflections on the Revolution in France*, Harmondsworth: Penguin

Buzan, B. (1991), *People, States and Fear*, New York: Harvester Wheatsheaf

Buzan, B., C. Jones and R. Little (1993), *The Logic of Anarchy*, New York: Columbia University Press

Buzan, B. and R. Little (1996), 'Reconceptualizing Anarchy', *European Journal of International Relations*, 2(4):403–39

Campbell, D. (1992), *Writing Security*, Minneapolis: University of Minnesota Press

Carnochan, W. B. (1993), *The Battleground of the Curriculum*, Stanford: Stanford University Press

Carr, E. H. (1945), *Nationalism and After*, London: Macmillan

Carr, E. H. (1964), *The Twenty-Years' Crisis, 1919–1939*, New York: Harper & Row

Carsten, F. L., ed. (1961), *The Ascendancy of France*, Cambridge: Cambridge University Press

Cartwright, J. (1774), *American Independence, the Interest and Glory of Britain*, London: Woodfall

Chandler, D. G. (1971), 'Armies and Navies', in J. S. Bromley, pp. 741–62

Cipolla, C. M., ed. (1974), *The Fontana Economic History of Europe: The Sixteenth and Seventeenth Centuries*, Glasgow: Collins

Citrin, J., E. B. Haas, C. Muste and B. Reingold (1994), 'Is American Nationalism Changing?', *International Studies Quarterly*, 38(1):1–33

Clough, S. B., ed. (1964), *A History of the Western World*, Boston: D. C. Heath

Coase, R. 'The Problem of Social Cost', *Journal of Law and Economics*, 3(1):1–44

Cobden, R. (1973), *The Political Writings of Richard Cobden*, New York: Garland

Cohen, W. I. (1995), *America in the Age of Soviet Power, 1945–1991*, Cambridge: Cambridge University Press

Coleman, J. S. (1990), *Foundations of Social Action*, Cambridge, Mass.: Belknap Press

Colley, L. (1992), *Britons: Forging the Nation*, New Haven: Yale University Press

Colinvaux, P. (1983), *The Fates of Nations*, Harmondsworth: Penguin

Corvisier, A. (1979), *Armies and Societies in Europe*, Bloomington: Indiana University Press

Cox, R. W. (1982), 'Production and Hegemony', in H. K. Jacobson and S. Sidjanski, eds, *The Emerging Industrial Economic Order*, Beverly Hills: Sage

Cox, R. W. (1987), *Production, Power and World Order*, New York: Columbia University Press

Crystal, D (1997), *English as a Global Language*, Cambridge: Cambridge University Press

Cumings, B. (1981), *The Origins of the Korean War I*, Princeton: Princeton University Press

Dahl, F. (1949), 'Amsterdam – Cradle of English Newspapers', *The Library*, pp. 166–78

Dahrendorf, R. (1959), *Class and Class Conflict in Industrial Society*, Stanford: Stanford University Press

Dallek, R. (1983), *The American Style of Foreign Policy*, New York: Oxford University Press

Daly, M. ed., (1994), *Communitarianism*, Belmont: Wadsworth

Dangerfield, G. (1961), *The Strange Death of Liberal England, 1910–1914*, New York: Putnam

Davies, D. W. A. (1961), *A Primer of Dutch Seventeenth Century Overseas Trade*, The Hague: Martinus Nijhoff

Davis, R. (1962), 'English Foreign Trade, 1700–1774', *Economic History Review*, 15(1)

Dehio, L. (1963), *The Precarious Balance*, London: Chatto & Windus

de la Court, P. (1702)[1662], *The True Interest and Political Maxims of the Republick of Holland*, London: (s.n.)

Department of State (1985a[1945]), 'Charter of the United Nations', pp. 95–110

Department of State (1985b)[1944], 'The Bretton Woods Agreements', pp. 745–67

Department of State (1985c)[1947], 'Recommendations on Greece and Turkey', pp. 530–4

Department of State (1985d)[1945], 'Fundamentals of United States Foreign Policy', pp. 915–18

Department of State (1985e)[1948], 'Charter on the International Trade Organization', pp. 788–800

Department of State (1985f)[1947], 'National Security Act of 1947', pp. 921–30

Department of State (1985g)[1947], 'Armed Forces for the United Nations', pp. 918–21

Der Derian, J. (1987), *On Diplomacy*, Oxford: Blackwell

Deudney, D. H. (1995), 'The Philadelphian System', *International Organization*, 49(2):191–228

Deutsch, K. W., S. A. Burrell, R. A. Kahn, M. Lee, M. Lichterman, R. E. Lindgren, F. L. Lowenheim and R. W. Van Wagenen (1957), *Political Community and the North Atlantic Area*, Princeton: Princeton University Press

Deutsch, K. W. (1970), *Political Community at the International Level*, New York: Archon Books

Dickens, C. (1985)[1864–65], *Our Mutual Friend*, Harmondsworth: Penguin

Dickens, C. (1986)[1849–50], *David Copperfield*, Harmondsworth: Penguin

Dickens, C. (1973), *Barnaby Rudge*, Harmondsworth: Penguin

Doyle, M. (1983a, b), 'Kant, Liberal Legacies and Foreign Affairs', I and II, *Philosophy and Public Affairs*, 12(3,4):205–35, 323–53

Draper, T. (1991), *A Very Thin Line*, New York: Hill & Wang

Drucker, P. (1998), *Peter Drucker on the Profession of Management*, Boston: Harvard Business School Publications

Dumas, A. (1993), *The Black Tulip*, Oxford: Oxford University Press

Dunn, J. (1985), '"Trust" in the Politics of John Locke', in *Rethinking Modern Political Theory*, Cambridge: Cambridge University Press

Durkheim, E. (1933)[1893], *Social Division of Labour in Society*.

Ellingsæter, A. L. (1992), *Part-time Work in European Welfare States*, Oslo: Institutt for samfunnsforskning

Elliott, J. H. (1977), *Imperial Spain*, New York: New American Library

Elliott, J. H. (1984), *Richelieu and Olivaries*, Cambridge: Cambridge University Press

Elliott, J. H. (1989), 'The Mental World of Hernan Cortes', in *Spain and its World, 1500–1700*, New Haven: Yale University Press, pp. 27–42

Engels, P. H. (1862), *De Belastingen en de Geldmiddelen van de Aanvang de Republiek tot op Heden*, Utrecht: Kemink en Zoon

Engels, F. (1976)[1878], *Anti-Dühring*, Peking: Foreign Languages Press

Etzioni, A. (1988), *The Moral Dimension*, New York: Free Press

Etzioni, A. (1996), *The New Golden Rule*, New York: Basic Books

Farrar, L. L., jun. (1977), 'Cycles of War', *International Interactions*, 3(1):161–79

Fawn, R. and J. Larkins, eds (1996), *International Society after the Cold War*, London: Macmillan

Feld, M. D. (1975), 'Middle Class Society and the Rise of Military Professionalism', *Armed Forces and Society*, 1(4):419–42

Fernandez-Santamaria, J. A. (1977), *The State, War and Peace: Spanish Political Thought in the Renaissance, 1516–1559*, Cambridge: Cambridge University Press

Finnemore, M. (1996), *National Interests in International Society*, Ithaca: Cornell University Press

Finney, J. (1989), *Invasion of the Body Snatchers*, New Brunswick: Rutgers University Press

Forrestal, J. (1951), *The Forrestal Diaries*, New York: Viking

Foucault, M. (1973), *The Order of Things*, New York: Random House

Friedrich, C. J. and Z. Brzezinski (1965), *Totalitarian Dictatorship and Autocracy*, Cambridge, Mass.: Harvard University Press

Fukuyama, F. (1989), 'The End of History', *The National Interest*, 16:3–18

Fukuyama, F. (1992), *The End of History and the Last Man*, New York: Free Press

Fukuyama, F. (1995), *Trust*, London: Hamish Hamilton

Gaddis, J. L. (1982), *Strategies of Containment*, New York: Oxford University Press

Gaddis, J. L. (1987), *The Long Peace*, New York: Oxford University Press

Gaddis, J. L. (1997), *We Now Know*, Oxford: Clarendon Press

Galbraith, J. K. (1992), *The Culture of Contentment*, Boston: Hill & Wang

Gallagher, J. and R. Robinson (1953), 'The Imperialism of Free Trade', *Economic History Review*, 6(1):1–15

Gambetta, D., ed. (1988), *Trust*, Oxford: Blackwell

Garner, J. F. (1994), *Politically Correct Bedtime Stories*, New York: Macmillan

Gates, S., T. L. Knutsen and J. M. Moses (1996), 'Democracy and Peace: A More Skeptical View', *Journal of Peace Research*, 33(1):1–10

Geyl, P. (1964), *The Netherlands in the Seventeenth Century*, London: Ernest Benn

Gibbon, E. (1994)[1814], *Memoirs of my Life and Writings*, Keele: Keele University Press

Gibbon, E. (1997)[1788], *The History of the Decline and Fall of the Roman Empire III*, Harmondsworth: Penguin

Gilpin, R. (1981), *War and Change in World Politics*, Cambridge: Cambridge University Press

Gilpin, R. (1987), *The Political Economy of International Relations*, Princeton: Princeton University Press

Godwin, W. (1985)[1793], *Enquiry Concerning Political Justice*, Harmondsworth: Penguin

Goldstein, J. (1988), *Long Cycles*, New Haven: Yale University Press

Goldsworthy, V. (1998), *Inventing Ruritania*, New Haven: Yale University Press

Goodwin, A., ed. (1965), *The American and French Revolutions*, Cambridge: Cambridge University Press

Gordon, J. S. (1997), *Hamilton's Blessing: The Extraordinary Life and Times of our National Debt*, New York: Walker

Gorbachev, M. (1987), *Perestroika*, New York: Harper & Row

Gough, J. W. (1973), 'Political Trusteeship', in *John Locke's Political Philosophy*, Oxford: Oxford University Press, pp. 154–93

Gramsci, A. (1971)[1947], *Selections from the Prison Notebooks*, London: Lawrence & Wishart

Green, W. S. (1985), 'Otherness Within: Towards a Theory of Difference in Rabbinic Judaism', in J. Neusner and E. S. Friedrichs, eds, pp. 46–69

Greenfeld, L. (1992), *Nationalism*, Cambridge, Mass.: Harvard University Press

Grotius, H. (1853)[1625], *De Jure Belli ac Pacis*, Cambridge: Cambridge University Press

Haas, P. M., ed. (1992), *Knowledge, Power and International Policy Coordination*, special issue of *International Organization*, 46(1)

Habermas, J. (1981), 'Modernity – An Incomplete Project', in *German Critique*, 22(1):3–15

Habermas, J. (1989), *The Structural Transformation of the Public Sphere*, London: Polity Press

Halberstam, D. (1969), *The Best and the Brightest*, New York: Random House

Halliday, F. (1983), *The Making of the Second Cold War*, London: Verso

Halstead, J. P. (1983), *The Second British Empire*, London: Greenwood Press

Hamilton, E. J. (1934), *American Treasures and the Price Revolution in Spain, 1501–1650*, Cambridge, Mass.: Harvard University Press

Hampson, N. (1968), *The Enlightenment*, Harmondsworth: Penguin

Harbutt, F. (1986), *The Iron Curtain*, New York: Oxford University Press

Hastings, A. (1997), *The Construction of Nationhood*, Cambridge: Cambridge University Press

Heckscher, E. (1931), *Mercantilism*, London: Allen & Unwin

Hegel, G. W. F. (1952), *Hegel's Philosophy of Right*, Oxford: Oxford University Press [1821]

Held, D. (1995), *Democracy and the Global Order*, Stanford: Stanford University Press

Hobbes, T. (1951)[1651], *Leviathan*, Harmondsworth: Penguin

Hobsbawm, E. J. (1978), *Industry and Empire*, Harmondsworth: Penguin

Hodgeson, G. (1973), 'The Establishment', *Foreign Policy*, 10(1):3–40

Hoffmann, S. (1968), *Gulliver's Troubles*, New York: McGraw-Hill

Hofstadter, R. (1948), *The American Political Tradition and the Men who Made It*, New York: Knopf

Hollinger, D. (1995), *Postethnic America*, New York: Basic Books

Holsti, K. J. (1991), *Peace and War*, Cambridge: Cambridge University Press

Holsti, K. J. (1996), *The State, War, and the State of War*, Cambridge: Cambridge University Press

Hooykaas, R. (1963), 'Science and Reformation', in G. S. Metraux and F. Couzet, eds, *The Evolution of Science*, New York: New American Library, pp. 258–91

Horelick, A. L. and M. Rush (1966), *Strategic Power and Soviet Foreign Policy*, Chicago: University of Chicago Press

Hughes, R. (1993), *The Culture of Complaint: The Fraying of America*, New York: Warner Books

Hume, D. (1985)[1777],'Of the First Principles of Government', in *Essays: Moral, Political and literary*, Indianapolis: Liberty Classics, pp. 32–41

Huntington, S. P. (1989), 'No Exit: The Errors of Endism', *The National Interest*, 17:3–11

Huntington, S. P. (1991), *The Third Wave: Democratization in the Late Twentieth Century*, Norman: University of Oklahoma Press

Huntington, S. P. (1997a), *The Clash of Civilizations and the Remaking of World Order*, London: Simon & Schuster

Huntington, S. P. (1997b), 'The Erosion of American National Interests', *Foreign Affairs*, 76(5):28–50

Israel, J. I. (1989), *Dutch Primacy in World Trade, 1585–1740*, Oxford: Clarendon Press

Israel, J. I. (1993), *The Anglo-Dutch Moment*, Cambridge: Cambridge University Press

Jeppeson, R. L., A. Wendt and P. Katzenstein (1996), 'Norms, Identity and Culture in National Security', in Katzenstein, ed., pp. 33–78

Jervis, R. (1997), *System Effects*, Princeton: Princeton University Press

Kant, I. (1991a)[1784], 'Idea for a Universal History with a Cosmopolitan Purpose', in H. Reiss, pp. 41–54

Kant, I. (1991b)[1793], 'On the Common Saying: "This May be True in Theory, But it Does not Apply in Practice"', in H. Reiss, pp. 61–92

Kant, I. (1991c)[1795], 'Perpetual Peace', in H. Reiss, pp. 93–131

Kant, I. (1991d)[1798], 'The Contest of Faculties', in H. Reiss, pp. 176–91

Kant, I. (1991e)[1797], 'The Metaphysics of Morals', in H. Reiss, pp. 131–76

Katzenstein, P. J., ed. (1996), *The Culture of National Security*, New York: Columbia University Press

Kennedy, P. (1987), *The Rise and Fall of the Great Powers*, New York: Random House

Kennedy, P. (1993), *Preparing for the Twenty-first Century*, London: HarperCollins

Kennedy, P. (1997), 'Noch fünf Jahre zum Feixen', in *Der Spiegel*, 36:174–77

Kenwood, A. G. and A. L. Lougheed (1971), *The Growth of the International Economy, 1820–1960*, London: Allen & Unwin

Keohane, R. O. (1982), 'Hegemonic Leadership and the US Foreign Economic Policy in the "Long Decade" of the 1950s', in D. P. Rapkin and W. P. Avery, eds, *America in a Changing World Political Economy*, London: Longman

Keohane, R. O. (1984), *After Hegemony*, Princeton: Princeton University Press

Keynes, J. M. (1919), *The Economic Consequences of the Peace*, New York: Little Brown

Kissinger, H. A. (1968), 'The White Revolutionary: Reflections on Bismarck', *Daedalus*, 4:888–925

Kissinger, H. A. (1969), *American Foreign Policy*, New York: Norton

Knorr, K. E. (1968), *British Colonial Theories*, Toronto: University of Toronto Press

Knorr, K. E. (1973), *Power and Wealth*, London: Basic Books

Knutsen, T. L. (1991), 'Answered Prayers: Fukuyama, Liberalism and the End-of-History Debate', *Bulletin of Peace Proposals*, 22(1):77–85

Knutsen, T. L. (1992), 'The Reagan Doctrine and the Lessons of the Afghan War', *Australian Journal of Politics and History*, 38(2):193–206

Knutsen, T. L. (1994), 'Re-reading Rousseau in the Post-Cold War World', *Journal of Peace Research*, 31(3):247–63

Knutsen, T. L. (1996), 'Norsk utenrikspolitikk som forskningsfelt', in T. Knutsen, G. Sørbø and S. Gjerdåker, eds, *Norges utenrikspolitikk*, Oslo: CMI/Cappelen akademisk, pp. 18–50

Knutsen, T. L. (1997), *A History of International Relations Theory*, Manchester: Manchester University Press

Kolko J. and G. Kolko (1972), *The Limits of Power*, New York: Harper & Row

Koreyu, W. (1993), *The Promises we Keep*, New York: St Martin's Press

Koselleck, R. (1988[1959]), *Critique and Crisis*, Cambridge, Mass.: MIT Press

Kossmann, E. H. (1961), 'The Dutch Republic', in F. L. Carsten, ed., pp. 275–300

Krasner, S., ed. (1983), *International Regimes*, Ithaca: Cornell University Press

Kratochwil, F. V. (1989), *Rules, Norms and Decisions*, Cambridge: Cambridge University Press

Kriedte, P. (1983), *Peasants, Landlords and Merchant Capitalists*, Cambridge: Cambridge University Press

Laclau, F. and C. Mouffe (1985), *Hegemony and Socialist Strategy*, London: Verso

LaFeber, W. (1989), *The American Age*, New York: Norton

Landes, D. (1969), *The Unbound Prometheus*, Cambridge: Cambridge University Press

Lasswell, H. (1936), *Politics*, New York: McGraw-Hill

Lebow, N. R. and B. S. Strauss, eds (1991), *Hegemonic Rivalry*, Boulder: Westview Press

Lenin, V. I. (1939)[1917], *Imperialism, the Highest Stage of Capitalism*, New York: Progress

Leonard, I. A. (1992)[1949], *Books of the Brave*, Los Angeles: University of California Press

Lippmann, W. (1944), *U.S. Foreign Policy: Shield of the Republic*, Boston: Little Brown

List, F. (1927)[1837], 'Das natürliche System der politischen Ökonomie', in *Werke IV*, Berlin: Reimar Hobbing, pp. 154–550

Lloyd, C. (1965), 'Armed Forces and the Art of War', in A. Goodwin, ed., pp. 174–217

Locke, J. (1960)[1689], *Two Treatises of Government*, Cambridge: Cambridge University Press

Locke, J.(1990[1664]), 'Does the Private Interest of each Individual constitute the foundation of the law of nature? It does not', in *Questions concerning the Law of Nature*, Ithaca: Cornell University Press, pp. 235–51

Lohbeck, K. (1993), *Holy War, Unholy Victory*, Washington, DC: Regnery

Lossky, A. (1971), 'International Relations in Europe', in J. S. Bromley, pp. 154–93

Lundestad, G. (1986), 'Empire by Invitation? The United States and Western Europe, 1945–1952', *Journal of Peace Research*, 23(3):263–77

Lundestad, G. (1990), *The American 'Empire'*, New York: Oxford University Press

Lundestad, G., ed. (1994), *The Fall of Great Powers: Peace, Stability, and Legitimacy*, New York: Oxford University Press

McKay, D. and H. M. Scott (1983), *The Rise of the Great Powers, 1648–1815*, London: Longman

McNeill, W. H. (1982), *The Pursuit of Power*, Chicago: University of Chicago Press

Machiavelli, N. (1961)[1532], *The Prince*, Harmondsworth: Penguin

Mackenzie, F. A. (1902), *American Invaders*, London: Grant Richards

Macpherson, C. B. (1973), *The Political Philosophy of Possessive Individualism*, Oxford: Clarendon

Mahbubani, K. (1993), 'The Dangers of Decadence', *Foreign Affairs*, 72(September/October)

Maitland, F. W. (1911), 'Trust and Corporation', in *Collected Papers III*, Cambridge: Cambridge University Press, pp. 321–404

Malthus, T. (1982)[1789], *An Essay on the Principle of Population*, Harmondsworth: Penguin

Mandelbaum, M. and S. Talbott (1987), *Reagan and Gorbachev*, New York: Vintage

Mandeville, B. de (1989)[1714], *Fable of the Bees*, Harmondsworth: Penguin

Mann, T. (1984)[1901], *The Buddenbrooks*, New York: Knopf

Martin, D. (1998), *Does Christianity Cause War?*, Oxford: Oxford University Press

Marx, K. H. (1977)[1867], *Capital*, New York: Vintage Books

May, E. R. (1976), *'Lessons' of the Past*, New York: Oxford University Press

Misztal, B. A. (1996), *Trust in Modern Societies*, Oxford: Polity Press

Mitchell, B. R. (1962), *Abstract of British Historical Statistics*, Cambridge: Cambridge University Press

Mitrany, D. (1933), *The Progress of International Government*, New Haven: Yale University Press

Modelski, G., ed. (1987), *Long Cycles in World Politics*, Seattle: University of Washington Press

Modelski, G. and W. R. Thompson (1988), *Sea Power in Global Politics, 1494–1993*, Basingstoke: Macmillan

Modelski, G. and W. R. Thompson (1989), 'Long Cycles and Global War', in M. I. Midlarski, *Handbook of War Studies*, Boston: Unwin Hyman, pp. 23–55

Modelski, G. and W. R. Thompson (1996), *Leading Sectors and World Powers*, Columbia: University of South Carolina Press

Montesquieu, C. L. de Secondat, baron de (1990)[1748], *The Spirit of the Laws*, Chicago: Encyclopædia Britannica

Moore, B., jun. (1969), *Social Origins of Dictatorship and Democracy*, Boston: Beacon Press

Morgenthau, H. J. (1978), *Politics among Nations*, New York: Knopf

Morison, S. E. (1972), *The Oxford History of the American People III*, New York: New American Library

Morison, S. E. (1974), *The Oxford History of the American People II*, New York: New American Library

Mosse, W. E. (1974), *Liberal Europe: The Age of Bourgeois Realism, 1848–1875*, London: Thames & Hudson

Mowat, R. B. (1928), *A History of European Diplomacy*, London: Edward Arnold

Moynihan, D. P. (1993), *Pandaemonium*, Oxford: Oxford University Press

Mueller, J. (1989), *Retreat from Doomsday*, New York: Basic Books

Mueller, J. (1995), *Quiet Cataclysm*, Reading, Mass.: Addison-Wesley

Muir, R. (1933), *The Interdependent World and its Problems*, London: Constable

Multatuli (1987)[1860], *Max Havelaar*, Harmondsworth: Penguin

Myrdal, G. (1944), *An American Dilemma*, New York

Naimark, N. N. (1995), *The Russians in Germany*, Cambridge, Mass.: Harvard University Press

Nato (1997), *Nato Handbook*, Brussels: Nato Information Service

Nau, H. (1990), *The Myth of America's Decline*, New York: Oxford University Press

Nef, J. U. (1963), *War and Human Progress*, New York: Norton

Nelson, R. R. and S. G. Winter (1982), *An Evolutionary Theory of Economic Change*, Cambridge, Mass.: Belknap Press

Neumann, I. B. (1996), 'Self and Other in International Relations', *European Journal of International Relations* 2 (2):139–74

Neusner, J. and E. S. Frerichs, eds (1985), *To See Ourselves as Others See Us*, Chico: Scholars Press

North, D. C. (1981), *Structure and change in Economic History*, New York: Norton

North, D. C. (1990), *Institutions, Institutional Change and Economic Performance*, Cambridge: Cambridge University Press

North, D. C. and R. P. Thomas (1973), *The Rise of the Western World*, Cambridge: Cambridge University Press

North, D. C. and B. Weingast (1989), 'The Evolution of Institutions Governing Public Choice in 17th Century England', *Journal of Economic History*, 49:803–32

Nye, J. S., jun. (1991), *Bound to Lead*, New York: Basic Books

O'Brian, P. K. (1988), 'The Costs and Benefits of British Imperialism 1846–1914', *Past & Present*, 120:163–200

O'Donnell, G., P. C. Schmitter and L. Whitehead (1988), *Transitions from Authoritarian Rule: Comparative Perspectives*, Baltimore: Johns Hopkins University Press

OECD (1992), *Annual Review: Structural Shifts in Major OECD Countries*, Paris: OECD

OECD (1997), *OECD Economic Outlook*:61, Paris: OECD

OECD (1997a), *OECD National Accounts 1983–1995*, Paris: OECD

Ogg, D. (1981), *Europe of the Ancien Regime, 1715–1783*, Glasgow: Fontana/Collins

Oldewelt, W. F. H. (1953), 'De Scheepvartstatistiek van Amsterdam in de 17e en 18e Eeuw', *Jaarboek Amstelodamum*, 45:114–53

Organski, A. F. K. and J. Kugler (1980), *The War Ledger*, Chicago: University of Chicago Press

Pagels E. (1995), *The Origin of Satan*, New York: Random House

Paglia, C. (1992), 'Rock as Art', in *Sex, Art, and American Culture*, New York: Vintage, pp. 19–22

Palmer, R. R. and J. Colton (1971), *A History of the Modern World*, New York: Knopf

Parker, G. (1974), 'The Emergence of Modern Finance in Europe, 1500–1730', in C. M. Cipolla, pp. 527–95

Parker, G. (1981), *The Dutch Revolt*, Harmondsworth: Penguin

Parkinson, F. (1977), *The Philosophy of International Relations*, Los Angeles: Sage

Plato (1987)[*c.* 368 BC], *The Republic*, Harmondsworth: Penguin

Plumb, J. H. (1950), *England in the Eighteenth Century*, Harmondsworth: Penguin

Poggi, G. (1978), *The Development of the Modern State*, Stanford: Stanford University Press

Polanyi, K. (1957), *The Great Transformation*, Boston: Beacon Press

Porter, R. (1982), *English Society in the Eighteenth Century*, Harmondsworth: Penguin

Porter, M. (1990), *The Competitive Advantage of Nations*, London: Macmillan

Postma, J. (1975), 'The Dutch Slave Trade: A Quantitative Assessment', *Revue française d'histoire d'outre-mer*, 62(226/27):232–44

Putnam, R. (1993), *Making Democracy Work*, Princeton: Princeton University Press

Putnam, R. (1995a), 'Bowling Alone: America's Declining Social Capital', *Journal of Democracy*, 6(1):65–79

Putnam, R. (1995b), 'Tuning In, Tuning Out: The Strange Disappearance of Social Capital in America', *PS*, (December):664–83

Randle, R. F. (1973), *The Origins of Peace*, New York: Free Press

Ranke, L. von (1872)[1833], 'Die grossen Mächte', in *Sämmtliche Werke*, Leipzig: Duncker & Humblot, XXIV:1–40

Reagan, R. (1990), *An American Life*, New York: Simon & Schuster

Redfield, R., ed. (1953), *The Primitive World and its Transformations*, Ithaca: Cornell University Press

Reich, R. B. (1991), *The Work of Nations*, New York: Knopf

Reiss, H., ed. (1991), *Kant: Political Writings*, Cambridge: Cambridge University Press

Rengger, N. (1997), 'The Ethics of Trust in World Politics', *International Affairs*, 73(3):469–89

Riley, P. (1996), *Leibniz' Universal Jurisprudence*, Cambridge, Mass.: Harvard University Press

Rittberger, V., ed. (1995), *Regime Theory and International Relations*, Oxford: Clarendon Press

Robinson, R. and J. Gallagher (1983), *Africa and the Victorians*, London: Macmillan

Rokkan, S. (1967), 'Geography, Religion and Social Class', S. M. Lipset and S. Rokkan, eds, *Party Systems and Voter Alignments*, New York: Free Press

Rosecrance, R. (1986), *The Rise of the Trading State*, New York: Basic Books

Rousseau, J.-J. (1971)[1762], 'Du contrat social', in *Oeuvres complètes II*, Paris: Editions du Seuil, pp. 518–80

Rowen, H. H., ed. (1972), *The Low Countries in Early Modern Times*, New York: Harper & Row

Roy, O. (1994), *The Failure of Political Islam*, Cambridge, Mass.: Harvard University Press

Ruggie, J. G. (1982), 'International Regimes, Transactions and Change', *International Organization*, 36(2):379–415

Ruggie, J. G. (1993), 'Territoriality and Beyond', *International Organization*, 47(1):139–75

Rupert, M. (1995), *Producing Hegemony*, Cambridge: Cambridge University Press

Russell, B. (1938), *Power: A New Social Analysis*, London: Allen & Unwin

Russett, B. (1990), *Controlling the Sword*, Cambridge, Mass.: Harvard University Press

Sahlins, P. (1989), *Boundaries*, Berkeley: University of California Press

Samuelsson, K. (1957), *Ekonomi och Religion*, Stockholm: KFs bokförlag

Sandel, M. J. (1996), *Democratic Discontent*, Cambridge, Mass.: Belknap Press

Schama, S. (1987), *The Embarrassment of Riches*, New York: Knopf

Scheler, M.(1961)[1919], *Ressentiment*, New York: Free Press

Schlesinger, A. M. jun. (1974), *The Imperial Presidency*, New York: Popular Library

Schlesinger, A. M. jun. (1992), *The Disuniting of America*, Knoxville: Whittle Direct Books

Schmitt, C. (1979)[1932], *Der Begriff des Politischen*, Berlin: Duncker & Humblot

Schmitt, C. (1985[1923]), *The Crisis of Parliamentary Democracy*, Cambridge, Mass.: MIT Press

Schmitthenner, H. (1938), *Lebensräume im Kampf der Kulturen*, Leipzig: Quelle & Heyer

Schnapper, D. and H. Mendras, eds (1990), *Six Manières d'être européen*, Paris: Editions du Seuil

Schroeder, P. (1996), *The Transformation of European Politics, 1763–1848*, Oxford: Clarendon Press

Schultz, T. (1961), 'Investment in Human Capital', *American Economic Review*, 51:1–17

Schumpeter, J. A. (1976)[1918], 'Die Krise der Steuerstaats', in R. Hinkel, ed., *Rudolf Goldscheid, Joseph Schumpeter: Die Ökonomie der Staatsfinanzen*, Frankfurt a. M.: Suhrkamp

Schumpeter, J. A. (1919), 'Zur Soziologie der Imperialismen', *Archiv für Sozialwissenschaft*, Tübingen

Schumpeter, J. A. (1954), *History of Economic Analysis*, London: Oxford University Press

Scott, J. B. (1934), *The Spanish Origin of International Law*, Oxford: Clarendon Press

Seligman, A. (1992), *The Idea of Civil Society*, Princeton: Princeton University Press

Seligman, A. (1997), *The Problem of Trust*, Princeton: Princeton University Press

Senghaas, D. (1985), *The European Experience*, Leamington: Berg

Small, M. and J. D. Singer (1982), *Resort to Arms*, Beverly Hills: Sage

Smith, A. (1965)[1776], *The Wealth of Nations*, New York: Modern Library

Smith, A. (1982)[1759], *The Theory of Moral Sentiments*, Oxford: Oxford University Press

Smith, A. D. (1991), *National Identity*, Harmondsworth: Penguin

Smith, J. Z. (1985), 'What a Difference a Difference Makes', in J. Neusner and E. S. Frerichs, eds, pp. 3–48

Smith, W. D. (1984), 'The Function of Commercial Centres in the Modernization of European Capitalism: Amsterdam as an Information Exchange in the Seventeenth Century', *Journal of Economic History*, 44(4):985–1005

Sorel, G. (1959), *Reflections on Violence*, London: Macmillan [190?]

Spruyt, H. (1994), *The Sovereign State and its Competitors*, Princeton: Princeton University Press

Staat van oorlog (annual report of the States General), The Hague: Rijksarchiv

Stavrianos, L. S. (1966), *The World since 1500*, Englewood Cliffs: Prentice-Hall

Steensgaard, N. (1970), 'European Shipping to Asia', *Scandinavian Economic History Review*, 18(1):1–11

Steel, R. (1981) *Walter Lippmann and the American Century*, New York: Vintage Books

Stein, A. (1978), *The Nation at War*, Baltimore: Johns Hopkins University Press

Stoye, J. (1980), *Europe Unfolding, 1648–1688*, Glasgow: Fontana/Collins

Strange, S. (1988), *States and Markets*, New York: Blackwell

Taft, J. (1989), *American Power*, New York: Harper & Row

Taylor, A. J. P. (1971), *The Struggle for Mastery in Europe, 1848–1918*, Oxford: Oxford University Press

Taylor, G. (1996), *Cultural Selection*, New York: Basic Books

Taylor, P. (1996), *The Way the Modern World Works*, New York: Wiley

ten Raa, F. J. G. and F. de Bas (1908–21), *Het Staatsche Leger I–V*, Breda: Koninklijke Militaire Academie

ten Raa, F. J. G. (1940–50), *Het Staatsche Leger VI–VII*, 's-Gravenhage: Martinus Nijhoff

't Hart, M. (1991), '"The Devil or the Dutch": Holland's Impact on the Financial Revolution in England, 1643–1694', *Parliaments, Estates and Representation*, 11:39–52

't Hart, M. (1993), *The Making of a Bourgeois State*, Manchester: Manchester University Press

Thompson, E. P. (1978), *Making of the English Working Class*, Harmondsworth: Penguin

Thompson, I. A. A. (1976), *War and Government in Habsburg Spain, 1560–1620*, London: Athlone Press

Thomson, D. (1974), *Europe since Napoleon*, Harmondsworth: Penguin

Thomson, D. (1978), *England in the Nineteenth Century*, Harmondsworth: Penguin

Tilly, C., ed. (1975), *The Formation of Nation States in Western Europe*, Princeton: Princeton University Press

Tilly, C. (1995), *Popular Contentions in Great Britain, 1758–1834*, Cambridge, Mass.: Harvard University Press

Tocqueville, A., de (1970)[1893], *Recollections: The French Revolution*, New Brunswick: Transaction Books

Todorov, T. (1989), *Nous et les autres*, Paris: Editions du Seuil

Toulmin, S. (1990), *Cosmopolis*, Chicago: University of Chicago Press

Toynbee, A. J. (1954), *A Study of War IX*, London: Oxford University Press

Triepel, H. (1938), *Die Hegemonie*, Stuttgart: Kohlhammer

Tudor, H. (1972), *Political Myth*, London: Pall Mall

Tucker, R. C., ed. (1978), *The Marx–Engels Reader*, New York: Norton (2nd edn)

US Bureau of the Census (1996), *Statistical Abstract of the United States 1996* (116th edn), Washington DC: US Government Printing Office

US Department of State, ed. (1985), *A Decade of American Foreign Policy: Basic Documents*, Washington, DC: GPO

Vattell, É., de (1863)[1758], *The Law of Nations or the Principles of Natural Law Applied to the Conduct and to the Affairs of Nations and of Sovereigns*, Philadelphia: Johnson

Vicens-Vives, J., ed. (1971), *Historia de España y America Social y Economia III*, Madrid

Vincent, J. (1986), *Human Rights and International Relations*, Cambridge: Cambridge University Press

Vitoria (1934a), 'On the Indians Recently Discovered', in J. B. Scott, Appendix A

Vitoria (1934b), 'On the Law of War made by the Spaniards on the Barbarians', in J. B. Scott, Appendix B

Vries, J. de and A. van der Woude (1997), *The First Modern Economy*, Cambridge: Cambridge University Press

Wallensteen, P. and M. Sollenberg (1997), 'Armed Conflicts, Conflict Termination and Peace Agreements 1989–96', *Journal of Peace Research*, 34(3):339–58

Wallerstein, I. (1974, 1980, 1989 and forthcoming), *The Modern World-System*, vols. I–IV. New York: Academic Press

Wallerstein, I. (1984), 'The Three Instances of Hegemony in the History of the Capitalist World-Economy', in *The Politics of the World-Economy*, Cambridge: Cambridge University Press, pp. 37–47

Wallis, J. J. and D. C. North (1986), 'Measuring the Transaction Sector in the American Economy, 1870–1970', in S. L. Engermann and R. E. Gallman (eds), *Long-term Factors in American Economic Growth*, Chicago: University of Chicago Press, pp. 95–161

Walt, S. P. (1991), 'Alliance Formation in Southwest Asia', in R. Jervis and J. Snyder, eds, *Dominoes and Bandwagons*, New York: Oxford University Press

Waltz, K. N. (1979), *Theory of International Politics*, Reading, Mass.: Addison-Wesley

Walworth, A. C. (1969), *Woodrow Wilson II*, Baltimore: Penguin

Watson, A. (1987), 'Hedley Bull, States Systems and International Societies', *Review of International Studies*, 13:147–53

Watson, A. (1992), *The Evolution of International Society*, London: Routledge

Watson, J. S. (1960), *The Reign of George III, 1760–1815*, Oxford: Clarendon Press

Webb, R. K. (1985), *Modern England*, London: Allen & Unwin

Weber, M. (1930), *The Protestant Ethic and the Spirit of Capitalism*, London: Allen & Unwin

Wedgwood, C. V. (1939), *The Thirty Years War*, New Haven: Yale University Press

Wendt, A. (1994), 'Collective Identity Formation and the International State', *American Political Science Review*, 88(2):384–96

Williams, E. E. (1896), *Made in Germany*, London: Heinemann

Williams, E. N. (1984), *The Ancien Regime in Europe*, Harmondsworth: Penguin

Williamson, A. (1894), *British Industries and Foreign Competition*, London: Simpkin Marshall

Wills, G. (1993), *Lincoln at Gettysburg*, New York: Simon & Schuster

Wilson, C. (1957), *Profit and Power*, London: Longman

Wolf, E. (1982), *Europe and the People without History*, Berkeley: University of California Press

Woodruff, W. (1967), *Impact of Western Man*, New York: St Martin's Press

World Bank (1997), *World Development Report 1997*, New York: Oxford University Press

Wright, Q. (1965)[1942], *A Study of War*, Chicago: University of Chicago Press

Yergin, D. (1991), *The Prize*, New York: Simon & Schuster

Yergin, D. and J. Stanislaw (1998), *The Commanding Heights*, New York: Simon & Schuster

Young, I. (1965), 'Russia', in A. Goodwin, ed., pp. 306–33

Zangwill, I. (1909), *The Melting Pot: A Drama in Four Acts*, New York: Macmillan

Zwitzer, H. L. (1984), 'The Dutch Army during the Ancien Regime', in *Revue internationale d'histoire militaire*, 58:15–37

Index